The Left Hemisphere

The Left Hemisphere

Mapping Critical Theory Today

Razmig Keucheyan

TRANSLATED BY GREGORY ELLIOTT

VERSO

London • New York

This work was published with the help of the French Ministry of Culture – Centre National du Livre

First published by Verso 2013
Translation © Gregory Elliott 2013
Originally published as *Hémisphère gauche. Une cartographie des nouvelles pensées critiques*
© La Découverte 2010

1 3 5 7 9 10 8 6 4 2

Verso
UK: 6 Meard Street, London W1F 0EG
US: 20 Jay Street, Suite 1010, Brooklyn, NY 11201
www.versobooks.com

Verso is the imprint of New Left Books

ISBN-13· 978-1-78168-102-2

British Library Cataloguing in Publication Data
A catalogue record for this book is available from the British Library

Library of Congress Cataloging-in-Publication Data
Keucheyan, Razmig.
  [Hémisphère gauche. English.]
  Left hemisphere : mapping critical theory today / Razmig Keucheyan ; translated by Gregory Elliott.
       pages cm
  Includes index.
  ISBN 978-1-78168-102-2 (alk. paper)
  1. Right and left (Political science)–History–20th century. 2. Right and left (Political science)–History–21st century. 3. Postmodernism. I. Elliott, Gregory. II. Title.
  JA83.K4613 2013
  320.501'9–dc23
                              2013013995

Typeset in Minion by Hewer Text UK Ltd, Edinburgh
Printed in the US by Maple Vail

Defeat is a hard experience to master: the temptation is always to sublimate it.

Perry Anderson, *Spectrum*

Contents

Michael Hardt and Toni Negri, or the 'Joy of Being

Communist': *Operaismo – Empire and Multitude – Towards a*

   Cognitive Capitalism?

The Revival of Theories of Imperialism: *Marxism and*

   Imperialism – Leo Panitch – Robert Cox – David Harvey

The Nation-State: Persistence or Transcendence?: *Benedict*

   Anderson and Tom Nairn – Jürgen Habermas and Étienne

   Balibar – Wang Hui – Giorgio Agamben

Capitalisms Old and New: *Critique of Cognitive Capitalism –*

   Robert Brenner – Giovanni Arrighi – Elmar Altvater –

   Luc Boltanski

Introduction

In his preface to *Aden Arabie*, Jean-Paul Sartre associates Paul Nizan with the rebellious youth of the 1960s. He suggests a community of revolt secretly linking his fellow-student of the 1930s with those who set out to storm the old world thirty years later. In the post-war period, Nizan had suffered a long eclipse. He had suddenly re-emerged and, more contemporary than ever, his work had been republished at the start of what were to be two revolutionary decades. 'As the years go by', writes Sartre, 'his hibernation has made him younger. Yesterday he was our contemporary; today he is theirs.'[1] For an oeuvre to go into hibernation in this way, and then attract the interest of new generations, requires precise conditions. It must somehow 'speak' to the young – that is, at the very least, cast a special light on the world in which they are immersed.

Determining what is contemporary is central to this book, as is the relationship between what is contemporary and what – temporarily or definitively – is not. Our subject, however, is not literature but the general theory of emancipation. More specifically, we shall be concerned with the new critical theories.

The term 'critical theory' has a long history. Traditionally – often in the singular and upper case – it refers to the thinkers of the Frankfurt School, the generations of philosophers and sociologists who have succeeded one another at the helm of that city's *Institut für Sozialforschung*.[2] However, it will be used in this work in a much broader sense and always in the plural. In the sense given it here, it covers both the queer theory developed by the North American feminist Judith Butler and the metaphysics of the event proposed by Alain Badiou, as well as Fredric Jameson's theory of postmodernism, Homi Bhabha and Gayatri Spivak's postcolonialism, John Holloway's 'open Marxism', and Slavoj Žižek's Hegelian neo-Lacanianism.

The new critical theories are *new* in as much as they appeared after the fall of the Berlin Wall in 1989. While most of them were developed prior to that event, they emerged in the public sphere in its wake. For example, we shall understand nothing of Michael Hardt's and Toni Negri's theory of 'Empire' and

---

1   Jean-Paul Sartre, preface to Paul Nizan, *Aden Arabie*, Paris: La Découverte, 2002, p. 13.
2   For a history of the Frankfurt School, see Martin Jay, *The Dialectical Imagination: A History of the Frankfurt School and the Institute of Social Research, 1923–1950*, Boston: Beacon, 1973.

'Multitude'[3] if we do not appreciate what it owes to the Italian current of Marxism that Negri belongs to – i.e. *operaismo* – which crystallized in the early 1960s.[4] In its current form, however, the theory only emerged at the end of the 90s. The novelty of critical theories is in part bound up with the renewal of social and political critique that began in the second half of the 1990s, with events like the French strikes of November–December 1995, the demonstrations against the WTO at Seattle in 1999, and the first World Social Forum at Porto Alegre in 2001.

Obviously, the issue of the extent to which a form of thought is 'new', and the criteria for assessing such novelty, is itself complex. It is a theoretical – and political – question in itself.[5] Should we opt for a purely chronological criterion, arguing that what is new is simply what comes 'after'? But in that case the most trifling, uninteresting idea which demarcates itself, however minimally, from existing currents of thought should be classified as 'new'. Chronology is therefore insufficient to define novelty. Is 'new', then, synonymous with 'important'? But important from what point of view – intellectual, political or both? And who judges this importance? The hypothesis advanced in this book is that we are currently going through a transitional period politically and intellectually; and that it is premature to venture unequivocal answers to such questions.

A new critical theory is *a theory*, not merely an analysis or interpretation. It not only reflects on what is, by describing past or present social reality in the manner of empirical social science. It also raises the issue of what is desirable. As such, it necessarily contains a political dimension. Critical theories reject the epistemological axiom of 'value neutrality' posited by Max Weber in the early twentieth century in his essays on the methodology of the social sciences.[6] In them the descriptive and the normative (i.e. the political) are inextricably linked.

Critical theories are theories that more or less comprehensively challenge the existing social order. The criticisms they formulate do not concern particular aspects of this order, like the imposition of a tax on financial transactions (the 'Tobin tax') or some measure relating to pension reform. Whether radical or more moderate, the 'critical' dimension of the new critical theories consists

---

3   See Michael Hardt and Toni Negri, *Empire*, Cambridge (MA): Harvard University Press, 2000, and *Multitude: War and Democracy in the Age of Empire*, New York: Penguin, 2004.

4   On the history of *operaismo*, see Steve Wright, *Storming Heaven: Class Composition and Struggle in Italian Autonomist Marxism*, London: Pluto, 2002.

5   See Stathis Kouvelakis, 'Le marxisme au 21e siècle: formes et sens d'une résilience', in Gérald Bronner and Razmig Keucheyan, eds, *La Théorie sociale contemporaine*, Paris: Presses Universitaires de France, 2011.

6   See Max Weber, *The Methodology of the Social Sciences*, ed. and trans. Edward A. Shils and Henry A. Finch, Glencoe: Free Press, 1949.

in the general character of their challenge to the contemporary social world.[7] This generality is itself variable. Some, like classical and contemporary Marxists, tend to adopt the standpoint of the 'totality', in the belief that the global character of capitalism requires that critique should itself be global. Others, like poststructuralists, challenge the very possibility of such a standpoint. But in every instance an increase in generality, which aims to go beyond the strictly local to the more global, is evident.

Until the second half of the twentieth century, the centre of gravity of critical thinking lay in western and eastern Europe. Today it has shifted to the United States, either because the relevant authors are natives of that country or, when they are not, because they teach in US universities. This involves a significant alteration in the geography of thinking, which (as we shall see) is not without its effects on the nature of contemporary critical theories.

Only a stubborn cultural bias, however, would have it that the future of critical theories is still being played out in the western countries. As Perry Anderson has suggested, it is highly likely that theoretical production follows the pattern of production *tout court*, or at any rate that the development of the two is not independent.[8] Not, as an unduly simplistic materialism might think, because the economy determines ideas 'in the last instance', but because new ideas arise where new problems are posed. And it is in countries like China, India and Brazil that these problems are already arising or will arise in the future.

The historical conjuncture in which theories are formed stamps them with their main characteristics. 'Classical' Marxism – initiated on Marx's death by Engels and notably comprising Kautsky, Lenin, Trotsky, Luxemburg and Otto Bauer – emerged against the background of profound political and economic turbulence, which led to the First World War and the Russian Revolution. Conversely, so-called Western Marxism, of which Lukács, Korsch and Gramsci were the initiators, and to which Adorno, Sartre, Althusser, Marcuse and Della Volpe in particular belong, developed in a period of relative stability for capitalism. The themes broached by these authors, but also their theoretical 'style', clearly register the effects of this. Thus, although they all pertain to the Marxist tradition, a gulf separates Hilferding's *Finance Capital* (1910) and Lenin's *State and Revolution* (1917) from Adorno's *Minima Moralia* (1951) and Sartre's *The Family Idiot* (1971–72).

---

7   The new critical theories include anti-Kantian currents, like those inspired by the works of Michel Foucault and Gilles Deleuze. Consequently, it would be unduly restrictive to limit the meaning of the work 'critique' to its Kantian sense. Nevertheless, this sense is frequently encountered – in particular, whenever a critique of 'categories' (social, racial, sexual) is involved.

8   See Perry Anderson, *In the Tracks of Historical Materialism*, London: New Left Books, 1983.

How do things stand with the world in which the new forms of critical thinking are being produced? If the collapse of the Soviet bloc created the illusion of a peaceful and prosperous 'new world order', the hope (for those for whom it was such) proved short-lived. Our epoch is characterized, among other things, by an unprecedented economic crisis, mass unemployment and general insecurity, by a global war against 'terrorism', by growing inequalities between North and South, and an imminent ecological crisis.

With its turbulence, today's world resembles the one in which classical Marxism emerged. In other respects, it is significantly different – above all, no doubt, in the absence of a clearly identified 'subject of emancipation'. At the start of the twentieth century, Marxists could count on powerful working-class organizations, of which they were often leaders, and whose activity was going to make it possible to surmount what was supposedly one of the ultimate crises of capitalism. Nothing similar exists at present or, probably, for the immediate future. How, in the light of this, are we to continue thinking radical social transformation? Such is the challenge facing contemporary critical theories.

PART I

Contexts

CHAPTER ONE

The Defeat of Critical Thinking (1977–93)

PERIODIZING

In the beginning was defeat. Anyone who wishes to understand the nature of contemporary critical thinking must start from this fact.

From the second half of the 1970s, the protest movements born in the late 1950s, but which were inheritors of much older movements, went into decline. The reasons are various: the oil shock of 1973 and the reversal of the 'long wave' of the *trente glorieuses*; the neo-liberal offensive with the election of Margaret Thatcher and Ronald Reagan in 1979 and 1980; the capitalist turn in China under the leadership of Deng Xiaoping; the decline of old forms of working-class solidarity; the Left's ascension to power in France in 1981 and, with it, ministerial prospects encouraging the conversion of leftist militants who had distinguished themselves in May 1968; the definitive loss of credibility of the Soviet and Chinese blocs; and so on and so forth. The Sandinista Revolution in Nicaragua in 1979 was probably the last event to exhibit the characteristics of a revolution in the traditional sense. The same year, the Iranian Islamic Revolution was the first of a series of political objects difficult to identify that filled subsequent decades.

This process of decline attained its clearest expression, if not its culmination, in the fall of the Berlin Wall. Clearly, something had come to an end around 1989. The problem is to know what and to identify the moment when what ended had begun.

If we attempt a periodization, several divisions are possible. Firstly, it might be argued that we had reached the end of a short political cycle, whose inception dated back to the second half of the 1950s. This cycle was that of the 'New Left'. This term refers to 'left-wing' organizations – in particular, Maoist, Trotskyist and anarchist – as well as the 'new social movements' of feminism and political ecology, for example. The New Left emerged around 1956, the year of the Suez crisis and the crushing of the Budapest uprising by Soviet tanks, but also that of Khrushchev's 'secret speech' on Stalin's crimes to the Twentieth Congress of the Communist Party of the Soviet Union. In France that year deputies (including the Communists) voted to grant special powers to Guy Mollet's government for 'pacifying' Algeria.

To belong to the New Left was to reject the alternative imposed in 1956 by the two established camps, while continuing to develop a radical critique of capitalism. In other words, it consisted in condemning both Anglo-French policy towards Egypt – and imperialism in general – and the Soviet intervention in Budapest. The apogee of the New Left occurred from around 1968 until about 1977 (the Italian autonomist movement). The French and Mexican 1968, the Italian 'extended' May and 'hot autumn' of 1969, the Argentinian 'Cordobazo' (1969),[1] and the Prague Spring – these were all part of the same international trend. A first option for periodization thus consists in arguing that what ended in 1989 was the cycle begun in 1956 by the Egyptian and Hungarian crises and the ensuing reactions on the radical Left. The Cuban Revolution (1959) and the Vietnam War are other events that helped drive this cycle.[2]

A second option dates the political cycle that ended around 1989 back to the Russian Revolution of 1917 or the 1914 war. This is what the historian Eric Hobsbawm has called the 'short twentieth century'.[3] The First World War, and the Bolshevik Revolution of which it was a condition of possibility, are then regarded as the 'matrices' of the twentieth century. The barbarism witnessed by this age, especially during the Second World War, is presented as a consequence of changes in the modality and intensity of collective violence that occurred during World War I. Other aspects of the century are related to these developments. The role of 'ideologies', for example, of which 1989 is supposed to have sounded the death-knell, while 1917 is alleged to have represented their 'totalitarian' intrusion into history.[4] In this second hypothesis the New Left is regarded as a sub-cycle subordinate to the broader cycle initiated in 1914 or 1917.

A third possibility consists in believing that 1989 ended a cycle initiated at the time of the French Revolution in 1789. This is a longer-range hypothesis, with weightier political and theoretical consequences. It is sometimes characterized as 'postmodern', with reference to the works of Jean-François Lyotard, Marshall Berman and Fredric Jameson in particular.[5] Postmodernism is based on the idea that the French Revolution lies at the beginning of political modernity. From this standpoint, subsequent revolutions – the Russian and Chinese,

---

1   This Argentinian protest movement, which formed on 29 May 1969 in the industrial city of Cordoba in Argentina, initiated the fall of Juan Carlos Onganía's dictatorship.

2   On the New Left see, for example, Van Gosse, *The Movements of the New Left, 1950 –1975: A Brief History with Documents*, New York: Palgrave Macmillan, 2008. A remarkable cinematic evocation of the period is Chris Marker's *Le Fond de l'air est rouge* (1977).

3   Eric Hobsbawm, *Age of Extremes: The Short Twentieth Century, 1914–1991*, London: Michael Joseph, 1994.

4   See Jean Baechler, *La Grande Parenthèse (1914–1991). Essai sur un accident de l'histoire*, Paris: Calmann-Lévy, 1993.

5   See Jean-François Lyotard, *The Postmodern Condition: A Report on Knowledge*, trans. Geoffrey Bennington and Brian Massumi, Minneapolis: University of Minnesota Press, 1984; Marshall Berman, *All That Is Solid Melts into Air: The Experience of Modernity*, London and New York: Verso, 1983; Fredric Jameson, *Postmodernism, or The Cultural Logic of Late Capitalism*, London and New York: Verso, 1991.

for example – represent sequels to that event. Yet in so far as the Communist regimes failed to realize the modern project inaugurated by the French Revolution, that whole project is regarded as compromised. This third hypothesis implies that the intellectual categories – reason, science, time, space – and political categories – sovereignty, citizenship, territory – peculiar to modern politics must be abandoned for new categories. 'Network' forms of organization, the importance ascribed to minority 'identities', or the supposed loss of sovereignty by nation-states in the context of globalization form part of this hypothesis.

Three beginnings – 1789, 1914–17, 1956 – for one ending: 1989. Different divisions are possible and can be superimposed on these. Postcolonial studies stress the major events of modern colonial history (the end of the Haitian Revolution in 1804 or the Sétif massacres of 1945 in Algeria, for example). The 1848 Revolution and the Paris Commune are likewise sometimes invoked as origins of the political cycle that came to a conclusion in 1989. The relative significance accorded events also varies depending on the region of the world considered. In Latin America, instances of national independence in the first half of the nineteenth century, the Mexican Revolution of 1910, and the Cuban Revolution of 1959 are central. In Europe, the end of the Second World War and the *trente glorieuses* can serve as reference-points, just as in Asia the proclamation of the People's Republic of China in 1949 can.

The new forms of critical thought are obsessed with these issues of periodization. In the first place, they involve thinking their own historical location in cycles of political struggle and theoretical development. Never has a set of critical theories devoted such importance to this problem. Obviously, Marxism has always posed the issue of its relationship to history in general and intellectual history in particular. This is the significance of the countless debates over the links between Marx and Hegel, Marx and the classical political economists, or Marx and the utopian socialists. It is also the meaning of discussions about the link between the emergence of Marxism and the revolutions of Marx's time: those of 1848 and the Paris Commune, in particular. But the problem is posed more sharply when, to employ a Shakespearean phrase of which Jacques Derrida was fond, time seems to be 'out of joint', as it is today.[6] It is true that prioritizing one or other of the cycles we have mentioned has different implications. The postmodern hypothesis, as has been indicated, has profound consequences, in that it assumes the disappearance of the modern form of politics. While the other two options do not involve such radical revision, they nevertheless lead to a serious reassessment of the doctrines and strategies of the Left since the early twentieth century.

---

6   This theme is developed in particular in Jacques Derrida, *Specters of Marx*, trans. Peggy Kamuf, London and New York: Routledge, 1994.

We shall return to the question of periodization and the answers offered by the new critical thinking. For now, it is crucial to assign due importance to the fact that these theories develop in a conjuncture marked by the defeat of the Left intent on social transformation. This defeat goes back to a cycle that began with the French Revolution, the Russian Revolution, or the second half of the 1950s. But in any event, it is well-attested and its scope is profound. It is decisive for understanding the new forms of critical thinking. It imparts a particular coloration and 'style' to them.

TOWARDS A GEOGRAPHY OF CRITICAL THINKING

In *Considerations on Western Marxism*, Perry Anderson has shown that the defeat of the German Revolution in the years 1918–23 led to a significant mutation in Marxism.[7] The Marxists of the classical generation had two main characteristics. Firstly, they were historians, economists, sociologists – in short, concerned with empirical sciences. Their publications were mainly conjunctural and focused on the political actuality of the moment. Secondly, they were leaders of parties – that is, strategists confronting real political problems. Carl Schmitt once claimed that one of the most important events of the modern age was Lenin's reading of Clausewitz.[8] The underlying idea is that to be a Marxist intellectual in the early twentieth century was to find oneself at the head of one's country's working-class organizations. In truth, the very notion of 'Marxist intellectual' made little sense, the substantive 'Marxist' being self-sufficient.

These two characteristics were closely linked. It is because they were political strategists that these thinkers required empirical knowledge to make decisions. This is the famous 'concrete analysis of concrete situations' referred to by Lenin. Conversely, their role as strategists nourished their reflections with first-hand empirical knowledge. As Lenin wrote on 30 November 1917 in his postscript to *State and Revolution*, 'It is more pleasant and useful to go through the "experience of the revolution" than to write about it.'[9] In this phase of Marxism's history the 'experience' and the 'writing' of revolution were inextricably linked.

The 'Western' Marxism of the subsequent period was born out of the erasure of the relations between intellectuals/leaders and working-class organizations that had existed in classical Marxism. By the mid-1920s, workers'

---

7   See Perry Anderson, *Considerations on Western Marxism*, London: New Left Books, 1976.

8   Carl Schmitt, *Theory of the Partisan*, trans. G.L. Ulmen, St. Louis: Telos Press, 2007. On Marxists' relationship to Clausewitz, see Azar Gat, 'Clausewitz and the Marxists: Yet Another Look', *Journal of Contemporary History*, vol. 27, no. 2, 1992.

9   V.I. Lenin, *Collected Works*, Vol. 25, London: Lawrence and Wishart, 1964, p. 492.

organizations had everywhere been beaten. The failure in 1923 of the German Revolution, whose outcome was regarded as crucial for the future of the work-ing-class movement, sounded a halt to hopes of any immediate overthrow of capitalism. The decline that set in led to the establishment of a new kind of link between intellectuals/leaders and working-class organizations. Gramsci, Korsch and Lukács were the first representatives of this new configuration.[10] With Adorno, Sartre, Althusser, Della Volpe, Marcuse and others, the Marxists who dominated the years 1924–68 possessed converse characteristics to those of the preceding period. For a start, they no longer had organic links with the workers' movement and, in particular, with the Communist parties. They no longer held leadership positions. In those instances where they were members of Commu-nist parties (Althusser, Lukács, Della Volpe), they had complex relations with them. Forms of 'fellow-travelling' can be observed, exemplified by Sartre in France. But an irreducible distance between intellectuals and party remained. It is not necessarily attributable to the intellectuals themselves: Communist party leaderships were often profoundly mistrustful of them.[11]

The rupture between intellectuals and working-class organizations charac-teristic of Western Marxism had a significant cause and a significant consequence. The cause was the construction from the 1920s of an orthodox Marxism that represented the official doctrine of the USSR and fraternal parties. The classical period of Marxism was one of intense debates over, in particular, the character of imperialism, the national question, the relationship between the social and the political, and finance capital. From the second half of the 1920s, Marxism became fossilized. This placed intellectuals in a structurally difficult position, since any innovation in the intellectual domain was hence-forth denied them. This was a major cause of the distance that now separated them from working-class parties. It confronted them with the alternative of maintaining allegiance or keeping their distance from the latter. With time the separation only grew, all the more so in that other factors aggravated it, like the increasing professionalization or academicization of intellectual activity, which tended to distance intellectuals from politics.

A notable consequence of this new configuration was that Western Marx-ists, unlike those of the previous period, developed abstract forms of knowledge. For the most part they were philosophers and often aestheticians or epistemolo-gists. Just as the practice of empirical science was bound up with the fact that

---

10   See Anderson, *Considerations on Western Marxism*, chapter 2. For different analyses of Western Marxism, see Russell Jacoby, *Dialectic of Defeat: Contours of Western Marxism*, Cambridge: Cambridge University Press, 2002, as well as Martin Jay, *Marxism and Totality: The Adventures of a Concept from Lukács to Habermas*, Berkeley: University of California Press, 1984.

11   See Frédérique Matonti, *Intellectuels communistes. Essai sur l'obéissance politique. La Nouvelle Critique (1967–1980)*, Paris: La Découverte, 2005.

the Marxists of the classical period played leadership roles within workers' organizations, so remoteness from such roles prompted a 'flight into abstraction'. Marxists now produced hermetic knowledge, inaccessible to ordinary workers, about fields without any direct relationship to political strategy. In this sense, Western Marxism was non-'Clausewitzian'.

The case of Western Marxism illustrates the way in which historical developments can influence the content of thinking that aspires to make history. More precisely, it demonstrates the way in which the type of development that is a political defeat influences the course of the theory which has suffered it.[12] The failure of the German revolution, Anderson argues, led to an enduring rupture between the Communist parties and revolutionary intellectuals. In severing the latter from political decision-making, this rupture led them to produce analyses that were increasingly abstract and less and less strategically useful. The interesting thing about Anderson's argument is that it convincingly explains a property of the content of the doctrine (abstraction) by a property of its social conditions of production (defeat).

Starting from this, the issue is to determine the relationship between the defeat suffered by political movements in the second half of the 1970s and current critical theories. In other words, it consists in examining the way that the critical doctrines of the 1960s and 70s 'mutated' on contact with defeat, to the point of giving rise to the critical theories which emerged during the 1990s. Can the defeat of the second half of the 1970s be compared with that suffered by the workers' movement in the early 1920s? Have its effects on critical doctrines been similar to those experienced by Marxism after the early 1920s and, in particular, to the 'flight into abstraction' characteristic of it?

FROM ONE GLACIATION TO THE NEXT

Today's critical theories are inheritors of Western Marxism. Naturally, they have not been influenced exclusively by it, for they are the product of multiple connections, some of them foreign to Marxism. Such, for example, is the case with French Nietzscheanism, particularly the oeuvres of Foucault and Deleuze. But one of the main origins of the new critical theories is to be found in Western Marxism, whose history is closely bound up with that of the New Left.

Anderson's analysis demonstrates that the significant distance separating critical intellectuals from working-class organizations has a decisive impact on the type of theories they develop. When these intellectuals are members of

---

12   On the relationship between defeat and theory, see Razmig Keucheyan, 'Figures de la défaite. Sur les conséquences théoriques des défaites politiques', *Contretemps*, new series, no. 3, 2009.

the organizations in question and, *a fortiori*, when they are leaders of them, the constraints of political activity are clearly visible in their publications. They are markedly less so when this bond weakens, as in the case of Western Marxism. For example, being a member of the Russian Social-Democratic Workers' Party at the start of the twentieth century involved different kinds of constraints than being on ATTAC's scientific committee.[13] In the second case, the intellectual concerned has plenty of time to pursue an academic career outside of his political commitment – something incompatible with member-ship in a working-class organization in the early twentieth century in Russia or elsewhere. Obviously, the academy has itself changed – more precisely, massified – considerably since the era of classical Marxism; and this has an impact on the potential trajectory of critical intellectuals. Academics were a restricted social category in late nineteenth- and early twentieth-century Europe. Today, they are much more widespread, which manifestly influences the social and intellectual trajectory of the producers of theory. To under-stand the new critical theories, it is crucial to grasp the character of the links between the intellectuals who elaborate them and current organizations. In chapter 3 we shall propose a typology of contemporary critical intellectuals intended to address this issue.

There is a geography of thought – in this instance, of critical thought. Clas-sical Marxism was essentially produced by central and east European thinkers. The Stalinization of that part of the continent cut off subsequent development and shifted Marxism's centre of gravity towards western Europe. This is the social space in which critical intellectual production was installed for half a century. During the 1980s, as a result of the recession of theoretical and political critique on the continent, but also because of the activity of dynamic intellec-tual poles like the journals *New Left Review, Semiotext(e), Telos, New German Critique, Theory and Society* and *Critical Inquiry*, the source of critique gradu-ally shifted to the Anglo-American world. Critical theories thus came to be most vigorous where they had not previously been.[14] While the old regions of production continue to generate and export important authors – it is enough to think of Alain Badiou, Jacques Rancière, Toni Negri or Giorgio Agamben – a fundamental shift has set in over the last thirty years, which is tending to relo-cate the production of critical theories to new regions.

---

13   On ATTAC see, for example, Bernard Cassen, 'On the Attack', *New Left Review* II/19, January–February 2003.

14   Anderson, *In the Tracks of Historical Materialism*, London and New York: Verso, 1983, p. 24. It is interesting to note that analytical philosophy followed the same trajectory towards the West. Its origins go back to Germany (Frege), Austria (Vienna Circle, Wittgenstein), and England (Russell, Moore), but its centre of gravity shifted in the second half of the twentieth century towards the United States (Quine, Putnam, Kripke, Davidson, Rawls).

It must be said that the intellectual climate deteriorated markedly for the radical Left in western Europe, especially France and Italy – the chosen lands of Western Marxism – from the second half of the 1970s. As has been indicated, Western Marxism succeeded classical Marxism when the Stalinist glaciation struck eastern and central Europe. Although different in numerous respects, an analogy can be established between the effects of this glaciation and what the historian Michael Scott Christofferson has called the 'anti-totalitarian moment' in France.[15] From the second half of the 1970s, France – but this also applies to neighbouring countries, especially those where the labour movement was powerful – saw a large-scale ideological and cultural offensive, which, on a different terrain, accompanied the rise of neo-liberalism with the election of Thatcher and Reagan, followed by that of François Mitterrand who, despite his 'socialist' pedigree, applied neo-liberal recipes without remorse. The movements born in the second half of the 1950s were stagnating. The initial oil shock of 1973 heralded difficult times economically and socially, with the first significant increase in the rate of unemployment. The Common Programme of the Left, signed in 1972 and uniting the Communist and Socialist parties, made the Left's arrival in government conceivable, but in the process directed its activity towards institutions, therewith stripping it of some of its former vitality.

On the publishing front, *The Gulag Archipelago* appeared in French translation in 1974. The media hype around Solzhenitsyn and other east European dissidents was considerable. They were not defended only by conservative intellectuals. In France, in 1977, a reception organized in honour of Soviet dissidents brought together Sartre, Foucault and Deleuze. Other famous critical intellectuals, like Cornelius Castoriadis and Claude Lefort, struck up the 'anti-totalitarian' anthem, the latter devoting a book entitled *Un homme en trop* to Solzhenitsyn.[16] It is true that from the 1950s *Socialisme ou barbarie* was one of the first journals to develop a systematic critique of Stalinism.[17] The 'anti-totalitarian consensus' that reigned in France from the second half of the 1970s extended from Castoriadis, via *Tel Quel* and Maurice Clavel, to Raymond Aron (obviously with significant nuances). From the other side of the stage, young 'entrants' into the intellectual field of the time – the 'new philosophers' – made 'anti-totalitarianism' their stock in trade. Nineteen seventy-seven – which we have selected as the

---

15   Michael Scott Christofferson, *French Intellectuals Against the Left: The Antitotalitarian Moment of the 1970s*, New York and Oxford: Berghahn, 2004.
16   Claude Lefort, *Un homme en trop. Essai sur l'Archipel du goulag de Soljenitsyne*, Paris: Seuil, 1975.
17   Philippe Gottraux, *Socialisme ou barbarie. Un engagement politique et intellectuel dans la France de l'après-guerre*, Lausanne: Payot, 1997.

starting point of the historical period dealt with in this chapter[18] – witnessed their consecration by the media. That year André Glucksmann and Bernard-Henri Lévy published *Les Maîtres penseurs* and *La Barbarie à visage humain*, respectively.[19]

The thesis of the 'new philosophers' was that any project for transforming society led to 'totalitarianism' – that is, regimes based on mass murder in which the State subjugates the whole social body. The accusation of 'totalitarianism' was directed not only at the USSR and the countries of 'real socialism', but at the whole labour movement. François Furet's 'revisionist' enterprise in the historiography of the French Revolution, and his subsequent analysis of the 'communist passion' in the twentieth century, rested on an analogous idea. During the 1970s certain 'new philosophers' – many of whom issued from the same Maoist organization, the *Gauche prolétarienne* – retained a certain political radicalism. In *The Master Thinkers*, Glucksmann counterposed the plebs to the (totalitarian) State, in libertarian accents that would not be disavowed by current supporters of the 'multitude', and which go some way to explaining the support he received at the time from Foucault.[20] Over the years, however, these thinkers gradually moved towards the defence of 'human rights', humanitarian intervention, liberalism and the market economy.

At the heart of the 'new philosophy' was an argument about theory. It derived from traditional European conservative thought, especially Edmund Burke. Glucksmann encapsulated it in a formula: 'To theorize is to terrorize'. Burke attributed the catastrophic consequences of the French Revolution (the Terror) to the 'speculative spirit' of philosophers insufficiently attentive to the complexity of reality and the imperfection of human nature. According to Burke, revolutions are the product of intellectuals prone to assign more importance to ideas than to facts that have passed the 'test of time'.[21] In a similar vein, Glucksmann and his colleagues criticized the tendency in the history of western thought that claims to grasp reality in its 'totality' and, on that basis, seeks to alter it – a tendency that goes back to Plato and which, via Leibniz and Hegel, issues in Marx and Marxism. Karl Popper, it is interesting to note, developed a similar thesis in the 1940s, in particular in *The Open*

---

18   Another possibility would have been to adopt as our end-point the appearance in 1976 of Christian Jambet and Guy Lardreau's *L'Ange. Ontologie de la révolution*, Paris: Grasset, 1976, which heralded the subsequent evolution of many leaders of *Gauche prolétarienne*.

19   André Glucksmann, *The Master Thinkers*, trans. Brian Pearce, Brighton: Harvester, 1980, and Bernard Henri-Lévy, *Barbarism with a Human Face*, trans. George Holoch, New York: Harper and Row, 1979.

20   See Peter Dews, 'The "Nouvelle Philosophie" and Foucault', *Economy and Society*, vol. 8, 1979.

21   For this conservative argument and various others, readers are referred to Ted Honderich, *Conservatism*, London: Hamish Hamilton, 1990.

Society and Its Enemies.[22] As is well known, Popper is one of the patron saints of neo-liberalism and his argument features prominently in its doctrinal corpus to this day. The assimilation of 'theorization' to 'terror' is based on the following syllogism: understanding reality in its totality amounts to wanting to subjugate it; this ambition inevitably leads to the gulag. In these conditions we can see why critical theories have deserted their continent of origin in search of more favourable climes.

The success of the 'new philosophers' may be regarded as symptomatic. It says a lot about the changes undergone by the political and intellectual field of the time. These were the years of the renunciation of the radicalism of 1968, the 'end of ideologies', and the substitution of 'experts' for intellectuals.[23] The creation by Alain Minc, Furet, Pierre Rosanvallon and others in 1982 of the Fondation Saint-Simon, which (in the words of Pierre Nora) brought together 'people who have ideas with people who have resources', symbolizes the emergence of a knowledge of the social world supposedly free of ideology.[24] *The End of Ideology* by the American sociologist Daniel Bell dates from 1960, but it was only during the 1980s that this leitmotif reached France and found expression in all areas of social existence. In the cultural sphere, Jack Lang and Jean-François Bizot – the founder of *Actuel* and Radio Nova – cast May 1968 as a failed revolution but a successful festival. In the economic domain, Bernard Tapie, future minister under Mitterrand, projected the firm as the site of every type of creativity. In the intellectual sphere, the journal *Le Débat*, edited by Nora and Marcel Gauchet, published its first issue in 1980; in an article entitled 'Que peuvent les intellectuels?', Nora advised the latter henceforth to confine themselves to their area of competence and stop intervening in politics.[25]

The atmosphere of the 1980s must be related to the 'infrastructural' changes affecting industrial societies after the end of the Second World War. One of the main changes was the importance assumed by the media in intellectual life. The 'new philosophers' were the first televised philosophical current. Certainly, Sartre and Foucault also appeared at the time in filmed interviews, but they would have existed, as would their oeuvres, in the absence of television. The same is not true of Lévy and Glucksmann. In many respects, the 'new philosophers' were media products, their works – as well as recognizable signs like white shirts, wayward locks, 'dissident' posture – being conceived with the

---

22   Karl Popper, *The Open Society and Its Enemies*, 2 vols, London and New York: Routledge, 2011.

23   François Cusset, *La Décennie. Le grand cauchemar des années 1980*, Paris: La Découverte, 2006.

24   On the history of 'expertise' in France, see Kristin Ross, *Fast Cars, Clean Bodies: Decolonization and the Reordering of French Culture*, Cambridge (MA): MIT Press, 1995.

25   See Perry Anderson, *The New-Old World*, London and New York: Verso, 2009, chapter 4.

constraints of television in mind.[26] The intrusion of the media into the intellectual field abruptly altered the conditions of production of critical theories. It is an additional element in explaining the hostile climate that developed in France from the late 1970s. Thus, one of the countries where critical theories had prospered most during the previous period – with the contributions of Althusser, Lefebvre, Foucault, Deleuze, Bourdieu, Barthes and Lyotard in particular – saw its intellectual tradition wither. Some of these authors continued to produce important works during the 1980s. Deleuze and Guattari's *Mille Plateaux* appeared in 1980, Lyotard's *Le Différend* in 1983, and Foucault's *L'Usage des plaisirs* in 1984. But French critical thinking lost the capacity for innovation it had once possessed. A theoretical glaciation set in, from which in some respects we have yet to emerge.

The phenomenon of the 'new philosophers' is certainly typically French, notably because its protagonists' sociological profile is intimately bound up with the French system of the reproduction of elites. But the general trend of abandoning the ideas of 1968, noticeable from the second half of the 1970s, is observable internationally, even if it assumes different forms in each country. A fascinating case, which still awaits an in-depth study, is that of the Italian Lucio Colletti. Colletti was one of the most innovative Marxist philosophers of the 1960s and 70s. A member of the Italian Communist Party from 1950, he decided to leave it at the time of the Budapest insurrection in 1956, which (as we have seen) was the occasion for a number of intellectuals to break with the Communist movement (though he did not actually make the break until 1964).[27] He became increasingly critical of Stalinism. Like Althusser in France (with whom he corresponded and who held him in high regard), and under the influence of his master Galvano Della Volpe, Colletti defended the idea that the break made by Marx with Hegel was sharper than commonly thought. This thesis is developed, in particular, in *Marxism and Hegel*, one of his best-known works.[28] Another of his influential works is *From Rousseau to Lenin*, which attests to the importance of Lenin's materialism in his thinking.

From the mid-1970s Colletti proved increasingly critical of Marxism and especially Western Marxism, of which he was one of the representatives and chief theoreticians. In an interview published at the time, speaking in a pessimistic tone that heralded his subsequent evolution, he declared:

---

26 Something spotted by Deleuze as early as 1977 in 'À propos des nouveaux philosophes et d'un problème plus général', in Gilles Deleuze, *Deux régimes de fous et autres textes (1975–1995)*, Paris: Minuit, 2003.

27 Steve Redhead, 'From Marxism to Berlusconi: Lucio Colletti and the Struggle for Scientific Marxism', *Rethinking Marxism*, vol. 22, no. 1, 2010.

28 Lucio Colletti, *Marxism and Hegel*, trans. Lawrence Garner, London: New Left Books, 1973.

The only way in which Marxism can be revived is if no more books like *Marxism and Hegel* are published, and instead books like Hilferding's *Finance Capital* and Luxemburg's *Accumulation of Capital* – or even Lenin's *Imperialism*, which was a popular brochure – are once again written. In short, either Marxism has the capacity – I certainly do not – to produce at that level, or it will survive merely as the foible of a few university professors. But in that case, it will be well and truly dead, and the professors might as well invent a new name for their clerisy.[29]

According to Colletti, either Marxism succeeds in reconciling theory and practice, and thus repairing the rupture provoked by the failure of the German revolution to which we have referred, or it no longer exists as Marxism. In his view, 'Western Marxism' was therefore a logical impossibility. In the 1980s Colletti moved towards the Italian Socialist Party, led at the time by Bettino Craxi, whose degree of corruption mounted vertiginously over the years. In the 1990s, in a final tragic shift to the right, he adhered to *Forza Italia*, the party newly created by Silvio Berlusconi, and became a senator for the party in 1996. Upon Colletti's death in 2001, Berlusconi saluted the courage he had demonstrated in rejecting Communist ideology and recalled his role in *Forza Italia*'s activities.

On the other side of the world, similar evolution characterized the 'Argentinian Gramscians'. Gramsci's ideas were soon in circulation in Argentina, by virtue of the cultural proximity between it and Italy, but also because his concepts were particularly useful in explaining the highly original and typically Argentinian political phenomenon of Peronism (for example, the notion of 'passive revolution').[30] A group of young intellectuals issued from the Argentinian Communist Party, led by José Aricó and Juan Carlos Portantiero, founded the journal *Pasado y Presente* in 1963, alluding to a series of fragments in the *Prison Notebooks* that bear this title.[31] Interestingly, ten years earlier (1952), a journal of the same name, *Past and Present*, was created in Britain around the Marxist historians Eric Hobsbawm, Christopher Hill and Rodney Hilton. As was bound to be true of Latin American revolutionaries in these years, the Argentinian Gramscians were influenced by the Cuban Revolution (1959), the hybridization of Gramsci's oeuvre and that event prompting theoretical developments of great fertility. At the time, the journal also acted as an interface between Argentina and the world by translating and/or publishing authors like Fanon, Bettelheim, Mao, Guevara, Sartre, and representatives of the Frankfurt School.

---

29   Lucio Colletti, 'A Political and Philosophical Interview', *New Left Review*, I/86, July–August 1974, p. 28.

30   Osvaldo Fernandez Diaz, 'In America Latina', in Eric Hobsbawm and Antonio Santucci, eds, *Gramsci in Europa e in America*, Bari: Laterza, 1995.

31   See Raul Burgos, *Les Gramscianos argentinos*, Buenos Aires: Siglo XXI, 2004.

In the early 1970s, when the class struggle took a more violent turn in Argentina, Aricò and his group moved towards the Peronist revolutionary Left, particularly the Montoneros guerrillas, who were a kind of synthesis of Perón and Guevara. The journal attempted to reflect the strategic questions faced by the revolutionary movement, concerning the conditions of armed struggle, imperialism, and the character of the dominant Argentinian classes. With the 1976 coup d'état, Aricò was forced into exile in Mexico, like a number of Latin American Marxists of his generation. Thereafter his trajectory, like that of his colleagues, consisted in a gradual shift to the political centre. To start with, they proclaimed their support for the Argentinian offensive during the Malvinas War in 1982. Some of them, including the philosopher Emilio de Ipola, would cast a highly critical retrospective eye over this. Ardent support-ers of Felipe Gonzales and the Spanish PSOE in the 1980s, they ended up backing the first democratically elected president after the fall of the Argen-tinian dictatorship, the (centre-right) radical Raúl Alfonsín. They formed part of a group of special advisers to the latter; the group was known as the 'Grupo Esmerelda' and theorized the idea of the 'democratic pact'. Their support for Alfonsin extended to adopting what was in some respects an ambiguous atti-tude to the odious *Leyes de Obedencia y Punto Final* amnestying the crimes of the dictatorship, which President Nestor Kirchner was to abrogate in the first decade of the 2000s.[32]

Examples of shifts to the right by intellectuals could be multiplied. The neo-liberal turn of China propelled by Deng Xiaoping in the late 1980s had a marked impact on Chinese critical thinking, leading to the appropriation (or re-appropriation) of the western liberal tradition by significant sectors of the intelligentsia, and the acclimatization of debates on John Rawls' theory of justice.[33] Another, similar case is that of many US neo-conservatives – among them Irving Kristol, often presented as the 'godfather of neo-conservatism' – who issued from the non-Stalinist Left. An instructive document in this regard is 'Memoirs of a Trotskyist' published by Kristol in the *New York Times*.[34]

Once again there is no question of claiming that these authors or currents are identical. The new philosophers, Colletti, and the Argentinian Gramscians are intellectuals of very different calibre; innovative Marxists like Colletti or Aricò obviously cannot be placed on the same level as an impostor like Lévy. Their intellectual trajectories are largely explained by the national contexts in which they occurred. At the same time, they are also the expression of a move

32   See Nestor Kohan, 'José Aricò, *Pasado y Presente*, y los gramscianos argentinos', *Revista N*, February 2005.

33   See Chen Lichuan, 'Le débat entre libéralisme et nouvelle gauche au tournant du siècle', *Perspectives chinoises*, 84, 2004.

34   'Memoirs of a Trotskyist', *New York Times Magazine*, 23 January 1977.

to the right by formerly revolutionary intellectuals that can be identified on an international scale.

The conclusion to be drawn from this is that the second half of the 1970s and the 1980s were a period of abrupt changes in the geography of critical thinking. It was then that the political and intellectual coordinates of a new period were gradually fixed.

THE GLOBALIZATION OF CRITICAL THINKING

At the same time as the 'closure of possibilities' in continental Europe, powerful currents of critical thinking emerged in peripheral regions of the international intellectual field. Not that theoretical critique had hitherto been restricted to the western world. The case of the Peruvian Marxist José Carlos Mariátegui, who died in 1930, indicates that innovative forms of critical thinking had long been produced outside the West. The interesting thing about Máriategui is that he adapted a theory (Marxism) developed in nineteenth-century Europe to the Latin America, and particularly the Andean world, of the early twentieth century.[35] The same is true of the West Indian from Trinidad and Tobago, C. L. R. James, whose *The Black Jacobins* (1938), about the Haitian Revolution, rivalled Mariátegui's *Seven Interpretive Essays on Peruvian Reality* (1928) in its subtlety. Or Frantz Fanon, whose *Les Damnés de la Terre* (1961) is one of the most influential works of the second half of the twentieth century and one of the sources of inspiration for postcolonial studies.

However, cases of this kind are comparatively rare. It was not until the last third of the twentieth century that a significant number of world-class critical theorists emerged from the periphery. Thus, some of the main contemporary critical thinkers originate on the margins of the 'world system'. Among them are the Palestinian Edward Said (d. 2003), the Slovenian Slavoj Žižek, the Argentinian Ernesto Laclau, the Turk Seyla Benhabib, the Ecuadorian Bolívar Echeverría, the Brazilian Roberto Mangabeira Unger, the Mexican Nestor Garcia Canclini, the Japanese Kojin Karatani, the Indian Homi Bhabha, the Cameroonian Achille Mbembe, the Chinese Wang Hui, or the Peruvian Anibal Quijano. There is no doubt that continental Europe is no longer, as it was until the 1970s, the principal producer of critical theories. It is even likely that this centre is gradually drifting away from the western world in general.

How are we to explain the globalization currently affecting critical theories? Such theories are subject to the general regime in the international circulation of ideas. If (to paraphrase Pascale Casanova) there exists a 'world

---

35   See Michael Löwy, ed., *Marxism in Latin America from 1909 to the Present*, trans. Michael Pearlman, New Jersey: Atlantic Highlands, 1992.

republic of letters', there also exists a 'world republic of critical theories'.[36] This republic is not homogeneous. It remains governed by a form of 'uneven development', in the sense that not every region makes an equal contribution to intellectual production. Among the determinants influencing the theoretical productivity of a region are, in particular, the nature of its university system, its level of economic development, and the vigour of its social movements. However, notwithstanding the evident existence of regional disparities, the issue of the conditions of production and circulation of critical thinking is posed at a global level today.[37]

If the centre of gravity of critical theories shifted in the course of the 1980s, in the Anglo-American world this phenomenon was not unrelated to the diversification in the national origins of their authors. Unlike French universities, whose self-enclosed character is notorious, the US academy is open to the world.[38] This openness is explained in the first instance by the fact that the United States is a country of migration and, in particular, intellectual migrations. Think of the famous refugee scholars who emigrated during the Second World War. Leo Strauss, Alfred Schütz, Hans Reichenbach, Rudolf Carnap, Erich Auerbach (who was Said's and Jameson's teacher), Theodor Adorno and Herbert Marcuse settled in the United States in the 1930s and 40s.[39] The US academy has retained an extrovert character that has doubtless increased since then and continues to attract a number of critical theorists for regular stints or permanent residence. Among them are Laclau, Walter Mignolo, Yann Moulier-Boutang, Étienne Balibar, Giovanni Arrighi, Said, Robin Blackburn, David Harvey, Unger, Boaventura de Sousa Santos, Bhabha, Spivak, Achille Mbembe, Badiou, Giorgio Agamben and so forth. The list could be extended indefinitely. Some have pursued their whole career in the United States, while others have settled there more recently. Some also teach in universities in other countries – for example, those of their country of origin. Others teach exclusively in the United States. But in every case they are received by North American universities, some of them the most highly reputed in the world.

36   Pascale Casanova, *The World Republic of Letters*, trans. M.B. DeBevoise, Cambridge (MA): Harvard University Press, 2004.

37   On the globalization of scientific thought, see Terry Shinn *et al.*, *Denationalizing Science: The Contexts of International Scientific Practice*, Dodrecht: Kluwer, 1992. On the impact of globalization on contemporary critical theory, especially postcolonial studies, see Arif Dirlik, 'The Postcolonial Aura: Third World Criticism in the Age of Global Capitalism', *Critical Inquiry*, vol. 20, 1994.

38   See Johan Heilbron, Nicolas Guilhot and Laurent Jeanpierre, 'Internationalisation des sciences sociales: les leçons d'une histoire transnationale', in Gisèle Sapiro, ed., *L'Espace intellectuel en Europe. De la formation des États-nations à la mondialisation, xixe-xxe siècles*, Paris: La Découverte, 2009.

39   See Lewis Coser, *Refugee Scholars in America: Their Impact and Their Experiences*, New Haven: Yale University Press, 1984.

Why is the United States so attractive to contemporary critical theorists? Conversely, why have universities in the United States, whose recent governments have not distinguished themselves by their particularly 'progressive' character, evinced such an interest in these theorists? Today more than ever, critical thinkers are academics. Trade unionists, community activists, journalists or guerrillas do sometimes produce critical theories. But in most cases the latter are developed by professors and, more precisely, professors in the humanities. From this it can be deduced that the dissociation between political organizations and critical intellectuals registered by Anderson in connection with Western Marxism has increased since the 1960s and 70s. The contemporary Lenins, Trotskys and Luxemburgs are academics, who often work in establishments that are highly rated on the international market. This amounts to saying that they in fact bear little resemblance to those figures of classical Marxism, of whom it has been observed that not one held an academic chair. This does not mean that today's critical intellectuals are not politically committed, or that they are less radical than the classical Marxists. But outside their engagement they are academics – something that is bound to impact on the theories they produce. We shall see in chapter 3 that among these intellectuals, rare are those who are fully fledged members of political or social organizations.

Once critical theorists mainly move in an academic milieu, they are subject to the laws governing it.[40] One of these laws is not in doubt: the domination of North American universities in the higher education and research global market when it comes to finance, publications and infrastructural facilities. The attraction for critical theorists held by these universities is a special case, generally valid for all intellectuals regardless of their political orientation. The American orientation of critical theorists is explained by the American orientation of theorists in general. Wholly integrated into the university system, contemporary critical thinkers in no way form an intellectual 'counter-society' like German social democracy's school for cadres in the early twentieth century or, later, the French Communist Party's. Parallel institutions of this type possibly exist today in an embryonic form.[41] It might also be thought that some Internet sites perform the role of intellectual 'counter-society'.[42] Generally speaking, however, contemporary critical intellectuals are situated in the 'ivory

---

40   For a sociology of contemporary academics, see Christine Musselin, *Les Universitaires*, Paris: La Découverte, 2008.

41   ATTAC's scientific committee, the 'popular universities' that are experiencing a renewed interest, or the 'nomad university' organized by editors of the journal *Multitudes* (close to Negri) are examples of this.

42   See, for example, the site close to the ideas of Noam Chomsky, organized in particular by Michael Albert: www.znet.org.

tower'. And this involves their submission to the rules and resources that govern this social field, which make US academic institutions irresistible attractors.

However, a more specific factor accounts for the hospitality shown the new critical theorists by North American universities. Since the 1960s, the United States has been the quintessential country of identity politics. This phrase refers to policies – governmental or otherwise – aimed at promoting the interest, or combatting the stigmatization, of some particular category of the population. Identity politics aim to rehabilitate the 'identity' of social groups hitherto discriminated against on account of the negative perception to which they are subject. Identity politics has two important characteristics.[43] The first is that it involves minorities who recognize themselves as such – that is, who do not have the mission of transforming themselves into a majority. In this regard they are opposed to entities like the 'people' or the 'working class', whose historical role was to coincide, in the more or less long term, with society as a whole. The struggle for recognition of homosexual identity, for example, does not necessarily aim to generalize this identity. It aims to put an end to the stigmatization of those concerned. The second characteristic of 'identity' thus conceived is that it is not a (uniquely) economic instance. It contains a decisive cultural dimension.

What is the relationship between identity politics and the US orientation of critical theories? As François Cusset has shown, through their reception in the United States from the 1970s, authors like Derrida, Deleuze and Foucault helped fuel academic and political debates over identity politics.[44] Obviously, across the Atlantic, intellectual traditions exist that are peculiar to oppressed minorities. Think of the importance of W. E. B. Du Bois (1868–1963) in the construction of a critical corpus on the condition of blacks or the powerful feminist tradition which is continuing to develop there.[45] However, a junction occurred between French (post)structuralism and the 'identitarian' concerns of a number of US intellectuals and social movements. It derived from the fact that (post)structuralism makes it possible to conceive the emancipatory potential of so-called minority-dominated groups, and also from the fact that some of its variants (to say the very least) formulate a critique of 'totality', in favour of a political

---

43   See Philip Gleason, 'Identifying Identity: A Semantic History', *The Journal of American History*, vol. 69, no. 4, 1983, and Michel Feher, '1967–1992. Sur quelques recompositions de la gauche américaine', *Esprit*, December 1992. For a critique of the notion of identity politics, see Craig Calhoun, 'The Politics of Identity and Recognition', in Calhoun, *Critical Social Theory*, Oxford: Blackwell, 1995.

44   François Cusset, *French Theory: How Foucault, Derrida, Deleuze, and Co. Transformed the Intellectual Life of the United States*, trans. Jeff Fort, Minneapolis: University of Minnesota Press, 2008. See also Craig Calhoun, ed., *Social Theory and the Politics of Identity*, Oxford: Blackwell, 1994.

45   See W. E. B. Du Bois, *The Souls of Black Folk*, London: Longmans, 1965, and Chris Beasley, *What Is Feminism? An Introduction to Feminist Theory*, London: Sage, 1999.

philosophy based on 'difference'. In France it is likely that the 'republicanism' derived from the French Revolution, intensified by the centrality assigned to the industrial working class at the expense of other oppressed categories by the Communist Party, prevented the emergence of analogous social movements. We shall return to the foundations of identity politics and their significance in the emergence of new critical theories. We shall see that the concept of 'identity' is today prioritized in the context of the crisis of the 'subject of emancipation' that has been brewing since the 1960s. Generally speaking, a 'recoding' of the social world in terms of 'identities' is noticeable from the 1980s.[46]

A PROLIFERATION OF REFERENCES

An important characteristic of the new critical theories is Marxism's loss of hegemony within them. Contrary to a received idea, Marxism today is a decidedly living paradigm. A number of contemporary critical theorists, among the most stimulating, identify with this tradition. It remains active not only in the domain of critical theories, but also in the social sciences. The work of the economist Robert Brenner; the geographer David Harvey; the sociologist Mike Davis; the historian Perry Anderson and his brother, the political scientist Benedict Anderson; or the sociologist Erik Olin Wright, among numerous others, attest to this. At the same time it is clear that Marxism can no longer claim the centrality it once possessed. From the second half of the nineteenth century until the early 1970s, for more than a century, Marxism was the most powerful critical theory. Its sway was undivided, even in regions where competing critical theories, such as anarchism, were firmly implanted. On the Left, the only doctrine that can stand comparison with Marxism in terms of diffusion and political impact is Keynesianism. (That said, Keynesianism refers to a set of economic policies, not a comprehensive world-view like Marxism.) On the Right, it is the neo-classical model and its generalization to all social spheres by Friedrich von Hayek, Milton Friedman and Gary Becker that is most comparable to Marxism in influence.

Marxism's success can be attributed to the fact that it involves a comprehensive paradigm, which no aspect of social – and, in a sense, physical – existence escapes. There is a Marxist perspective in all the disciplines of human sciences: economics, geography, sociology, political science, philosophy, linguistics and so on. There are even several. For example, a sociologist can adopt the standpoint of 'analytical' Marxism – say, that of Olin Wright – or an approach inspired by the Frankfurt School and Sartre – like that of Jameson.

---

46   Rogers Brubaker, 'Au-delà de l'identité', *Actes de recherche en sciences sociales*, no. 139, September 2001.

Another reason for the success of Marxism during the previous century is the subtle mix of objectivity and normativity that characterizes it. Marxism offers both an analysis of the social world and a political project, which makes it possible to imagine the contours of a possible different world. This ambivalence between the factual and the normative, which the best representatives of the tradition have known how to exploit, explains its hegemony in the history of modern critical theories.

The situation changed considerably in the last third of the twentieth century, and the 1970s represent a turning-point in this respect, with the concurrent flourishing of structuralism – a school that is perhaps the only one since Marxism to combine as subtly the objective and the normative, the scientific and the political, and also the only one to offer a 'totalizing' viewpoint on the social and natural world. With the emergence of structuralism, Marxism for the first time in its history confronted a rival worthy of the name, and lost the theoretical hegemony it had hitherto possessed on the Left.[47] From the outset, hybrid forms of Marxism and structuralism emerged; Althusser's oeuvre is sufficient testimony to this. Consequently, to present these two currents as rivals on all points would be an exaggeration; in some respects they developed in tandem. Even so, we are dealing with paradigms that rely on different assumptions. Today, a number of critical theorists identify with one form or another of structuralism or poststructuralism, conceiving it as an alternative to Marxism.

Marxism and structuralism are not the only intellectual traditions mobilized by the new critical theories. Far from it. We live in a time of the proliferation of the most diverse references, whereas the critical canon of the 1960s and 70s was unquestionably more standardized. More precisely, in the 1960s and 70s a 'canon' existed and, while it was accompanied by a proliferation of references, they were situated on the margins, by contrast with today. This eclecticism can be interpreted as an additional consequence of the defeat suffered by the radical Left from the second half of the 1970s. The advocates of a defeated theory often look to the oeuvre of thinkers external to it for resources with which to re-equip it. Anderson has shown that this was one of the main theoretical operations out of which Western Marxism developed.[48] The influence of Weber on Lukács, Croce on Gramsci, Heidegger on Sartre, Spinoza on Althusser, or Hjelmslev on Della Volpe, afford so many examples. Marx and classical Marxism are themselves inconceivable without taking their relations with exogenous traditions into consideration: Hegel and classical political economy in the case of Marx; Clausewitz, Hobson and Ernst Mach in the case of Lenin. This recourse to external sources is explained by the fact that they occupy a central position in

---

47   See Anderson, *In the Tracks of Historical Materialism*, chapter 2.
48   Anderson, *Considerations on Western Marxism*, chapter 3.

the debates of the era considered. Any intellectual, whether Marxist or not, who had no opinion on Croce's oeuvre in pre-war Italy would isolate himself from the most important discussions of his time. The same is true of any French thinker in the 1940s and 50s who ignored phenomenology. Through these external sources the authors in question sought to impart new impetus to theories that were in difficulty, precisely on account of the rout they had suffered.

How do things stand with the new critical theories? Defeat has impacted on the diversification of references in at least two ways. Firstly, it has led to the rehabilitation of old concepts. Among them we find, for example, 'utopia', 'sovereignty' and 'citizenship'. As Daniel Lindenberg points out, the use of these concepts would have provoked mockery from critical thinkers – especially Marxists – in the 1960s and 70s.[49] 'Citizenship' and 'sovereignty', which we find, for example, in the highly fashionable phrase 'food sovereignty', would have been regarded as belonging to the vocabulary of 'bourgeois' democracy. For its part 'utopia' would have been dismissed on account of its unduly 'idealist' connotations. However, these concepts are frequently employed today. One of the most debated notions within current critical theories was also absent from the conceptual repertoire of the 1960s and 70s. This is the notion of 'multitude' developed by Negri, Paolo Virno and Álvaro García Linera.

In addition to the rehabilitation of old concepts, defeat has prompted the emergence within critical theories of new references, positive or negative. Among them, in particular, figure Hannah Arendt and John Rawls. The former's analysis of totalitarianism and the latter's theory of justice are doubtless the themes that have generated the most debate during the 1980s and 90s. On these grounds it is understandable that they feature in the writings of critical thinkers. Daniel Bensaïd, Judith Butler, Agamben and Zygmunt Bauman have offered analyses of Arendt, whereas Alex Callinicos, Philippe van Parijs, Benhabib, Anderson and Olin Wright have attended to Rawls. Furthermore, in the new critical theories we find references to a series of figures from democratic and national liberation movements. The writings of Thomas Jefferson have been the object of a new edition presented by Michael Hardt.[50] In *Multitude*, Hardt and Negri draw inspiration from another 'founding father' of the United States, James Madison.[51] For his part, Balibar evokes Gandhi, claiming that the major 'missed encounter' of the twentieth century was his with Lenin.[52] Robespierre's

49   Daniel Lindenberg, 'Le marxisme au XXe siècle', in Jean-Jacques Becker and Gilles Candar, eds, *Histoire des gauches en France*, Paris: La Découverte, 2005, vol. 2, p. 642.

50   Thomas Jefferson, *The Declaration of Independence*, introduced by Michael Hardt, London and New York: Verso, 2007.

51   Michael Hardt and Antonio Negri, *Multitude: War and Democracy in the Age of Empire*, London: Penguin, 2005.

52   Étienne Balibar, 'Lenin and Gandhi: A Missed Encounter?', *Radical Philosophy*, no. 172, March–April 2012.

speeches have been reprinted, with an introduction by Žižek, as have Saint Just's complete works presented by Miguel Abensour.[53] And this is to ignore the innumerable 'returns to Marx' which aim to rediscover the spirit of the author of *Capital* 'beyond' Marxism. The scale of a defeat is also measured by the quantity of thinkers to whom people feel compelled to 'return'.

One of the authors on whom critical theorists draw merits particular attention: Carl Schmitt. This conservative jurist with a Nazi past is a major influence on thinkers of the radical Left. References to his oeuvre can be found in Agamben, Bensaïd, Negri and Balibar, in particular. Schmitt has become so popular among radical thinkers that a specialist in his work, Jean-Claude Monod, has devoted considerable space to what he calls 'left-wing neo-Schmittians' – that is, authors who use Schmitt in their attempt to re-found theoretical and political critique.[54] Systematic reference to Schmitt in critical theories dates from the 1990s. References to his concepts nevertheless appeared in Italian *operaismo*. One of the founders of that current, Mario Tronti, published an essay in 1977 entitled *Sull'autonomia del politico*, in which he referred to Schmitt's oeuvre. As the book's title indicates, it aided him in conceptualizing the problem of the 'autonomy of the political' in a Marxist framework where politics is generally regarded as subordinate to economics. Well before the *operaisti*, Walter Benjamin had felt Schmitt's influence. Several references to the latter occur in *The Origin of German Tragic Drama* (1925). A theoretical connection exists between Schmitt and thinkers of the Frankfurt School. It derives from the similarity of their historical experience, starting with the Weimar Republic.

We shall not understand Schmitt's attraction for thinkers of the radical Left if we do not appreciate that he had himself experienced the influence of intellectuals and leaders of the labour movement. In his oeuvre, Schmitt refers to Marx, Lenin, Trotsky and Mao; and his *Theory of the Partisan*, for example, is directly influenced by them. As is well known, for Schmitt politics essentially consists in defining the boundary between 'friend' and 'enemy'. Schmitt's interest in Marxists derives from the fact that, according to him, they invented a new type of 'enemy' – namely, the 'class enemy'. In drawing on Schmitt, present-day critical theorists are therefore simply rediscovering themes originally derived from Marxism. The reference to Georges Sorel is equally interesting. It occurs in certain contemporary critical thinkers, among them Laclau. Schmitt explicitly invokes Sorel, regarding him as the Machiavelli of the twentieth century. Now, there clearly exists a Marxism of Sorelian descent, of which Gramsci and Mariátegui, two authors with considerable influence on the new critical

---

53   See, respectively, Maximilien Robespierre, *Virtue and Terror*, trans. John Howe, London and New York: Verso, 2007, and Saint Just, *Oeuvres complètes*, Paris: Gallimard, 2004.

54   Jean-Claude Monod, *Penser l'ennemi, affronter l'exception. Réflexions critiques sur l'actualité de Carl Schmitt*, Paris: La Découverte, 2006.

theories, count among the representatives.[55] Schmitt's impact on these theories is therefore not only direct, but also 'mediated' by the influence he had on thinkers who are themselves influential on them.

Within the new critical theories we also observe numerous references to religious phenomena. Various contemporary critical thinkers bolster their analyses with doctrines or figures from Christianity. Surprising as it is, this is nothing new. We need only think of Pascal's influence on Lucien Goldmann, who maintained that adhesion to Marxism rested on an act of faith similar to religious faith,[56] or Ernst Bloch's study of *Thomas Münzer: Theologian of Revolution* (1921) and the revolutionary millenarianism that marked peasant revolts in the sixteenth century. For his part, Mariátegui devoted a text to Joan of Arc as early as 1929.[57] References to theology were, however, comparatively marginal in twentieth-century critical theories. They were made by authors who were certainly far from negligible, but who did not have a central place in the 'canon' of the revolutionary Left. Moreover, they were more frequent in Western than classical Marxism.

Things are quite different now. The authors who invoke religious doctrines in their oeuvres count among the main contemporary critical thinkers. Thus, Badiou has written an important work on Saint Paul.[58] In it he puts to Paul's test the idea that the 'subject' is constituted in fidelity to an 'event', which can be political, scientific, artistic, or even amorous in kind. The relationship between subject and event is developed more systematically in *Being and Event* and *Logics of Worlds*, in which references to religious thinking (especially Paul) also figure. Agamben has also devoted a meditation to Saint Paul, in the form of a commentary on the Epistle to the Romans entitled *The Time that Remains*. Agamben's erudition in theological matters is unrivalled among current critical thinkers. In his works there are frequent references to Roman religious law (in *Homo sacer*), the Jewish tradition, or particular aspects of Christian eschatology. In *Empire*, Negri and Hardt turn for support to the '*poverello*', Saint Francis of Assisi. Moreover, Negri has devoted a work to the Book of Job, entitled *The Labor of Job*. Several of Žižek's books refer to religious problematics – for example, *The Fragile Absolute*, subtitled *Or, Why Is the Christian Legacy Worth Fighting For?*, and *The Puppet and the Dwarf*, subtitled *The Perverse Core of*

---

55   On Sorel, see Jacques Julliard and Shlomo Sand, eds, *Georges Sorel en son temps*, Paris: Seuil, 1985.

56   Michael Löwy, 'Lucien Goldmann, ou le pari communautaire', *Recherche sociale*, September 1995.

57   On the relationship between Marxism and religion, see Roland Boer, *Criticism of Heaven: On Marxism and Theology*, Leiden and Boston: Brill, 2007.

58   Alain Badiou, *Saint Paul: The Foundation of Universalism*, trans. Ray Brassier, Stanford: Stanford University Press, 2003.

Christianity.[59] In Žižek the invocation of religion performs the function not so much (as in Badiou and Negri) of a resource for reconstructing the project of emancipation, as of defending Christianity for its own sake, in so far as it forms part of the history of emancipation. The Pascalian tradition persists in current critical theories – for example, in Bensaïd's *Le Pari mélancolique.* In it Bensaïd, whose variety of Marxism André Tosel characterizes as 'Pascalian Marxism', presents revolutionary commitment as analogous to Pascal's famous wager. Following in the wake of Mariátegui, Bensaïd is also the author of a book on Joan of Arc, *Jeanne de guerre lasse.* Enrique Dussel, a philosopher of Argentinian origin living in Mexico, bases his thought on the founding intuitions of Latin American 'liberation theology'. One of the most influential thinkers on that continent, Dussel is the author of the monumental *Etica de la liberacion,* in which he compares his intuitions with the works of Karl-Otto Apel and Charles Taylor in particular.[60] The relationship between religion and politics in Latin America is different from that in Europe and North America; and an analysis specific to the continent is required here.

How are we to explain the presence of theology at the very heart of the new critical theories? The relationship between critical thinking and religion is far from incidental. In particular, it will have a decisive impact on the alliances that will – or will not – be forged in the future by progressive or revolutionary movements with religious currents, in the western world and elsewhere. That Marxism – to be precise, a schematic Marxism – regarded religion (in a celebrated formula) as the 'opium of the people' has obviously had an influence not only on theories, but also on the strategies pursued by the labour movement. If we take the case of the revolutions which have unfolded in the Arab world since late 2010, it is clear that something important is being played out there in terms of the relations between religion and emancipation. The Islamist currents, which are highly diverse, are shot through with contradictions. Some are conservative; others are ready to work for the democratization of religion by allying with 'progressive' movements. The way the latter represent themselves, agreeing to make alliances with Islamist currents or not, will largely determine the outcome of those revolutions. In short, the way that forms of critical thought theorize the religious is a crucial strategic question.

We shall confine ourselves to two aspects of the problem. Firstly, the overwhelming majority of religious references in current critical thinking deal with a specific problem: belief. This is the case with the references to

---

59   Slavoj Žižek, *The Fragile Absolute,* London and New York: Verso, 2000, and *The Puppet and the Dwarf: The Perverse Core of Christianity,* Cambridge (MA): MIT Press, 2003.

60   Enrique Dussel, *Etica de la liberacion en la edad de la globalizacion y de la exclusion,* Madrid: Trotta, 1998. On liberation theology, see Michael Löwy, *The War of the Gods: Religion and Politics in Latin America,* London and New York: Verso, 1996.

Saint Paul, Job and Pascal. These theological figures raise the question of how it is possible to continue believing or hoping when everything seems to run counter to belief, when circumstances are radically hostile to it. It is only natural that critical thinkers should feel the need to offer an answer to it. Experiments in constructing a socialist society have all ended tragically. The Marxist conceptual and organizational framework, which dominated the labour movement for more than a century, has collapsed. In such conditions, how is one to continue believing in the feasibility of socialism, when the facts have brutally and repeatedly invalidated the idea? Theology offers plentiful resources for thinking this problem – belief in the non-existent is its speciality – and from this point of view it is understandable that critical thinkers have seized on them.

A second aspect of the question is more sociological. The current resurgence of religion is obviously not exclusively attributable to critical thinkers. It is imposed on them by the world in which they live. Alternative hypotheses about the 'return of the religious' or, conversely, the 'disenchantment of the world' are the subject of fierce debates among specialists. If its everyday practice seems to be continuing on its secular decline in Europe, religion appears to be making a strong comeback in the political field, with, for example, radical Islam and American fundamentalist currents. In this regard, contending for the religious phenomenon with fundamentalists, demonstrating that progressive, even revolutionary, forms of religiosity exist, is a smart strategy. It involves confronting the opponent on his own ground. Typical in this regard is the new introduction to the *Gospels* published by Terry Eagleton, under the appetizing title *Terry Eagleton Presents Jesus Christ*.[61]

One consequence of defeat is that it has altered the pantheon of critical authors of the 1960s and 70s. Some of the authors who were then situated at the top of the doctrinal hierarchy have been downgraded, or even disappeared from it, while others who were at the bottom have moved to the top. During the 1960s and 70s Benjamin was a not insignificant author in the Marxist tradition. The first article devoted to him in *New Left Review* – a good indicator of theoretical trends – dates from 1968. But compared with figures like Mao, Marcuse, Lenin or Wilhelm Reich, Benjamin was secondary. The 1960s and 70s were highly political and the significance of an author was assessed at the time by the strategic use that could be made of him. When the neo-liberal counter-revolution set in, Benjamin's 'rating' gradually increased. Within Marxism the author of the *Theses on the Concept of History* is, *par excellence*, the one who makes it

---

61   *The Gospels: Terry Eagleton Presents Jesus Christ*, London and New York: Verso, 2007. On the 'theological turn' in contemporary critical thinking, see also Göran Therborn, *From Marxism to Post-Marxism?*, London and New York: Verso, 2009.

possible to think defeat. His considerations on the 'tradition of the vanquished' – salvaging and transmitting the memory of struggles – have since then been put to work.[62]

Another thinker whose importance has continued to grow over the years is Gramsci.[63] The author of the *Prison Notebooks* has always occupied a special place in the pantheon of twentieth-century critical thinkers, particularly – obviously – in Italy. His influence has nevertheless manifestly increased over the last two or three decades. The reason for this is, firstly, that Gramsci is a thinker of 'superstructures'. In other words, he is the author in the Marxist tradition who makes it possible to pose the problem of culture more sharply. Thus, Gramsci has been transformed into an unavoidable reference-point for several intellectual currents, among them cultural studies, whose main figures include Raymond Williams and Stuart Hall, and whose specialism is the study of 'popular culture'. Moreover, with his concept of 'hegemony', Gramsci makes it possible to understand the specificity of the forms of domination prevalent in certain political contexts. As a result, critical intellectuals in different parts of the world – for example, the Argentinian Gramscians and the Indian 'subalternists' – have developed a special relationship with his oeuvre.[64]

In 1993 Derrida's *Specters of Marx* appeared. It was the first work to signal a certain revival of theoretical critique in France and stimulated important debates internationally. This was also the date of the publication of Bourdieu's *La Misère du monde*, which had an unanticipated sales success for a scholarly work of over a thousand pages. A revival of critical thinking ensued in one of the countries, if not *the* country, which had generated the most of it in the 1960s and 70s, with the different variants of critical Marxism and (post)structuralism. These works (and others) connected up with debates underway in other countries, where critical thinking had remained alive throughout the period, particularly in the Anglophone world. There is no doubt about it: *Specters of Marx* was more discussed in the United States than in its author's own country.[65] (However, Bourdieu was influential in France at the time.) No doubt it might even be said that Derrida's integration into the American academy was a condition of possibility of that work.

The revival of critical theories currently underway does not mean that we have done with defeat. The radical Left manifestly remains on the defensive.

---

62   See Daniel Bensaïd, *Walter Benjamin, sentinelle messianique à la gauche du possible*, Paris: Plon, 1990; Terry Eagleton, *Walter Benjamin: Towards a Revolutionary Criticism*, London and New York: Verso, 1981; and Michael Löwy, *Fire Alarm: Reading Walter Benjamin's 'On the Concept of History'*, trans. Chris Turner, London and New York: Verso, 2005.

63   On the international circulation of Gramsci's oeuvre, see Michele Filippini, *Gramsci globale. Guida pratica alle interpretazioni di Gramsci nel mondo*, Bologna: Odoya, 2011.

64   See Burgos, *Les Gramscianos argentinos*, and Jean-Loup Amselle, *L'Occident décroché. Enquête sur les postcolonialismes*, Paris: Stock, 2008.

65   See Michael Sprinker, ed., *Ghostly Demarcations*, London and New York: Verso, 1999.

What distinguishes political defeats from military and sporting defeats is that they are potentially interminable. In an armed confrontation the balance of forces turns in favour of one of the belligerents at some point, and the fighting stops. In sport the scale of the defeat is always limited by the exhaustion of the time allocated to the contest. In the political domain, by contrast, defeat can continue indefinitely, which amounts to saying that the gains of the labour movement – democratic and social rights – are infinitely destroyable. Whatever might be said of the revival in critical thinking, it is only right not to neglect this parameter. The new critical theories remain largely subject to it.

CHAPTER TWO

A Brief History of the 'New Left' (1956–77)

The new critical theories have not been developed by 'new' theorists, if by that is meant biologically young intellectuals. There are, of course, young authors producing innovative critical thinking today, but the critical thinkers recognized in the public sphere are in most cases over 60 years of age and often over 70. The implications of this are not insignificant. However 'contemporary', these authors' analyses are mainly the fruit of political experiences belonging to a previous political cycle – that of the 1960s and 70s. Negri's ideas are more influenced by the Italian 'extended May' and 'years of lead' than by the demonstrations at Genoa and the Mumbai Social Forum. The same is true of those of Badiou or Rancière, which (by their own admission) are to be related much more to May 1968 than to the strikes of December 1995.

The new critical theories thus represent an attempt by intellectuals formed during a previous political cycle to think the beginning of a new cycle – the one initiated sometime between the Zapatista uprising of 1994, the strikes of December 1995 in France and the Seattle demonstrations of 1999. This historical discrepancy is hardly surprising. Prior to his imprisonment in 1926, Gramsci, one of the initiators of Western Marxism, exhibited characteristics similar to those of the classical Marxists – in particular, that of being a leader of the Italian Communist Party. The remark also applies to Lukács, who was education commissar in the Hungarian Soviet Republic in 1919, and to Korsch, who was a deputy in the Thuringian Diet in 1923. It was only later that thinkers who had gravitated to Marxism in the context of the new cycle emerged. What is valid for Western Marxism also applies to the current period. The new critical theories have been developed by 'veterans' of critical thinking – that is, by thinkers whose sociological characteristics and ideas were originally associated with the previous period.

That is why an understanding of the new critical theories must involve examination of the theoretical traditions from which these authors derive. In other words, it presupposes an analysis of the 'old' critical theories, those which these authors were developing, along with the dominant thinkers of the time who are now dead, during the 1960s and 70s. The distinction between 'old' and 'new' critical theories is certainly not clear-cut. Some of what passes for new today dates back to theoretical problematics that emerged during the 1960s or even earlier. The history of ideas does not necessarily keep the same time as the history of political events. As a result, there is no reason to suppose that the fall of the Berlin Wall set theoretical counters back to zero. On the other hand, the defeat suffered by the Left from the second half of the 1970s is so profound that there can be no doubt that a break has occurred. The aim of this chapter is to determine the precise relationship between the new critical theories and the old ones.

ALIENATION AND THE CRISIS OF THE SUBJECT OF EMANCIPATION

Western Marxism made many innovations in the Marxist tradition. Some are exogenous, such as those deriving from psychoanalysis, which gave rise to the 'Freudo-Marxism' of Reich, Marcuse and Erich Fromm. Others are endogenous, like Gramsci's development of the concept of 'hegemony', already present in Russian socialists like Plekhanov and Axelrod.[1] The most significant of the changes undergone by Marxism in these years resulted from the publication in the early 1930s of the young Marx's writings – in particular, the 1844 Paris *Manuscripts*. On account of the war it was only from the second half of the 1940s that the theoretical effects of this text made themselves felt. Their impact was at its height during the 1960s and 70s. Several representatives of Western Marxism were influenced by them, especially Lefebvre, Marcuse, Lukács, Della Volpe and Colletti. This influence proved decisive even when the texts were cited only to be rejected. Thus Althusser regarded the *Manuscripts* as 'pre-materialist' – external to the corpus of dialectical materialism.[2] However, they were what enabled the author of *Pour Marx* to advance the hypothesis of the 'epistemological break' which, from *The German Ideology* (1845–6) onwards, separated the 'young Marx' from the scientific Marx.

The interest aroused by the *Manuscripts* was bound up with the crisis Marxism was experiencing. They created the impression that it was possible to contribute to the development of a Marxism adapted to the new conjuncture. The publication during the twentieth century of unpublished writings by Marx – Volumes Two and Three of *Capital*, the *Grundrissse* – prompted original interpretations of his whole oeuvre and a reformulation of the political project underlying it.[3]

---

1   On the history of this concept, see Perry Anderson, 'The Antinomies of Antonio Gramsci', *New Left Review*, I/100, November 1976–January 1977, and Peter D. Thomas, *The Gramscian Moment: Philosophy, Hegemony and Marxism*, Leiden and Boston: Brill, 2009.

2   See Louis Althusser, *For Marx*, trans. Ben Brewster, London: Allen Lane, 1969.

3   See André Tosel, 'The Development of Marxism: From the End of Marxism-Leninism to a Thousand Marxisms – France–Italy, 1975–2005', in Jacques Bidet and Stathis Kouvelakis, eds, *Critical Companion to Contemporary Marxism*, Leiden and Boston: Brill, 2008.

The *Manuscripts* resonated with an experience typical of the period 1945–77: *alienation*. In fact, they placed that concept at the heart of their analysis.[4] As Pierre Nora has shown, alienation was the 'word of the moment' corresponding to this period: 'The moment of alienation was the crystallization of a broad, diffuse and spontaneous social sensibility, corresponding to the massive effects of growth and rapid changes in French society, under the goad of a spearhead of intellectual critique.'[5] What Jean Fourastié was subsequently to dub the *trente glorieuses* – the 'long wave' of economic growth following the Second World War – accelerated the rural exodus, raised living standards, generalized leisure and created a 'new working class', analyzed in particular by Serge Mallet and Alain Touraine. The massification of higher education increased the discrepancy between subjectively perceived social opportunities and real social opportunities. The feeling of 'alienation' lodged in this discrepancy. In 1965 George Perec published *Les Choses*, '*the* novel of alienation' according to Nora. This work gave expression to the growing rupture between individual aspirations to 'authenticity' and the alienating character of society.[6] May 1968, whose protagonists would seek to repair this rupture, was not far off.

The 'diffuse sense' of alienation fuelled, and was nourished by, a series of theoretical elaborations. Among them was Henri Lefebvre's *Critique de la vie quotidienne*, whose first volume was published in 1947. A decade earlier, Lefebvre had published *Le Matérialisme dialectique*, in which the influence of the 1844 *Manuscripts* already made itself felt. Over and above their differences, Jean Baudrillard's *La Société de consommation* (1970), Guy Debord's *La Société du spectacle* (1967), Jacques Ellul's *Technique ou l'enjeu du siècle* (1954), and Jean-Yves Calvez's *La Pensée de Karl Marx* (1956) formed part of this trend. It originated in Lukács, in particular the Lukács of *History and Class Consciousness* (1923), one of whose central concepts was 'reification'. This concept, proximate to that of 'alienation', had already appeared in Marx, in *The Poverty of Philosophy* and then Volume Three of *Capital*. However, it was in the form given it by Lukács in the central chapter of his work – 'Reification and the Consciousness of the Proletariat' – that it was to exercise most influence.[7]

The importance assumed by the notion of 'alienation' within the Left of the time is also explained by other factors. Within 'standard' Marxism – that taught, for example, in the cadres' schools of the Communist parties ('conformist'

4   On this see Stéphane Haber, *L'Aliénation. Vie sociale et dépossession*, Paris: Presses Universitaires de France, 2007.

5   Pierre Nora, 'Aliénation', in Anne Simonin and Hélène Clastres, eds, *Les Idées en France, 1945–1988*, Paris: Gallimard, 1989, p. 493.

6   On Perec's *Les Choses*, see also Bernard Pudal's analysis 'Ordre symbolique et système scolaire dans les années 1960', in Dominique Damamme *et al.*, *Mai–juin 68*, Paris: L'Atelier, 2008.

7   On this intellectual tradition, see Russell Jacoby, *Dialectic of Defeat: Contours of Western Marxism*, Cambridge: Cambridge University Press, 1981.

Marxism, in Russell Jacoby's formulation; 'traditional' Marxism, in Moishe Postone's)[8] – the concept of *exploitation* was fundamental. Exploitation is the extraction of surplus-value – that is, the portion of labour performed by wage-labourers for which they are not remunerated by capitalists. It is an economic concept, even if its consequences extend far beyond this sphere as traditionally conceived. This notion, like the representation of the social world that goes with it, tends to assign centrality to economic oppression – that suffered by the industrial working class – and to regard other forms of oppression, like male domination or colonialism, as secondary. This is what Marxists once called the problematic of 'secondary fronts', the 'main' front being the opposition between capital and labour. Contrary to a current but erroneous retrospective view, 'qualitative' themes – this is an important point – were never absent from Marxism and the labour movement. But in it exploitation nevertheless played the role of organizing concept.

The second half of the twentieth century saw a proliferation of 'secondary fronts'. Among them, notably, were women's struggles (so-called second-wave feminism), national liberation movements, homosexual demands and nascent political ecology. Even where these fronts were also conceived as anti-capitalist, this tended to weaken the centrality of economic oppression and indicate the need for a more inclusive concept than 'exploitation'. The notion of 'alienation' was to play this role. The loss of centrality of economic oppression is also attributable to the stabilization of capitalism during the *trente glorieuses*. It contradicted predictions banking on an imminent collapse of the system. Leading to a redistribution of wealth in the developed countries, it also tended to render cultural problematics more visible. That is why critical theories prioritizing analysis of 'superstructures' multiplied during the 1960s and 70s: the 'culturalist' Marxism of Thompson and Hill, the cultural studies of Williams, Hall and Hoggart, the Marxist aesthetics of Jameson and Eagleton, and Bourdieu's sociology of culture. Anderson argues that concentration on the 'superstructures' is typical of Western Marxism.[9] In fact, it is typical of the whole set of critical theories developed in the course of the 1960s and 70s.

The relative importance assumed by cultural themes, it should be noted, varied from country to country. In the United States the absence of mass working-class parties has always contributed to exorbitant importance being ascribed to the 'cultural front' (to use Michael Denning's phrase), from the 1930s to the

---

8   See Moishe Postone, *Time, Labor, and Social Domination: A Reinterpretation of Marx's Critical Theory*, Cambridge: Cambridge University Press, 1993.

9   Perry Anderson, *Considerations on Western Marxism*, London: New Left Books, 1976, chapter 4.

counter-culture of the 1960s and 70s.[10] Without the possibility of integrating themselves into specifically political party structures, activists turned to art, culture or the academy. Moreover, this partially explains the persistence of radical currents in the USA after the collapse of such party structures in other regions. Elsewhere, the existence of popular parties created a distinct relationship between culture and politics.[11]

Added to these factors was a growing mistrust of the industrial working class and of the political and trade-union apparatuses supposed to represent it. A number of activists turned away from traditional organizations and began to envisage the emancipatory potential of new social subjects: women, the colonized, students, the insane (see Foucault's works on the history of madness, but also anti-psychiatry and institutional psycho-therapy at the La Borde clinic directed by Jean Oury and Félix Guattari), 'outcasts' (e.g. in Marcuse), or prisoners (once again Foucault with the *Groupe d'information sur les prisons*). Currents also emerged that looked to unorganized sections of the working class, which consequently escaped the grasp of the Communist parties and trade unions, for elements of revolutionary dynamism. In France the discourse developed by the Maoists around the figure of the 'semi-skilled worker', and later the 'immigrant worker', forms part of this trend.[12] In Italy the theory of the 'mass worker' developed by *operaismo* (Tronti, Negri, Romano Alquati) – that is, the worker from the south of the country employed in the factories of the north, who, not being 'organized', can exhibit revolutionary spontaneity – belongs to the same tendency.[13]

In this context the concept of 'alienation' served as a 'coagulant' making it possible to think the unity of these various struggles. If, in the economic sense of the word, these new social subjects cannot be called 'exploited' (since exploitation as a rule concerns the working class), all can be said to be 'alienated' in one respect or another. The concept of alienations extends to making contact with progressive sections of the Catholic Church. One of the great books devoted to Marx in this period was *La Pensée de Karl Marx* (1956) by the Jesuit Jean-Yves Calvez, who precisely proposed a re-reading of Marx's oeuvre in the light of the concept of 'alienation', in accordance with certain aspects of the

10   See Michael Denning, *The Cultural Front*, London and New York: Verso, 1998. See also Stathis Kouvelakis, 'Le marxisme au 21e siècle: formes et sens d'une résilience', in Gérald Bronner and Razmig Keucheyan, eds, *La Théorie sociale contemporaine*, Paris: Presses Universitaires de France, 2011.

11   For the French case, see Frédérique Matonti, 'Arts, culture et intellectuels de gauche au xxe siècle', in Jean-Jacques Becker and Gilles Candar, eds, *Histoire des gauches en France*, vol. 2, Paris: La Découverte, 2005.

12   See Romain Bertrand, 'Mai 68 et l'anticolonialisme', in Damamme *et al.*, *Mai–juin 68*.

13   See Steve Wright, *Storming Heaven: Class Composition and Struggle in Italian Autonomist Marxism*, London: Pluto, 2002.

Church's social doctrine.[14] It can therefore be said of this concept that it brings about a convergence at a theoretical level between scattered social and political struggles. In this sense the two characteristics of the New Left mentioned up to this point – namely, the crisis of the 'subject of emancipation' and the importance of the notion of 'alienation' – are intimately linked. If the latter assumed such significance for it, it was because of the multiplication of subjects of emancipation and the 'coalizing' effects it had on them.

THE QUESTION OF POWER

An important feature distinguishing the New Left from the old involves the question of power. During the first half of the twentieth century, the predominant conception of power in critical theories, and especially Marxism, was inspired by the Russian revolutions of 1905 and 1917.[15] It assigns paramount importance to the capture, and then withering away, of state power. The state is regarded as an instrument of the domination of the bourgeoisie, which the proletariat must consequently seize through armed insurrection. The way in which the clash between bourgeoisie and working class is conceived is military. The assault on the state is led by the party, which embodies the interests of the proletariat at the point at which a crisis in the existing regime sets in. This crisis is the product of the internal contradictions of the system, but also derives from the power gradually accumulated by the working class. This is the classical Marxist theme of 'dual power'. As Trotsky puts it in his *History of the Russian Revolution*,

> The historic preparation of a revolution brings about, in the pre-revolutionary period, a situation in which the class which is called to realise the new social system, although not yet master of the country, has actually concentrated in its hands a significant share of the state power, while the official apparatus of the government is still in the hands of the old lords. That is the initial dual power in every revolution.[16]

The development of this conception of power during the 1960s and 70s is complex. However, there can be no doubt that a change occurred. From the post-war period the Communist parties were integrated into the political

---

14   On the relationship between Christianity and Marxism in French thought from the 1950s–70s, see Mark Poster, *Existential Marxism: From Sartre to Althusser*, Princeton: Princeton University Press, 1977.

15   In the case of social democracy the experience of the Popular Front was decisive, just as the Spanish Civil War was in the case of anarchism.

16   Leon Trotsky, *The History of the Russian Revolution*, trans. Max Eastman, London: Pluto, 1977, p. 224. Obviously, the issue of strategy in classical Marxism is not confined to this aspect.

landscape of the western democracies – something that led them to abandon in fact, if not in principle, the idea of taking power via the insurrectionary road. This trend gave rise to 'Eurocommunism', which emerged in France, Spain and Italy during the 1970s. Eurocommunism consisted in a more or less public break by European Communist parties with the Soviet model, both in the field of foreign policy and as regards respect for liberties.[17] Its promoters advocated a gradual, 'democratic' transition to socialism, which authorized a strategy of alliance with social democracy, even with Christian Democracy in Italy. Eurocommunism was to lead to such experiments as the Union of the Left in France and the Historic Compromise in Italy. Although legitimizing itself with certain statements by Lenin, and even if there existed more or less radical versions (like that defended by Nicos Poulantzas),[18] it was clearly distinct from Bolshevism.

The Leninist model remained in force in 'leftist' organizations. We shall leave to one side the question of how far the Leninist self-conception of these groups corresponded to their reality. The *Ligue communiste révolutionnaire* (LCR), one of the main French Trotskyist currents, doubtless experienced the influence of the libertarian spirit of May 1968 more than that of 'democratic centralism'. However, its discourse was strongly imprinted with Leninism. As regards Third Worldist movements, the predominant strategic model, inspired by the Chinese Revolution, was the 'protracted people's war' theorized by Mao or the Algerian and Cuban revolutionary experiences. Maoism allocated a certain role to the peasantry, on account of the weak urbanization of the countries where it was applied. Conceived in a context of prolonged confrontation, it added to dual power a dual territoriality, which takes concrete form in 'liberated zones'. This model was also adopted – in theory, at any rate – by leftist organizations during the 1960s and 70s, for example Maoist or Third Worldist ones.

The conditions of political struggle in western countries during the second half of the twentieth century obviously had little in common with those that obtained in Russia or China in the first half. Neither the political regime nor the social structure was the same. This led a number of thinkers to develop theories of power adapted to the advanced democracies. Within Marxism this was notably true of Gramsci, Adorno and Althusser. Althusser's 'ideological state

---

17   See Carl Boggs and David Plotke, *The Politics of Eurocommunism: Socialism in Transition*, Boston: South End Press, 1999.

18   See, for example, Nicos Poulantzas, *State, Power, Socialism*, trans. Patrick Camiller, London: New Left Books, 1978. In passing, we may signal that there exists in contemporary Marxism a significant current identified with Poulantzas, of which Bob Jessop is a well-known representative. For example, see the latter's *State Power: A Strategic-Relational Approach*, Cambridge: Polity, 2007.

apparatuses' (family, school, church), distinguished from the 'repressive state apparatus' (police and army), aimed to bring out the diffuse forms of power. The same is true, in a very different context, of Adorno and Horkheimer's 'culture industry'. From the mid-1920s Gramsci elaborated a conception of power that assigns an increasingly important role to its non-state component, therewith anticipating theoretical developments in the 1960s. That is one of the reasons why he figures (as we have said) among the most cited authors in new critical thinking. The famous paragraphs of the *Prison Notebooks* on the relationship between state and civil society attest to it – among them, the following:

> In Russia the State was everything, civil society was primordial and gelatinous; in the West, there was a proper relation between State and civil society, and when the State trembled a sturdy structure of civil society was at once revealed. The State was only an outer ditch, behind which there stood a powerful system of fortresses and earthworks.[19]

For Gramsci power is not only concentrated in institutions or condensed in the state, but also disseminated throughout the whole social body. This difference in the nature of power between 'East' and 'West' – two concepts which, in the sense given them by Gramsci, are not merely geographical, but specifically political – has important political implications. In particular, it presupposes that in the West a 'war of movement' is insufficient on its own for the overthrow of the socio-political order – that a 'war of position', of which a war of movement is only one aspect, must be conducted. The war of position contains an essential 'cultural' dimension. The author of the *Prison Notebooks* forms the link between the Leninist moment in the theory of power and subsequent approaches to the latter. Lenin was unquestionably aware of the fact that power is not concentrated exclusively in the state; and Gramsci obviously does not deny the importance of state power, as is demonstrated by his concept of 'integral state'.[20] Generally speaking, the most recent Gramscian historiography shows that Gramsci was profoundly Leninist in his own way.[21] But the growing interpenetration of state and 'civil society' during the twentieth century, the ever greater blurring of the boundaries between the two, forced him to take the Marxist theory of power in new directions.

The thinker who accounts most clearly for this changed conception of power is probably Foucault. Within today's critical theories, Foucault's approach

19   Antonio Gramsci, *Selections from the Prison Notebooks*, ed. and trans. Quintin Hoare and Geoffrey Nowell Smith, London: Lawrence and Wishart, 1971, p. 238.

20   See Christine Buci-Glucksmann, *Gramsci and the State*, trans. David Fernbach, London: Lawrence and Wishart, 1980.

21   See Thomas, *The Gramscian Moment*.

to power has the influence possessed by the Leninist model during the first half of the twentieth century. Foucault assigns decisive importance to the idea of micro-power. According to him, power is dispersed throughout society, not concentrated in a state from which domination supposedly proceeds unilaterally. This 'ascendant' conception underscores the inscription of power in 'intermediate' institutions like schools, hospitals, the army and prisons, which produce individuals who are always-already integrated into power relations. From this follows the idea – typically structuralist – that, strictly speaking, power has no subject. In the Leninist model the subject of power is the state and, in the last instance, the bourgeois class it represents (in complex fashion).

The strategic implications of this philosophy are significant. Confronting the state only makes sense if the latter concentrates a significant portion of power. Once it is dispersed to the four corners of the social world, the struggle against it necessarily is too. For Foucault the spaces of contestation are multiple, like the actors who invest them. In this kind of approach the struggle is interminable – that is, none of the protagonists conclusively wins the day. Within the labour movement, on the contrary, the dominant idea was that, when the time comes, an ultimate clash decides one way or the other – something illustrated by the phrase 'the final struggle'. The absence of any climax in Foucault's theory of power does not prevent the antagonists developing on contact with one another. Alternatively put, power – and the resistance to it – has a history. The doctrine of power developed by Foucault is therefore relational, not substantive. Most structuralist and poststructuralist thinkers defend approaches of this type. The concept of 'rhizome' developed by Deleuze and Guattari, like the idea of 'societies of control', is an example of it.[22]

Foucault's theory of power is typical of the New Left, even if Foucault was critical of the latter in many respects. As Ingrid Gilcher-Holtey puts it, 'if one believes the conceptions of this New Left, socialism must not so much be achieved by means of political and social revolution, by the seizure of power and the nationalization of the means of production, as aim to liberate man from alienation: in everyday life, in the family, in sexual relations and in relations with others.'[23] Foucault does not employ the notion of 'alienation' and is hesitant about the idea that sexuality should in some way be 'liberated'.[24] He nonetheless

---

22   See Gilles Deleuze and Félix Guattari, *A Thousand Plateaus: Capitalism and Schizophrenia*, trans. Brian Massumi, London: Athlone, 1988, and Gilles Deleuze, 'Post-scriptum sur les sociétés de contrôle', *Pourparlers*, Paris: Minuit, 1990.

23   Ingrid Gilcher-Holtey, 'La contribution des intellectuels de la nouvelle gauche à la définition du sens de Mai 68', in Geneviève Dreyfus-Armand, Robert Frank, Marie-Françoise Lévy and Michelle Zancarini-Fournel, eds, *Les Années 68. Le Temps de contestation*, Paris: Complexe, 2000.

24   See Michel Foucault, *The History of Sexuality*, vol. 1, trans. Robert Hurley, London: Allen Lane, 1979. In this book Foucault opposes the 'repressive hypothesis' about sexuality, which

shares with the New Left the desire to break with 'statocentrism'. The New Left politicized aspects of existence hitherto regarded as external to the political field. The politicization of sexuality is one example; and we know the significance it was to assume during the 1970s, particularly within feminist and homosexual movements. That is why the 'critique of everyday life' dear to Lefebvre is a central theme of the period. It results in a challenge to traditional forms – social-democratic and democratic-centralist – of organizing the Left, in favour of less hierarchical, more flexible organizations. The reticular, horizontal organization of the '*altermondialiste*' movement of the 1990s, often presented as having emerged with it, actually long predates it, just like the theories of 'anti-power' supposedly peculiar to it.

THE RESONANCE OF STRUCTURALISM

One characteristic of the New Left is the proliferation of currents to which it has given rise. It is probably necessary to go back to the years following the 1830 revolution, described by Rancière in *La Nuit des prolétaires*, to encounter a doctrinal proliferation comparable to that which occurred from the 1960s onwards.[25]

Among the theories that circulated within the New Left, it is appropriate to distinguish between those which were linked to political groups and those which were not directly. Structuralism belongs to the second category, in the sense that there was no party or movement corresponding to this paradigm. The same applies to existentialism or the Frankfurt School, which were not organized political currents. This does not mean that these currents had no 'social base', in the broad sense of the term. The relationship between structuralism and the rise of technocracy in France was classically analyzed by Lefebvre.[26] It simply means that these paradigms did not have the mission of becoming embodied in organizations.

The situation of Communism, Trotskyism, Maoism, *operaismo*, situationism, anarchism, council communism, feminism, political ecology and their numerous variants, is different. Each of these rubrics refers not only to a more or less homogeneous critical theory, but also to parties, associations, trade unions, avant-gardes – in short, organizations identifying with those theories. The organizations in question can vary in size. The militants of the French or

---

differentiates him from a number of critical thinkers of the period and the general prevailing climate. We shall pass over this point, which is secondary from our point of view here.

25 Jacques Rancière, *The Nights of Labor: The Workers' Dream in Nineteenth-Century France*, trans. John Drury, Philadelphia: Temple University Press. On this period see also David Harvey, *Paris: Capital of Modernity*, London and New York: Routledge, 2003.

26 Henri Lefebvre, *L'Idéologie structuraliste*, Paris: Seuil, 1975.

Italian Communist Party were long numbered in the hundreds of thousands; those of Debord's Situationist International in some dozens at most. Their operating principle can also differ. The Women's Liberation Movement had a decidedly non-centralized structure, at the outset at any rate.[27] By contrast, the Socialist Workers' Party, one of the branches of British Trotskyism, is a hierarchical party, as well as being relatively homogeneous doctrinally. In both cases, however, an interaction has occurred between ideas and a 'social base', which raises the issue of the relationship between critical theories and 'repertoires of action' or activist 'know-how'.

The fact that an intellectual current is not embodied in organizations does not mean it has no influence on the period under consideration. In the case of structuralism this influence was profound. The paradigm was one of the pillars of the theoretical 'moment' of the 1960s and 70s.[28] In subsequent decades it was diffused throughout the world and irrigated the whole set of critical theories. Along with Marxism, structuralism is the sole current to have influenced all sectors of thought and to have been so systematically 'hybridized' with other currents. Thus, just as there exists a Marxist feminism, ecology and literary studies, there are forms of feminism, ecology and literary studies that derive inspiration from structuralism. Accordingly, it is crucial to specify the contours of this paradigm and examine its relations with the political movements of the 1960s and 70s.

Four main theoretical operations underlie structuralism.[29] The first is the importation into the social sciences of models in force in linguistics – more especially, the model of structural linguistics. Saussure is the main initiator of this current. His ideas passed through Roman Jakobson and the Prague School of literary studies to finally reach the founder of French structuralism – namely, Claude Lévi-Strauss. Structural linguistics was first applied by Lévi-Strauss to kinship structures. The author of *Anthropologie structurale* (1958) equated these structures with a language and regarded the exchange of women between groups as a form of communication. Starting from this initial application to a social phenomenon, the linguistic model was set to work by the structuralists in the analysis of the whole range of human phenomena. In *Les Quatre concepts*

---

27   See Dominique Fougeyrollas-Schwebel, 'Le féminisme des années 1970', in Christine Fauré, ed., *Encyclopédie politique et historique des femmes*, Paris: Presses Universitaires de France, 1997.

28   On the notion of theoretical 'moment', see Frédéric Worms, 'Le moment philosophique des années 1960 en France. De la structure à la différance', *Esprit*, May 2008.

29   See Perry Anderson, *In the Tracks of Historical Materialism*, London: New Left Books, 1983, chapter 2. See also François Dosse, *History of Structuralism*, vol. 1, trans. Deborah Glassman, Minneapolis: University of Minnesota Press, 1997. It goes without saying that a current as rich as structuralism cannot be reduced to four theoretical operations, however fundamental. However, it would be equally mistaken to claim that nothing unites the different variants of the school.

fondamentaux de la psychanalyse (1964) Lacan defended the notion that the unconscious is structured like a language. The semiology developed by Barthes conceived the social world as a whole as a system of signs, as illustrated by the studies collected in *Mythologies* (1957). The tendency to generalize the linguistic model reached its apogee with the principle stated by Derrida in *De la grammatologie* (1967), and then clarified in *La Dissémination* (1972), that '*il n'y a pas de hors-texte*'. Derrida dismissed the Saussurean hypothesis that language is a stable 'system of differences', therewith marking one of the ways in which the transition from structuralism to poststructuralism was made. From his point of view the signifier is inevitably 'floating'. The transition from the model of structural linguistics to Derridean 'textuality' does not, however, presuppose abandonment of the primacy assigned to language.[30] Within poststructuralism it possesses a centrality to which Foucault's analyses of the 'order of discourse' likewise attest.

A second characteristic of structuralism is its relativism – that is, the critique of truth in which it engages. Saussurean linguistics is based on an 'internalist' conception of signification. It defends the idea that the signifier acquires its meaning through its position in the structure of the language, by differentiating itself from other signifiers and being contrasted with them. The instance of 'reference' – what the signifiers refer to in reality – is bracketed by Saussure, because it does not enter into the determination of 'linguistic value'. The French structuralists radicalize this evacuation of reality. In their view no simple 'correspondence' governs the relations between language and reality. Derrida's idea that 'there is nothing outside-text' signifies precisely that, as does Foucault's notion that the link between 'words and things' is mediated by an *episteme*.[31] Structuralism's subversion of truth is part of a more general trend, typical of the 1960s and 70s, critical of modern science and its presuppositions. This tendency is itself the expression of the hypothesis of the end of 'metanarratives' prophesied by Lyotard in *La Condition postmoderne* in 1979.[32]

The third element underlying structuralism is its relationship to causality and the progressive insistence of its representatives on the contingent character of history. In 1960s structuralism – that of such classical works as *Anthropologie structurale*, *Mythologies*, *Les Mots et les choses* and *Lire le Capital* – a form of historical determinism and objectivism was predominant. It was expressed in the attention devoted to analyzing the *longue durée* and the 'structural

---

30   Anderson, *In the Tracks of Historical Materialism*, p. 42.

31   See Michel Foucault, *The Order of Things*, London: Tavistock, 1970.

32   Jean-François Lyotard, *The Postmodern Condition: A Report on Knowledge*, trans. Geoffrey Bennington and Brian Massumi, Minneapolis: University of Minnesota Press, 1984. On the social critique of science, see Michel Dubois, *La Nouvelle Sociologie des sciences*, Paris: Presses Universitaires de France, 2001.

invariants' constitutive of the social world. In many respects, structuralism is the inheritor of the French positivist (Comte, Durkheim) and Saint-Simonian traditions. Obviously, Marxism also influenced structuralism in this regard.

Over time, however, contingency became ever more salient in structuralist theory. May 1968, which none of the authors concerned had anticipated, and whose irruption contradicted its theses outright, was not irrelevant to this development.[33] Thus, the event ended up occupying an increasingly decisive place in their analyses. In 'vitalist' vein, one of the emblematic authors of the years after May 1968, Deleuze, stressed the unbounded creativity of desire. In this respect the appearance of *Anti-Oedipus* in 1972 constitutes a moment of transition to poststructuralism. In Althusser an initial implacable structuralism gradually gave way to an 'aleatory materialism' or 'materialism of the encounter'. In an interview with Glucksmann and Maurice Clavel, Foucault adopted the latter's idea that the philosopher should become a 'transcendental journalist'. The original determinism of structuralism thus gradually made way for a philosophy of history placed under the sign of contingency and the event. Today's theorists of the 'event' – Badiou, Žižek and Rancière – are inheritors of this problematic.

The fourth theoretical operation characteristic of structuralism is its critique of the 'subject', which results in its famous 'anti-humanism'. In the conclusion to *Les Mots et les choses* (1966), Foucault announced the death of man 'like a face drawn in sand at the edge of the sea': 'man is neither the oldest nor the most constant problem that has been posed for human knowledge . . . As the archaeology of our thought easily shows, man is an invention of recent date. And one perhaps nearing its end.'[34] For his part, Althusser employed the phrase 'theoretical anti-humanism', notably during a debate with the 'humanist' Roger Garaudy prior to the meeting of the Central Committee of the Communist Party at Argenteuil in 1966.[35] For Althusser, history is a 'process without a subject or goal'. While there is indeed a class struggle, there is no subject of emancipation who serves as the conscious motor of it. In *Mythologiques*, Lévi-Strauss refers to the subject as 'that intolerable spoilt brat who for too long has occupied the philosophical stage and prevented any serious work by demanding undivided attention'.[36] The target of the 'anti-humanism' of Foucault, Althusser and Lévi-Strauss was humanism in general, but more particularly Sartrean existentialism. Sartre was the

33   As perceived by Lefebvre in *L'Idéologie structuraliste*. See also Kristin Ross, *May 68 and Its Afterlives*, Chicago: University of Chicago Press, 2002.

34   Foucault, *The Order of Things*, pp. 386–7.

35   See Matonti, 'Arts, culture et intellectuels de gauche au XXe siècle', in Becker and Candar, eds, *Histoire des gauches en France*.

36   Claude Lévi-Strauss, *L'Homme nu*, Paris: Plon, 1971, pp. 614–15.

rival from the previous philosophical generation with whom the structuralists constantly clashed in these years.

It is interesting to note that a critique of humanism, with different presuppositions and conclusions, was developed at the same time by another current of thought – namely, the Frankfurt School. In the late 1940s, Adorno and Horkheimer conducted a problematization of the emancipatory potential of reason and universalism, which they called 'dialectic of Enlightenment'.[37] The thesis they proposed is that the founding values of the Enlightenment – progress, liberty, individual autonomy – gradually came to backfire on themselves. While they were emancipatory when compared with the *ancien régime* and obscurantism, they had made themselves complicit with the worst atrocities in the twentieth century. In particular, the extermination camps were presented by Adorno and Horkheimer as the product of the degeneration of reason into sheer 'instrumental' rationality.

'1968 THOUGHT' REVISITED

The relationship between structuralism and the New Left has been much debated. It involves the question of to what extent the political movements of the 1960s and 70s were 'on the same wavelength' as that intellectual school. Two hypotheses clash on this score. The first is that of '1968 thought', formulated in the book of that name by Luc Ferry and Alain Renaut, whose subtitle is 'Essay on Contemporary Anti-Humanism'. For Ferry and Renaut, structuralism – Lacan, Foucault, Bourdieu and Derrida, in particular – is '1968 thought'. In other words, this doctrine has an affinity with the political moment of the 1960s and 70s, in the sense that they are the 'symptom of the same cultural phenomenon'.[38] The operator that creates the link between the two is 'anti-humanism'. According to Ferry and Renaut, slogans such as *jouir sans entraves* (whatever turns you on), or *il est interdit d'interdire* (it is forbidden to forbid), which are among the most celebrated of 1968, are expressions of this critique of the classical 'subject'. Their main argument consists in distinguishing classical humanism from contemporary individualism: 1968 was an individualistic event, but not a humanist one. This is because in their view 'the subject dies with the advent of the individual'.[39] Whatever their intentions, the protagonists of 1968 were thus supposedly working for the emergence of an 'era of the void', to use Gilles Lipovetsky's phrase.

---

37   See T. W. Adorno and Max Horkheimer, *Dialectic of Enlightenment*, trans. John Cumming, London and New York: Verso, 1979. (*Dialektik der Aufklärung* first appeared in 1947.)

38   Luc Ferry and Alain Renaut, *La Pensée 68. Essai sur l'antihumanisme contemporain*, Paris: Gallimard, 1985, p. 23.

39   Ibid., p. 123.

The second hypothesis maintains that 1968 was radically opposed to structuralism. This hypothesis is notably defended by Lefebvre, Rancière, Castoriadis and, more recently, Kristin Ross. An amusing cinematic expression of it can be found in Godard's film *La Chinoise*, in which Anne Wiazemsky, playing a Maoist militant, throws tomatoes at Foucault's *Les Mots et les choses*. For these authors the movements of the 1960s and 70s were anti-structuralist on two counts. First of all, by virtue of the theme of 'alienation': there is nothing more humanist than this critical theme, which aims to restore – or realize for the first time – an 'essence' peculiar to man, who has been corrupted by capitalism.[40] The second characteristic of 1968 which caught structuralism out was that the latter, stressing the *longue durée* and 'structural invariants', is the converse of a conceptualization of the event. The idea that an event can abruptly change the course of history is foreign to it. As a slogan of the epoch adopted by Goldmann put it, 'structures do not take to the streets'.

Which hypothesis is correct? In favour of Ferry and Renaut's thesis are arguments that attest to a link between structuralism and the movements of the 1960s and 70s. First of all, publishing chronology: Foucault released *Histoire de la folie* in 1961, *Les Mots et les choses* in 1966 and *L'Archéologie du savoir* in 1969. *Pour Marx* and *Lire le Capital* by Althusser and his pupils both came out in 1965. *Lénine et la philosophie*, originally a lecture given by Althusser at the Sorbonne, appeared in February 1968. Derrida's *L'Écriture et la différance* and *De la grammatologie* were published in 1967, Lacan's *Écrits* in 1966, Bourdieu and Passeron's *Les Héritiers* in 1964. These books were not only published, they were also bought in large quantities. The second half of the 1960s and the first half of the 1970s were a golden age of publishing in the social sciences. Foucault's *Les Mots et les choses* sold 20,000 copies between April and December 1966. Five-thousand copies of Lacan's *Écrits* – not the simplest of texts – sold in less than fifteen days. Obviously, the fact that books are bought does not mean that they are read; and the fact that they are read does not mean that they have a real influence on the way individuals act. We can advance the hypothesis that the content of works of this kind, fairly 'technical', circulated widely among the population, but no doubt it circulated more via press reviews than via direct reading. At the time, certain papers or magazines (for example, *Le Nouvel Observateur* or *L'Express*) made a speciality of addressing the new educated audiences which the massification of higher education and increases in living standards – and hence in cultural consumption – created in western societies after the Second World War.[41]

40   On this see the analysis by Norman Geras, *Marx and Human Nature: Refutation of a Legend*, London and New York: Verso, 1983.

41   See Philippe Olivera, 'Les livres de Mai', in Damamme *et al.*, *Mai–juin 68*.

Nevertheless, it is clear that Ferry and Renaut neglect much of the thinking and event of 1968. The years prior to 1968 were equally marked by booming non- or even anti-structuralist publishing activity. In 1967 Debord's *La Société du spectacle* and Raoul Vaneigem's *Traité de savoir-vivre à l'usage des jeunes générations* appeared. Mustapha Khayati's *De la misère en milieu étudiant* was published in 1966. These texts derived from Situationist circles, issuing from the crossing of a libertarian Marxism and the tradition of the French avant-gardes, Dadaist, Surrealist and Lettrist in particular. Sartre and existentialism were also topical in 1968, even though the Sartrean philosophical moment had no doubt passed. When Sartre spoke in the great amphitheatre of the Sorbonne in May 1968, he was heckled by some of the audience, but was also shown great respect by the students. We could multiply the examples of philosophical, sociological, artistic or other currents which had a greater or less impact on 1968: the New Wave, the numerous variants of Marxism, psychoanalysis, left-wing Roman Catholicism, and so on. From a general standpoint, the idea that an event on the scale and of the complexity of May 1968 can be assigned a single, homogeneous 'thought' is methodologically mistaken.

Added to this is the fact that if structuralism was '1968 thought', the development of poststructuralism after 1968 would be unintelligible. We have remarked of the latter that it abandons conceiving language as a stable structure and attributes an ever greater significance to contingency. The structuralism of the 1960s, by contrast, regarded language as an enduring system of differences and defended a determinist approach to history. It was obviously May 1968 that destabilized high structuralism and once again rendered the historically unforeseen conceivable, in the eyes of the very people who had elaborated it. Classical structuralism corresponds to the 1950s and 60s, a period when France was 'modernizing' and when, while social change was definitely occurring, it seemed to be inscribed in fixed frameworks. The thunder clap of May abruptly altered the perception of politics and history, obliging structuralists to reassess their positions. Structuralism is not '1968 thought' because May 1968 compelled it to move towards poststructuralism.

TOWARDS NEW CRITICAL THEORIES

These elements of a history of the New Left enable us to frame a hypothesis that is important for understanding the genesis of the new critical theories. As we have seen, two of the main characteristics of the critical thinking of the 1960s and 70s were, on the one hand, the proliferation of subjects of emancipation and, on the other, the gradual abandonment of the 'statocentric' conception of power in favour of a 'decentralized' approach. They derived from the crisis experienced at the time by the traditional political and trade-union organizations of the working class. They also flowed from the multiplication of 'secondary fronts', notably around feminism, anti-colonialism and ecology. Now, these characteristics are also very much present in today's critical theories, which emerged in the second half of the 1990s. Thus, one of the debates within the latter concerns the concept of 'multitude' and whether it has replaced the working class as a new subject of emancipation. The contemporary authors who broach questions of identity, like representatives of queer theory (Judith Butler, Eve Sedgwick), theorists of recognition (Axel Honneth, Nancy Fraser), or postcolonial thinkers, are themselves in search of new political subjects. Over and above the diversity of their approaches, the problem that unites them is identifying who will be the actors in future social transformations and how their 'identity' will influence the nature of these transformations. For their part, Laclau, Benedict Anderson, Tom Nairn, Balibar and Habermas examine the concept of the 'people' in its relationship to globalization (Nairn), European construction (Balibar and Habermas), and the emergence of antagonisms within nations (Laclau). In their view, as in the modern age, the people remain the principal vector of emancipation. Thinkers of the 'event' such as Badiou and Žižek, for whom the 'subject' is constituted in fidelity to a founding event, also participate in this quest.

The conclusion to be drawn from this is simple. The crisis of the subject of emancipation, and the multiplication of possible subjects of emancipation, does not date from the fall of the Berlin Wall, but from the 1960s. The terms of the debate have certainly changed over the last half-century. The salience once accorded the theme of madness, and the emancipatory potential of the insane, has decreased. The struggles of women and homosexuals have undeniably progressed, which implies that their modalities have changed. However, it is the same debate, about the same crisis of the subject of emancipation. No hegemonic subject having arrived to take the place of the working class, contemporary critical theorists remain in search of potential substitutes or new articulations.

An analogous argument can be made as regards the issue of power. We note a tendency among a number of present-day critical theorists (Holloway, Virno, Negri) to assert that struggle in its various forms – social, trade-union, institutional, armed – must be replaced by exile, defection, nomadization – in short, a set of 'indirect' strategies aimed at keeping the state apparatus at a distance, as opposed to confronting it directly. As asserted in a famous statement by Deleuze, and often adopted by these authors: 'To flee, but in fleeing to seek a weapon.'[42] This body of doctrine is commonly referred to as theories of 'anti-power'. Bartleby, Herman Melville's famous character, is often regarded by it as exemplifying the strategy of circumventing power relations. In Melville's short story,

---

42   Gilles Deleuze and Claire Parnet, *Dialogues*, Paris: Flammarion, 1977, p. 164.

Bartleby the scrivener systematically answers 'I would prefer not to' to each of his employer's orders, which gradually leads the latter to give up seeking to impose on him.[43] The thinkers who develop theories of anti-power explicitly counterpose it to Leninism, regarded as bankrupt on account of the catastrophic experience of the USSR. Here too the problematic is far from novel. The wall came down, the political movements suffered profound defeats, but the problems posed in the 1960s have survived underground and are re-emerging today, more burning than ever.

---

43   Bartleby has attracted the interest of a number of contemporary thinkers. Gilles Deleuze devoted a text to him entitled 'Bartleby, or The Formula', in *Essays Critical and Clinical*, trans. D.W. Smith and Michael A. Greco, London and New York: Verso, 1998. See also Giorgio Agamben, *Bartleby, ou la création*, Paris: Circé, 1998, and Slavoj Žižek, *The Parallax View*, Cambridge (MA): MIT Press, 2006.

CHAPTER THREE

Contemporary Critical Intellectuals: A Typology

With the decline of oppositional movements in the second half of the 1970s, several reactions occurred in the intellectual field. The set of these reactions forms the outline of a typology of contemporary critical thinkers. Six categories of response by the latter can be identified in this period. I shall name these categories 'converts', 'pessimists', 'resisters', 'innovators', 'leaders' and 'experts'. The 'ideal-typical' character (in Weber's well-known sense) of these rubrics is obvious. Any intellectual will invariably be found straddling several of them. Some of the categories tend to be mutually exclusive – if not logically, then at least in practice. Generally speaking, however, most combinations of them are conceivable.

The determinants influencing critical intellectuals' membership in one or other of the categories vary. The first factor inflecting their trajectory is bound up with the overall development of the intellectual field, especially the academic field, alterations in which have impacted on their political convictions in recent decades. To be a critical thinker – Marxist in a majority of cases – in a French university when Althusser delivered a lecture on *Lénine et la philosophie* at the Sorbonne (February 1968) was one thing. To be one twenty years later, when the neo-liberal counter-revolution was in full swing, and the overall percentage of critical intellectuals had significantly declined, was quite another. The 'realignment' of academia during the 1980s and 90s swept up a number of formerly oppositional theorists, and reduced the likelihood of young theorists becoming such. Once again, this demonstrates that intellectuals are not exempt from the general laws governing the social field in which they operate.

A second factor influencing the course of intellectuals is the fate of the organizations to which they belonged. The self-dissolution in 1973 of the *Gauche prolétarienne*, one of the principal French Maoist organizations, manifestly had an impact on the trajectory of its members, regardless of whether they were intellectuals. The same applies to the Situationist International in 1972 or *Potere operaio* – Negri's organization – in 1973.

The third factor behind the trajectory of critical thinkers in recent decades is doctrinal in kind. The 'new philosophers', who furnish a sizeable contingent for the category of 'converts', were mainly recruited from Maoist ranks, especially those of the *Gauche prolétarienne*. How is this to be explained? As Michael Scott Christofferson has shown, the *Gauche prolétarienne* was distinguished from other leftist groups of the 1970s by its 'moralistic' conception of class struggle.[1] This clearly emerges from the terms in which, in its paper *La Cause du people*, the deeds of the dominant classes were denounced. This denunciation frequently took the form of condemnation of bourgeois 'immorality', in a vocabulary its militants regarded as likely to be understood by workers. The substitution of ethics for politics is a typical feature of the 'new philosophers'. In this sense the Maoism of the *Gauche prolétarienne*, and the ethics of 'human rights' defended by Glucksmann, Lévy and their colleagues, are ultimately not antithetical.

Naturally, this does not mean that Maoism automatically led to abandonment of the radicalism of the 1960s and 70s. The cases of Badiou and Rancière, likewise issuing from Maoist currents, prove the opposite, as do those of Immanuel Wallerstein, Giovanni Arrighi and Samir Amin. The correlation between doctrinal orientation in the 1960s and 70s and subsequent political trajectory definitely exists, but it is complex. It requires a case-by-case analysis.

CONVERTS

'Converts' are thinkers who stopped engaging in critical thinking with the change in the political conjuncture in the second half of the 1970s. We have already referred to them when evoking the trajectories of the 'new philosophers', Colletti, and the Argentinian Gramscians. Not all converts became conservative, even if some have moved from one end of the political spectrum to the other, without a break, in record time. The trajectories of Glucksmann and Alain Finkielkraut in France, Irving Kristol and Norman Podhoretz in the United States, or Colletti in Italy, are exemplary in this respect. Even when these thinkers remained attached to progressive positions, they no longer challenged capitalism. They therefore ceased to be critical theorists: they no longer investigated the conditions of possibility of a different world.

The conversion in the 1990s of part of the Regulation School to a moderately heterodox form of the neo-classical paradigm called 'economics of conventions' must be included in this history.[2] The Regulation School, whose founding act was the publication by Michel Aglietta in 1976 of *Régulation et crises du capitalisme*, originally identified with Marxism. Aglietta himself was a member of the Communist Party, while other regulationists were close to

---

1   Michael Scott Christofferson, *French Intellectuals Against the Left: The Antitotalitarian Moment of the 1970s*, New York and Oxford: Berghahn, 2004, p. 59.
2   See, for example, André Orléan, ed., *Analyse économique des conventions*, Paris: Presses Universitaires de France, 2004, and the special issue of *Revue économique*, vol. 40, no. 2, 1989.

Maoism (Alain Lipietz) or the independent leftist *Parti Socialiste Unifié*.[3] An initial 'realignment' occurred with the arrival of the Left in power in 1981, which led some members of the school to transform themselves into advisers to the Prince. Of all academic disciplines, economics is doubtless the one subject to most pressure from the dominant ideology. This is explained by its proximity to power, which has made economists the quintessential 'experts', especially since the end of the Second World War, and by the ideological function currently performed by this discipline. The economic 'creed' is at the heart of neo-liberal hegemony, meaning that it is particularly susceptible to anything that derives from it.

Within the category of converts we need to distinguish two types of intellectual. The first comprises those whose conversion to liberalism was the result of a long process, often the outcome of an internal critique of Marxism. During the 1950s and 60s, Claude Lefort was a prominent figure in the one of the most influential political and intellectual collectives of the time, *Socialisme ou Barbarie*,[4] whose name alluded to the famous alternative indicated by Rosa Luxemburg, and which had its origins in the Trotskyist tradition – more precisely, the *Parti communiste internationaliste* (PCI). The protagonists of *Socialisme ou Barbarie* left the PCI before adopting this name, on account of a disagreement about the character of the USSR. Trotskyists regarded the latter as a 'degenerated workers' state' – that is, a workers' state whose economy was post-capitalist, but whose revolution had been 'betrayed' by its leaders, first and foremost Stalin. For Lefort and Castoriadis, by contrast, the USSR represented a form of state capitalism, whose originality was that a specific social class – the bureaucracy – had replaced the bourgeoisie. The difference was considerable, since it concerned the essence of the regime and, consequently, the strategy to be adopted towards it.

After this split *Socialisme ou Barbarie* moved towards positions of a 'conciliar' – i.e. anti-Leninist and *autogestionnaire* – variety. This accounts for the success its theses met with among rebellious students in May 1968 and thereafter. Lefort's development led him to an increasingly liberal position, prompting him to structure his political philosophy around the opposition between

---

3   See Michel Aglietta, *A Theory of Capitalist Regulation: The US Experience*, trans. David Fernbach, London: New Left Books, 1979. On the evolution of the Regulation School, see Michel Husson, 'The Regulation School: From Marx to the Saint-Simon Foundation', in Jacques Bidet and Stathis Kouvelakis, eds, *A Critical Companion to Contemporary Marxism*, Leiden and Boston: Brill, 2008.

4   The history of this collective runs from 1949–67. The other significant figure in it was Castoriadis. The list of thinkers who at one stage or another of their career coincided with *Socialism ou Barbarie* is sizeable. In particular, we find Debord, Vincent Descombes and Lyotard. See Philippe Gottraux, '*Socialisme ou Barbarie*'. *Un engagement politique et intellectuel dans la France de l'après-guerre*, Paris: Payot, 1997.

'democracy' and 'totalitarianism'. He now defended the idea that in a democratic regime power is an 'empty place', whereas totalitarianism is characterized by the 'closure' of society on itself.[5] Between the foundation of *Socialisme ou Barbarie* in 1949 and the publication of his essay on Solzhenitsyn in 1975, a quarter-century had passed, which witnessed the author of *L'Invention démocratique* make the transition from 'leftist' positions to liberalism. Lefort gave his support to the 'Juppé plan' for pension reforms in 1995, in support of which he published a column in *Le Monde* entitled 'The dogmas are over'.[6]

The trajectory of the 'anti-totalitarian' intellectuals referred to earlier is different from that of Lefort. In their case conversion to the dominant order occurred in fast motion. This is indicated by the case of the politico-literary collective *Tel Quel*, of which Philippe Sollers, Julia Kristeva and Jean-Pierre Faye were among the best-known members. The transition of *Tel Quel*, founded in 1960, from a radical form of Maoism to the 'new philosophy' occurred between autumn 1976 and spring 1977.[7] As in the case of the *Gauche prolétarienne*, to which *Tel Quel* was close doctrinally, and on account of the social profile of its members, certain elements nevertheless prepared this rapid conversion to the dominant order. Firstly, *Tel Quel*'s Maoism – officially, at any rate – was anti-authoritarian, in contrast to that of other organizations of the same observance, like the *Parti communiste marxiste-léniniste de France* or Badiou's *Union des communistes de France marxiste-léniniste*, which were more tightly structured. The libertarian, even individualistic component of *Tel Quel*'s Maoism, which notably emerged in its members' interpretation of the Cultural Revolution, is especially eloquent. This individualism was reinforced by the fact that the journal always defended a 'modernist' conception of art, refusing to subordinate the latter's 'autonomy' to any political role. This explains the unstable line of *Tel Quel*, which at one time (around 1967) even gravitated towards the Communist Party and *Les Lettres françaises*. It was but a small step from this individualistic Maoism to the subsequent anti-totalitarian liberalism; and the winter of 1976–77 sufficed for it to be taken.

There is a category of intellectuals whom it is interesting to compare with the converts – namely, the 'radicalized'. It is not sizeable enough numerically to warrant a separate rubric in our typology. But it is symptomatic of developments in the intellectual field in recent decades. The radicalized are intellectuals who in the 1970s defended what, by comparison with the revolutionary orientations of their colleagues, were 'reformist' positions. However, they were radicalized during the 1980s and 90s. In other words, they took the

---

5   See Claude Lefort, *L'Invention démocratique*, Paris: Fayard, 1981.
6   Claude Lefort, 'Les dogmes sont finis', *Le Monde*, 4 January 2006.
7   See Christofferson, *French Intellectuals Against the Left*, p. 201.

opposite course from that of the converts, moving to the left. Among the radicalized are Derrida and Bourdieu. *The Inheritors* (published in 1964) was one
of the important books of May 1968. However, Bourdieu's political involve-
ment was belated. The sociologist was always distrustful of the leftisms of the
1960s and 70s, regarding them as 'unrealistic'.[8] His engagement became public
on the occasion of a petition of support for the Polish trade union Solidarity
in 1981, launched with Foucault. But it was during the strikes of December
1995 that Bourdieu positioned himself as part of the tradition of 'committed'
intellectuals which, initiated during the Dreyfus Affair, extends to Sartre and
Foucault. In subsequent years, until his death in 2002, the sociologist consist-
ently castigated neo-liberalism and offered his support to social movements.
He thereby contradicted the 'value neutral' attitude (in Weber's formula) he
had himself theorized in previous decades. In all likelihood it was not that
Bourdieu's political positions had changed during the 1980s and 90s. Rather,
the general 'realignment' of the political and intellectual fields made them
appear more radical.

The same might be said of Derrida. In the 1960s and 70s the author of
Dissemination was not among the most politically active French philosophers.
He was on the margins of visible engagement, whether in working-class organizations, 'leftist' groups, or innovative associations like the *Groupe d'information
sur les prisons*, in which two of his fellow philosophers – Foucault and Deleuze
– were prominent.[9] This did not prevent him from adopting public political
positions, as in May 1968. The philosopher was also arrested and briefly impris-
oned in Czechoslovakia in 1981 for having gone there to support dissidents. The
publication of *Spectres de Marx* in 1993 nevertheless marked a turning-point.
More than a publishing event, it was a political event.

At the time, Marx was regarded as bad company to keep. That a philosopher of Derrida's importance should devote a lengthy book to him, in which
he asserted the actuality of Marx's thought, conferred a new legitimacy upon
him.[10] 'Whether they wish it or know it or not, all men and women, all over
the earth, are today to a certain extent the heirs of Marx and Marxism', wrote
Derrida.[11] There followed a profound meditation on the meaning of the
Marxian legacy, the opposition between ontology and 'hauntology' (the
science of what haunts – the 'communist promise'), and spectres which, like

8   See Serge Audier, *La Pensée anti-68. Essai sur une restauration intellectuelle*, Paris: La
Découverte, 2008, pp. 245–53.
9   On Derrida's relationship to politics, see Christian Delacampagne, 'The Politics of
Derrida: Revisiting the Past', *MLN*, no. 121, 2006.
10   Jacques Derrida, *Specters of Marx*, trans. Peggy Kamuf, New York and London:
Routledge, 1994. On the debate sparked by Derrida's interpretation of Marx, see Michael Sprinker,
ed., *Ghostly Demarcations*, London and New York: Verso, 1999.
11   Jacques Derrida, *Specters of Marx*, p. 91.

Marx's, never die. Derrida's line was not particularly radical. But in the political context of the 1990s, the very fact of writing a book on Marx attested to a process of radicalization.

PESSIMISTS

A second category of critical intellectuals is pessimists. It should be noted that a form of pessimism also characterizes the thinkers who figure in the previous category: converts. It is because they regard the transformation of society as impossible or dangerous that numerous erstwhile critical intellectuals have become reconciled with the existing order. In this sense their conversion is a consequence of their pessimism.

Pessimism is a general characteristic of the current conjuncture. It derives from the fact that political change has become difficult to conceive. As Jameson puts it, today it is easier to imagine the end of the world than the end of capitalism, as indicated by recent Hollywood films, which contain a number of catastrophic scenarios but none that anticipates a form of post-capitalism.[12] The prevailing pessimism also has its origin in the experience of the great disasters of the twentieth century – colonialism, Nazism, Stalinism – whose gradual assimilation in the collective consciousness put paid to the optimism that prevailed in progressivist circles before the First World War and then, in a different form, in the 1960s and 70s.[13]

The category of 'pessimists' contains intellectuals who combine pessimism and radicalism. In contrast to the converts, pessimism does not lead them to renounce their convictions. It coexists with them. Pessimists continue to produce forms of critical theory, while evincing scepticism about the possibility of overthrowing capitalism in the foreseeable future. They do not exclude the possibility, but regard it as currently improbable. Critical thinking has always included major pessimists, even though pessimism is a political sentiment traditionally situated on the side of conservatism.[14] Gramsci's well-known watchword, 'pessimism of the intellect, optimism of the will', is indicative of this. To restrict ourselves to the twentieth century, the term 'pessimist' suits Adorno perfectly. He was not only one of the most important Marxists of the twentieth century, but also one of the founders of contemporary thinking about culture and the media, with whom thinkers like Hall, Bourdieu and Jameson have been in continuous debate. By virtue of this, Adorno was unquestionably a critical thinker. At the same time,

---

12   Fredric Jameson, 'Future City', *New Left Review*, II/21, May–June 2003.

13   According to Perry Anderson, pessimism is characteristic of much of Western Marxism. See his *Considerations on Western Marxism*, London: New Left Books, 1976, pp. 88–9.

14   See Ted Honderich, *Conservatism*, London: Hamish Hamilton, 1990.

Minima Moralia, his grand 'reflections from damaged life', scarcely exude optimism. The dedication to Horkheimer with which the book opens is evidence enough:

> The melancholy science from which I make this offering to my friend relates to a region that from time immemorial was regarded as the true field of philosophy, but which, since the latter's conversion into method, has lapsed into intellectual neglect, sententious whimsy and finally oblivion: the teaching of the good life. What the philosophers once knew as life has become the sphere of private exist-ence and now of mere consumption, dragged along as an appendage of the process of material production, without autonomy or substance of its own . . . Our perspective of life has passed into an ideology which conceals the fact that there is life no longer.[15]

Debord, in particular the post-Situationist Debord following the dissolution of the Situationist International in 1972, is a figure comparable to Adorno in this respect. Works like *Considérations sur l'assassinat de Gérard Lebovici* (1985), *Cette mauvaise réputation . . .* (1993), or Volume One of *Panégyrique* (1989) are characterized by an extremely pessimistic view of the balance of political forces. Debord's historical pessimism sometimes borders on an anthropological pessi-mism – that is, pessimism about human nature. However, this did not prevent him from maintaining and even accentuating the radicalism of his critique of the 'society of the spectacle' over the years. His *Commentaires sur la société du spectacle* in 1988 is certainly no less radical than *La Société du spectacle* in 1967. Pessimism and radicalism are therefore conjoined in Debord, just as they co-exist in Adorno.

The case of Debord points to a typical characteristic of political pessimism. It sometimes approximates to a form of 'dandyism' or 'decadentism'. These terms designate an 'aristocratic' renunciation of politics, based on a 'catastrophic' diagnosis of the irremediably corrupt character of society. The 'disappearance' of Debord, his stubborn refusal of all visibility and any social base – 'I don't do politics', he asserted in *Cette mauvaise réputation*[16] – exemplifies this. In short, pessimists subject the social world to critique, but do not formulate proposals or act as strategists with a view to changing it.

Who are the contemporary pessimistic critical intellectuals? Jean Baudril-lard, who died in 2007, unquestionably belongs in this category. His ideas have had a major impact internationally, to the extent that a journal called

---

15 Theodor Adorno, *Minima Moralia: Reflections from Damaged Life*, trans. E. F. N. Jephcott, London: New Left Books, 1974, p. 15.
16 See Guy Debord, *Cette mauvaise réputation*, Paris: Gallimard, 1993, p. 22.

Baudrillard Studies devoted to their interpretation appeared in 2004. Baudrillard was originally a follower and collaborator at Nanterre of Lefebvre, one of the most original French Marxists of the second half of the twentieth century. His analyses in *The Consumer Society* (1970), his most famous book, form part of the tradition of the critique of 'reification'. From the 1980s, however, he gradually turned towards a form of political 'nihilism', evinced by texts like *La Guerre du Golfe n'a pas eu lieu* or *L'Esprit du terrorisme*.[17] They describe the situation we find ourselves in as suffocating and punctuated by 'non-events' (which, appearances to the contrary notwithstanding, have not occurred), such as the Gulf War and the attacks of 11 September 2001. 'The collapse of the towers of the World Trade Center', claimed Baudrillard, 'is unimaginable, but that is not enough to make it a real event. A surplus of violence is insufficient to open onto reality. For reality is a principle and it is this principle that has been lost.'[18]

The philosophical foundations of Baudrillard's nihilism emerge in one of his main works, *Simulacres et simulation*. In it he defends the idea that 'reality is not what it was'. Our age is characterized by the proliferation of 'simulacra': a 'replacement of reality by signs of reality'. In all domains – art, science and politics – the regime of 'simulation' has supplanted that of 'representation'. The precondition of the latter was 'fixed frames of reference' – in other words, objects capable of being represented. But these frames of reference have now disappeared. By the same token, the separation between the 'real' and the 'imaginary' has collapsed. From this Baudrillard deduces that '[i]t is . . . the map that precedes the territory – precession of simulacra – that engenders the territory.'[19] For Baudrillard, despite their artificial character, simulacra are all-powerful. Thus, the critique of 'simulation' does not issue in any strategic considerations. This is because for Baudrillard there is nothing to counterpose to simulacra, which are conceived as a non-transcendable horizon. This is the theme of the 'end of politics' – of the ineffectuality of collective action in current conditions. In Baudrillard's writings we thus find a mixture, typical of left-pessimists, of radical critique of the existing order and scepticism about the possibilities of changing it.

Perry Anderson is another major contemporary pessimist, but in a very different way from Baudrillard. In an editorial in *New Left Review*, he writes:

17   See Jean Baudrillard, *The Gulf War Did Not Take Place*, trans. Paul Patton, Sydney: Power Publications, 1995, and *The Spirit of Terrorism*, trans. Chris Turner, London and New York: Verso, 2002.

18   Jean Baudrillard, 'L'esprit du terrorisme', *Le Monde*, 2 November 2001.

19   Jean Baudrillard, *Simulacra and Simulation*, trans. Sheila Glaser, Ann Arbor: University of Michigan Press, 1994, p. 1. The 'map' and the 'territory' refer to a short story by Borges in which geographers construct a map on a scale of 1:1.

The only starting-point for a realistic Left today is a lucid registration of historical defeat . . . For the first time since the Reformation, there are no longer any signifi-cant oppositions – that is, systematic rival outlooks – within the thought-world of the West; and scarcely any on a world scale either, if we discount religious doctrines as largely inoperative archaisms.

He added that neo-liberalism was 'the most successful ideology in world history'.[20] This text dates from 2000. Thus, it preceded the first World Social Forum at Porto Alegre (2001), as well as the attacks of 11 September 2001. Some of its claims are open to challenge and elicited strong reactions.[21] Ten years after its publication, neo-liberalism is no longer what it was, at all events as regards its ideological hegemony – which does not prevent the policies inspired by it from still obtaining the world over. Moreover, to dismiss current religious movements – especially Islam and evangelical currents – as mere 'archaisms' is rather peremptory. But be that as it may, Anderson has in no way modified the radicalism of his critique of capitalism since the 1960s. His positions on the war in Iraq, the degeneration of the French Left and French thought, or the UN cede nothing to those formerly adopted by him. However, his style of thinking and the content of his articles betray a pessimism of the intellect seemingly deserted by optimism of the will.

RESISTERS

The third category of critical intellectuals includes those who stuck to their guns after the defeat of the second half of the 1970s. It involves thinkers who, having identified at the time with some form of Marxism, anarchism or whatever, have remained attached to it – and this regardless of whether these thinkers have remained members (if they were) of organizations inspired by these doctrines.

However loyal to their initial commitments, resisters have naturally adapted their theories to the current conjuncture. Firstly, defeat has led them to down-grade the most 'ambitious' part of their political project. In addition, new political phenomena have emerged in recent decades, such as the ecological crisis or the return of the religious in the public sphere, vis-à-vis which they have had to situate themselves. In this sense, changes have occurred even among those intellectuals closest to the positions of the 1960s and 70s.

The category of 'resisters' partially intersects with the following one – that of 'innovators'. All innovators are resisters – thinkers unreconciled to the existing

20   Perry Anderson, 'Renewals', New Left Review, II/1, January–February 2000, pp. 16–17.
21   See Gilbert Achcar, 'Perry Anderson's Historical Pessimism', and Boris Kagarlitsky, 'The Suicide of New Left Review', both in International Socialism, no. 88, 2000.

order. But the converse is not true: not all resisters are necessarily innovators. To belong to the latter category, it is necessary not only to have maintained a certain radicalism, but also to have innovated theoretically.

Let us take two contemporary theorists of anarchism, Chomsky and Daniel Colson. Since the 1960s, Chomsky has defended an anarchism inspired by the Spanish Civil War and the powerful 'anarcho-syndicalist' current that emerged in it.[22] The basis of his political theory is an optimistic conception of human nature. For Chomsky, the latter is naturally disposed towards freedom. Consequently, any constraint is illegitimate, except in special cases, where the burden of proof lies with those exercising it. This libertarian conception of human nature was inspired in Chomsky by his studies in linguistics, in particular by the 'generative grammar' he has refined. According to him, on the basis of a finite number of grammatical rules the human brain is capable of generating an infinite number of sentences. For Chomsky, this unlimited propensity for creation applies not only to language, but to human behaviour in general. The best political system is consequently the one that allows this faculty to flourish most fully – namely, anarchism.

For his part, Daniel Colson is one of the most interesting anarchist philosophers at the present time.[23] Professor at the University of Saint-Étienne and activist in the Lyon region, he is one of the thinkers endeavouring to renew this current. In his work, this renewal is essentially based on one author: Deleuze. In a passage from *Mille plateaux*, Deleuze and Guattari define anarchism as 'not the unity of the One, but a much stranger unity that applies only to the multiple'.[24] According to Colson, Deleuze's conceptualization of the 'multiple' makes it possible to advance the anarchist project and to conceive and create a multiplicity of ways of being without hierarchy or domination. In his view, starting from this reference – and also from Spinoza and Nietzsche – a new anarchism can emerge.

Chomsky pertains to the category of 'resisters', whereas Colson belongs more with the 'innovators'. The US linguist characterizes his positions as 'traditionally anarchist', situating them in the wake of the Enlightenment and classical liberalism. By contrast, Colson is unquestionably innovative. It goes without saying that the relationship between these categories is fluid; often the difference is not marked. Each thinker inclines *more* to one side or *more* to the other,

---

22   See Robert Barsky, *Noam Chomsky: A Life of Dissent*, Cambridge (MA): MIT Press, 1998. Readers are also referred to the dialogue between Chomsky and Foucault dating from 1971, reproduced as *Chomsky versus Foucault: A Debate on Human Nature*, New York: New Press, 2006.

23   See Daniel Colson, *Petit lexique de philosophie anarchiste. De Proudhon à Deleuze*, Paris: Le Livre de poche, 2001, as well as 'L'anarchisme aujourd'hui', *Solidarités*, no. 102, 2007.

24   Gilles Deleuze and Félix Guattari, *A Thousand Plateaus: Capitalism and Schizophrenia*, trans. Brian Massumi, London: Athlone, 1988, p. 175.

but elements of theoretical innovation and conservation exist on both. Further-more, a theory is not necessarily truer or more interesting because it is more recent. After all, one of the most stimulating critical theories at present remains that of Marx . . .

Among 'resisters', we find Marxists. The question of who is a Marxist today is highly complex. It always has been, because this current has always been plural. What is there in common between Marxists of a 'positivist' tempera-ment, like Kautsky, and those who regard theology as a legitimate source of inspiration for materialism, like Benjamin or Goldmann? Moreover, all contem-porary critical theories are, in a sense, 'post-Marxist'. Marxism was so dominant in the twentieth century that no theory escaped its influence. It is therefore wholly legitimate for André Tosel to use the phrase (borrowed from Immanuel Wallerstein) 'a thousand Marxisms' to characterize the period 1989–2005.[25]

Among Marxists, Trotskyists furnish a sizeable contingent of the resisters. Communists were orientated to the USSR and its satellite countries, Maoists to China, Third Worldists to Algeria or Cuba, and social-democrats to the Scandi-navian countries. Trotskyists have never been able to relate to a 'really existing' regime of this type, except in the early years of the Russian Revolution. This partly accounts for their numerical weakness throughout the twentieth century, but also means that they were largely unaffected by the collapse of real social-ism. Trotskyism has always been a developing current, which counterposed a form of revolutionary authenticity to Stalinist 'betrayal'.[26]

What impact does this characteristic have doctrinally? It leads Trotskyists to inscribe their theoretical activity in a dialectic combining conservation and innovation. There is no better illustration of this than Daniel Bensaïd's refer-ence, in a collection of texts dating from 2001, to the figure of the 'Marrano'.[27] The Marranos were Sephardic Jews forcibly converted to Christianity under the Inquisition, but who clandestinely preserved their Jewish faith and practised its rites in secret. The Marrano faith was maintained for several centuries and produced some significant figures, including Spinoza. For Bensaïd, the Marrano combines loyalty to his tradition with patience about the possibilities for its fulfilment. Loyalty to tradition does not exclude alterations in the relationship to it over time. The dialectic between continuity and rupture with the past is at the heart of the 'Marrano communism' on which Bensaïd pins his hopes. But

25   See André Tosel, 'The Development of Marxism: From the End of Marxism-Leninism to a Thousand Marxisms – France–Italy, 1975–2005', in Bidet and Kouvelakis, eds, *Critical Companion to Contemporary Marxism*.

26   A version of this argument is advanced by Philippe Raynaud, *L'Extrème gauche plurielle. Entre démocratie et révolution*, Paris: Autrement, 2006.

27   See, for example, Daniel Bensaïd, *Résistances. Essai de taupologie générale*, Paris: Fayard, 2001.

even so, it assumes that the invariant core of the tradition is handed down from one generation to the next. The relevant core comprises the basic principles of Marxism. Patience – the 'slow impatience' that provides Bensaïd's autobiography with its title[28] – reveals revolutionaries' capacity to 'hang on' in periods when the balance of political forces is against them.

This is attested in a very different way by the works of another 'resister' – namely, Alex Callinicos, professor at King's College, London, and one of the leading intellectuals of the British Socialist Workers' Party (SWP). The hypothesis formulated by him is that the rupture between theory and practice characteristic of Western Marxism might be overcome in the future: 'are we already beginning to emerge from a period of severe but temporary defeats for the workers' movement, and entering an era when the new struggles stimulated by neoliberalism will allow classical Marxism once again to become a material force?'[29] According to Callinicos, Western Marxism is a parenthesis in the history of the workers' movement. The rupture between intellectuals and Marxist organizations provoked by the failure of the German revolution could turn out to be merely temporary, and Marxism might restore the 'unity of theory and practice' in the near future. It goes without saying that Callinicos does not advocate a return, pure and simple, to yesterday's Marxism. His hypothesis is that social conditions similar to those conducive to the emergence of classical Marxism could re-appear in different forms.

INNOVATORS

One condition of theoretical innovation is *hybridization*. An intermingling of heterogeneous references is a common feature of those we shall call 'innovators'. Thus, the works of Negri and Hardt are characterized by an admixture of Marxism and 'Deleuzo-Foucaultianism'. For his part, Žižek is a veritable machine for hybridizing theories. The Slovenian thinker aspires to re-found Marxism-Leninism by basing himself on Hegel and Lacan, while drawing on Christian theology. Butler and Laclau – two privileged debating partners of Žižek's[30] – are likewise influenced by poststructuralism (Lacan and Derrida, in particular), whose services they call on to develop their own respective 'post-Marxisms'. However, Butler inclines hers towards feminism, giving rise to queer theory, whereas Laclau privileges the Gramscian problematics of 'hegemony' and

---

28   See Daniel Bensaïd, in French *Une lente impatience*, Paris: Stock, 2004. In English, *An Impatient Life: A Memoir*, London and New York: Verso, 2014 (forthcoming).

29   Alex Callinicos, 'Where Is Anglo-Saxon Marxism Going?', in Bidet and Kouvelakis, eds, *Critical Companion to Contemporary Marxism*, p. 94.

30   See Judith Butler, Ernesto Laclau and Slavoj Žižek, *Contingency, Hegemony, Universality: Contemporary Dialogues on the Left*, London and New York: Verso, 2000.

'populism'. Seyla Benhabib, a member together with Axel Honneth and Nancy Fraser of the third-generation Frankfurt School, is another representative of feminism. However, she associates her variant of this with Habermas's 'communicative ethics' and Arendt's republicanism. Silvia Rivera Cusicanqui, a Bolivian sociologist of Aymara ancestry, is one of the introducers of Subaltern Studies from India into Latin America.[31] In this way she reunites two traditions that originally drew on the same sources – namely, the indigenous Marxism of Mariátegui, who was influenced by Sorel, and Subaltern Studies, which owes a number of its concepts to Gramsci, on whom Sorel was an important influence. John Bellamy Foster, Joel Kovel and Paul Burkett have undertaken a vast revision of Marxism, which consists in getting it to measure up to the ecological challenges facing humanity in the twenty-first century. The resulting 'eco-socialism' is among the most stimulating of contemporary critical themes.[32]

Will this series of hybridizations generate new currents, just as in the nineteenth century an unanticipated synthesis of German philosophy, British political economy and French socialism gave birth to Marxism? It is too soon to tell. Some of them will remain within the existing paradigmatic frameworks, while others will emerge from them to form new frameworks. In this respect, as in others, we are in a transitional phase. On the other hand, what is certain is that hybridization is a product of defeat. Yesterday as today, the supporters of a vanquished theory are looking outside their tradition for resources with which to develop it.

A second factor in theoretical innovation is the emergence of new objects. Political ecology is among these, having emerged in the second half of the twentieth century, particularly under the impetus of the works of André Gorz, Ivan Illich and Nicholas Georgescu-Roegen.[33] The appearance of new objects often presupposes confrontation with new currents, or the reinterpretation of old currents in the light of new problematics. The issue of law is another theme that has assumed importance in recent decades, mobilizing authors such as Habermas, Boaventura de Sousa Santos, Unger and Agamben.[34] This importance is explained by the 'judiciarization' of contemporary societies and also by changes in international law since the attacks of 11 September 2001.

Among the themes debated within critical theories is the 'ethnic' question.

---

31   See Silvia Rivera Cusicanqui and Rossana Baragan, eds, *Debates postcoloniales. Una introduccion a los estudios de la subalternidad*, La Paz: SEPHIS, 1997.

32   See Carolyn Merchant, *Radical Ecology: The Search for a Liveable World*, London and New York: Routledge, 2002.

33   See Hicham-Stéphane Afeissa, *Qu'est-ce que l'écologie?*, Paris: Vrin, 2009.

34   Derrida has also reflected on law: see, for example, his *Force de loi*, Paris: Galilée, 1994. There is an abundant literature on 'human rights' in new critical thinking. See, for example, Jacques Rancière, *On the Shores of Politics*, trans. Liz Heron, London and New York: Verso, 1995, and Slavoj Žižek, 'Against Human Rights', *New Left Review*, II/34, July–August 2005.

The British sociologist of Guyanese origin, Paul Gilroy, a representative of post-colonial studies, takes it as one of his subjects. In a famous book entitled *Black Atlantic* (1993), Gilroy revised the history of modernity, starting out from the idea that at its heart is the Atlantic Ocean.[35] According to Gilroy, the historiography of modernity is characterized by its methodological 'nationalism' – that is, by the fact that the nation has always been regarded as the elementary unit of its unfolding. A break with this nationalist historiography casts the role of blacks – slaves, but also musicians and intellectuals – in the formation of the modern world in a new light. Hence the idea of a *black* Atlantic. The thinking of Du Bois, Fanon and C. L. R. James can only be understood in as much as it was trans-Atlantic. For example, at the end of the nineteenth century Du Bois lived in Berlin, where he followed the teaching of Gustav von Schmoller, one of the leading lights of the German historical school. His conception of the condition of American blacks was influenced by the latter.

Analysis of the media also figures prominently, with three major types of critique. The first has its origins in Great Britain. This is the tradition of cultural studies inaugurated by thinkers like Hoggart, Williams, Hall and Dick Hebdige. Under Gramsci's influence, Hall developed a model of the reception of cultural products called 'encoding/decoding'.[36] It argues that an audience's reception of a text or images can conform to the intention of their author, or challenge it, or involve a compromise between these two positions. Contrary to the assumptions of Adorno and Horkheimer's theory of the 'culture industry', Hall shows that audiences are never passive in the face of information.

A second form of critique of the media has Chomsky as its figurehead.[37] As well as being an anarchist thinker and the most important linguist of the second half of the twentieth century, Chomsky has also produced an influential theory of the media. It is based on the idea that the circulation of information in public opinion passes through 'filters' such as private ownership of the press or television chains, or the ideology that serves the interests of those who own them. Chomsky's 'propaganda model' thus demonstrates the systematically biased character of news reporting.

The third type of critique of the media is that practised by Bourdieu and his collaborators. Here journalism is analyzed using concepts developed by the sociologist in connection with other domains – in particular, those of 'field' and 'capital'. In *Sur la télévision*, Bourdieu shows that the journalistic field is

---

35   See also Paul Gilroy, *Against Race: Imagining Political Culture beyond the Color Line*, Cambridge (MA): Belknap, 2000.

36   See Stuart Hall, 'Encoding/Decoding', in Hall *et al.*, eds, *Culture, Media, Language*, London and New York: Routledge, 1980.

37   Noam Chomsky and Edward Hermann, *Manufacturing Consent: The Political Economy of the Mass Media*, New York: Pantheon, 1988

characterized by a 'circular circulation of information', which leads each producer of information to refer to the information produced by the others, and thus to perpetuate errors and produce ideologically homogeneous information.[38]

Theoretical innovation may also result from an updating of old themes by contemporary authors. This is the case with value theory, which authors like Moishe Postone, Robert Kurtz and Anselm Jappe – representatives of the 'critique of value' – have developed afresh. In *Time, Labor and Social Domination*, Postone proposes a novel interpretation of this theory, which has prompted important debates and the emergence of an original trend of thinking.[39] According to Postone, labour is not a trans-historical category, applicable to all societies, which capitalism alienates by transforming it into a commodity. It is a specifically capitalist category, the capitalist system being defined by the fact that it is underpinned by value: 'Marx's "labour theory of value" . . . is not a theory of the unique properties of labor in general, but is an analysis of the historical specificity of value as a form of wealth, and of the labor that supposedly constitutes it.'[40] What allows qualitatively different commodities to be exchanged in a market is their embodiment of a certain labour-time. This time is abstract, because it is solely by dividing it into discrete, comparable temporal units that commodities become commensurable. This abstraction creates a power structure specific to capitalism, whose effects have hitherto been underestimated.

For Postone, 'traditional' Marxism erred in regarding Marx's project as a critique of capitalism from the *standpoint* of labour or the working class. Marx developed a critique *of* labour. The 'value critics' reject the idea, widespread in the labour movement, that the principal capitalist contradiction consists in the increasingly social character of production and its private appropriation by employers. This idea imparts a positive connotation to production and the working class behind it, and maintains that the switch to socialism will occur when production has attained a certain level of development. For Postone, the contradiction is located in the sphere of production itself, whence derives the reified structure of capitalist societies, which is over-determined by labour-value. This thesis has considerable strategic implications. It assumes that the overthrow of capitalism cannot be the deed of the proletariat, because the latter is a symptom of the omnipotence of the value-form in a capitalist regime. Such an overthrow presupposes the abolition of the working-class condition, not its universalization.

38   Pierre Bourdieu, *On Television and Journalism*, trans. Priscilla Parkhurst Ferguson, London: Pluto, 1998.

39   See Moishe Postone, *Time, Labor and Social Domination: A Reinterpretation of Marx's Critical Theory*, Cambridge: Cambridge University Press, 1993. See also Anselm Jappe, *Les Aventures de la marchandise. Pour une nouvelle critique de la valeur*, Paris: Denoël, 2003.

40   Postone, *Time, Labor and Social Domination*, p. 26.

In capitalism we are governed by abstractions – what Marx and, following him, the German Marxist Alfred Sohn-Rethel called *real abstractions*. As Marx puts it in the *Grundrisse*, under capitalism 'individuals are now ruled by *abstractions*, whereas earlier they depended on one another.'[41] Domination is certainly not an invention of capitalism. On the other hand, what is novel is the fact that individuals are dominated not by other individuals, or even groups of individuals (what Postone calls 'manifest' domination), but by abstractions. According to Postone, capitalism immerses individuals in an abstract time and labour that become the measure of everything. In other words, it generalizes the fetish form of the commodity to social reality in its entirety.

It might seem purely theoretical, but Postone's approach to value theory can be applied to the analysis of real political phenomena. In the light of it, Postone has advanced an original analysis of modern anti-Semitism.[42] For him it is a mistake to regard the latter as a simple continuation, albeit in virulent form, of traditional European anti-Semitism. It is different in kind. Modern anti-Semitism cannot be separated from a 'conspiracy' theory of the role of Jews in history. This view attributes certain characteristics to the Jewish people – elusiveness, abstraction, universality, mobility – which are in fact characteristics of value. The figure of the Jew is therefore the embodiment or personification of value in the eyes of the modern anti-Semite. More precisely, the opposition between Aryan and Jew is the reflection in Nazi ideology of the opposition between concrete and abstract, whose form emerges with capitalism and the labour underpinning it. A precondition of modern anti-Semitism, Postone concludes, is the possibility of fetishism.

EXPERTS

During the 1980s a new type of critical intellectual emerged: the 'expert', or, rather, 'counter-expert', whose analyses aimed to contradict the dominant discourse. In the first instance, counter-expertise possesses the peculiarity that it rests on an 'internal' critique of the dominant discourse – a critique situated on the same terrain as the analyses it challenges and formulated in the name of the same scientific norms. This approach is different from one that seeks, for example, to demonstrate the ideological role played by the discourse being criticized.

Counter-expertise is invariably practised in disciplines of a highly empirical cast. What form could counter-expertise take when it comes to issues in

---

41   Karl Marx, *Grundrisse*, trans. Martin Nicolaus, Harmondsworth: Penguin/NLR, 1973, p. 164.

42   See Moishe Postone, 'Anti-Semitism and National Socialism', in J. Zipes and A. Rabinach, eds, *Germans and Jews since the Holocaust*, New York: Holmes and Meier, 1986.

political philosophy or even sociological theory? In these domains there are certainly antagonisms, but they pertain to a logic that is distinct from counter-expertise, one referring more to irreconcilable 'world-views' than disagreements over precise statistics and analytical categories. That is why the intellectuals belonging to the category of 'counter-experts' are mainly economists and empirical sociologists. This is true of most members of ATTAC's scientific committee, who conduct studies in areas in which this anti-globalization organization intervenes. Its members are appointed by the association's administrative council in accordance with two criteria: their activist commitment and their 'recognized expertise in one or several areas'.[43] Economists and sociologists form a large majority on it, even if there are also some philosophers and trade unionists. The over-representation of these disciplines in sites of counter-expertise is explained by the fact that they are at once more 'factual' and more standardized methodologically.

Counter-expertise is only conceivable in a context where a significant fraction of critical intellectuals are academics. It involves the employment by the antagonists – experts and counter-experts – of the same scientific rules, which are none other than the norms governing academic disciplines. In this sense, the proportion of counter-experts among critical intellectuals is a function of their incorporation into academic institutions.

The emergence of 'counter-experts' is also explained by the appearance of new themes referred to earlier. This is true of ecology, a domain that involves mastery of often complex issues. Thus, a number of scientists – biologists, physicists, chemists – figure in the category of counter-experts. One of the best known is the Indian Vandana Shiva. A physicist by training, in 1982 Shiva set up the Research Foundation for Science, Technology and Ecology – an institute specializing in ecological issues that collaborates with village communities in northern India.[44] It has been very prominent in the struggle against 'biopiracy' – the patenting of living things and indigenous knowledge by pharmaceutical and food-processing multinationals, on which Shiva has published a book.[45] This has led her to develop a radical critique of the relationship between science and capitalism, and to militate in favour of a form of 'eco-feminism'. The case of Jacques Testart is similar. Testart is a French biologist who helped in the birth of the first test-tube baby at the start of the 1980s. He is a member of ATTAC's scientific committee, a columnist on the journal *La Décroissance*, and a determined critic

---

43   See the presentation of the scientific committee on ATTAC's web site: attac.org.

44   See Chiara Bonfiglioli, 'Vandana Shiva, la lute altermondialiste entre écologie et féminisme', in Chiara Bonfiglioli and Sébastien Budgen, eds, *La Planète altermondialiste*, Paris: Textuel, 2006.

45   See Vandana Shiva, *Biopiracy: The Plunder of Nature and Knowledge*, Dartington: Green Books in association with the Gaia Foundation, 1998.

of GMOs and the 'commodification' of living things. Once again, his status as a biologist means that he possesses the prestige and competence required to defend his views.

The fight against AIDS has witnessed a new form of activist counter-expertise, at once political and scientific. The aim of the relevant associations is not only to assert the interests of sufferers and help circulate information, but also to involve them in treating the epidemic. This has entailed challenging the monopoly on treatment possessed by doctors and questioning the power they have arrogated in its name.[46] Thus, several associations for fighting AIDS have specialized in 'therapeutic counter-expertise'. ACT UP, *Aides*, *Arcat* and several others created the collective 'TRT-5' for 'Treatment Research Therapy' in 1992.

The political and epistemological principles underlying the activity of these groups in the face of medical power go back to the feminist and homosexual movements of the 1960s and 70s. For example, feminists practiced 'unofficial expertise' in gynaecological matters. It aimed to constitute the object of traditional gynaecology – the woman – as a subject of knowledge of her own body, in other words, to make her 'the informed expert on herself'.[47]

Another historical source of counter-expertise is the 'specific' intellectual theorized by Foucault in the 1970s. In a famous interview with Deleuze, Foucault contrasted the specific intellectual with the 'universal' intellectual.[48] The latter – from Zola to Sartre – pronounces on any and every subject and, to do this, relies on (supposedly) universal values like the good, truth, justice or reason. By contrast, the specific intellectual only intervenes in his own area of competence, basing his interventions on a particular knowledge. Foucault himself practised this kind of commitment when he founded the *Groupe d'information sur les prisons* in 1972, with the aim of collecting and publicizing information on prison conditions.

One of the thinkers who contributed to the legitimation of counter-expertise is Bourdieu. Even if he did not regard himself as an 'expert', his conception of sociology drew him towards this kind of intervention. In 1997, in the wake of his support for the strikers during the major French strikes of December 1995, Bourdieu founded the association and collection *Raisons d'agir*. It is one of the centres of counter-expertise in France, similar in its *modus operandi* to ATTAC's scientific committee. An interesting feature of Bourdieu's sociology is that it is based on a strict distinction between *doxa* and *episteme* – that is, between

---

46   See Nicolas Dodier, *Leçons politiques de l'épidémie du Sida*, Paris: Éditions de l'École des Hautes Études en Sciences Sociales, 2003.

47   See Elsa Dorlin, *Sexe, genre et sexualités*, Paris: Presses Universitaires de France, 2008, p. 12.

48   See 'Intellectuals and Power', in Michel Foucault, *Language, Counter-Memory, Practice: Selected Essays*, trans. Donald F. Bouchard and Sherry Simon, Oxford: Blackwell, 1977.

common-sense opinion and scientific knowledge. As a result, only sociologists can attain to the objectivity of the social world, because they alone possess the tools – in particular, statistical ones – that enable them to release themselves from enslavement to current opinions. Consequently, their work consists in achieving this objectivity and then placing it at the disposal of social actors. The 'overarching' position conferred by this conception of sociological knowledge on those exercising it is not distinct from that claimed by 'experts'.

LEADERS

The sixth category of intellectuals is 'leaders'. In this category are thinkers who perform leadership roles in a political party or social movement, and who have simultaneously or subsequently made a significant contribution to critical theory. As we have seen, the dominant tendency since the 1920s has clearly been to a disconnection between intellectuals and working-class organizations. Among contemporary critical theorists, some nevertheless play a leadership role in parties. Bensaïd is among those who maintained a Marxist position proximate to that of previous decades in the 1980s and 90s, continuing to draw mainly on references from that tradition. At the same time, in the 1960s he was one of the founders of the *Ligue communiste révolutionnaire* and was an influential member of the *Nouveau Parti anticapitaliste* (NPA). An analogous case, likewise mentioned above, is that of Callinicos, a member of the SWP's leadership. But these organizations are microscopic when compared with those led by Marxists in the classical age. At most they contain several thousand members – a figure that pales into insignificance beside the million members enrolled by German social democracy in the early twentieth century, or the half million members of the French Communist Party as late as the 1970s.

Álvaro García Linera, current vice-president of Bolivia, is perhaps the sole thinker referred to in this book who is an innovative critical intellectual and a front-rank political leader. In this respect he is a rare specimen, a kind of lost 'classical Marxist' in an age that supposedly no longer produces them.[49] In the first instance he is the inheritor of the powerful Bolivian labour movement, long embodied in the Bolivian Workers' Centre (COB) that notably asserted itself in the 1952 revolution, which issued in a 'state capitalism' strongly coloured by nationalism and survived until the neo-liberal reforms of the mid-1980s. García Linera is a Marxist by formation: Marx's writings on 'peoples without a history' and India, or those of Lenin, on whom he has written a book, hold no

---

49   For a presentation of the career and ideas of Álvaro García Linera, see Pablo Stefanoni and Marc Saint-Upéry, 'Le laboratoire bolivien', in García Linera, *Pour une politique de l'égalité. Communauté et autonomie dans la Bolivie contemporaine*, Paris: Les Prairies ordinaires, 2008.

secrets for him. But he is also the product of indigenist movements (even though he himself comes from a white middle-class family), especially the 'Katarist' movement, named after the native rebel Tupac Katari (1750–1781).[50] Katarism holds that Spanish colonialism was succeeded by an 'internal' colonialism established by the country's elites. It advocates the defence of Aymara and Quechua identity and traditions. His immersion in this movement has enabled García Linera to supplement a 'classist' Marxist approach with an 'identitarian' one. This mixture of Marxism and indigenism, very pronounced in contemporary Latin America, had already been initiated by Mariátegui.

In the early 1990s, García Linera belonged to a guerrilla group called the Tupac Katari Guerrilla Army. He was arrested in 1992 and spent five years in prison. Once released, he became a sociology professor – he was originally a mathematician – in a university in La Paz. In 2000, the 'water war' broke out in the region of Cochabamba, following a hike in the price of water following its privatization. The social struggles waged by pauperized new urban strata, often Indian in origin, multiplied, in particular blockades of La Paz – a city surrounded by mountains and easy to cut off. García Linera was the main theorist of these new forms of struggle, which he sought to conceptualize by drawing on the works of Negri and Bourdieu in particular. In 2005, Evo Morales chose him for the post of vice-president of Bolivia, a post he has held since then. Since his accession to power, García Linera has developed the controversial concept of 'Andean capitalism'. According to him, a transition to socialism is not on the current agenda in Bolivia. Its presupposition is an extended period in which the emergence of a 'virtuous' national capitalism must be encouraged.[51]

A related case to that of García Linera is Subcomandante Marcos, leader of the Mexican Zapatista Army of National Liberation (EZLN). Marcos is a former philosophy professor at the National Autonomous University of Mexico. He is the author of a teeming oeuvre since the 1994 Zapatista uprising in Chiapas made him famous. This oeuvre takes up several volumes and has mainly taken the form of articles published in the Mexican daily *La Jornada*. Marcos' writings contain analyses of Mexican and global politics, articulated in an ironic style inspired by the 'magical realism' of writers of the Latin American literary 'boom' (Gabriel Garcia Marquez, Alejo Carpentier). 'El Sup' is a radical critic of the neo-liberalism and neo-colonialism suffered by Latin America. However, he is not, strictly speaking, a theorist, in as much as he does not develop an original intellectual system. In his writings we find no trace of concepts and theories belonging specifically to him.

---

50 Ibid., p. 28.
51 See the interview with García Linera, 'No estamos pensando en socialism sino en revolución democratizadora', *Pagina*, no. 12, 10 April 2006.

This does not prevent them from containing precise political views. In a famous passage of his work he indicates the reason for his celebrated balaclava, referring to the question of who Marcos is:

> Marcos is gay in San Francisco, black in South Africa, Asian in Europe, a Chicano in San Isidro, an anarchist in Spain, a Palestinian in Israel, an Indian in the streets of San Cristóbal, a kid gang member in Nez, a rocker in the Cité universitaire, a Jew in Germany, an ombudsman in Sedena [Defence Ministry], a feminist in political parties, a communist in the post–Cold War, a pacifist in Bosnia, a Mapuche in the Andes . . . In short, Marcos is any old human being on this planet. Marcos is all the rejected and oppressed minorities, who resist, explode and say '*Ya basta!*' He is every minority now finding its voice and every majority obliged to shut up and listen to the storm. He is every excluded group in search of words, their own words – something that will ultimately give a majority to the eternally separate, us. Everything that troubles power and clear consciences – that's what Marcos is.[52]

The political theory of Zapatistism comprises two elements. The first is indigenism. Marcos militates in favour of the integration of Indians into the Mexican nation, on the basis of the postulate that, notwithstanding their 'formal' integration, they are still victims of profound segregation. During his press conferences Marcos often speaks with a Mexican flag behind him, which implies a conception of the 'fatherland' significantly different from that of the Latin American Marxist guerrillas of previous decades. Marcos is a representative of 'minority' thinking – that is, promotion of the status of minority – one of whose origins lies in poststructuralism. In this sense he embodies the encounter of this current – which he practised during his philosophical years in Mexico, devoting his thesis to Althusser – with Mexican indigenist demands.

Furthermore, Marcos is strongly influenced by theories of 'anti-power' – in particular, that developed by the Mexico-based Scottish philosopher John Holloway in his book *Change the World without Taking Power*, published in 2002. The basic idea underlying theories of anti-power is that the transformation of society by the seizure of state power on 'Leninist' lines is an illusion, which always results in regimes more detestable than those confronted. On the basis of this assessment, Holloway advocates renouncing seizure of power and changing the world by exploiting the spaces of freedom inevitably produced by capitalism. In line with this idea, and contrary to the Latin American guerrillas influenced by the Cuban model, the Zapatistas have never sought state power.

---

52 Subcomandante Marcos, 'The Majority Disguised as the Resented Minority', *EZLN Press Release* (31 May 1994).

When they go to Mexico City, it is to get their demands heard and occupy the media terrain. A famous saying by Subcomandante Marcos runs: 'We do not want state power, we want power.'

An interesting case of a 'leader' is Edward Said. From 1977–91, Said was a member of the Palestinian National Council, the legislative assembly of the Palestine Liberation Organization (PLO). He left this body in 1991 in protest at the Oslo Accords, which were in the offing. Thereafter his relations with the Palestinian Authority in general, and Yasser Arafat in particular, degenerated to the point where the latter banned the distribution of Said's works in the autonomous territories. In 2002, Said helped set up the 'Palestinian Initiative' led by Mustafa Barghouti, an attempt to create a third political force – progressive and secular – alongside Fatah and Hamas. Although he defined himself as a Palestinian 'patriot', Said was close to Anglo-American radical circles throughout his life. His commitment was not of the same order as that of Bensaïd and Callinicos, in the sense that he was not the leader of a revolutionary party in a national political arena. Nor was he a member of a government like García Linera, or head of a guerrilla movement like Subcomandante Marcos. However, he was one of the few critical intellectuals who had an influence on real political processes during the 1980s and 90s.

Several hypotheses have been advanced in Part One of this book. It is worth briefly recalling them before embarking on Part Two. The first is that the new critical theories have developed within the framework of political coordinates inherited from the 1960s and 70s. This means that some of the main debates in these theories emerged in those years. In particular, this is true of debates over the nature of the subjects of emancipation and the issue of power. In both cases, problems arising from the crisis of the classical models and theories of the labour movement in the late 1950s still exist today. From this we have deduced that, in a certain respect, we are still situated in the historical sequence which began then. Moreover, the new critical theories must be conceived in connection with the political cycle of the 1960s, for they are the product of the defeat of the movements of the time. We shall understand nothing of the current political and theoretical situation if we do not see that it is suffused with the pessimism characteristic of periods marked by defeat.

A second hypothesis is that current critical theorists in contact with real political processes are a rarity. In most cases the thinkers we are concerned with in this book have little or no relationship with political, industrial or community organizations. Moreover, this applies to the most radical among them as well as the most moderate. In sum, this is a structural problem. The new critical theories have accentuated a tendency inaugurated in the mid-1920s by Western Marxism, described by Anderson, leading to a disconnection between theory and practice.

A third hypothesis is the internationalization of critical thinking. It will increasingly hail in the future from regions on the periphery of the world-system, like Asia, Latin America and Africa. Europe and the Western world have lost the (quasi-)monopoly they once had on the production of critical theories. This does not exclude the central character of the United States and its universities in the 'world republic of critical theories'. For today's critical theorists, US universities constitute a site of recognition comparable to Paris for writers in the first half of the twentieth century.

The fourth hypothesis is that innovation in current critical theory is mainly the product of two mechanisms. The first is hybridization, which sees old references from the critical corpus combined in an original way or associated with new actors or currents. In addition, innovation results from the introduction of new objects of analysis, like the media or ecology. This involves a renewal of the conceptual apparatus on which the relevant forms of critical thinking rely.

PART II

Theories

The purpose of Part Two of this book is to offer a map of contemporary forms of critical theory. This task is at once impossible to acquit and indispensable. Impossible, because these forms of critical thought are in the process of being developed and it is therefore not possible to grasp them in the way one can grasp past intellectual currents. Necessary, because the construction of 'cognitive maps', however provisional and incomplete, is (as Jameson has suggested) part of the process whereby the Left will overcome the defeats it has suffered in recent decades. Acting in the world involves initially – in fact, simultaneously – representing it to oneself, however partially. Part Two hopes to make a (modest) contribution to an overall review of, and sketch of the prospects for, the critical thinking that has emerged since the fall of the Berlin Wall.

We shall first present the way that the new forms of critical thought conceive the nature of the global system and its development since the last quarter of the twentieth century ('System'). What analyses of the current global economic, political and cultural system are being produced by critical thinkers? Several problematics will emerge, among them imperialism, capitalism, the construction of Europe, and ecology. We shall then turn to the issue of subjects of emancipation ('Subjects'). Our concern here will be to identify the actors whom critical thinkers regard as potential candidates for the role of 'operators' of social transformation. Obviously, the nature of the social transformation depends on the actors prioritized. We shall see that the diversity of potential candidates is commensurate with the crisis of the subject of emancipation, which (as we have said) has persisted as a general coordinate of the period.

Why choose these thinkers rather than others? Any selection runs the risk of excluding important elements of the problem considered. Mine doubtless contains its share of arbitrariness. I have tried to combine several criteria, in an inevitably imperfect manner. Some of the authors selected are unavoidable on account of their celebrity. This criterion pertains to what Vincent Descombes once called the 'clamorous' conception of intellectual history.[1] Others have been selected because they are regarded as particularly productive. Still others seemed to me to exemplify certain key features of the period, like the

---

1 Vincent Descombes, *Modern French Philosophy*, trans. Lorna Scott-Fox and J. M. Harding, Cambridge: Cambridge University Press, 1981, p. 2.

connection between the problematics of social classes and indigenism established by García Linera.

The geographical provenance of the thinkers selected is diverse. We shall refer to an African (Achille Mbembe), two Asians (the Chinese Wang Hui and the Indian Gayatri Spivak), two Latin Americans (Laclau and García Linera). Seyla Benhabib is Turkish – a native of a country which, depending on the geopolitical epoch and conjuncture, has been regarded as European or Asian. As for the rest, the dominant component is European and North American. Although the current trend is towards an internationalization of critical thinking, Europe and the United States remain the hegemonic powers in the field. However, there is no doubt that the days of their hegemony are numbered.

CHAPTER FOUR

System

The most widely discussed critical theory since the fall of the Berlin Wall is probably Hardt and Negri's theory of Empire and the Multitude. Debates over it have lessened in intensity in the last few years, but, like the current they are part of – sometimes characterized as 'Negrian' – they represent one of the most influential forms of critical thinking in these years. The theory is mostly developed in two books: *Empire*, published in 2000, and *Multitude*, published in 2004.[1] It involves a 'totalizing' form of thought, which no aspect of reality escapes. One of its undeniable strong points, which accounts in part for its success, is that it blends philosophical reflection with the analysis of concrete social movements. The multiplicity of references it makes – from St. Francis of Assisi, via Madison and Lenin, to Foucault – adds to the charm of a doctrine that evinces an eclecticism typical of current critical theories. No doubt this is one of the characteristics by which periods of reconstruction can be recognized.

While Hardt and Negri became globally famous with the appearance of *Empire*, they are the products of a tumultuous history. From the 1960s, Negri was one of the leading figures in an innovative school of European Marxism – namely, Italian *operaismo*. His current theses derive from this tradition and it is therefore important to take a look at them, all the more so because Negri is not the sole inheritor of *operaismo* today. Whereas other currents from the past have little impact on contemporary critical thinking, *operaismo* is among the doctrines of the 1960s and 70s with the most productive legacy. Certain themes tackled by its representatives in those years – for example, the relationship between the economy and knowledge – are prominent in today's debates. Among the contemporary thinkers who in one way or another intersected with the trajectory of *operaismo* are Virno, Agamben and Arrighi, as well as Yann Moulier-Boutang. But many other authors who at the time did not belong to this tendency, like Holloway or García Linera, have been influenced by it. As a result of

---

1   Michael Hardt and Antonio Negri, *Empire*, Cambridge (MA): Harvard University Press, 2000, and *Multitude: War and Democracy in the Age of Empire*, London: Penguin, 2004.

Negri's exile in France from the early 1980s, *operaismo* came into contact with French (post)structuralism,[2] in particular the oeuvres of Foucault and Deleuze. They exercised a decisive influence on Hardt and Negri's current ideas.

Operaismo

Operaismo emerged at the start of the 1960s with the creation by Raniero Panzieri of the journal *Quaderni rossi* (Red Notebooks). Panzieri, who was soon joined by other intellectuals like Mario Tronti, Romano Alquati and Massimo Cacciari (future mayor of Venice), was a theorist and trade-union activist excluded from the Italian Socialist Party because of his opposition to any agreement with Christian Democracy. Interestingly, the foundation of *Quaderni rossi* occurred under the influence of *Socialisme ou barbarie*, Lefort and Castoriadis's journal created in the late 1940s.[3] The history of *operaismo* was to be punctuated by the creation of new journals and new collectives, among them *Classe operaia*, founded by Tronti, Negri and Alquati following their break with Panzieri (who died prematurely in 1964), and *Potere operaio*, led by Negri, which was the rival of *Lotta continua*, led by Adriano Sofri. The leader of a dissident group in the PSI in the Veneto, Negri joined *Quaderni rossi* from its second issue.

The emergence of *operaismo* must be understood in relation to the 'years of lead' – that is, the rebellions by Italian workers and students in the 1970s and their repression by the state, especially the 'Hot Autumn' of 1969. These revolts outflanked the traditional organizations of the Italian working class, particularly the PCI, openly positioning themselves in opposition to them. In 1973, another important group in this current emerged – *Autonomia operaia* – led by Negri, which had a decisive influence on the powerful student movement of 1977. Negri was condemned for his alleged 'intellectual responsibility' for the 'terrorism' of these years – that perpetrated by the Red Brigades, for example. That is why he went into exile in France, returning to Italy to serve his sentence in the late 1990s and finally being freed in 2003. The history of *operaismo* extends to our days, and its influence is evident in many sectors of the Italian and European Left. The daily paper *Il Manifesto*,

---

2   The trajectory of Félix Guattari was decisive in the exchanges between the French and Italian radical Lefts in the 1970s. On this see François Dosse, *Gilles Deleuze and Félix Guattari: Intersecting Lives*, trans. Deborah Glassman, New York: Columbia University Press, 2010.

3   Steve Wright, *Storming Heaven: Class Composition and Struggle in Italian Autonomist Marxism*, London: Pluto, 2002, p. 23. *Quaderni rossi* was also influenced by C. L. R. James' Correspondence Publishing Committee.

launched in 1969, was started under the impetus of, among others, intellectuals from this current.[4]

Operaismo is a variegated tendency, the positions of whose main representatives have developed considerably over the years. *Operaismo* means 'workerism'. In countries like France the term refers to the (over)valuation – not free of anti-intellectualism – of the industrial working class, its culture and organizations. In Italy its meaning is the converse. It refers to the revolutionary spontaneity of fractions of the dominated classes that are not (yet) organized. *Operaismo* regards the factory as the 'centre of gravity' of the class struggle. The confrontation between workers and employers is held to occur at the very point of production, without the mediation of trade unions or parties. *Operaismo* is an anti-trade union, spontaneist current. Even if they often referred to Lenin, and although the issue of organization was central to their debates, its representatives were hostile to Leninism as traditionally conceived. The latter argued that the subjectivity of the working class must be completed or enriched by the party. Left to itself, it tends towards class compromise. The *operaisti*, by contrast, believe that the raw subjectivity of the workers contains the 'truth' of the class struggle.

Two features of 1960s Italy account for this position. The first is the bureaucratization of the organizations of the Italian working class and the compromises they entered into. The *Partito Comunista Italiano* is famous for having been the most 'liberal' of the European Communist parties. At the same time, its strategy consisted in moving progressively closer to other Italian parties – an orientation that culminated in the 'historic compromise' with Christian Democracy in the early 1970s.[5] As one commentator has remarked, the PCI practically saved Italian capitalism by delivering its electorate and its prestige into the hands of the country's corrupt institutions.[6] This induced in *operaismo* a visceral distrust of the organized working class, the union bureaucracies, the PCI and PSI; and opposition to its main theoretician, Gramsci, especially in the authorized interpretation of him by Palmiro Togliatti, the principal PCI leader of the time. Whereas in other countries – Argentina and Britain, for example – the author of the *Prison Notebooks* represented a theoretical resource in the 1960s in the face of a sclerotic Marxism-Leninism, in Italy it was rare to find an 'extra-parliamentary', revolutionary collective and/or intellectual invoking his legacy.

---

4   Maria Turchetto, 'From "Mass Worker" to "Empire": The Disconcerting Trajectory of Italian *Operaismo*', in Jacques Bidet and Stathis Kouvelakis, eds, *A Critical Companion to Contemporary Marxism*, Leiden and Boston: Brill, 2008.

5   For a history of the evolution of the Italian Left, readers are referred to Perry Anderson, *The New Old World*, London and New York: Verso, 2009, chapter 6.

6   Alex Callinicos, 'Toni Negri in perspective', *International Socialism*, second series, 92, Autumn 2001.

A second process underlying *operaismo*'s spontaneist, anti-trade union position was bound up with internal migration in Italy in the 1950s and 60s. The country's economic development proceeded in the twentieth century around a division between an industrialized north and a more rural south. In the postwar period the migration from the south of unskilled workers who were hired in the factories of the north intensified. This gave rise to the emergence of a new working class, sociologically distinct from the old Italian working class. The trade unions' reaction to this new class was a defence of 'professionalism' – that is, a form of corporatism which consisted in controlling the entry of new proletarians into the labour market.[7] By contrast, the *operaisti* regarded this new class as symptomatic of changes underway in capitalism and the subaltern categories, and defended the idea that it represented a potential new subject of emancipation.

This gave rise to the theory of the *mass worker*. The concept referred to a new type of worker, unskilled, coming from the south and implanted in the factories of the north, who performed simple productive tasks, and whom the *operaisti* positioned at the heart of the mode of production that developed in Europe after the Second World War.[8] The mass worker had neither the professional competence of the skilled worker, nor the 'class consciousness' transmitted from one generation to the next that resulted from it. However, the revolutionary potentialities of this new subject were considerable, if we are to believe *operaista* texts from the late 1960s, for reasons that were both strategic and basic. The mass worker was rejected by the organizations of the working class, making it possible to turn them into battering rams against the 'union bureaucracies'. From a structural point of view, through their lack of qualifications they destroyed existing forms of work organization, especially Fordism. As a result, the mass worker represented a weapon against the division of labour.

The discourse about 'semi-skilled workers' developed by certain tendencies in French Maoism in the same years is close to that of the *operaisti* in some respects. The semi-skilled worker was contrasted with the skilled worker, structurally integrated into post-war capitalism, with an occupation and a subjectivity fashioned by non-combative trade unions. Like the mass worker, the unskilled worker was the source of a social conflictuality the Maoists sought to encourage. Moreover, the Maoists and *operaisti* employed a similar repertoire of action, a centre-piece of which was the 'workers' inquiry'. This practice forms part of a tradition inaugurated in the labour movement in the nineteenth century, of which the workers' inquiry proposed by Marx himself in 1880 is a striking example. It attests to the importance assigned by these currents to the

---

7   Wright, *Storming Heaven*, p. 297.
8   Ibid., p. 107.

'subjective factor' – that is, the way the dominated classes subjectively live the domination they suffer. However, there are also differences between the *operaisti* and Maoists. One of the main ones is that the former were sophisticated theorists, whereas the French Maoists produced no innovative theories in these years (the works of Badiou and Rancière came later) and even regarded theoretical production with contempt.

Operaismo contradicted a dogma widely diffused in working-class organizations, whether Communist or social-democratic – namely, belief in the necessarily positive character of technological progress. From the outset, especially in Panzieri, it developed a critique of the apologetic conception of science and technology prevalent in the labour movement and the USSR, and made them a central instance of the domination of capital. The idea that the development of the productive forces was a vector of progress, and would gradually lead in and of itself to the appearance of socialism, was demolished by Panzieri. This situated *operaismo* in its initial phase within what Bloch called the 'warm currents' of Marxism – that is, those where an anti-technicist, 'romantic' dimension prevailed.[9] This dimension is consistent with the *operaista* critique of the old working class, repository of a technical knowledge inseparable from the division of labour.[10]

However, the attitude of the *operaisti* to technology gradually altered. In the fourth issue of *Quaderni rossi*, Panzieri introduced a reference to a text that remains fundamental to *operaismo* to this day – namely, the 'fragment on machines' from Marx's *Grundrisse*. The idea contained in this text (as interpreted by the *operaisti*) is that knowledge – mainly, but not exclusively, scientific knowledge – becomes the principal factor of production in late capitalism. In the standard Marxist model it is labour that is the source of value. With the ascendancy of knowledge-value, the worker ceases to be the central actor in the process of production and is progressively 'satellized' by it. The concept of 'general intellect' is introduced by Marx to describe this phenomenon:

> The development of fixed capital indicates to what degree general social knowledge has become a *direct force of production*, and to what degree, hence, the conditions of the process of social life itself have come under the control of the general intellect and been transformed in accordance with it.[11]

9 See Ernst Bloch, *The Principle of Hope*, 3 vols, trans. Neville Plaice, Stephen Plaice and Paul Knight, Oxford: Blackwell, 1986.

10 In addition to the workers' inquiry, sabotage of the productive apparatus is a characteristic of the *operaista* repertoire. See Razmig Keucheyan and Laurent Tessier, 'Du sabotage au piratage. Entretien avec Toni Negri', *Critique*, nos 733–4, 2008.

11 Karl Marx, *Grundrisse*, trans. Martin Nicolaus, Harmondsworth: Penguin/NLR, 1973, p. 706.

'Fixed capital' refers to the capital incorporated into machines. In this sense it designates a technical knowledge transformed into an instrument of production. For its part, the 'general intellect' refers to individuals' collective intelligence and their capacity for cooperating in economic production and, more generally, social existence. It involves a 'general social knowledge' that is anonymous and dispersed throughout the social body, which includes fixed capital, without being reducible to it, and which locates knowledge and know-how at the heart of capitalism, but also of possible challenges to it. This idea is the core of the hypothesis of 'cognitive capitalism' formulated by the inheritors of *operaismo* today.

In addition to the 'general intellect', another important concept of *operaismo* is *class composition*. This refers to the mixture of technical objectivity and political subjectivity contained in a given political struggle. This mixture makes it possible to characterize a historical period and identify a principal actor in it. Thus, the mass worker is the dynamic figure corresponding to 1970s capitalism, in that it is both the product of structural changes in the latter and the bearer of a capacity for challenging its operation. Capital responds to each 'class composition' with a profound restructuring.

Unlike other variants of Marxism, which allocate to capital primacy over labour in determining the course of history, the *operaisti* argued that working-class struggles hold the initiative and that capitalism is always reactive or lagging behind. The most influential work in which this idea was developed was Tronti's *Operai e capitale* (*Workers and Capital*, published in 1966), one of the great classics of *operaismo*. In a chapter entitled 'The Strategy of Rejection', Tronti claims, for example, that

> the working class *does* what it *is*. It is both the *articulation* and the *dissolution* of capital. The power of capital seeks to use the will of workers to oppose them, to make them the motor of its own development. The workers' party must start from this same real mediation of the capitalist interest that occurs on the side of the workers, to organize it into antagonism, into a terrain of tactical struggle, into a strategic possibility of destruction.[12]

In other words, workers' struggles compel the system to constantly reform itself. This logically leads Negri to maintain that the movements of the 1960s and 70s were not defeated, contrary to the commonly held opinion (which is also that expressed in chapter 1 of this book), but on the contrary won their battle against the capitalism of the time. Present-day capitalism is, in his view, the result of the changes imposed on the system by these movements.

---

12   See also Alberto Toscano, 'Chronicles of Insurrection: Tronti, Negri, and the Subject of Antagonism', *Cosmos and History*, no. 5, 2009.

The *operaisti* gradually abandoned the idea that the factory is the site where the class struggle unfolds. The history of *operaismo* is punctuated by reversals of this kind, and just as technology passed from its status as the core of domination to that of the motor of capitalist development and its contestation (with the theory of the general intellect), from the second half of the 1970s Negri began to theorize the idea that the class struggle unfolds in society as a whole. The thesis underpinning this position is that the factory gradually extends its logic to the whole of society and that, as a result, the exploitation to which workers are subject now affects the whole population.[13] In Negri's subsequent evolution, this thesis was to intersect with a concept developed by Foucault – 'biopower' – which refers to the government of populations and bodies that Foucault believed had emerged in the nineteenth century.

In this new configuration, the mass worker is replaced by a different dynamic figure: the *social worker*. Negri registers the crisis experienced by the 'working class' as an analytical category and a reality.[14] This concurs with analyses made at the same time in France by authors like Gorz, whose *Adieu au prolétariat* dates from 1980.[15] Two processes account for this development in Negri's view. The first is the general rise in the educational level of the population. This means that individuals are decreasingly 'massified' and increasingly 'singularities'. In addition, the *operaisti* defend the hypothesis of the 'tertiarization' of society – that is, the ascendancy of the tertiary sector. Here too they form part of a general 'post-Marxist' trend, to which authors like Touraine and Mallet also belong. Education and tertiarization combine to confer an ever increasing importance on intellectual or 'immaterial' labour in production.

Empire and Multitude

From his specifically *operaista* period until his exile in France in 1983 and the appearance of *Empire* in 2000, Negri published a series of works – among them *Marx au-delà Marx* (based on a seminar given at the Ecole normale supérieure at Althusser's invitation in 1978), *L'Anomalie sauvage* devoted to Spinoza, and *Le Pouvoir constituant*.[16] Increasingly, Negri distanced himself from Marxism as traditionally conceived. He now set about developing a theory of power and

---

13   Wright, *Storming Heaven*, p. 300.
14   Ibid., p. 163.
15   André Gorz, *Farewell to the Working Class: An Essay on Post-Industrial Socialism*, trans. Michael Sonenscher, London: Pluto, 1982.
16   See Toni Negri, *Marx beyond Marx: Lessons from the Grundrisse*, trans. Harry Cleaver, Michael Ryan and Maurizio Viano, London: Pluto, 1991; *The Savage Anomaly: The Power of Spinoza's Metaphysics and Politics*, trans. Michael Hardt, Minneapolis: University of Minnesota Press, 1991; *Insurgencies: Constituent Power and the Modern State*, trans. Maurizia Boscagli, Minneapolis: University of Minnesota Press, 1999.

subjectivity. Negri gradually distanced himself from *Capital*, which he regarded as an 'objectivist' text conforming to economism, and counterposed to it the *Grundrisse*, presented as more in tune with the recent developments in capitalism. In the early 1990s, together with the former Trotskyist Jean-Marie Vincent, he founded the journal *Futur antérieur*, which was to echo his new concerns.[17]

In his reflections on power, Negri developed a key distinction inspired by Spinoza. This is the distinction between *potere* and *potenza* (or between *pouvoir* and *puissance*). The first notion refers to power in the usual sense of the term – that is, 'power *over*'. In this meaning of the word, A possesses power over B if she can make him perform an act he would not otherwise have performed, or not perform an act he wished to perform. On a collective level, this meaning of power refers to the constraints that institutions – for example, governmental ones – exercise over one or more individuals. The second meaning of 'power' is 'power *to*', understood in the sense not of domination or the use of force, but of the capacity or faculty to perform an act. One or several individuals are 'powerful' in this sense if they realize the potential they possess. For example, I realize the human potential to swim if I actually learn to swim.

These two meanings of power are closely related but opposite. Power in the first sense consists in separating individuals from their potential – that is, what they would be capable of doing. Conversely, to realize a potential consists in freeing oneself from the constraints imposed by power. This distinction has a libertarian connotation. The Multitude is situated on the side of power as potential – that is, cooperation and creativity. For its part, Empire is on the side of power as constraint, in that, to exist and prosper, it needs constantly to harness the powers of the Multitude. The following passage from *Empire* provides a glimpse of the theme:

> Once again in postmodernity we find ourselves in Saint Francis's situation, posing against the misery of power the joy of being. This is a revelation that no power will control – because biopower and communism, cooperation and revolution remain together, in love, simplicity, and also innocence. This is the irrepressible lightness and joy of being communist.[18]

Let us turn, then, to the interconnected concepts of Empire and Multitude. The success of the former, and the book of the same name, rests in part on a misunderstanding. *Empire* appeared in 2000 and owes its popularity to the aggressive resurgence of US imperialism after 11 September 2001, which gave rise to the

---

17   See the interesting archives of *Futur antérieur* at http://multitudes.samizdat.net. A history of this journal and its influence on the radical Left remains to be written.

18   Hardt and Negri, *Empire*, p. 413.

military adventures in Afghanistan and Iraq. However, what Hardt and Negri call 'Empire' is very different from what is usually understood by 'imperialism'. Imperialism implies one or several centres and peripheries. It assumes the existence of dominant regions (historically, Europe, followed by the United States), and dominated regions which are the victims of imperialism. Thus conceived, imperialism classically consists in the projection of the power of the central states onto the world stage, which implies – notably in Lenin's conception – the existence of inter-imperialist conflicts.

Hardt and Negri reject this conception of global geopolitical and economic relations. According to them,

> In contrast to imperialism, Empire establishes no territorial center of power and does not rely on fixed boundaries or barriers. It is a *decentered* and *deterritorializing* apparatus of rule that progressively incorporates the entire global realm within its open, expanding frontiers.[19]

Hardt and Negri register the inexorable decline of nation-states in the era of globalization. In their view, the latter abolishes national sovereignty and the regulatory capacities possessed by states during the modern age. The authors share the viewpoint of analysts – on the Left and Right – who believe that globalization radically challenges the state form. This does not mean that the problematic of sovereignty has disappeared. But it is now situated at a higher level, which is precisely that of Empire. As this passage states, imperial sovereignty is defined by the fact that it has no centre and is not territorial. Empire is a 'smooth space', as Hardt and Negri put it with reference to a concept coined by Deleuze. It does not experience the 'asperities' that are the borders or political and/or economic inequalities characteristic of the national *ancien régime*. Power certainly exists, but it is literally without a site: 'In this smooth space of Empire, there is no place of power – it is both everywhere and nowhere.'[20]

However, global actors involved in power strategies are not absent from Empire. Transnational corporations receive the lion's share in the ontology of the contemporary political world proposed by Hardt and Negri. Far from being dependent on state constraints, they 'directly structure and articulate territories and populations. They tend to make nation-states merely instruments to record the flows of the commodities, monies and populations that they set in motion.'[21] By dint of their reticular, mobile character, transnationals therefore possess primacy in the context of Empire, reducing states to the rank of mere

---

19   Ibid., p. xii.
20   Ibid., p. 190.
21   Ibid., p. 31.

'instruments'. Hardt and Negri outline the structure of Empire by drawing on the description of the Roman Empire offered by the historian Polybius (second century BCE). This structure is composed of three parts. At the summit are 'monarchical' bodies – for example, the United States (whose power is, in spite of everything, acknowledged by the authors), alliances like the G-8, and international organizations such as the IMF, NATO and the World Bank. Next come 'aristocratic' bodies such as transnational firms and nation-states of average and weak power. The potential impact of the action of the latter on the system as a whole is less than that of the higher-level organs. 'Democratic' bodies like the General Assembly of the UN or NGOs, supposed to represent the people, round off this structure.

Hardt and Negri stress the importance assumed by international law within Empire. Military interventions by the 'international community' – with the US at its head – since the fall of the Berlin Wall (Iraq, Kosovo, Somalia, Libya . . .) have been carried out in the name of nascent international law, rather than by invoking great power interests. Even when they were not, the determination of the interested parties – for example, the Bush administration in the case of Iraq in 2003 – to convince the UN Security Council of their legitimacy demonstrates the constraining power over state action now represented by the international juridical apparatus. This is one of the arguments advanced by the authors to reject the equation of Empire with classic forms of imperialism, which were without international legality. As well as being bound up with an alteration in the global legal order, the emergence of Empire possesses an economic substratum. It is tributary to the profound changes undergone by capitalism since the 1970s. This economic dimension of Empire leads Hardt and Negri to formulate the hypothesis of the emergence of a 'cognitive capitalism'.

Empire confronts the Multitude. For Hardt and Negri, the latter is the new subject of emancipation, which has replaced the working class in this role. One of the major recurrent debates in recent social movements – especially the anti-globalization movement – is the issue of whether the working class remains an operative subject – and concept – or whether it must be replaced by different subjects, among them the Multitude. The European Social Forum at Saint-Denis in 2003, for example, witnessed a clash over this question in a debate between Callinicos and Negri – then just freed from his Italian prison – that was attended by hundreds of young people. The concept of multitude is very old. Although difficult to identify precisely, its first use in modern political philosophy probably dates back to Machiavelli. It was then employed by Spinoza and Hobbes. Among contemporary critical theorists, in addition to the authors of *Empire*, Virno and García Linera make use of the concept.[22]

---

22   The best introduction to the political and conceptual issues raised by the concept is

As the term indicates, the concept of multitude refers to a multiplicity of individuals. This multiplicity possesses no unity. The individuals who make it up do not necessarily have anything in common, such as, for example, being workers, women, blacks or homosexuals. In this sense, the idea of irreducible multiplicity is the bedrock of the multitude. At the same time, such lack of unity does not prevent the multitude from persevering in being; in other words, it does not lead to its dissolution. The multitude is the mode of existence of multi-plicity, which, in order to exist, does not need to be unified or reduced to a common denominator of those belonging to it. This characteristic distinguishes the multitude from two modern concepts and political subjects – namely, the 'people' (and the nation) and 'social classes'. The multitude is contrasted with the people in that the latter refers to the population always-already governed or 'informed' by the state. Contrary to the multitude, the people possesses a prin-ciple of unity, which is the (supposed) 'social contract' made between the state and citizens, whatever form it takes in modern theories of the state (Hobbes, Rousseau). The advocates of the multitude are hostile to use of the concept of 'people', frequent in the history of the labour movement. In their view the multi-tude is situated beneath or 'before' the people; it is what refuses to let itself be captured by the state.

It is for the same reason that the multitude is counterposed to 'social classes', especially the 'working class'. Social classes possess a unifying principle, even if tendential or relative, of an economic kind. Members of any social class are often diverse as regards their sex or ethnicity. Nevertheless, one factor unites them – namely, the position of the individuals concerned in the socio-economic structure: workers, managers, bourgeois and so on. This is what 'objectively' legitimates the unification of the class by the party. By contrast, the multiplicity inherent in the multitude is left as it is, without any attempt at unification, for it is deemed irreducible and regarded as virtuous.

The concept of Multitude developed by Hardt and Negri is both sociologi-cal and political. Its success derives from the fact that it captures certain decisive elements of the current state of the dominated classes, which (accord-ing to these authors) the concept of social class can no longer grasp. Over the last thirty years, the wage-earning class has fragmented. Whereas identities and statuses within it were relatively clearly established after the war, the crisis of the early 1970s, and the neo-liberal turn at the end of the decade, led to their multiplication, making the condition of wage-earners ever more heterogene-ous. The crisis of the labour movement derives in part from the difficulty of mobilizing on the basis of old repertoires of action connected to old social

Paolo Virno, *A Grammar of the Multitude: For an Analysis of Contemporary Forms of Life*, trans. Isabella Bertoletti, James Cascaito and Andrea Casson, Los Angeles: Semiotext(e), 2004.

statuses, rendering the crisis at once objective and 'representational'. With the fragmentation of the wage-earning class and mass unemployment has also come general job insecurity. The permanent contract, although still legally central in a number of countries, has lost its normative power.

Added to the now plural character of the wage-earning condition is another form of multiplicity, a more political one. The second half of the twentieth century was characterized by the proliferation of what used to be called 'secondary fronts' – that is, struggles other than the 'main front' constituted by the opposition between capital and labour, like feminism, ecology, anti-colonialism, or the homosexual movement. As the century progressed, 'minority politics' tended to be increasingly promoted. The hegemonic, centralizing practices of organizations issued from the labour movement, and the catastrophes they produced in the East as in the West, had much to do this trend. But the dynamic of fragmentation and proliferation of political identities also represents a basic tendency of modernity. The concept of 'Multitude' seems capable of grasping the current multiplicity of forms of identity, oppression and resistance. From Argentinian *piqueteros*, to Mexican Zapatistas, French *sans-papiers*, social centre activists in Italy, and queers, the concept captures aspects of this infinite multiplicity, while seeking not to dissolve its potentially transformative impact on the system.

What are the relations between Empire and the Multitude? For Negri, struggles always hold the initiative. This means that they put the system in crisis: in other words, the profit rate and forms of power decline as the intensity of struggles increases. This is what is sometimes called a 'voluntarist' theory of crisis, which maintains that the crisis derives not from the objective contradictions of capitalism, but from the degree of combativeness of those contesting it. Hardt and Negri adopt this schema in their formulation of the relations between Empire and the Multitude. In their view, in order to exist, Empire needs to harness the potential of the Multitude. Empire is a 'parasitic' structure, which feeds off the Multitude's capacity for creation and cooperation: 'The power of the proletariat imposes limits on capital and not only determines the crisis but also dictates the terms and nature of the transformation. *The proletariat actually invents the social and productive forms that capital will be forced to adopt in the future.*'[23] The relationship between Empire and Multitude is ambiguous. On the one hand, Empire needs to absorb the elements of innovation stemming from the Multitude.[24] On the other, Empire's actions towards the Multitude tend to inhibit its creativity, in favour of fixed or already existing forms. This way of

---

23   Hardt and Negri, *Empire*, p. 268.

24   On this point, Hardt and Negri are close to the position of Luc Boltanski and Eve Chiapello in *The New Spirit of Capitalism*, London and New York: Verso, 2007 trans. Gregory Elliott, to which we shall return.

conceiving the relationship between Empire and Multitude predates Hardt and Negri. In Hobbes, the constitution of Leviathan has as its precondition – even its *raison d'être* – the multitude, in the sense that its objective is to discipline the latter and reduce the risks of civil war inherent in it.

What is the Multitude's attitude towards Empire? One of the criticisms frequently made of Hardt and Negri is the absence of any strategic reflection in their work. This criticism is justified, but it can be addressed to the overwhelming majority of contemporary critical theorists (strategic reflection requires particular conjunctural conditions). In fact, we do find the initial outlines of strategic reflection in Hardt and Negri. Thus, one of the points stressed by the authors is the *nomadic* character of the Multitude. The theory of 'nomadism' is highly fashionable at present. It derives from Deleuze and Guattari, in particular from a famous chapter of *Mille Plateaux* (1980) entitled 'Treatise of Nomadology'. The state is a territorial entity. It makes sense only if it controls a territory and filters the population flows of those circulating in it. In this regard it is an instance of resistance to movement. By contrast, the Multitude is situated on the side of movement – that is, as Deleuze and Guattari, and then Hardt and Negri, put it, on the side of 'deterritorialization'. In the authors of *Mille Plateaux*, this concept is fundamentally bound up with desire. Desire is always on the side of deterritorialization, vitality and flows, whereas power and the state constantly seek to re-territorialize it so as to subjugate it. The interesting thing is that, in contrast to national sovereignty, the new form of sovereignty represented by Empire is likewise on the side of deterritorialization. Empire is deterritorialized in as much as the contemporary forms of capital underpinning it are mobile.

Towards a Cognitive Capitalism?

The economic context in which Empire emerges is not irrelevant. After all, even if *operaismo* is an original variant of it, Negri is a representative of Marxism and, by that very token, obliged to allocate a role to the economy. The economic hypothesis accompanying the theory of Empire and the Multitude is 'cognitive capitalism'. The French philosopher and economist Yann Moulier-Boutang has offered the most rigorous characterization of it.[25] The hypothesis of cognitive capitalism starts out from the idea that a 'third age' of capitalism has recently emerged, succeeding mercantile capitalism (seventeenth and eighteenth centuries) and industrial capitalism (nineteenth and twentieth centuries) – namely, cognitive capitalism. This is principally defined by the fact that 'immaterial' or

---

25 See Yann Moulier-Boutang, *Cognitive Capitalism*, trans. Ed Emery, Cambridge: Polity, 2012.

'cognitive' labour is predominant in it. At present, commodities contain more knowledge and know-how than previously; and this tendency is growing with the passage of time. It applies to all sectors of the economy, not only the technology sector. Thus, the increasingly immaterial character of capitalism is observed in one of the oldest human activities: agriculture. The cognitive composition of agricultural products today involves chemical fertilizers whose development has often required long periods of laboratory research, agronomical know-how on the ground, but also certification and marketing techniques of great sophistication. The importance of knowledge-value is in this sense increasing and that of labour-value as traditionally conceived – measured by labour time – is tending to decline. This thesis is obviously to be related to the *general intellect*.

The rise of knowledge-value provokes a crisis in the traditional Marxist 'critique of political economy'. One of the basic axioms of political economy and its critique is the scarcity of material resources. It is because they are scarce that they are the object of a struggle for their appropriation between individuals or social classes. The communist society heralded by Marx and others has material abundance as its main characteristic. In order to attain it, however, it is necessary to transcend the scarcity inherent in capitalism. The transition from labour-value to knowledge-value complicates the situation. Knowledge is what economists call a 'non-rival' good. In other words, the fact that one person possesses it does not prevent another from also possessing it; and its value does not diminish as a result. Thus, unlike a piece of meat or a dwelling, the formula $E = MC^2$ can be possessed by an infinite number of people without losing its value. Even more than that, it is likely that this type of good has more value the greater the number of people who possess it. In fact, the cooperation of the greatest number is what makes it possible for knowledge – in this instance, scientific knowledge – to develop. The relationship between the number of owners and the value of the entity considered is inversely proportional in the case of material objects, and proportional in the case of cognitive objects. If one starts from the hypothesis that knowledge-value is in the process of replacing labour-value, the change entailed in the operation of capitalism and the structure of ownership is considerable. The break with scarcity would pitch us into 'post-capitalism'. Empire and its economic bedrock – cognitive capitalism – therefore contain the seeds of the new society that Hardt and Negri persist in characterizing as 'communist'.

The development of capitalism also brings about changes in the nature of social classes. Once knowledge-value replaces labour-value, a new social class based on the new form of value, and the exploitation of whose activity grounds the new capitalist regime, should appear, just as the exploitation of the industrial working class formerly enabled industrial capitalism to function. Negri and Moulier-Boutang call this new class of the 'exploited' the 'cognitariat', a neologism constructed from a contraction of 'cognitive' and 'proletariat'. The cognitariat is composed of all those who possess nothing but their brain and their training, and who contribute to immaterial production. The cognitariat is an extension of the 'social worker', which (as we have seen) replaced the 'mass worker' in the late 1970s. Contract workers in the entertainment industry, who enjoy legal protection depending on the country they are in, are an example of this. They produce the immaterial good *par excellence* – namely, culture. They are indispensable components in theatrical, televisual, musical or cinematic production. At the same time, for the most part they are casualized, as was demonstrated by the debates in France over the alteration of their status in 2003. This also applies to the computer scientists trained in industrial quantities in India and other Asian countries, or the workforce in 'call centres' in the countries of the Maghreb, who are often highly qualified young people. A high level of cultural capital and casualization are what characterizes members of the cognitariat.

In the regime of cognitive capitalism the distinction between labour and non-labour tends to fade.[26] The production of material goods assumes the performance of a series of tasks that are more or less complex but defined. These tasks are performed in the workplace, which presupposes that labour-time is discrete and measurable, and that its boundary vis-à-vis 'outside-work' is clearly marked. In the production of goods with a high cognitive content, the measurement of labour enters into crisis. A contract worker in the theatre will certainly participate in rehearsals, beginning and ending at particular times. But an essential part of her work will consist, for example, in learning the text of the play she is in – work that will most likely be done at home, and which cannot be precisely measured. Another example is how to calculate the hours of a doctoral student in biology, whose education (by reading articles or attending conferences) occurs at any time of the day and night, and who contributes by his labour to scientific and economic innovation. Cognitive capitalism thus tends to blur the distinction between work and non-work, with work extending over the whole day – which signifies that 'work' is now synonymous with 'life'. That is why many supporters of the hypothesis of cognitive capitalism are firm defenders of a 'guaranteed income' or 'basic income'.[27] In their view such unconditional income, uncoupled from work, is the only thing that can provide a solution to the growing absence of any separation between work and non-work – that is, to the problem of measuring labour and its remuneration. Since labour cannot be measured, it is appropriate to uncouple a wage from possession of a job and allocate a 'basic income' to everyone.

---

26   Ibid., p. 119.
27   On this see Jean-Marc Ferry, *L'Allocation universelle. Pour un revenu de citoyenneté*, Paris: Cerf, 1995, and Philippe van Parijs, *Real Freedom for All: What (if Anything) Can Justify Capitalism?*, Oxford: Clarendon, 1997.

THE REVIVAL OF THEORIES OF IMPERIALISM

The issue of imperialism is central to the new critical theories. Obviously, this is attributable to the geopolitical conjuncture. The issue of the new global balance of power in general, and imperialism in particular, has become decisive today, including among thinkers on the Right.[28] The problematic of imperialism has a long history, from Hobson (on whom drew Lenin in his brochure on imperialism as the 'highest stage' of capitalism), via Luxemburg, Bukharin and Guevara, to Fanon. The issue has been reconfigured in recent decades but has never disappeared from the concerns of critical thinkers. One change is a decline in the influence of economic theories of imperialism – theories explaining imperialism by factors inherent in the logic of capitalism – in favour of analyses stressing different explanatory factors – for example, the political or cultural dimension of the phenomenon. Postcolonial studies, for example, are an expression of this development.

Marxism and Imperialism

A first group of authors whom we should mention comprises theorists of imperialism who have criticized the conceptions of Hardt and Negri. Among them we find Atilio Boron, Bensaïd, Callinicos, Malcolm Bull, Gopal Balakrishnan and Ellen Meiksins Wood. In most cases these authors pertain to the category of what, in the typology of contemporary intellectuals presented in chapter 3, we have called 'resisters'. They are defined by their proximity to the Marxism of the 1960s and 70s (even if the Marxism of these years was itself diverse). Given Hardt and Negri's distance from the Marxist conception of imperialism, it is understandable that these thinkers are prominent critics of them. What are their criticisms of Hardt and Negri? Here we shall confine ourselves to the objections addressed to the theory of Empire and shall turn to those formulated in connection with the concept of Multitude later.

First of all, in the opinion of its critics, the theory of Empire underestimates the inter-imperialist contradictions that exist at present. This theory maintains that Empire is a supra-national entity which has transcended the division of the world into nation-states. This is the full meaning of the term 'smooth space' that recurs in the writing of Hardt and Negri. Yet clashes between great powers have manifestly not disappeared. The war in Iraq in 2003, in particular, demonstrated that the national interests of the United States and the European countries do

---

28   See, for example, Niall Ferguson, *Colossus: The Rise and Fall of the American Empire*, London: Penguin, 2005.

not necessarily coincide. The emergence of China as an economic power, and the conflictual relations it already has with the United States, will in all likelihood have geopolitical consequences in the future. Taiwan could be a reason for crystallization of this conflict. Low-intensity wars in Africa or Asia, which are in large part the expression of imperial rivalries on those continents, likewise demonstrate the decidedly non-'smooth' character of the global space. The antagonisms that can be observed in the early twenty-first century thus in many respects resemble those that structured the nineteenth and twentieth centuries.

This leads to a second criticism of the theory of Empire. There is little doubt that the globalization of the economy has had an impact on the international order. The emergence of non- or supranational entities such as transnational firms or NGOs means that states must now reckon with the presence of influential actors alongside them. In the second half of the nineteenth century and in the twentieth century, this was not the case (or was the case to a lesser extent); and the power of states in international affairs was unquestionably greater. At the same time, to argue (as do Hardt and Negri) that the state form is currently undergoing an inexorable decline, that states today are mere 'instruments' of transnational corporations, that they have lost any efficacy of their own, seems excessive, to say the least.

Globalization proceeds from an expansionary tendency intrinsic to capitalism but is also a policy deliberately implemented by the most powerful states. Increased world trade in part responds to the fall in internal demand in the main global economic powers from the 1970s onwards. Moreover, what is commonly called the 'deregulation' or 'opening up' of sectors of the economy that is constitutive of the process of globalization has dictated an expansion, not a reduction, in the quantity of legislation. But who legislates if not states, including when it comes to international legislation? In addition, whatever their degree of internationalization, transnational corporations remain closely connected to their country of origin, which in most cases is western. The leadership of these firms invariably derives from the elites of the country concerned, as indicated by sociological analyses of social classes in globalization.[29] One of the key elements in the classical Marxist theory of imperialism was the argument that in the capitalist regime, economic and state logics are profoundly integrated. This means that state power is more or less directly 'in the service' of its capitalists and, conversely, that the latter serve the geopolitical designs of their state. Imperialism results from the interpenetration of these two logics. Given the conflicts in the world, critics of Hardt and Negri maintain, there is little reason to call this model into question.

---

29   See Anne-Catherine Wagner, *Les Classes sociales dans la mondialisation*, Paris: La Découverte, 2007.

Leo Panitch: Chronicle of the US Super-power

Nothing would be more mistaken than to present contemporary Marxist approaches to imperialism as mere repetition of the classical theories of Lenin, Bukharin and Luxemburg. Debates are rife between representatives of this tradition over the nature of the 'new imperialism', to adopt the title of a work by David Harvey. A significant part of the debate has crystallized around Leo Panitch's iconoclastic theses. Professor of political science at York University in Canada, Panitch edits an important publication in the contemporary Marxist constellation, *Socialist Register*, founded in the 1960s by Ralph Miliband, father of the current leader of the British Labour Party, and the labour historian John Saville. In a series of texts co-written with Sam Gindin, Panitch proposes rethinking the classical Marxist theory of imperialism in the light of recent developments.[30]

His first criticism of this theory is that it overestimates the influence of economic factors in explaining imperialism and underestimates its political dimension. According to Panitch, contrary to Lenin and Bukharin, imperialism is not the direct product of the internal contradictions of capital accumulation. It derives from the will to power of states as such, not exclusively from the material interests of their capitalist classes. In this, Panitch's position approximates to that of 'neo-Weberian' theorists of the state like Michael Mann and Anthony Giddens.[31] From this standpoint, the theory of imperialism must be conceived as an extension of the theory of the state, not as an extension of the theory of economic crises, as in classical Marxism. The problem, adds Panitch, is that the theory of the state – and, more generally, of politics – has always been a weak point in Marxism. The fact that it is located among the 'superstructures' has in effect led Marxists to neglect it in favour of 'infrastructural' – economic – problematics. According to Panitch, the weakness of the Marxist theory of imperialism results from this shortcoming.

The hypothesis of the state's 'relative autonomy' from the economy is central to Panitch's analysis of imperialism. The state is 'not . . . autonomous from capitalist classes or the economy, but rather [has] capacities to act on behalf of the system as a whole, while their dependence on the success of overall accumulation for their own legitimacy and reproduction nevertheless leaves these capacities bounded'.[32] Panitch continues to identify with Marxism. As a result,

30   See, in particular, Leo Panitch and Sam Gindin, 'Global Capitalism and American Empire', *Socialist Register*, vol. 40, London: Merlin, 2004.

31   See, for example, Michael Mann, *The Sources of Social Power: The Rise of Classes and Nation-States, 1760–1914*, Cambridge: Cambridge University Press, 1993.

32   Leo Panitch and Sam Gindin, 'Superintending Global Capital', *New Left Review*, II/35, September–October 2005, p. 102.

he is led to base political processes on economic processes. But at the same time, he aims to complicate the link, hitherto simplistically conceived in his view, between these two instances and thus to affirm the 'relative autonomy' of the political from the economic. This expression signifies that states project themselves militarily on the world stage for political and economic reasons, or a mixture of the two, but that economic reasons never lead mechanically in and of themselves to imperialism. Even when economic reasons are involved, they are 'mediated' by political decisions.

Drawing on Polanyi, Panitch argues that capitalism is characterized by the progressive separation of economics and politics. Prior to the emergence of this system, these domains were 'embedded' in one another, to such a degree that any event pertaining to the one had an impact on the other; or, more precisely, any phenomenon always conjointly pertained to both. The separation of these spheres implies that what occurs in the one does not necessarily have repercussions in the other. In other words, these spheres tend to become autonomous, and this applies at national and international levels alike. As a result, there is no reason for the economic competition engaged in by national bourgeoisies, transnational firms or other economic actors to be translated systematically into inter-imperialist (political) conflicts. The 'standard' Marxist model, by contrast, maintains that politics is never 'disembedded' from the economy and that the processes which occur within the latter always have (geo)political repercussions.

Furthermore, Panitch claims that globalization has gradually dissolved the coherence of national bourgeoisies. The latter were the locus where, from the eighteenth century onwards, the interests of capital and national interests met and mixed. Hence the idea of the 'national' bourgeoisie. Now that these bourgeoisies have lost their coherence, and (as Panitch thinks) a 'transnational' dominant class has emerged, there is less reason for inter-imperialist rivalries to exist. In fact, it was the structural divergence in the interests of national bourgeoisies that caused such rivalries. This argument of Panitch's in some respects resembles the position of Hardt and Negri. They defend the idea that globalization abolishes the state form and the whole of the apparatus – including national bourgeoisies – which accompanies it. In this sense they concur with the thesis that the dominant classes have a transnational character today.[33] However, Panitch's position differs from that of the authors of *Empire* on two points. On the one hand, Panitch disagrees with the idea that states are in the process of being liquidated on account of globalization. For him the latter is, among other things, the product of state policy. On the other hand, Panitch argues that the

---

33 Following Boltanski and Chiapello, this is the meaning of the concept of 'connexionist elite' developed by the latter.

American empire is more powerful now than ever. In particular, the international institutions that Hardt and Negri claim limit US imperial power are for Panitch active supports of that power, in the sense that it dominates the world through their agency.

It is doubtless for his position on US imperialism that Panitch is best known today. Within the new critical thinking, the dominant thesis on this issue maintains that the United States is currently subject to an inexorable decline, notably because of the disastrous situation of its economy and the emergence of new great powers, among them China. Among the supporters of this thesis, we find in particular Giovanni Arrighi. Thus, Arrighi claims that recent decades have led to 'a relative and absolute loss of the US's capacity to retain its centrality within the global political economy'.[34]

Panitch opposes the hypothesis of the end of American hegemony. His arguments are predominantly quantitative. US economic growth in the years 1984–2004 was 3.4 per cent – that is, higher than all periods of growth preceding the 'golden age' of 1953–74 (when it was 3.8 per cent), but also higher than the other counties of the G-7 in the same period.[35] In the same era, the productivity of the US economy grew by 3.5 per cent; expenditure on research and development was higher than that of Japan, Germany, Great Britain, Italy and Canada combined; the volume of exports was situated at a level markedly higher than that of its main competitors. Statistically, the decline announced by a number of analysts is therefore not observable. More generally, Panitch argues that the crisis of profitability that began in the early 1970s at the time of the oil shock, and the onset of the crisis of the Keynesian/Fordist model, has been resolved under the auspices of the United States thanks to the neo-liberal model. By contrast, authors like Arrighi and Brenner think that the crisis has not been resolved and that American deficits are symptomatic of the US's inability to establish a new mode of regulation of capitalism. For them, neo-liberalism is a factor of economic and financial instability; it has never succeeded in ensuring the conditions for a dynamic accumulation.

Panitch also maintains that the relations between the United States and competing powers like Japan, the European Union and China cannot be compared with those that existed in the early twentieth century between the US and Britain, the previous dominant power. One of Arrighi's arguments is that the handover we are currently witnessing from the US to China is of the same order as that which previously occurred between Britain and the US. In particular, the possession by the new power of colossal quantities of the old

---

34   Giovanni Arrighi, 'Hegemony Unravelling-I', *New Left Review*, I/32, March–April 2005, p. 74.

35   See Panitch and Gindin, 'Superintending Global Capital', pp. 113–14.

one's debt is the sign of a hegemonic transition. In the past century, such a transition was made at the cost of a cycle of unprecedented violence – in particular, two world wars – and it cannot be excluded that it will occur in tragic conditions this time as well.

According to Panitch, the economies of the leading powers are interpenetrated to such a degree that no risk of conflict exists for the foreseeable future. It is a mistake to represent their relations in the manner of old inter-imperialist rivalries. More precisely, the American economy has so profoundly penetrated that of its potential rivals – through direct foreign investment – that any challenge on their part is difficult to conceive. Moreover, the massive US trade deficit with countries like Japan or China is not a sign of weakness. On the contrary, it is a sign of strength. This deficit has existed for a quarter of a century, which indicates that it is different in kind from the deficit that might affect 'normal' countries. Added to this is the fact that holding debt is one thing, and transforming such financial power into political and military power quite another; and China is far from having done so to this day. According to Panitch, the United States consequently still has no serious opponent globally and will not have one in the immediate future.

Robert Cox: The Neo-Gramscian Theory of International Relations

The question of imperialism is formulated in different terms by Robert Cox. Cox has played various leadership roles in the International Labor Organization (ILO), based in Geneva. He has also developed one of the most innovative theories of international relations in the second half of the twentieth century, known as the 'neo-Gramscian' theory of international relations. It employs notions developed by Gramsci – hegemony, transformism, historical bloc, passive revolution – to analyze the global geopolitical order. Cox's theory is one of the best known in its discipline and, like realism, liberalism, neo-institutionalism and constructivism, is the subject of a chapter in many of the academic textbooks in the field.

In the wake of Cox, the neo-Gramscian theory of international relations has undergone important developments over the last twenty years.[36] Stephen Gill, of British origin but employed in Canada, is one of the preeminent representatives of this current in North America. In particular, he is the author of *Power and Resistance in the New World Order*, in which he examines the resistance to neo-liberal globalization, drawing on not only Gramsci but also

---

36   See Andrea Bieler and Adam Morton, 'A Critical Theory Route to Hegemony, World Order and Historical Change: Neo-Gramscian Perspectives in International Relations', *Capital and Class*, no. 82, 2004.

Foucault's conception of power – something that demonstrates the fertility of a cross between two conceptions of power.[37] The neo-Gramscian approach to international relations has also undergone interesting developments in the Netherlands, in particular in the work of Kees van der Pijl and Henk Overbeek.[38] The Dutch neo-Gramscians – the Amsterdam School, as it is called – have notably examined the emergence of the European Union in its relationship with the formation of transnational elites, the structure of continental finance and industrial capital, and neo-liberal ideology.

What is Gramsci's relationship to international relations? According to Cox, the author of the *Prison Notebooks* makes it possible to think afresh geopolitics in general and imperialism in particular.[39] Cox's approach is opposed to the doctrine that dominated international relations in the twentieth century – namely, realism. The latter is based on two main axioms. Firstly, the basic unit of international relations is the state. To analyze geopolitics and the events which occur in it – wars, treaties, international institutions, trade, diplomacy – we must start out from the principle that the world is composed of states with interests, whose main activity consists in trying to realize them. Significantly, states are regarded by realists as 'black boxes'. They do not examine what occurs within states, be it the nature of their regimes (democracy or dictatorship), the relations between social classes, or other characteristics. For realists every state ultimately behaves in the same way: it seeks to increase its power in order to achieve its ends. The second axiom advanced by the realists is that the international system is 'anarchic'. There is no planetary authority superior to states that could moderate potential conflicts between them. In particular, realists believe that international organizations have no causal power of their own. They are nothing other than the scene of clashes between great powers.[40]

Cox formulates several criticisms of realism. The first concerns the 'ahistorical' character of the doctrine. Realism is an abstract theory, supposedly valid for all time and any place. That is why it licenses a significant degree of formalization, illustrated by its representatives' interest in logic and game theory. For Cox, by contrast, international relations constitute a dynamic system, which amounts to saying that they have a history. Cox places his analyses under the banner of 'historicism'.[41] He adopts the term 'historical

37   See Stephen Gill, *Power and Resistance in the New World Order*, New York: Palgrave Macmillan, 2008.

38   See Kees van der Pijl, *Transnational Classes and International Relations*, London and New York: Routledge, 1998.

39   Robert Cox, 'Gramsci, Hegemony, and International Relations: An Essay in Method', *Millennium: Journal of International Studies*, vol. 12, 1983.

40   The most convincing contemporary formulation of realism is John Mearsheimer's in *The Tragedy of Great Power Politics*, New York: Norton, 2001.

41   Timothy Sinclair, 'Beyond International Relations Theory: Robert Cox and Approaches

materialism', which he nevertheless takes care to distinguish from 'reduction-ist' versions of that doctrine. Cox's historicism consists in the fact that, for him, social formations develop over time. As a result, the international system may be based on different 'basic units' in different epochs, with the nation-state as we have known it for two centuries being only one of the modalities of the system's organization. More generally, while inscribing his work in a line of descent from Braudel and analysis of the *longue durée*, Cox acknowledges the possibility of profound structural changes in global geopolitics. In addi-tion, his historical materialism – like all materialisms – assigns primacy to 'production'. From this standpoint the international system is regarded as influenced by the 'mode of production' that obtains in the given epoch. However, production is conceived by Cox in a broad sense; it is not synony-mous with economic production. Institutions, norms and ideas are just as much component parts of production as industry or finance.

The main concept adopted by Cox from Gramsci is hegemony. In Gramsci it refers to a particular type of domination exercised by one class over the others, or by one section of society over the latter as whole. Registering the differences between the Tsarist Russia confronted by Bolsheviks and west European societies, Gramsci argues – anticipating Foucault's analyses – that power is much more diffuse in the latter; that the state in the strict sense does not concentrate the bulk of it, as in Russia. In western Europe, the bourgeoisie had attained such a degree of 'hegemony' over the other classes that it could even sometimes permit itself not to govern directly, while never surrendering control over the actual conduct of affairs. As Gramsci says, in the West the state is 'an outer ditch, behind which there stood a powerful system of fortresses and earthworks'.

The strategic consequences of this thesis are significant. It entails that taking state power – supposing such a thing to be possible when the boundaries between the latter and civil society are fainter (Gramsci thought it was) – is insufficient to overturn the established order. Activity directed towards 'civil society', 'culture' and 'common sense' is indispensable. Thus, Gramsci asserts 'the necessity for new popular beliefs, that is to say a new common sense and with it a new culture and a new philosophy which will be rooted in the popular consciousness with the same solidity and imperative quality as traditional beliefs'.[42] According to the author of the *Prison Notebooks*, hegemony is inscribed in bodies and minds, through 'intermediate' institutions like the church, the press or schools. The fact that a majority of members of a society

---

to World Order', in Robert Cox and Timothy Sinclair, eds, *Approaches to World Order*, Cambridge: Cambridge University Press, 1996.

42   Antonio Gramsci, *Selections from the Prison Notebooks*, ed. and trans. Quintin Hoare and Geoffrey Nowell Smith, London: Lawrence and Wishart, 1971, p. 424.

regards these institutions as legitimate is what ensures the foundation of a particular hegemony.

How does the concept of hegemony apply to the analysis of international relations? Cox replaces the idea of the hegemony of one class over others by that of a state over the rest of the international community. Thus, 'to become hegemonic, a state would have to found and protect a world order which was universal in conception, i.e., not an order in which one state directly exploits others but an order which most other states (or at least those within reach of the hegemony) could find compatible with their interests'.[43] Hegemony differs from domination. There are situations of domination without hegemony and others where the latter obtains. What distinguishes hegemony from domination is that the countries subject to domination consent to it – that is, domination does not operate solely through the brute force deployed by the dominant country. This consent rests on military protection, economic prosperity, or a combination of the two, which the dominant country is in a position to guarantee for the relevant community of states. As the quotation indicates, states subject to hegemony must believe that it is in their interests. Moreover, hegemony possesses the characteristic that the hegemonic state represents a political and cultural model for the others, whose elites seek to copy the functioning of its institutions. From the Roman Empire to the United States, examples of this phenomenon are not wanting. The cultural dimension of hegemony implies that it does not lie on the surface of states. It penetrates the innermost core of societies under hegemony – their economy, their customs and their beliefs.

A rapid glance at modern history makes it possible to indicate the alternation of hegemonic and non-hegemonic periods. From 1845 to 1875 Great Britain was the unchallenged centre of the world economy. Its domination was hegemonic in that it guaranteed the geopolitical balance, and the dynamism of its economy brought a certain prosperity to the regions (their elites) it dominated. At the time Britain also represented a cultural model whose institutions and customs were diffused internationally. The second period – 1875–1945 – is non-hegemonic. It witnessed the decline of British power, the rise of the United States, the replacement of free trade by protectionism, the break-up of several empires (Ottoman, Hapsburg), the whole crowned by two world wars. None of the powers of the time was in a position to impose its domination on the others, still less to elicit their consent.

The third period extends from 1945 to 1975. The United States then took charge of a new hegemony, which included unprecedented economic growth and the wide-scale spread of a cultural model of production and consumption. A characteristic of this new hegemony is that the domination of the United

---

43   Cox, 'Gramsci, Hegemony and International Relations', p. 136.

States was secured through the agency of international organizations like the
UN, the World Bank and the IMF. These represent the international equivalent
of 'intermediate' institutions like the church and schools. They make it possible
to 'sweeten' domination by rendering it legitimate in the eyes of those subject to
it – that is, precisely by transforming domination into hegemony. The fourth
period began in 1975. This date heralds the decline of American hegemony as a
result of the exhaustion of post-war growth, but also defeat in Vietnam and the
emergence of a Third World making its voice heard even within international
organizations. Cox coincides with authors like Arrighi in arguing that US
hegemony entered into crisis in the mid-1970s.

As a general rule, countries that succeed in imposing their hegemony on
the international community are those which have experienced a profound
internal political and technological revolution. According to Cox, an international hegemony is the translation onto the world stage of the hegemony
acquired by the dominant class of a state. The institutions established by this
class are then diffused throughout the globe. Consequently, Cox assigns what
occurs within states primacy in the constitution of the international – a position
which is also that of Gramsci in the several passages in the *Prison Notebooks*
where he refers to geopolitics. This model is distinguished from other analyses,
like Wallerstein's theory of world-systems, which locate the origin of change at
the international level and regard what occurs within states as derivative. Cox
employs another Gramscian concept to conceive the effects of the diffusion of
the hegemonic model in dominated countries – namely, 'passive revolution'. A
passive revolution is one whose origin is external to the country concerned. In
other words, it is not the fruit of social upheavals in that country. For example,
in nineteenth-century Italy the bourgeois class of the north of the country was
too weak to preside over the country's unity. That unity was 'imported' and
imposed from without by Napoleonic arms. 'Passive revolution' is indeed a
'revolution', since it leads to a change in the political structure of the country
considered. However, it is 'passive' in as much as it is not endogenous.

David Harvey: Spatial Fix and Accumulation by Dispossession

The most elegant theory of imperialism currently available is doubtless Harvey's,
developed, in particular, in his book *The New Imperialism*, which appeared in
2003. Harvey is a geographer by training, who in the 1960s wrote a thesis on
hop production in nineteenth-century England. After work on the epistemology of geography, he moved towards Marxism, of which he has developed a
geographical variant called 'historical-geographical materialism'. Traditionally,
Marxists have taken little account of the spatial dimension of capitalism.
Harvey's originality consists in having explored its contours. One of the

influences acknowledged by the author of *Spaces of Capital* and *Social Justice and the City* is the French philosopher Henri Lefebvre, one of the most innovative heterodox Marxists of the second half of the twentieth century (he died in 1991). In particular, Lefebvre was the author of *La Production de l'espace*, as well as reflections on the 'right to the city', which provide inspiration for Harvey's analyses.[44] Harvey is not the only one to relate social processes and spatial processes from a critical standpoint. We find in several journals, one of the best known of which is *Antipode: A Radical Journal of Geography*, much work along these lines. Moreover, we may note a revival of interest in spatial themes in contemporary critical thought, with authors like Edward Soja, Neil Smith, Doreen Massey and Saskia Sassen.

Harvey has undertaken a magisterial reconstruction of Karl Marx's theory of space.[45] Like all nineteenth-century thinkers, Marx was a thinker of time; and an important part of his work consisted in seeking to understand historical evolution. However, we also find in Marx a consideration of space, which Harvey has sought to bring out and develop. Marx's conception of space is closely connected with the problematic of imperialism. This is what Marx has to say in a passage from the *Grundrisse*:

> While capital must on one side strive to tear down every spatial barrier to intercourse, i.e. to exchange, and conquer the whole earth for its market, it strives on the other side to annihilate this space with time, i.e. to reduce to a minimum the time spent in motion from one place to another. The more developed the capital, therefore, the more extensive the market over which it circulates, which forms the spatial orbit of its circulation, the more does it strive simultaneously for an even greater extension of the market and for greater annihilation of space by time.[46]

There are two ideas in this splendid passage. Firstly, Marx maintains that capitalism is global from its inception. Its tendency to conquer the whole planet and transform it into a market is inherent in it. It is neither contingent nor recent, contrary to what conventional talk about 'globalization' would have us believe. As Marx puts it in a passage of *Capital*, 'the world market is contained in the very notion of capital'. Capitalism's global expansion nevertheless comes at a price. The greater the distance between the site of production and the site

44   For an introduction to Lefebvre's oeuvre, see Stathis Kouvelakis, 'Henri Lefebvre, Thinker of Urban Modernity', in Jacques Bidet and Stathis Kouvelakis, eds, *A Critical Companion to Contemporary Marxism*, Leiden and Boston: Brill, 2008.

45   David Harvey, 'The Geography of Capitalist Accumulation: A Reconstruction of Marx's Theory', in *Spaces of Capital: Towards a Critical Geography*, Edinburgh: Edinburgh University Press, 2001.

46   Karl Marx, *Grundrisse*, trans. Martin Nicolaus, Harmondsworth: Penguin/NLR, 1973, p. 539.

of sale ('realization') of the commodity, the more its cost increases, because transport is not free. This implies that capitalism must constantly accelerate the 'speed of turnover' of commodities in order to minimize the cost of their transportation and maximize the profit derived from them by the capitalist. The profit reaped by the latter results from increasing this velocity. This is the phenomenon referred to by Marx with the mysterious phrase 'annihilation of space by time'. In the capitalist regime, abolishing space by accelerating the circulation of commodities – time – is a vital necessity. It leads to a 'compression' of space whose effects make themselves felt in the very representation individuals have of it.

Capitalism's tendency to penetrate and exploit new spaces has its origin in the crises it periodically undergoes. For want of any coordination between producers, the system generates more capital – including, but not exclusively, in the form of commodities – than it can absorb, which leads to their periodic devaluation. This is what Marxists call 'crises of over-accumulation', which are generally accompanied by financial bubbles that temporarily generate the illusion that they are a substitute for real profitability. However, capitalism possesses the means to resolve (temporarily) these crises. In and through the destruction of capital it induces, the crisis is a way of causing the profit rate to increase again. Harvey has drawn attention to a different way of resolving crises of over-accumulation, which he refers to with the concept of 'spatial fix'. This concept has two senses – one literal, the other metaphorical.[47] The literal sense refers to the idea that capital is a spatial or 'territorialized' entity, which invests – fixes – and transforms its environment by taking concrete form in machines, forms of transport and modes of communication. To adopt a term of which Lefebvre was fond, capital 'produces' space; it is not an abstract entity that makes do with pre-existing space. The metaphorical meaning of the concept 'spatial fix' refers to the idea of a 'solution' to the problem of the over-accumulation of capital. Harvey thus suggests that one of the ways that capital resolves crises is through space – more precisely, the implantation of capital in spaces hitherto void of capitalist relations.

One of the influences acknowledged by Harvey is Luxemburg. In 1913 she published a work entitled *The Accumulation of Capital: A Contribution to An Economic Explanation of Imperialism*, where she developed an original theory of imperialism.[48] According to Luxemburg, imperialism is explained by the under-consumption created by the exploitation of workers in the countries at

---

47   See David Harvey, *The New Imperialism*, Oxford: Oxford University Press, 2003, p. 115. See also 'The Spatial Fix: Hegel, von Thünen, and Marx', in *Spaces of Capital*.

48   The other major influence on Harvey's conception of imperialism is Hannah Arendt, *The Origins of Totalitarianism*, Cleveland and New York: Meridian, 1962, Part Two, 'Imperialism'.

the centre of the world economy. This exploitation creates insufficient demand, incapable of absorbing production, which leads the countries concerned to shift the surplus commodities to other regions of the world. Imperialism is born out of this imperative. If necessary, the terms of trade are imposed by force. For Luxemburg, capitalism always needs a non-capitalist 'exterior' to resolve its crises. So that they are not themselves subject to crises of over-production, and are able to 'amortize' those of others, the regions to which the over-produced commodities are transferred must not be capitalist. Consequently, the global system requires that they be maintained in a non-capitalist state – that is, prevented from developing. In this sense the under-development of whole swathes of the world is functional from the standpoint of capital accumulation on a world scale.

Harvey rejects the idea that under-consumption is the cause of capitalist crises. In his view, as in that of most contemporary Marxist economists, over-accumulation of capital and the crisis of profitability it generates constitute the main explanatory factor in crises. At the same time, Harvey points to an element of truth in the Luxemburgist theory of imperialism. It is correct to argue that capitalism needs an 'exterior' to overcome the crises it experiences. This 'exterior' serves not mainly as a receptacle for commodities produced in surplus quantities, but to absorb unprofitable capital. This new framework of accumulation precisely constitutes a *spatial* fix: it is both a solution (temporary, by definition) to the crisis of over-accumulation and a concrete place subject to a new 'production of space' via machines, forms of transport, factories, telecommunications, dams – in short, everything a dynamic industrial environment comprises.

Today, China is a global spatial fix *par excellence*. Its transition to the market economy in the late 1970s was a magnet for colossal quantities of foreign capital. The rural exodus yielded constant renewal of a labour force available at a cost defying competition, while the internal market also grew, with average income in the towns increasing by ten per cent per annum. The development of China has obvious spatial implications. The multiplication of gigantic cities, but also ecological devastation – including that wreaked by the construction of dams – demonstrates that capitalism is literally a producer of space.

Capital's tendency to over-accumulation implies that, after having absorbed surplus capital, the spatial fix will likewise begin to generate some of its own. Following the Second World War, on account of reconstruction requirements, Germany and Japan were the targets of significant foreign investment. However, from the 1960s onwards they were in a position to compete with the United States and the other economic super-powers on the world market. For several more years or decades China will likewise be a receptacle for global capital. But it is certain that its current growth rate cannot be maintained indefinitely.

Accordingly, capitalism will be led to seek new spaces of profitability. When a spatial fix ceases to be dynamic, capital deserts it. This is what happened to the historic European and US centres of capital accumulation. The post-industrial landscapes of factories abandoned as a result of relocation, and populations racked by mass unemployment awaiting unlikely redevelopment, are instances of this phenomenon. As Harvey puts it, 'If capital does move out, then it leaves behind a trail of devastation and devaluation; the deindustrializations experienced in the heartlands of capitalism (such as Pittsburgh, Sheffield, the Ruhr), as well as in many other parts of the world (such as Bombay), in the 1970s and 1980s are cases in point.'[49]

For Luxemburg, capital always needs an 'exterior' to overcome its crises of over-accumulation. That is why capitalism and imperialism are inextricably linked, the second being a precondition for the survival of the former. The problem, claims Harvey, is that in the era of 'late' capitalism, few regions of the world still escape the logic of capitalism. Consequently, it is difficult to find places devoid of capitalist relations in which to invest surplus capital. However, it is possible to 'fabricate' such places from scratch. This is what is implied by a second concept – which complements that of spatial fix – developed by Harvey: *accumulation by dispossession*. This concept refers to cases where a non-capitalist sector of society is more or less brutally transformed into a capitalist sector. This assumes a 'dispossession' of populations, for the private logic of the market expels the older, generally more 'collective' mode of social organization.

Several types of accumulation by dispossession can be identified. The privatization of public services is one. In this case, a sphere hitherto insulated from competition by the state – education, health, energy – is opened up to capital. The community of citizens is then dispossessed in favour of private operators. Another type of accumulation by dispossession is war. The destruction wrought by armed conflicts – like the war in Iraq, which is referred to in *The New Imperialism* – destroys the capital already invested (infrastructure, economic fabric), and makes it possible to invest new capital. In this sense, crises of over-accumulation are closely connected with war. A third type of accumulation by dispossession is migration, whether external or internal. The expulsion of the peasantry and privatization of its land in countries like Mexico or India, and the formation of urban sub-proletariats in the slums of global megalopolises, is an example of it.[50]

Accumulation by dispossession draws on what Marx in *Capital* called 'original accumulation'. This refers to the (violent) appropriation of a common good

---

49   Harvey, *The New Imperialism*, p. 116.
50   See Mike Davis, *Planet of Slums*, London and New York: Verso, 2007.

by a fraction of the population at the expense of the greatest number. The enclosure of land previously exploitable by all in eighteenth- and nineteenth-century Europe is a classic example of original accumulation. What accumulation by dispossession reveals is that original accumulation must periodically be repeated in order to 're-launch' capitalism – that is, restore the profit rate to an acceptable level. Contrary to what Marx thought, original accumulation is not confined to the origins of capitalism. It occurs regularly in different regions of the world, on account of the system's need to discover outlets for surplus capital. The concept of 'accumulation by dispossession' is interesting in that it makes it possible to expand the traditional notion of imperialism and, in particular, to connect an 'internal' imperialism and an 'external' imperialism. Dispossession affects not only 'peripheral' territories that are still alien to capitalism, but also sectors where capitalist relations already obtain, in which they are nevertheless destroyed – by privatization, war, exodus – so as to be re-launched. Original accumulation therefore follows capital like its shadow.

Accumulation by dispossession is resisted by its victims. Struggles for the defence of public services since the 1980s in France, or the movements of landless peasants in Brazil, indicate that battles are being fought over the ownership and mode of administration of common goods. An argument that associates Harvey with Marx is that not every dispossession is negative; that it can even contain 'progressive' aspects. Thus, 'political movements, if they are to have any macro and long-run impact, must rise above nostalgia for that which has been lost and likewise be prepared to recognize the positive gains to be had from the transfer of assets that can be achieved through limited forms of dispossession'.[51] Marx regarded capitalism as progress when compared with feudalism and maintained that it was a painful but necessary step towards socialism. For Harvey, the position of the author of *Capital* is too unilateral. Capitalism often destroys egalitarian social relations without bringing about the slightest progress. At the same time, Harvey recognizes with Marx that 'limited forms of dispossession' sometimes make it possible to abolish feudal arrangements and improve the life of the population. In such conditions it would be dogmatic to reject them.

THE NATION-STATE: PERSISTENCE OR TRANSCENDENCE?

Hardt and Negri argue that in the era of globalization, nation-states have been structurally undermined by global actors such as transnational firms and international organizations. This leads the authors of *Empire* to allocate limited causal power to nation-states and to argue that their power is set to be further undermined in coming decades.

---

51   Harvey, *The New Imperialism*, p. 178.

The problematic of the nation-state actually contains two problematics, which are closely connected but nevertheless distinct. The first is that of the nation and nationalism. It involves the issue of the extent to which nationalism – understood not in its extremist (right-wing) sense, but as the ideology that accompanies the division of the world into nations – remains a vigorous ideology, as has been the case since the French Revolution. The second problematic is the state. This concerns the form and function of the modern state in its relationship, for example, with capitalism, civil society or geopolitics. These two themes are obviously interlinked because modern nations have mostly assumed the form of states. However, there are exceptions, like diasporas, which are nations without a state. Moreover, in the past, nation and state were not so closely connected, and today state or quasi-state 'supra-national' forms, such as the European Union, are emerging. This section mainly deals with the issue of nations and nationalism, as well as their possible supersession by new political forms. The issue of the state form will, however, be broached in the last part via the theory of the 'permanent state of exception' developed by Agamben.

Benedict Anderson and Tom Nairn: Nation-States Faced with Globalization

The most widely discussed theory of nationalism in the last quarter-century, within critical theory but also more generally, is unquestionably Benedict Anderson's. Brother of Perry Anderson, professor of international relations at Cornell University in New York State, Anderson was originally an Asian specialist. His latest work is about the Philippines and, in particular, the literary oeuvre and political activity of the father of the country's independence, José Rizal.[52] In 1983, Anderson published *Imagined Communities: Reflections on the Origin and Spread of Nationalism*, a book that has since become a classic. In it he developed the idea that nations are 'imagined communities'. Anderson's conception of nationalism, like that of other authors to whom we shall refer, developed in an intellectual context dominated by Marxism, even if it differs from the latter in many respects. Nationalism, like religion, has always represented a problem for Marxism. As is well known, the latter advocates proletarian internationalism. This did not prevent many Marxists of the classical generation – Lenin at their head – from recognizing peoples' right to self-determination. Recognition of this right was either tactical or regarded as a necessary stage en route to internationalism.

52   Benedict Anderson, *Under Three Flags: Anarchism and the Anti-Colonial Imagination*, London and New York: Verso, 2006. See also Razmig Keucheyan, 'Éléments d'astronomie politique. À propos de Benedict Anderson, *Under Three Flags: Anarchism and the Anti-Colonial Imagination*', *Contretemps*, no. 20, 2006.

The problem is that, like religion, nationalism by no means disappeared during the twentieth century. Not only did it grow in strength, but it 'absorbed' socialism by compelling attempts to build socialism to cast themselves in the mould of the nation-state. The starting-point of Anderson's theory of nationalism lies in this observation: 'the "end of the era of nationalism", so long prophesied, is not remotely in sight. Indeed, nation-ness is the most universally legitimate value in the political life of our time.'[53] During the 1970s and 80s, the persistence of nationalism, a veritable anomaly from a Marxist point of view, prompted a revival of attempts to understand the phenomenon by critical thinkers. Tom Nairn, whose analyses we shall refer to shortly, starts from an assessment similar to Anderson's.

Anderson offers a celebrated definition of the nation. For him it is 'an imagined political community – and imagined as both inherently limited and sovereign.'[54] According to Anderson, nations are 'imagined' in that they are not based on anything 'objective', unlike social classes, which possess greater ontological substance (obviously, this thesis associates Anderson with Marxism). In truth, nations acquired such substance over time, but it has been constructed retrospectively on the basis of an ideology (an 'imaginary') imposed by proto-national elites, via such institutions as censuses, museums or cartography. Anderson's stress on the notion of 'imagination' indicates that for him the nation is a matter of 'representations', even if the latter are embodied in a concrete social reality that generates feedback effects on those representations. The members of nations – even the smallest of them – will never have the opportunity to know the majority of their fellow citizens directly. Yet despite this absence of real relations, in the mind of each of them there is what Anderson calls an 'image of their communion' – that is, a representation of each individual as belonging to the same national community. Anderson cites another theoretician of nationalism from the 'historicist' tradition to which he belongs, Ernest Gellner, who maintains that 'Nationalism is not the awakening of nations to self-consciousness: it *invents* nations where they do not exist.'[55]

Aside from its 'imagined' character, three further elements feature in Anderson's definition of the nation: the fact that it is lived as 'limited', as 'sovereign' and as a 'community'. The limited character of the nation derives from the fact that, even if its borders are elastic, they are not infinitely so. Nations are territorial entities whose peripheries can change hands on the occasion of wars and treaties, but which are nevertheless geographically stable. The territorialization of power is one of the elements that distinguishes modern forms of power

53   Benedict Anderson, *Imagined Communities: Reflections on the Origin and Spread of Nationalism*, London and New York: Verso, 1991, p. 3.

54   Ibid., p. 6.

55   Quoted in ibid., p. 6.

from those of the *ancien régime*. The 'limited' character of nations is not exclusively 'objective'. At the level of subjectivity, or the 'imagination' of citizens, it presupposes the existence of an 'outside' that separates national citizens from foreigners. No nation is coextensive with the whole of humanity, not even potentially. This is what distinguishes nations from social classes, particularly the working class, whose vocation from a Marxist standpoint is ultimately to become identified with the 'human race' in its entirety.

'Sovereignty' is what characterizes modern nation-states by comparison with old nations. The aristocracies of the *ancien régime* were highly internationalized – that is, more precisely, Europeanized. Anderson recalls that Great Britain has not been ruled by an English dynasty since the eleventh century. It has witnessed the succession to its throne of the Plantagenets (Norman), the Tudors (Welsh), the Stuarts (Scottish), the House of Orange (Dutch), and the Hanoverian dynasty (German). Obviously, this is inconceivable in the context of modern nations. As Gellner had already noted, they are characterized by the endogenous formation of their elites. In other words, the latter derive from the population present on the national territory (most of the time from the highest social classes). In this sense, modern governments are supposed to be the expression of the national will, even when the prevailing political regime is not democratic.

The final element in the definition offered by Anderson is this: a nation is a 'community' in that membership of it takes priority – once again, in the 'imagination' of those concerned – over the 'factions' it might contain, whether the latter be social classes, religious groups or other types of collective. The 'fraternity' between fellow citizens, on which nations are supposed to be based, is what 'makes it possible . . . for so many millions of people, not so much to kill, as willingly to die' for their country.[56] This capacity for sacrifice, which nations and nationalism nurture in individuals, is what has made them so powerful for two centuries.

According to Anderson, nationalism cannot be understood if we do not appreciate that its emergence coincides with the large-scale diffusion of printing. In the eighteenth century, what he calls 'print capitalism' gradually emerged. From this period onwards, printing became a lucrative activity that attracted capitalist investment. The advance of literacy increased the proportion of the population engaged in reading, and social institutions were established – such as the literary and political societies that were to have a decisive impact on the French Revolution and hence modern nationalism – which encouraged the development of this practice. These factors converged to give rise to the emergence of a market in printed matter.

---

56   Ibid., p. 7.

The advent of this market had two consequences for the spread of nationalism. First, it contributed to the emergence of increasingly standardized national languages. The capitalist character of printing impelled editors to publish works that could be read by the maximum number of people so as to increase their profits. This desacralized Latin and reduced its influence. In addition, the fact that the language was printed tended to stabilize it, rendering its evolution more gradual. This conferred on it greater historical 'depth', which facilitated identification by contemporaries with past periods in the national history. Such standardization also created a felt need for greater correctness in expression, leading to the promotion of institutions – for example, academies – charged with producing orthographic and syntactical norms. From a general point of view, this standardization implied that a growing number of people spoke an ever more closely related language. These people would increasingly tend to regard themselves as co-citizens, the common language being a criterion – not the sole one – of membership of a nation.

A second effect of print capitalism is more specifically bound up with the press and journalism. According to Anderson, the press played a paramount role in the emergence of modern nations. The reading of national periodicals enabled every individual to obtain knowledge of events occurring in all parts of the country. A Parisian and a Marseillais reading the same account in a newspaper will tend to conceive themselves as belonging to the same collective, even if they have never met face to face. Papers thus confer a sense of 'simultaneity' on the citizens of a nation; they 'synchronize' representations and temporalities that were previously more local (feudal) at country level. The 'image of communion' underpinning modern nations therefore possesses a concrete social basis, situated in the development of capitalism and, in particular, the relationship between capitalism and culture (broadly construed). As a result it would be mistaken to regard Anderson's theory of nationalism as 'idealist' on the grounds that it stresses the 'imagined' character of modern nations – that is, the role of ideas in their appearance. For the imaginary in question is, in the last instance, the product of a process of an infrastructural kind.

From a Marxist standpoint, the main problem raised by nationalism is its persistence. Why does this phenomenon persist, even growing in strength (judging from the number of countries recognized each year by the international community), when it is archaic? How is it, moreover, that the internationalism heralded by modern socio-economic development has not really ended up competing with nationalism? The beginnings of an answer to this question lie in the following idea: 'in Western Europe the eighteenth century marks not only the dawn of the age of nationalism but the dusk of religious modes of thought. With the ebbing of religious belief, the suffering which belief in part composed did not disappear.'[57] According to Anderson, in the modern age nationalism took over some of the functions previously performed by religion. This does not mean that nationalism is the direct result of secularization. But one of the factors explaining its emergence and persistence is the fact that it responds to 'existential' questions akin to those answered by religions: 'Why was I born blind? Why is my best friend paralysed? Why is my daughter mentally impaired? The religions attempt to explain. The great weakness of all evolutionary/progressive styles of thought, not excluding Marxism, is that such questions are answered with impatient silence.'[58] For Anderson, nationalism gives individuals a sense of continuity – something that 'progressivist' doctrines, which are often characterized by some form or other of materialism, do not (or do insufficiently). This enables a country's citizens to inscribe their existence in a totality that transcends them. In support of this thesis, Anderson cites Régis Debray, who describes the logic of nationalism as follows: 'Yes, it is quite accidental that I am born French; but after all, France is eternal.'[59]

A similar starting-point to Anderson's leads another critical thinker, Tom Nairn, to different conclusions about nationalism. Nairn is professor of political science in Melbourne, Australia. Like Anderson, he belongs to the generation of the British New Left. One characteristic of this generation was that it set the problematic of the 'national question' back to work, following its long eclipse in the Marxist tradition after the trauma of the 1914 war (it is virtually absent from Western Marxism). Prior to this date, prominent Marxists, in particular those in the Austrian and Russian empires (Bauer and Lenin, to look no further), tackled the issue head on. The vigour of their debates was commensurate with the obstacles to proletarian internationalism represented by the nationalist movements of the time. After the Great War, the issue became ossified theoretically, particularly as a result of the fact that Stalin himself had written on it (his book on *Marxism and the National Question* dates from 1912), but also because of the divisions it had created during the war. Nairn is Scottish by birth. By his own admission, this is not without significance for understanding his interest in the issue and renders his situation similar in some respects to that of Marxists reflecting on nationalism in the context of a multinational state like the Austro-Hungarian Empire. Scotland did not develop such a powerful nationalist movement as Ireland; and one of the aims of Nairn's investigation is to understand why.

With Perry Anderson, Nairn is the author of a set of theses that were the subject of much debate in the 1960s – what became known as the

---

57   Ibid., p. 11.
58   Ibid., p. 10.
59   Quoted in ibid., p. 12.

'Nairn–Anderson Theses'. They claimed that Great Britain had experienced a premature revolution in the seventeenth century, whose consequence was the persistently archaic character of the British state. Because bourgeois elements were virtually absent from society at the time, this revolution was in the main led by the landed aristocracy. In the nineteenth century the English bourgeoisie, terrified by the effects of the French Revolution but also by the power of its own proletariat – tested, for example, on the occasion of Chartism in the 1830s and 40s – did not develop an identity of its own and did not as such play a leading role economically or culturally.[60] For Anderson and Nairn, this explains the 'abnormal' character of Great Britain compared with other national formations and led Nairn to announce the 'twilight' of the British state in a series of articles from the late 1970s. Nairn's principal publications include *The Break-up of Britain* (1977), *Faces of Nationalism* (1997) and *Global Nations* (2006).

Like Benedict Anderson, Nairn registers the difficult relationship between Marxism and nationalism: 'The theory of nationalism', he asserts at the start of one of his articles, 'represents Marxism's great historical failure.'[61] And like Anderson, Nairn elaborates a 'materialist' – an adjective he prefers to 'Marxist' – conception of nationalism. For him, the decisive element in understanding its emergence in the modern world is not the print capitalism prioritized by Anderson. It is a different phenomenon of an infrastructural kind – namely, 'uneven and combined development'. The theory of uneven and combined development, which is found in particular in Trotsky, refers to the idea that the development of 'advanced' countries has as its inevitable counterpart the under-development of 'laggard' countries. In other words, the lag in question is not in fact a lag, but strictly contemporaneous with the 'advance' of the western countries. In this sense, the under-development of some is the direct result of the development of others – hence the idea of 'combined' uneven development. This thesis has significant strategic consequences. Among other things, it assumes breaking with the idea that a country must be 'mature' for socialist forces to unleash a revolution in it. Such 'maturity' is impossible to achieve, since under-developed countries are maintained in a state of under-development. This idea has been developed by 'world-systems' theorists, among them Wallerstein and Arrighi.

According to Nairn, nationalism is a reaction by the countries of the periphery to uneven and combined development. In such conditions they have no choice but to try to create, in voluntarist fashion, the conditions for their

---

60   This thesis about the 'peculiarity' of Great Britain was criticized by E. P. Thompson: see 'The Peculiarities of the English', in Thompson, *The Poverty of Theory and Other Essays*, London: Merlin, 1978. For the version of it developed by Tom Nairn, see 'The Twilight of the British State', *New Left Review*, I/101–102, January–April 1977.

61   Tom Nairn, 'The Modern Janus', *New Left Review*, I/94, November–December 1975, p. 3.

own development so as to extricate themselves from the cycle of forced under-development induced by their mode of integration into the world economy. This resistance to under-development has occurred in ambivalent fashion. On the one hand, the dominated countries have implemented original develop-ment strategies – for example, socialist ones. On the other, they have copied the models operative in the centre, but in a capitalist international environment now very different from the one in which the 'advanced' countries took off. However that may be, the application of one or other of these options has neces-sitated the mobilization of colossal social forces in the dominated countries, which has taken the form of modern nationalism. In order to achieve this mobi-lization, the proto-nationalist bourgeoisies that were in the process of being formed had to build on what existed. They did not have at their disposal any of the social institutions characteristic of capitalism in the metropolitan countries. What were available were local particularisms: customs, folklore, languages, religions and so forth.

According to Nairn, modern nationalism was born out of the galvanization of these particularisms. It was the product of their collision with uneven and combined development. By definition the content of these particularisms is specific to each region. In this sense, any nationalism contains an idiosyncratic aspect. At the same time, however, the way that these particularisms are mobi-lized is universal (as indicated by the –ism in 'nationalism'). In order to account for the dual nature of nationalism, Nairn uses the term 'modern Janus'. As is well known, Janus was the Roman god with two faces, one turned towards the past and the other turned towards the future. Thus, nationalism is based on elements from old traditions, but it transforms them to construct a modern phenomenon out of them.

Nairn is not the first to relate the emergence of nationalism to develop-ment. Gellner, whose theory of nationalism we have already referred to, argues that nationalism is the quintessential modernizing ideology. For Gellner, nationalism is a by-product of industrialization. The latter involves the appear-ance of a standardized education system and, more generally, of an 'exo-socialization' – that is, a socialization common to a large number of indi-viduals. This socialization, undertaken by the state, is necessitated by constant economic growth, which requires mutual understanding and coordination between ever more numerous producers. In this perspective, any region that industrializes creates nations and nationalism. For Nairn, by contrast, national-ism does not invariably accompany industrialization. It is the fruit of under-development in the countries of the periphery: 'England and France and the United States did not invent "nationalism"; they did not need to, originally.'[62]

---

62   Ibid., p. 15.

The interesting thing about Nairn's theory is that, according to him, nationalism emerged in the periphery and only returned to the centre – western Europe – subsequently. In so far as the periphery contains the overwhelming majority of the world's population, nationalism became an ineluctable phenomenon in world history. While seeking to extricate themselves from under-development, the countries of the periphery were integrated into the world economy and, in so doing, transformed the latter. The scope of capitalism's activity consequently went on expanding. What is more, once it had arrived in the centre, nationalism combined with the state institutions that existed there and was thus reinforced. The encounter between the state and modern nationalism, according to Nairn, is comparatively belated. Nationalism is therefore originally 'anti-imperialist'. However, the author is careful to emphasize that it is not the political or cultural level, but precisely socio-economic aspects that explain its emergence. The 'materialist' dimension of this analysis consists in the fact that the main factor explaining nationalism is located in the world economy.

This does not prevent Nairn, like Anderson, from acknowledging the importance of 'subjective' elements in explaining nationalism: 'The subjectivity of nationalism is an important objective fact about it'.[63] An 'objective' analysis of nationalism must grasp subjective elements it contains. Anderson argues that nations are 'imagined communities' – that is, they presuppose the existence of representations, material in origin, which are embodied in institutions and transform social reality. The same is true for Nairn. Although nationalism is the product of 'objective' processes (uneven and combined development), the precondition of its success is that it takes possession of the 'identity' of the individuals involved, that it appeals to their 'feelings'. The emotional charge contained in the phenomenon explains its 'romantic' and 'populist' accents. Nationalism is an 'inter-class' phenomenon, which assumes an alliance between the social classes in a territory. As Nairn puts it, in order to achieve their goals, proto-national bourgeoisies have had to 'invite the masses into history' – that is, create space for them in their national project. But for that, he adds, 'the invitation-card had to be written in a language they understood' – hence the need to rely on a traditional culture known by them and, in particular, by the majority rural populations in the countries of the South.[64] Nationalism blends the most archaic aspects with the most modern.

All of this leads Nairn to be critical of 'abstract internationalism', which he claims to detect in many representatives of Marxism. For him, the defeats suffered by internationalism at the hands of nationalism during the nineteenth

---

63   Ibid., p. 8.
64   Ibid., p. 13.

and twentieth centuries, and, in particular, the fact that all socialist experiments have had no choice but to cast themselves in the mould of nation-states, are not accidental. They were inevitable for the reasons invoked above. The world capitalist economy generates uneven and combined development; and uneven and combined development generates nationalism: 'There was never any chance of the new universal class which figured in Marxist doctrine emerging *as* "proletarians", rather than "Germans", "Cubans", "Irishmen" and so on.'[65] Nationalism is neither accidental nor provisional. It is part and parcel of the very logic of the world capitalist economy.

Moreover, Nairn regards nationalism as a positive phenomenon in many respects. He is distrustful of 'cosmopolitanism' – for example, the version recently given currency by Ulrich Beck – which he argues is a creation of intellectuals, without any relationship with reality. In his view, universalism emerges from the encounter and mixing of different cultures and is in no instance given *a priori*. In this sense it presupposes the 'difference' which, in the modern world, tends to attach itself to states to produce nation-states.[66] From this point of view, Nairn does not regard the proliferation of nations witnessed over the last twenty years as necessarily negative. Acknowledgement of the positive effects of nationalism is obviously not unqualified on his part. He distinguishes between 'civic' nationalism and 'ethnic' nationalism. The second is the vector of the evils generally attributed to nationalism and to its most aggressive form, which is fascism. The hypothesis is that nationalism is dangerous when the majority of the population involved is rural. This is what, in one of his articles, he calls 'the curse of rurality'.[67] From his point of view, peasants are more inclined to develop 'ethnic' forms of nationalism. The reason for this is the brutality of the changes visited on the peasantry by the transition to capitalism, as well as their lower level of education. By contrast, within urban populations nationalism is often virtuous.

Nairn also stresses the fact that the smallest states – 'micro-states' – are generally the most effective ones and those best equipped to respond to the challenges of globalization. For example, he refers to a table of the most prosperous countries constructed by the journal *Foreign Policy*.[68] This table synthesizes several criteria – economic, social and cultural – relative to the 'well-being' of populations. Among the twenty highest placed countries, we find in particular Singapore, Switzerland, Denmark, the Czech Republic and New

---

65   Ibid., p. 22.

66   See Tom Nairn, 'Globalization and Nationalism: The New Deal', *Open Democracy*, 7 March 2008, p. 8; available at opendemocracy.net.

67   Tom Nairn, 'The Curse of Rurality: Limits of Modernization Theory', in *Faces of Nationalism: Janus Revisited*, London and New York: Verso, 1997.

68   See 'Globalization and Nationalism', p. 6.

Zealand. This is explained by the increased 'cohesion' of these small nations and by the greater control they have over their environment. In the postmodern concert of nations, Nairn claims, small is beautiful. It will be understood why for him globalization is in nowise the swan song of nation-states. *Pace* Hardt and Negri, nations remain its ineluctable actors.

Jürgen Habermas and Étienne Balibar: The Question of Europe

Anderson and Nairn believe that the world will long continue to be organized on the basis of nation-states. This does not exclude the emergence of more or less integrated coalitions of states at a supra-national level, any more than it does international organizations with greater or lesser margins of manoeuvre.

For their part, Habermas and Balibar try to conceptualize the emergence of supra-national 'blocs' that are irreducible to the parts – the nation-states – which make them up. This does not mean that in their view the consolidation of these blocs has been accomplished, or that their multiplication on a planetary scale is irreversible. Nor does it mean that nation-states are losing their influence in globalization. But for Habermas and Balibar, the second half of the twentieth century saw the emergence of unprecedented political entities, neither states nor empires, which are possibly leading the political history of humanity into uncharted territory.

Habermas is one of the best known of all the authors dealt with in this book. Successor of Adorno and Horkheimer at the head of the Frankfurt School, author of a sociology of modernity and a general theory of human action (the theory of 'communicative action'), he is one of the major thinkers of the second half of the twentieth century. His oeuvre integrates and synthesizes in an original fashion the main currents of modern thought, from Marxism, via analytical philosophy, systems theory and Kantianism, to pragmatism. His first well-known book, published in 1962, dealt with the emergence of the 'public sphere' in eighteenth-century Europe. His *magnum opus, The Theory of Communicative Action* (1981), is an attempt to think the conditions of emergence of consensus – of an 'ethic of discussion' – by means of a 'communicative' rationality that is distinct from 'instrumental' rationality.

Alongside his academic activity, Habermas has constantly intervened in public post-war debates. The issue of German responsibility for the atrocities committed during the Second World War has taken up a significant amount of his energy. This made him one of the protagonists in the 'historians' controversy' ('*Historikerstreit*'), which set him against Ernst Nolte in the 1980s. Habermas has also debated with Joseph Ratzinger, the future Pope Benedict

XVI, then head of the Congregation for the Doctrine of the Faith.[69] Habermas is the main representative of the liquidation of the legacy of the old Frankfurt School, that of 'Critical Theory'. He has 'normalized' this theory by bringing it, in the company of Rawls' theory of justice and the communitarianism of Michael Walzer and others, into the canon of the 'political philosophies' of the era. At the same time, some of the hypotheses he advances retain a considerable subversive charge.

For Habermas, the alliance between local particularisms and modernism, which Nairn regards as the essence of nationalism, is currently dissolving before our very eyes. The two faces of the 'modern Janus' are, in other words, in the process of separating: 'With this decoupling of shared cultural identity from the formation of society and the form of the state, a nationality that has certainly become more diffuse becomes detached from nationality in the sense of citizenship in a nation'.[70] According to Habermas, modern nation-states always combine a dominant 'cultural identity' with a state structure. 'Nationality' – an individual's membership in a nation – proceeds from the conjunction of these two elements. More or less sizeable minorities exist in many countries, and they coexist peacefully or are repressed by the representatives of the dominant identity. In some states, like Switzerland or Belgium, several cultures co-exist, whereas the same culture can be extended over several states, like Aymara identity, which runs across Peru, Bolivia and Argentina. In general, however, nation-states rest on a dominant culture that is in many respects 'fantasized' – the fruit of a historical construction – but whose effects are real.

For Habermas, the equation of a cultural identity with a state is tending to disappear today. In the contemporary world, the issues of cultural identities and state institutions are increasingly posed independently of one another, thus putting an end to a centuries' old shared history. Cultural pluralism is now the state's normal mode of existence. Hence the idea that the 'nation-state' form, which combines these two instances, has ceased to be politically relevant. One of the works that Habermas devotes to this issue is significantly entitled in French *Après l'État-nation*. In some respects, Habermas shares Hardt and Negri's diagnosis of the subversion of nation-states in the context of globalization. For Habermas, the latter opens a new era in the history of political forms, which must result in posing the question of sovereignty at a higher level. However, from this diagnosis Habermas draws different conclusions from those of the authors of *Empire*.

---

69   See Joseph Ratzinger and Jürgen Habermas, 'Les fondements pré-politiques de l'État démocratique', *Esprit*, no. 306, July 2006.

70   Jürgen Habermas, 'Historical Consciousness and Post-Traditional Identity', in Habermas, *The New Conservatism: Cultural Criticism and the Historians' Debate*, ed. and trans. Shierry Weber Nicholsen, Cambridge: Polity, 1989, p. 256.

An initial argument facilitating Habermas's hypothesis of the decline of the nation-state is technological and military in kind. The modern nation-state cannot be separated from nationalist ideology. The latter regards the nation as the highest political value and requires of its nationals, where necessary, the supreme sacrifice. The two world wars of the twentieth century, as well as countless continental wars, attest to the mobilizing power of nationalism. Yet this primacy of the nation in the scale of political values no longer obtains – in western countries, at any rate – and its mobilizing capacity has declined. One reason for this is developments in weaponry, which render 'military service' paradoxical: 'Today, anyone who actually uses the weapons with which he threatens another country knows that he is destroying his own country in the same moment.'[71] According to Habermas, it has become impossible to 'defend one's fatherland' as required by nationalism, because defending it amounts to destroying it. The possession by adversaries of nuclear weapons implies that in the event of the unleashing of hostilities, they will destroy one another. This phenomenon is dubbed MAD by nuclear strategists – an acronym for Mutually Assured Destruction. Underpinning the balance of terror in the Cold War was each side's certainty that it would be wiped off the map by its opponent's nuclear missiles as soon as it employed its own. This is why, notwithstanding their proliferation, atomic weapons have only been used twice.

According to Habermas, the full implications of this strategic situation for politics and, in particular, the evolution of nation-states have not been realized. Once war can lead to the destruction of the nation, not merely its weakening with a view to its capitulation, the will to 'defend' loses its sense, for this defence risks leading the nation to perdition. For the sake of the fatherland's survival, it is advisable not to engage militarily. Thus, pacifism becomes the patriotic attitude *par excellence*, whereas militarism is impossible to sustain. The problem is that, in ceasing to be militarist, nationalism loses one of its mainsprings. Mobilizing the population in defence of the fatherland was invariably a way for nationalism to assert its precedence. Hence the idea that one of the pillars on which it rested has collapsed.

This argument is interesting in that it is 'technologistic'. It maintains that technological change is capable of reshaping the social world in a certain way. In other words, the cause of a social phenomenon – in this instance, the decline of nationalism – is attributed to a technological phenomenon – namely, the appearance of nuclear weapons. This argument is perhaps a residue of the influence on Habermas of the original Frankfurt School. Reflection on technology and its effects occupied a prominent position in the thought of Adorno and Horkheimer, as illustrated by their analyses of the 'culture industry'.

---

71   Ibid., pp. 257–8.

A second argument advanced by Habermas to explain the decline of nationalism deals with developments in perceptions of otherness in the second half of the twentieth century. Because of growing international migration, but also on account of mass media and the democratization of tourism, individuals have more contact with foreign cultures. This has two significant consequences. First of all, migration has transformed the 'ethnic' composition of societies. Whereas national populations were hitherto (relatively) more homogeneous culturally and religiously, migration has introduced diversity. This implies that no cultural identity has remained intact, if it ever was. Given that the existence of a dominant identity cannot be separated from the formation of nation-states, we can say that migration has subverted one of their foundations. But the contact with otherness also pertains to the order of representations. The images of remote countries conveyed by the media have progressively induced in the minds of citizens a 'relativism' about their own traditions. It prompts them to regard their culture as simply one possible way of life. Since nationalism regards the nation – its nation – as the supreme political value, this relativism is bound to undermine it. Habermas argues that 'over and above' particularisms, relativism has also brought out the universalism contained in each national tradition. To recognize the culture of the other as a possible way of life amounts to assigning it equivalent value to one's own culture.

A third argument offered by Habermas deals with the relationship between the sciences – particularly the human sciences – and nationalism. The human sciences, and historiography first and foremost, have always performed the function of constructing the 'national narrative'. Since the origins of nationalism, they have been hand in glove with the dominant classes and charged with legitimating the existing order. This legitimation takes the form of highlighting significant moments in the national history while passing over that history's dark hours in silence. The national narrative developed by historians is transmitted to the mass of citizens by way of educational textbooks. However, during the second half of the twentieth century (although the process started considerably earlier), the human sciences distanced themselves from power. Two phenomena contributed to this. The first was the professionalization of scientific activity, which enabled researchers to enjoy the protection – in particular, the financial protection – of universities and thus to sever the link with power. Professionalization also generated stricter, less political norms of scientific production – Weber's 'value neutrality' – which led researchers to become autonomous. A second factor helping to increase the distance between historical science and power is the internationalization of research. Historians have become increasingly interested in countries other than their own. This has rendered historiography more 'objective', as a result of the distance separating historians from political issues in the country studied. The fact that the main specialist on Vichy France is the American Robert Paxton illustrates the point.

All this leads Habermas to formulate the hypothesis of the emergence of a 'post-national political identity'.[72] It is indeed an 'identity', in the sense that it mobilizes representations and affects alike. Its content is nonetheless distinct from national identities, for it does not rest on a particular history and traditions, but on 'the political order and the principles of the basic law'. The object of patriotism is now not a culture, but abstract principles like human rights or the rule of law. That is why Habermas characterizes this new patriotism as 'constitutional'. According to the philosopher, individuals are no longer attached to their national tradition as such. This does not mean, obviously, that they do not value some particular aspect of this tradition – for example, food, sport or music. But the nation as 'concrete totality' no longer functions as the source of meaning in western countries. It is no longer able to excite passions as it did in the nineteenth and twentieth centuries. What citizens are now attached to are the principles of 'living together', freedom of conscience and speech, the right to vote and circulate freely, or equal treatment before the law. Thus, 'the abstract idea of the universalization of democracy and human rights forms the hard substance through which the rays of national tradition – the language, literature, and history of one's own nation – are refracted'.[73] In the framework of 'constitutional patriotism', the form becomes the content of patriotism.

The emergence of a post-national political identity is a revolution in the order of political identities. In particular, the universalism underpinning it makes it possible once again to pose the question of 'cosmopolitanism', on which Habermas (in characteristically Kantian fashion) has his heart set. Contrary to Nairn, who argues that the universal derives from the hybridization of particularisms, Habermas defends the idea that national traditions must wane and the general principles of existence in society must be abstracted from them if the universal is to emerge. Nairn develops a 'creative' conception of the universal, whereas Habermas proposes a 'subtractive' conception of it. In this connection, he regards the construction of Europe as a prefiguration of post-national cosmopolitanism. He is one of the contemporary thinkers who takes Europe most seriously, seeking to provide it with solid political foundations. This prompted him to come out in favour of the European constitutional treaty in 2005.[74] In his view, that constitution was capable of mobilizing the peoples of Europe around a common project and, above all, of conferring a political

72   For an approach that is similar in some respects, see Anthony Appiah, 'Cosmopolitan Patriotism', *Critical Inquiry*, vol. 23, no. 3, 1997.

73   Habermas, 'Historical Consciousness and Post-Traditional Identity', p. 262.

74   See the comment column 'À nos amis français' signed by Habermas together, notably, with Günter Grass and Wolf Biermann, in *Le Monde*, 3 May 2005.

content on a Europe widely perceived as bureaucratic. The need to transcend the stage of mere 'common market', by creating a European 'public sphere', was especially emphasized by Habermas.

For his part, Balibar opposed the constitutional treaty of 2005. The reason was its neo-liberal orientation, but also the absence to this day of a 'constituent power' in Europe that might render it legitimate. Balibar started out as a Marxist, a collaborator of Althusser in his youth and one of the authors, with Jacques Rancière, Pierre Macherey and Roger Establet, of *Lire le Capital*. Like all the co-authors of that work, Balibar subsequently distanced himself from Althusserianism and even Marxism. But he remains one of the leading experts in France on Marx's oeuvre, on which he published a book entitled *La Philosophie de Marx* in 1993.[75] Like Althusser, Balibar was a member of the French Communist Party (PCF), but he was expelled following the affair of the Vitry and Montigny-lès-Cormeilles bulldozers in 1980 and 1981. The Communist mayors of those towns – Paul Mercieca and Robert Hue – had the dwellings of immigrant workers forcibly cleared. Balibar published an article entitled 'From Charonne to Vitry' in which he made a connection between the PCF's attitude during decolonization and its subsequent positions on immigration. Balibar's interest in the problematic of nationalities, 'ethnicity' and migration, with which his work on Europe is bound up, is therefore longstanding. The co-author of *Reading Capital* has made relating this problematic to that of social classes his speciality. In 1988 he published a book on the subject – *Race, Nation, Class* – with Immanuel Wallerstein.[76]

Balibar's reflections on Europe are organized around the concept of *border*, and one of his major contributions is that he has made this a genuine philosophical problem. We know little of what European citizenship will be in the future, but it will obviously be a 'citizenship of borders'. Europe is a pile of intertangled borders: 'Europe is itself a border . . . or, more precisely, a superimposition of borders, and hence of relations between the histories and cultures of the world (or at least a large number of them), which it reflects within itself'.[77] The site of encounters and conflicts between cultures, languages, religions, and intellectual and political traditions, Europe strictly speaking has no borders because it is itself a border. This distinctive status derives from the central place occupied by the continent in the modern world and, in particular, from its past (and present) imperialism. The global projection it had (has)

75   Étienne Balibar, *The Philosophy of Marx*, trans. Chris Turner, London and New York: Verso, 1995.

76   Étienne Balibar and Immanuel Wallerstein, *Race, Nation, Class: Ambiguous Identities*, trans. Chris Turner, London and New York: Verso, 1991.

77   Étienne Balibar, *L'Europe, l'Amérique, la guerre. Réflexions sur la médiation européenne*, Paris: La Découverte, 2003.

means that Europe contains in condensed form the relations between civilizations such as they exist on a planetary scale. The longstanding presence on its territory of immigrant populations of diverse origins is a result of this. It cannot but have an influence on European citizenship and, ultimately, on the very idea of citizenship.

The centrality of the 'border paradigm' in the construction of Europe also derives from the importance of territory in the continent's political and juridical history. Basing himself on Carl Schmitt, a constant source of inspiration,[78] Balibar shows that in European public law the territory has primacy in defining sovereignty. In this perspective, he who controls the territory and, consequently, the populations circulating in it, is sovereign. This is what Schmitt calls the 'nomos of the Earth' – that is, the normativity that follows from control over territory. From this derives the determinant character of borders, in as much as they define the territory and hence sovereignty. From this point of view, the sovereign is the one who possesses power over borders, who decides on entry into the territory and exit from it, whether of human beings, commodities or information. However, the construction of Europe leads to a crisis in this European juridical tradition. Its vocation was to regulate the functioning of a continent divided into independent states. But what becomes of the 'nomos of the Earth' when these states enter into a process of political unification? The status of the territory and its borders in defining sovereignty changes dramatically. Recurrent debates about the 'limits' of Europe are symptomatic of this fact.

The collapse of the Soviet Union has altered the conditions in which the construction of Europe is occurring. It has made Europe the sole supra-national entity on the continent, whereas it previously shared this status with the USSR (the USSR was a supra-national entity of an imperial kind). The fall of the USSR has transformed the 'environment' of the European Union. That environment is now composed of countries that could enter it and has raised the issue of the modalities of their integration. Russia, the Caucasus, the Balkans or Turkey – are they destined to enter the European Union? What of the relations between the latter and the Mediterranean world, with which the countries of Europe have links dating back to Antiquity? For Balibar, to pose the problem in terms of 'destiny' is fallacious, because it amounts to 'essentializing' membership in Europe. In any event, there can be no question of responding to it by claiming that the borders of Europe run through some particular location rather than another. To say of European citizenship that it is a 'citizenship of borders' is tantamount to refusing to dissolve the problem and to maintaining that the future of Europe is being played out in these regions.

---

78   See his preface to Carl Schmitt, *Le Léviathan dans la doctrine de l'État de Thomas Hobbes*, entitled 'Schmitt's Hobbes, Hobbes' Schmitt', Paris: Seuil, 2002.

All forms of citizenship have hitherto been based on a 'rule of exclusion'. It separates those individuals who find themselves inside the community from those who are outside. In the ancient city, the criterion of membership was statutory or 'objective', in the sense that citizenship was transmitted hereditarily. In modern nations, this criterion tends towards a universalism of rights, applied by a state in a given territory. Over and above their differences, the presence of a 'rule of exclusion' is a common feature of both of these different senses of citizenship. There is no citizenship that is coextensive with the whole of humanity (proletarian internationalism never adopted the concept of citizenship). But European citizenship requires that a new form of citizenship be conceived, based on a 'principle of openness' or 'non-exclusive membership'. It has to be commensurate with the constitutive pluralism of Europe – its character as a continent-border – and it must develop a mode of membership that breaks with the millennial opposition between 'inside' and 'outside'. Balibar does not conceal the difficulty of the task. A non-exclusive citizenship is a 'logically enigmatic and [historically] unprecedented idea', affirms the philosopher, who nevertheless suggests points of comparison in the history of empires and multinational states.[79]

What Balibar calls the 'borders of Europe' are not necessarily situated on the geographical edges of the continent. They can run through its centre as well. In particular, the borders of Europe run through major towns and cities. That is where police operations most often occur to check the identity and residence permits of immigrants. The border is a political entity; it is located where public powers position it. Power relations are therefore at stake in it. A recurrent hypothesis in Balibar's writings on Europe is the existence of a *European apartheid*. Along with Badiou and Emmanuel Terray in particular, Balibar is one of the French intellectuals actively engaged in the defence of the *sans-papiers* and, more generally, immigrants. The notion of 'apartheid' refers to the situation in South Africa, a re-emergence of which Balibar perceives in different forms in Europe. The repression of people who have illegally entered European territory is on the increase, an index of the formation of a 'fortress Europe'. However, the problem goes deeper than selective immigration policies. It ultimately affects the foundations of the project of constructing Europe.

A foreigner in a European country was formerly regarded as the national of another state (whether European or not). With the coming into force of the Maastricht Treaty (1992), the status of foreigners underwent a qualitative change. A distinction was henceforth made between 'community' foreigners – the citizens of another country that was a member of the Union – and

---

79   See Étienne Balibar, *Politics and the Other Scene*, London and New York: Verso, 2002, p. 112.

'extra-community' foreigners. According to Balibar, 'discrimination is written into the very nature of the European Community, which in each country directly leads to the definition of two categories of foreigners with unequal rights.'[80] European citizenship – the 'rule of exclusion' – is defined by Maastricht as the sum of national citizenships. Any individual who is the citizen of a member-state is a European citizen. The problem is that this definition creates an aporia at the 'aggregate' level, which leads to the pejoration of the condition of foreigners within the Union. From this Balibar deduces that European citizenship cannot be the mere transposition to a community level of the 'national' model of citizenship. To be meaningful, it must provide individuals – foreigners or otherwise – with new rights. The rupture with the national model of citizenship is manifest. Political modernity was characterized by the equation 'citizenship = nationality'. Enjoyment of political and social rights was bound up with membership in a national community. These two elements are now going to have to evolve separately. On this point Balibar's analyses coincide with those of Habermas.

The problems encountered in European construction largely derive from the absence to date of a 'European people'. Europe is a sovereignty 'without a subject', whose impact on the lives of Europeans is growing without it resting on any real political legitimacy. The process of European integration oscillates between the two tendencies of 'contractualism' and 'naturalism'.[81] Contractualism conceives Europe as a contract. That is, it regards European integration as being in the interest of member countries and seeks to progress applications through the strategy of the lowest common denominator. The treaties concluded hitherto, and especially the workings of the Convention chaired by Valéry Giscard d'Estaing that drafted the 2005 constitutional treaty, exemplify this approach. On the other hand, European construction is marked by 'naturalism'. It maintains that the member countries are 'naturally' destined to unite by virtue of their common Graeco-Roman and/or Judeo-Christian origins. The equivocations over Turkish entry into the Union illustrate this aspect. In this perspective, legitimation of European construction derives not from the 'rationality' of the contracting parties, but from the supposedly common 'descent' of those concerned.

Each of these ways of legitimating the Union poses a problem. Balibar's opposition to the 2005 constitutional treaty stemmed, in particular, from the excessively 'contractualist' approach that underlay its drafting. A European constitution is certainly necessary. It would help impart political content to

---

80   Étienne Balibar, '*Es Gibt Keinen Staat in Europa*: Racism and Politics in Europe Today', *New Left Review*, I/186, March–April 1991, p. 6.

81   Étienne Balibar, *Droit de cité*, Paris: Presses Universitaires de France, 2002, p. 50.

largely bureaucratic European structures. However, a constitution is by definition the product of a 'constituent power' – that is, of a 'people' which constitutes the political order.[82] 'Constituent power' arises most frequently in situations of revolution or civil war, as illustrated by the English, American and French cases in the seventeenth and eighteenth centuries. The process of ratifying the European constitutional treaty assumed that precisely what was in question – namely, the existence of a power from which the constitution derived – had been settled. For its part, 'naturalism' is based on a mythological conception of Europe. Europe is not an eternal entity. It has a history that Balibar dates back to William of Orange (late seventeenth century),[83] when the term 'Europe' replaced that of 'Christendom' in the language of diplomacy. Christendom obviously referred to a quite different geographical entity, which indicates that the current representation of Europe as a coherent whole is a recent one.

According to Balibar, the 'contractualism' and 'naturalism' that are current in European construction pertain to the same general tendency. Both are opposed to a political conception of Europe, which the philosopher ardently desires, and which would make it the product of a 'general will'. The bureaucratic character of the European Union leads to a proliferation of juridical and administrative measures that are not presented as emanating from a legitimate sovereign state. In these conditions it is understandable that 'fictive ethnicities' – nationalist, even racist, tendencies – are re-emerging within the Union. Nationalism and racism can only be combated effectively by reviving, in voluntarist fashion, politics at a European level. Such a politics must be based on the idea of common collective fate – 'community of fate' is an expression that Balibar adopts from Arendt (and Ernest Renan) – which counterposes a *demos* orientated towards the future to an *ethnos* harking back to a mythical past.

Balibar indicates several 'worksites' for the purposes of making Europe more democratic. In the wake of Bourdieu, for example, he suggests encouraging the organization of trade-union and community movements at a European level.[84] For a bureaucratic structure to be politicized, a civil society situated at the same level must address demands to it. Balibar also suggests demanding the 'democratization of borders' – that is, making decisions about entry to and exit from the Union less arbitrary and more subject to democratic control. His most striking proposal concerns the issue of languages and translation: 'the "language of Europe" is not a code but a constantly transformed system of crossed usages;

---

82   The concept of 'constituent power' has its origins in Sieyès and is developed by Schmitt and Negri in particular.

83   See Balibar, *We, the People of Europe?: Reflections on Transnational Citizenship*, Princeton: Princeton University Press, 2003, p. 6.

84   See Pierre Bourdieu, 'Pour un mouvement social européen', *Le Monde diplomatique*, June 1999.

it is, in other words, *translation*.[85] The language of Europe is none of the so-called working languages of the Union. Nor is it English, the language most widely shared by Europeans. The language of Europe is translation – that is, the capacity to pass from one of the languages spoken on the continent (or elsewhere) to the others. This idea is obviously to be related to what we said about the plurality of cultures represented in Europe. Balibar's proposal, which draws on the work of Umberto Eco, consists in educating young Europeans more in linguistic inter-comprehension. This does not involve teaching several languages to each individual, but ensuring that everyone can speak in their own language while making themselves understood by others. This requires an understanding of the 'genius' or 'spirit' of each language, not necessarily of a specific grammar and vocabulary. It might be that the fate of Europe lies in the ability of its inhabitants to apprehend such a spirit.

Wang Hui: 'Consumerist Nationalism' and the Emergence of a Chinese New Left

China's national trajectory is of universal relevance in the early twenty-first century. The two most important events at the end of the last century were doubtless the disappearance of the Soviet bloc – thus closing the historical cycle that began with the 1917 revolution – and China's turn to capitalism, which started in the late 1970s under the leadership of Deng Xiaoping. If there is one country where the fiction of spontaneously emerging and self-regulating markets fools no one, it is China. Neo-liberal reforms were imposed there by a strong state and in a context of national self-assertion (it is true that this fiction was already scarcely credible in the Chile of the Chicago boys and Augusto Pinochet). According to Wang Hui, a representative of the 'Chinese New Left', the regime in power in China takes the form of a 'consumerist nationalism'.[86] 'Nationalism' because, while (as we have seen in the case of Habermas) there may be doubts about the persistence of national sentiment in European countries, there can scarcely be any in present-day China. 'Consumerist' because the political radicalism of China's twentieth century has given way to an '*Enrichissez-vous!*' that Guizot would not have disowned. The new possessing classes are past masters in the art of ostentatious consumption; the state is run by technocrats for whom ideology is no longer of any interest;[87] and the collusion between

---

85   Balibar, *We, the People of Europe?*, p. 178.
86   See Wang Hui, *The End of the Revolution: China and the Limits of Modernity*, London and New York: Verso, 2009.
87   On the formation of the Chinese Communist Party's cadres, see the enlightening article by Emilie Tran, 'Ecole du parti et formation des élites dirigeantes en Chine', *Cahiers internationaux de sociologie*, vol. 122, 2007.

economic and political elites has generated considerable levels of corruption, while workers and peasants, hitherto at the heart of the imagined community, have been expelled from it.

Wang Hui (born in 1959) started out as a literary specialist. He is the author of a thesis on the writer Lu Xun (1881–1936), one of the sources of inspiration for the Chinese New Left; Lu was close to the Communist movement in his time and his writings were admired by Mao himself. Wang took an active part in the Tiananmen Square events of 1989 and during the ensuing repression was sent to a 're-education' camp for a year in a province in the country's interior.[88] Like a number of Chinese intellectuals of his generation, he then undertook research in the United States. This was the prelude to an internationalization of his career and work, which has made him one of the 'official' representatives of China's New Left in the West. While continuing to write on literature, Wang is increasingly concerned with the history of ideas and social theory. Thus he is the author of the monumental (untranslated) *Rise of Modern Chinese Thought* in four volumes.[89]

From 1996 to 2007, together with the sociologist Huang Ping, Wang was responsible for editing the journal *Dushu* (*Reading*), whose readership rose to 100,000, and which was a focal point for the political, economic and cultural debates of the period. This journal was founded in 1979 on the basis of the watchword 'Nothing off-limits in the domain of reading'. The growing influence of *Dushu* led its publishing house, probably under pressure from the authorities, to dismiss its two editors from their posts in 2007. In 1997, Wang published a striking article entitled 'Contemporary Chinese Thought and the Question of Modernity', which was translated into English the following year by the journal *Social Text*.[90] In it he offered a subtle account of the relationship between China's social and intellectual history in the 1980s and 90s. With the Japanese Kojin Karatani, author of *Transcritique: On Kant and Marx*,[91] and the South Korean Paik Nak-Chung, Wang is one of the most fertile Asian critical thinkers today.

The 'Chinese New Left' is not a homogeneous bloc, any more than the western New Left was in the 1960s and 70s. Originally, 'New Left' was a term given currency by its detractors, who accused its representatives – including, in addition to Wang Hui, Wang Shaoguang, Cui Zhiyuan, Wang Xiaoming, Gan Yang and Qian Liqun – of seeking to return China to the time of the Cultural

88   See Pankaj Mishra, 'China's New Leftists', *New York Times*, 15 October 2006.

89   See Zhang Yongle, 'The Future of the Past: On Wang Hui's *Rise of Modern Chinese Thought*', *New Left Review*, II/62, March–April 2010.

90   Wang Hui, 'Contemporary Chinese Thought and the Question of Modernity', *Social Text*, no. 55, Summer 1998.

91   Kojin Karatani, *Transcritique: On Kant and Marx*, Cambridge (MA): MIT Press, 2005.

Revolution. At least three elements unite the advocates of the New Left. First of all, they subject the neo-liberalism and authoritarianism of the Chinese state to concerted criticism. In other words, they believe that these are two aspects of the same phenomenon. Chinese liberals, who have been very powerful since the 1980s (and the 'new Enlightenment' following the country's opening up by Deng), criticize the absence of civil and political liberties in the country, but support the neo-liberal reforms. They simply suggest extending economic liberalism to the political field.[92] The New Left is opposed to this conception. In its view, authoritarianism and the neo-liberal reforms form a system. Those reforms are not the consequence of increased freedom in the economy, attributable to the state's withdrawal and the emergence of an autonomous civil society. They have been implemented in authoritarian fashion by the state. Authoritarianism and neo-liberalism are therefore not antithetical. Quite the reverse. In China the state and civil society interpenetrate in many ways, to the extent that making a clear distinction between them is difficult.

From a more general point of view, the New Left condemns the reigning fetishism of growth and the teleology of 'modernization' in China and their disastrous social and ecological effects: deepening inequalities between social classes, town and country, and men and women; massive privatization of public enterprises; dreadful living conditions for internal migrants; the commodification of culture, and so on. The public space occupied by the New Left corresponds in some respects to that occupied during the twentieth century by European social democracy – the old social democracy, not present-day social liberalism – even if some of its representatives are more left-wing than social-democractic. One example of the measures it advocates is the establishment in China of the kind of social security found in the western welfare states since the end of the Second World War. Social democracy never materialized in China in the twentieth century. Will it perhaps do so in the twenty-first, in the wake of the country's economic development?

A second feature of the New Left is closely linked to the first. For its representatives, the Chinese revolutionary tradition of the twentieth century, including Maoism, is unfinished business. The New Left condemns the collective amnesia, skilfully orchestrated by the Chinese Communist Party (CCP), which has gripped the country since the reforms of the Deng period. Naturally, it does not regard all of Mao's policies (for example, the Great Leap Forward of the 1950s) as worth defending – far from it. But as Wang Hui points out, whether one likes it or not, Marxism represented the Chinese road to modernity. Conducting a serious examination of its various dimensions

---

92   See Wang Chaohua, 'Minds of the Nineties', in Wang, ed., *One China, Many Paths*, London and New York: Verso, 2003.

and implications is consequently the only way for the country to project itself into the future.[93]

It is worth noting in this connection that, despite the efforts of its elites, China's revolutionary legacy remains powerful among oppressed social categories. The trade-union struggles that have proliferated over the last decade, giving rise to a new working class at the centre of the social stage, are based on the egalitarian imaginary – 'communism' is the exact term – which prevailed during the last century. To this day, that imaginary remains the 'grammar' in which demands and protests against the injustices suffered by the population are formulated. To adopt the terms of the sociologist Ching Kwan Lee, the 'spectre of Mao' therefore continues to haunt class struggles in China.[94]

A third characteristic of China's New Left is that it is one of the main agents – though not the only one – of the importation into China of a series of authors who have met with considerable success: Braudel, Foucault, Heidegger, Marcuse, Deleuze, Jameson, Lyotard, Derrida and others. In other words, the New Left is, among other things, the Chinese branch of the new critical thinking, in the sense that it shares a set of theoretical references with the latter.[95] For example, Cui Zhiyuan is influenced by the 'critical legal studies' of Roberto Mangabeira Unger, with whom he has co-authored some texts.[96] Wang Xiaoming is the author of a 'Manifesto for Cultural Studies', which proposes applying to contemporary Chinese culture the approach founded by Hall and Hoggart.[97] The examples could be multiplied.

As regards the relationship between the Chinese New Left and the new forms of critical thought, three clarifications are in order. First, the acclimatization of the new critical thinking in China is absolutely dependent on the fact that the country's official ideology remains Marxism. This is bound to influence the way these authors are read. The reception of Jameson, who is affiliated with Marxism, but a Marxism that has little to do with that taught in the CCP's training schools, cannot occur in the same way in China as in other countries. Secondly, the Chinese intellectual field is highly internationalized, as a result of the fact that a number of Chinese intellectuals (whether critical or not) live in the diaspora, and in some instances have done so for a long time. This means

---

93 Wang Hui, *The End of the Revolution*, pp. 4–5.

94 See Ching Kwan Lee, 'From the Specter of Mao to the Spirit of the Law', *Theory and Society*, vol. 32, no. 2, 2002. See also the same author's *Against the Law: Labor Protests in China's Rustbelt and Sunbelt*, Berkeley: University of California Press, 2007.

95 On the reception of various forms of critical thought in China, see Wang Ning, 'The Mapping of Chinese Postmodernity', *boundary 2*, vol. 24, no. 3, 1997.

96 See Cui Zhiyuan, 'Whither China? The Discourse on Property Rights in the Chinese Reform Context', *Social Text*, no. 55, 1998.

97 See Wang Xiaoming, 'A Manifesto for Cultural Studies', in Wang Chaohua, ed., *One China, Many Paths*.

that a number of the debates among the New Left occur not only in mainland China, but also in Taiwan or the United States.

Thirdly, the modalities of the professionalization/academicization of Chinese intellectuals are specific. Among the 'three differences' that Chairman Mao proposed to struggle against during the Cultural Revolution was the division between mental and manual labour (the other two being between rulers and ruled and town and country). As Wang Hui points out, the reconciliation of theory with practice was a constant concern of the Maoist era, leading in some cases to widespread maltreatment of intellectuals. From the end of the 1970s, Deng called for respect for competence and made 'experts' one of the pillars of the new regime. Thereafter, a class of intellectuals and a competitive university system were established. The structural separation from practice that affects contemporary critical thought in the rest of the world now also extends to the Chinese Left. This does not prevent some of its representatives from being fairly closely linked with social, trade-union or ecological movements in particular.[98] But like other national intellectual fields, the Chinese intellectual field is now relatively autonomous from the political field.

One of Wang Hui's most trenchant analyses is of the Tiananmen Square events. According to Wang, the perception of these events in the West was ideologically biased, over-determined both by the neo-liberal hegemony prevalent in the 1980s and by their coincidence with the collapse of the Soviet bloc.[99] The media presented the movement as mainly composed of students and as demanding the introduction of democratic rights. This demand was indeed present, but it was far from the only one. Many sectors of society took part in the movement, and their demands were socio-economic as well as political. The Tiananmen events involved the whole range of urban social categories – peasants were comparatively absent from it – who had paid the price for the preceding decade of neo-liberalism. Tiananmen was as much a rebellion against the corruption and social injustice attributable to privatization as a demand for freedom of expression and a multi-party system. That is why the events in many respects anticipated the movements against neo-liberal globalization and the international institutions that implement it – the IMF, the World Bank, the WTO and so forth – which emerged throughout the world in the late 1990s, and which were to culminate in Seattle, Genoa and Porto Alegre. In this sense, Tiananmen was the first anti-globalization event.

---

98   See Leslie Hook, 'The Rise of China's New Left', *Far Eastern Economic Review*, April 2007.

99   See Wang Hui, 'Aux origines du néolibéralisme en Chine', *Le Monde diplomatique*, April 2002, and *China's New Order: Society, Politics and Economy in Transition*, Cambridge (MA): Harvard University Press, 2003, chapter 1.

Accordingly, 1989 was a pivotal year in more than one respect. On the one hand, it represented the end of the cycle of October and the final act of the 'obscure disaster' (to borrow Badiou's phrase) represented by actually existing socialism.[100] But at the same time, through the agency of the Tiananmen events, it heralded the birth of a new cycle of global struggles. That the starting signal for this cycle was given in China, future centre of capital accumulation on a world scale, is a fact which will assume its full significance in coming decades.

Many contemporary critical thinkers are concerned with the emergence of supra-national political entities. As we have seen, this is true of Habermas with his theory of 'constitutional patriotism'. As we shall see later, it is also true of Achille Mbembe, who, via the concept of 'Afropolitanism', envisages the appearance of an Africa-wide cosmopolitanism. In a similar vein, Wang Hui argues that something essential is being played out today around the notion of 'Asia'. That is why during his term of office at the head of *Dushu* the journal gave pride of place to thinkers from other Asian countries.

The notion of 'Asia' was originally a colonial invention, like that of the 'Orient' deconstructed by Said.[101] During the modern era, Asia was subjected to the will to power of European colonizers and the will to knowledge of European scholars – geographers, writers, philosophers. The colonial representation of Asia was not confined to intellectuals in government service. The idea of an 'Asiatic mode of production', crucial in Marx's classification of modes of production, indicates that a certain essentialism about the continent permeated the modern *episteme* whatever the political sensibility.

Starting in the nineteenth century, anti-colonial movements altered this tendency by investing 'Asia' with a positive connotation. The People's Republic of China and its founder obviously played a central role in anti-colonialism by participating from the start, for example, in the non-aligned movement and by inventing a strategic model – 'protracted people's war' – that was to be adopted by a number of anti-colonial movements. The last quarter of the twentieth century, however, represented a moment of reassertion by China of its national aspirations. The dichotomy that counterposed China to the West in a binary fashion is once again structuring the political thinking of the country – of its elites but also of significant sections of the population. The emergence of 'neo-Confucianism' as the regime's ideological foundation cannot be understood outside this context.[102] It seeks to prove that modernization is endogenous to China, that it is not the product of a graft from the West.

---

100   Alain Badiou, *Of an Obscure Disaster*, Maastricht: Jan van Eyck Academie, 2009.

101   See Wang Hui, 'Les Asiatiques réinventent l'Asie', *Le Monde diplomatique*, February 2005.

102   See Arif Dirlik, 'Confucius in the Borderlands: Global Capitalism and the Reinvention of Confucianism', *boundary 2*, vol. 22, no. 3, 1995.

For Wang Hui, to conceive the possibility of an Asia-wide international solidarity, of a finally decolonized Asian imaginary, is the only way of escaping 'consumerist nationalism'. A different integration of China into globalization involves the country rethinking its relations with surrounding countries. But for that, the path to an alternative modernity – a more socially just one – will have to be explored.[103]

Giorgio Agamben: The Permanent State of Exception

Within the problematic of the nation-state it remains to deal with changes in the state form in recent decades. This issue has numerous dimensions, from changes in the relations between state and market, to the new territoriality induced by globalization and the construction of transnational networks (transnational firms, diasporas, NGOs), to the emergence of a 'penal state' (in Loïc Wacquant's phrase).[104] We shall confine ourselves to one aspect of the problem – namely, the emergence in the twentieth century of what Agamben has called a 'permanent state of exception'.

Agamben is one of the most stimulating contemporary philosophers. He belongs to a generation of Italian thinkers with worldwide influence, including Negri, Arrighi, Virno, Roberto Esposito and Gianni Vattimo. It would be interesting to examine in more detail the sociological and intellectual determinants that led to the emergence of this generation. Author of a protean oeuvre, in which reference to theology plays a key role, Agamben is influenced by thinkers such as Heidegger (by whom he was taught), Benjamin, Arendt, Foucault and Debord, whom he knew and the Italian translation of some of whose works he has prefaced.[105] His impact on young intellectuals and militants is on the increase. For example, the 'Invisible Committee', author of L'Insurrection qui vient, is greatly influenced by his ideas.[106]

Reflection on the 'state of exception' goes back to the Roman conception of dictatorship, invoked by Marx when he refers to the 'dictatorship of the proletariat'.[107] However, it gained considerable momentum in the twentieth century as a result of multiplying cases of the suspension of the constitutional order. The state of exception was the subject of a notable debate between

---

103   On this see Wang Hui's latest work, *The Politics of Imagining Asia*, Cambridge (MA): Harvard University Press, 2011.

104   See Loïc Wacquant, *Punishing the Poor: The Neoliberal Government of Social Insecurity*, Durham (NC): Duke University Press, 2009.

105   For an introduction to Agamben's thought, see Stanley Grelet and Mathieu Potte-Bonneville, 'Une biopolitique mineure. Entretien avec Giorgio Agamben', *Vacarme*, no. 10, 2000.

106   The Invisible Committee, *The Coming Insurrection*, Cambridge (MA): MIT Press, 2009.

107   See Karl Marx, 'Critique of the Gotha Programme', in *The First International and After: Political Writings Volume Three*, London and New York: Verso, 2010.

Benjamin and Schmitt. In 1922, Schmitt published *Political Theology*, in which he tackled the issue of the nature of 'exceptional situations' in politics. In a famous sentence, the German jurist asserted: 'Sovereign is he who decides on the exception.'[108] The previous year, Schmitt had published *Dictatorship*, a work in which he distinguished between the 'dictatorship of commissars' (aimed at maintaining existing law) and 'sovereign dictatorship' (aimed at constituting a new legal order). The same year, Benjamin wrote an essay entitled 'Critique of Violence', where the problem of the exception is posed via the relationship between law and violence. In his theses 'On the Concept of History', published twenty years later, Benjamin once again invoked the state of exception:

> The tradition of the oppressed teaches us that the 'state of exception' in which we live is not the exception but the rule. We must attain to a conception of history that is in keeping with this insight. Then we shall clearly realize that it is our task to bring about a real state of exception, and this will improve our position in the struggle against Fascism.[109]

The paradoxical observation that the state of exception is increasingly tending to become the norm is the starting-point of Agamben's analyses.

A state of exception or emergency is classically defined as the provisional suspension of the constitution and the law in order to save them from peril. Two things legitimate it. The first is absolute necessity. The republic must be confronted with a danger that is imminent and of such a magnitude that its protection requires the interruption of the normal procedures of political decision-making and their replacement by a 'dictatorship' (in the classical sense, which predates the twentieth century). As a legal adage frequently employed in this debate puts it, *necessitas non habet legem* (necessity knows no law) – that is to say, necessity authorizes suspension of the law. In this perspective, the state of exception is not opposed to law, but a condition of its possibility, since without it the legal order would disappear, rendering any legislative act impossible. The second element underlying classical doctrines of the state of exception is its temporary character. When society has been rescued from the danger threatening it, the dictatorship is discharged and the law restored. In principle, the institution authorized to suspend the law – particularly in the French tradition – is none other than the one that makes it in normal times: parliament.

The state of exception was therefore originally placed under the sign of time on two counts: the danger must be *imminent* and the dictatorship can only

---

108   Carl Schmitt, *Political Theology: Four Chapters on the Concept of Sovereignty*, trans. George Schwab, Chicago: University of Chicago Press, 2006, p. 5.
109   Walter Benjamin, 'Theses on the Philosophy of History', in Benjamin, *Illuminations*, ed. Hannah Arendt and trans. Harry Zohn, London: Fontana, 1992, pp. 248–9 (translation modified).

be temporary. These two aspects define the possibility of a 'constitutional dicta-torship'. Some countries (France and Germany) provide in their constitution for the possibility of its suspension. Others (Britain and the United States) do not, in the belief that envisaging in law the possibility of its negation is dangerous. The problem in this second case is that, when an exceptional situation arises, a radical lawlessness is liable to be established. It is interesting to note that the ambiguous relationship between the state of exception and the law is also observed in the case of the 'right of resistance'. In situations of oppression, as during the Second World War, citizens can assert their legitimate right to resist in the name of a conception of the law and justice which they deem to have been flouted. They then oppose the law in the name of the law.

According to Agamben, the state of exception has today become a veritable 'paradigm of government'.[110] It has been released from the temporal constraints referred to above and transformed into an enduring politico-juridical order. The attacks of 11 September 2001 and the unleashing of the 'war on terror' – a war 'without end' in the words of its instigators – represent a turning-point in this respect, which has not left any national or international legislation untouched.[111] But the constitutive elements of the permanent state of exception were put in place during the First World War, which saw the belligerent coun-tries introducing exceptional laws that profoundly affected the law. The emergence of the permanent state of exception is first of all indicated by the collapse of the separation of powers, one of the foundations of modern politics. For Agamben, we have been dragged back to a time when this separation did not exist, when power was concentrated or undivided. As the philosopher puts it, when the West starts giving the whole planet lessons in 'democracy', it begins to depart, perhaps irremediably, from its democratic tradition.[112] In the perma-nent state of exception, executive power absorbs legislative and judicial power. 'Totalitarian' regimes, in which government interferes not only with the other powers, but also in civil society, illustrate this.

But this also affects democratic regimes. Thus, for some decades we have been witnessing an expansion of 'government by decree'. A decree is a norm with the force of law that issues from the executive, not the legislature. Most often it requires retrospective validation by parliament, but its source is govern-mental. According to Agamben, government by decree is becoming established

110   Giorgio Agamben, *State of Exception*, trans. Kevin Attell, Chicago: University of Chicago Press, 2005, chapter 1. Agamben's reflections on the state of exception should be related to those of Negri on 'constituent power'. See Toni Negri, *Insurgencies: Constituent Power and the Modern State*, trans. Maurizia Boscaglia, Minneapolis: University of Minnesota Press, 1999.

111   See Jean-Claude Paye, *La Fin de l'État de droit. La lutte antiterroriste, de l'état d'exception à la dictature*, Paris: La Dispute, 2004.

112   Agamben, *State of Exception*, chapter 1.

today as a normal technique, whereas it is supposed to be employed only on an exceptional basis. Italy seems to be the country that has gone furthest down this road – decrees have become 'an ordinary source of law' – but its generalization extends to the totality of democracies.

The permanent state of exception is embodied in new types of space, new 'heterotopias', as Foucault would put it.[113] Guantánamo Bay prison, where those whom the United States regards as 'enemy combatants' or 'illegal combatants' are locked up, is an example. Characterization as a 'prisoner of war' has existed since laws of war came into being. It confers a legal status on prisoners and guarantees them certain rights. By contrast, the term 'enemy combatants' given currency by the Patriot Act (October 2001) deprives prisoners of any rights. It sucks the person into a legal vacuum where he is at the mercy of the sheer power of his jailers, and from which he will (possibly) re-emerge only at their pleasure. Characterization as an 'illegal combatant' makes an individual 'a legally unnameable and unclassifiable being'. According to Agamben, 'The only thing to which it could possibly be compared is the legal situation of the Jews in the Nazi *Lager*, who, along with their citizenship, had lost every legal identity, but at least they retained their identity as Jews . . . [I]n the detainee at Guantánamo, bare life reaches its maximum indeterminacy.'[114]

The notion of 'bare life' is developed by Agamben in his book *Homo Sacer*, of which *State of Exception* is the second volume (the third being *Remnants of Auschwitz*).[115] It refers to the ancient distinction between *zôé* (bare life), which designates the 'mere fact of living', and *bios*, which refers to 'qualified life', to the particular mode of existence of an individual or group. This distinction occurs in the context of the debate initiated by Foucault with his concept of 'biopolitics'.[116] For Agamben, sovereign power is exercised over bare life, without any mediation. This appears most clearly in situations where, as in the case of the 'illegal combatants' in Guantánamo, individuals are not only stripped of rights, but regarded as not being subjects of law, as being external to any legality. To assert that the state of exception is a 'paradigm of government' amounts to arguing that such spaces, and the 'exiles' they produce – the *sans-papiers* are another obvious example – are currently proliferating. The relationship between sovereignty (the law) and life is at the centre of Agamben's thought: 'if the law

---

113   Michel Foucault, 'Des espaces autres', in *Dits et écrits*, Vol. I, Paris: Gallimard, 2001.
114   Agamben, *State of Exception*, pp. 3–4.
115   Giorgio Agamben, *Homo Sacer: Sovereign Power and Bare Life*, trans. Daniel Heller-Roazen, Stanford: Stanford University Press, 1998, and *Remnants of Auschwitz: The Witness and the Archive*, trans. Daniel Heller-Roazen, Cambridge (MA): MIT Press, 2002.
116   See, for example, Michel Foucault, *The Birth of Biopolitics: Lectures at the Collège de France, 1978–1979*, trans. Graham Burchell, London and Basingstoke: Palgrave Macmillan, 2008.

employs the exception – that is the suspension of law itself – as its original means of referring to and encompassing life, then a theory of the state of exception is the preliminary condition for any definition of the relation that binds and, at the same time, abandons the living being to law.'[117]

A contributory factor in the emergence of the permanent state of exception is humanity's entry into the 'atomic age'. This point was notably highlighted by the US constitutionalist Clinton Rossiter.[118] Nuclear power creates a new range of 'systemic' risks, which are unprecedented on account of the dangers they entail and the scale of those dangers. Management of such risks presupposes establishing gigantic administrative and techno-scientific structures, which have led to a significant expansion of the state. These structures regulate the production and circulation of nuclear energy in its civil and military aspects, including emergency plans in the event of a catastrophe. The atomic age has increased the perimeter of state secrecy and *raison d'état*, in which, for example, atomic plants are shrouded, restricting the perimeter of the public sphere accordingly. In addition, it has profoundly altered the nature of armed conflicts. The balance of terror between nuclear powers has led to a proliferation of 'low-intensity' wars: civil wars, insurgencies and counter-insurgencies, the war on 'terrorism' or 'drugs', 'international policing' operations, and so forth. One result of this is the abolition of the clear dichotomy between war and peace, which gives way to 'states of violence' wherein war and peace can no longer be distinguished.[119]

According to Agamben, the state of exception is in nowise the expression of a residue of monarchism or absolutism within democratic societies. In other words, it does not indicate the persistence of the *ancien régime* within modernity. It is a pure product of the 'democratic-revolutionary' tradition, since its modern form derives from the French Revolution.[120] In reality, this is self-evident because, if the state of exception consists in the suspension of the democratic legal order, it can only make its appearance when such an order exists. Once this is accepted, the real question is what conclusions are to be drawn about the nature of democratic regimes. The state of exception has followed democracy like its shadow throughout the modern age; and today this shadow is growing ever longer. For Agamben, it reveals the intimate, necessary links between violence and law. Law is not that which protects against violence; it contains a potential for violence whose realization is the state of exception. In this perspective, what must be done is to separate these two instances in such a

---

117   *State of Exception*, p. 1.
118   See, for example, Clinton Rossiter, 'Constitutional Dictatorship in the Atomic Age', *The Review of Politics*, vol. 11, October 1949.
119   See Frédéric Gros, *États de violence. Essai sur la fin de la guerre*, Paris: Gallimard, 2006.
120   *State of Exception*, pp. 4–5.

way as to render the violence contained in law innocuous: 'One day humanity will play with law just as children play with disused objects, not in order to restore them to their canonical use but in order to free them from it for good.'[121] Only transformative (revolutionary) political activity can conduce to this outcome, for it is precisely defined by its ability to intervene and sever the link between violence and law. To engage in such activity is to bring about what Benjamin called the 'real state of exception'.

CAPITALISMS OLD AND NEW

Marxism traditionally combines economic analysis with political and/or cultural theory. According to this paradigm, the base determines (in complex fashion and through mediations) the superstructures, which presupposes that these two instances must be studied conjointly, on pain of missing the overall logic of the system. What Marxists called 'economics', moreover, only coincides in part with what classical economists understand by the term. When they argue that the economy 'determines' the superstructures, Marxists are not claiming that everything is explained by economic processes as ordinarily conceived. As it determines the superstructures, the 'economy' changes its nature and enters into a relationship of mutual (dialectical) influence with them. However that might be, in the classical forms of Marxism, economics and politics and/or culture are closely intertwined.

With Western Marxism there emerges a tendency to autonomize the analysis of the superstructures. In Gramsci, Lukács, Sartre and Althusser, the economy is less salient than in the preceding generation of Marxists. The reasons for this autonomization are various. For example, they stem from the 'glaciation' of Marxist economics – the fact that it was increasingly placed under the control of the Communist parties. Autonomization also derives from the professionaliza-tion of the 'profession' of economist (and other disciplines in the human sciences), which tends to reduce interdisciplinarity. It is interesting to note in this regard that the authors who will be discussed in this section on contemporary capitalism are mostly professional (academic) economists.

The disconnection between economic and political and/or cultural theory is further accentuated in current critical thinking. In other words, the latter has continued the tendency to autonomization initiated by Western Marxism. For example, Jameson relies on the analysis of 'late capitalism' formulated by the Marxist economist Ernest Mandel, but it plays an 'auxiliary' role, rather than being the veritable motor of his analysis. Today there exist remarkable studies of the development of capitalism, undertaken by such authors as Robert

---

121   Ibid., p. 64.

Brenner, Claudio Katz, François Chesnais, Robert Pollin, Elmar Altvater, Robert Wade, and Gérard Duménil and Dominique Lévy. We also find studies of the superstructures, whether politics or culture. But these two domains of critique are now disjoined. An interesting question is whether this disjunction might in the future be reduced and, if so, on what conditions. A certain pessimism is in order here. This issue is part of a more general problem, which is the critique of the division of labour, of which the division of intellectual labour is one aspect.

Critique of Cognitive Capitalism

As we have seen, a hypothesis advanced by Negri and his school involves the emergence of a 'cognitive capitalism'. Many economists have raised doubts about this hypothesis. That the knowledge of wage-earners is valorized by capitalism is self-evident. But it has always known how to extract profit from it, whatever the epoch or economic sector concerned. Even at the time of the most radical 'Taylorism' – the wholesale rationalization of productive tasks – workers' knowledge was mobilized in production. The cognitive content of labour depends on the occupation. An engineer and an unskilled worker definitely do not perform the same intellectual operations. But a cognitive dimension is present in both instances; and the same goes for all occupations. There is therefore no real transition from labour-value to knowledge-value. The second is already contained in the first.[122]

Supporters of the 'cognitive' hypothesis tend, moreover, to limit their analyses to the developed countries. On a planetary scale it is the figure of the classically exploited that is predominant, not the cognitively exploited. The salient fact of recent decades in economic affairs is the integration of China into the world market and its impact on the global labour force. It is manifestly not the cognitive worker who is hegemonic in Chinese factories, even if China is not merely the 'workshop of the world', but trains, for example, more than a million engineers a year. The integration of other 'giants' like India or Brazil, as well as the 'original accumulation' that is rife in the ex-Soviet countries, exercises a downwards pressure on working conditions in the countries of the North. In addition, the neo-liberal turn of the late 1970s has led to a resurgence of the most brutal forms of capitalist exploitation.

The 'flexibilization' of the labour market, successive 'reforms' of pension regimes extending the period of contribution, the weakening of protection in case of unemployment – these illustrate the trend. In short, the 'progressive' wage relation based on the 'Fordist-Keynesian' compromise has deteriorated

---

122 See Michel Husson, 'Sommes-nous entrés dans le capitalisme cognitif?', *Critique communiste*, nos 169–70, Summer–Autumn 2003.

sharply. This set of measures is an attempted response to the fall in the profit rate resulting from the reversal of the 'long wave' of economic growth during the 1970s. In some respects, the socio-economic and juridical changes of recent decades take us back to a 'pre-industrial' form of capitalism. This is what Michel Husson calls 'pure' capitalism.[123] The emergence of an organized labour movement starting in the second half of the nineteenth century had counteracted the system's most savage tendencies and stabilized conditions for capital accumulation. The dislocation of the Fordist wage relation has prompted a revival of capitalism's most regressive aspects.

There is no question of denying that technological developments, but also a general rise in educational levels, increase the cognitive composition of labour. The sectors at the forefront of innovation, like information technology, have seen their relative importance in the economy enhanced. Far from the 'convivial' image projected by firms like Google, Microsoft and the 'start-ups' that proliferated in the 1990s, such sectors have generated new forms of oppression and alienation. These should cause us to revise our conception of the nature of the dominated classes in contemporary capitalism. However, this trend coexists with older forms of exploitation, so that capitalism integrates several temporalities at the same time. Through new forms of organization and technological innovation, Taylorism seems to have discovered a 'second youth': 'The workforces employed are in fact growing at both ends: on the one hand, workforces composed of cognitive workers are growing very rapidly, but the mass of jobs created are to be found in the low-skill posts of sales and personal service.'[124] The 'dual' structure in the economy is particularly evident in the United States, a country that combines sectors with high cognitive value – of the Silicon Valley variety – with situations of exploitation of extreme brutality.

For a number of critical economists the (Marxist) law of value must be retained and cannot be replaced by a 'cognitivist' theory of value. (That law, as we know, states that the value of a commodity is bound up with the quantity of labour it contains.) In their view, it remains hegemonic in contemporary capitalism. One implication of this is that the opposition between 'capital' and 'labour' remains formative at present. A hypothesis advanced by the 'cognitivists', which they share with authors like Jeremy Rifkin or Gorz, is the 'end of work'. It suggests that the civilization of work, in which 'self-realization' occurs through work and income is bound up with the latter, is nearing its end. The idea of the 'end of work' is based on two premises. First of all, according to its supporters, full employment has now become unattainable. Unemployment is here to stay; it is part and parcel of the structure of societies and not

123   Michel Husson, *Un pur capitalisme*, Lausanne: Page Deux, 2008.
124   Husson, 'Sommes-nous entrés dans le capitalisme cognitive?', p. 2.

attributable to a passing crisis or inappropriate economic policies. One reason that 'cognitivists' favour universal income is that a reduction in unemployment below a certain threshold is, in their view, unlikely. Consequently, work and income must be uncoupled so as to guarantee everyone minimum resources. The second hypothesis, which in part justifies the first, is that a growing proportion of the work once done by human beings is now performed by technology. The decline of employment is thus in part due to the fact that labour is replaced by machines. This development is positive according to the cognitivists; it makes it possible to envisage a civilization finally released from work and hence from exploitation.

For Michel Husson, the argument that full employment has become unattainable is baseless. It is an unwarranted extrapolation from the current conjuncture. Thus, the economic 'bright spell' of the years 1997–2001 led to the creation of ten million jobs in Europe, which prompted a return to discussion of full employment.[125] Moreover, technological development is not in itself destructive of employment. For example, machines have to be conceived, built and maintained, which assumes that they embody human labour. Cognitivists can be criticized for their fascination with technology. This fascination derives from the current of *operaismo*, which is the source of this hypothesis. Technology is not 'progressive' in itself; its positive or negative effects are always conditional on power relations. In any event, it is certain that it will not abolish capitalist exploitation solely through its own development, for labour is not simply an occupation but, in the last instance, a social relationship.

Against the cognitivists who defend the slogan of 'universal income', Husson advances the slogan: 'All wage-earners for abolishing the wage-earning class!' Here it is not universal income but a reduction in working time that is the radical measure appropriate to the present period. It will enable everyone to find a job, and hence allow societies to restore full employment, so as subsequently to envisage ways and means for collectively abolishing the wage-earning class. Among other things, full employment will make it possible to reduce the pressure on wages by diminishing the 'industrial reserve army'. A reduction in working hours represents a veritable incursion into the sphere of private property. If capitalist value derives from the capitalist's appropriation of a portion of wage-labour, this reduction represents a form of expropriation.

In the *Grundrisse*, a text cognitivists like to quote, Marx makes free time the real measure of wealth. Be that as it may, it is pointless to demand a universal income without changing anything in the operation of the commodity sphere. For this income could serve to generate still more flexibilization in the labour market. Once income ceases to be proportional to working hours,

---

125   Ibid., p. 3.

extension of the latter no longer has a cost for the firm. Added to this is the fact that, to be financially viable, universal income would have to be introduced at the expense of other forms of social income: pensions, family and unemployment benefits, health benefits.[126] Consequently, it may turn out to be a source of impoverishment for wage-earners – something suggested by the fact that economists on the Right, like Milton Friedman, are in favour of some forms of guaranteed income.

Robert Brenner: The Long Downturn

The most influential critical economist internationally over recent years is probably the American Robert Brenner. A professor at UCLA, a member of the editorial committee of *New Left Review* as well as *Against the Current*, the organ of the US political oranization Solidarity, Brenner is primarily known for his analysis of the 'long downturn' experienced by the global economy starting in the 1970s. For a time Brenner was close to 'analytical Marxism'. The variant of Marxism he has developed is also sometimes characterized as 'political' Marxism, a rubric shared with Ellen Meiksins Wood which was originally coined by the French Marxist Guy Bois, who challenged Brenner's theory of capitalism.[127] Inspired by E. P. Thompson's criticism of the base/superstructure metaphor highly influential in certain traditional forms of Marxism (Thompson critiqued the determinist aspects of the latter), political Marxism maintains that social change occurs principally in the relations of production, in as much as they are fundamentally political. This applies especially to the transition from feudalism to capitalism, which we shall turn to in a moment. One of the characteristics of capitalism, says Wood, is that it separates the economic from the political, thus creating the impression that they are autonomous spheres. Against any standpoint that would 'naturalize' this separation, she asserts the need for

> a conception of the 'economic', not as a 'regionally' separate sphere which is somehow 'material' as opposed to 'social', but rather as itself irreducibly social – indeed, a conception of the 'material' as constituted by social relations and practices. Furthermore, the 'base' . . . is not just 'economic' but also entails, and is embodied in, juridical-political and ideological forms and relations that cannot be relegated to a spatially separate superstructure.[128]

---

126   On the costs of universal income, see René Passet's calculations in *L'Illusion néo-libérale*, Paris: Fayard, 2000.

127   See Paul Blackledge, 'Political Marxism', in Jacques Bidet and Stathis Kouvelakis, eds, *Critical Companion to Contemporary Marxism*, Leiden and Boston: Brill, 2008.

128   Ellen Meiksins Wood, *Democracy against Capitalism: Renewing Historical Materialism*, Cambridge: Cambridge University Press, 1995, p. 61.

Brenner was originally a historian of capitalism. He proposed a thesis on capitalism that gave rise to an important debate known as the 'Brenner debate'. A book of this title, collecting contributions from leading economic historians, was published by Cambridge University Press.[129] The articles that prompted this debate appeared in the 1970s in *Past and Present*, an academic journal founded and edited by British Marxist historians close to the Communist Party such as Hobsbawm, Thompson and Hill. Brenner is also the author of *Merchants and Revolution* (1993), in which he studies the role of London merchant companies in the English Revolution.

Starting in the 1960s, a new intellectual trend crystallized in critical political economy, which can be designated by the generic term 'Third Worldist'. It includes both the theory of 'dependency' developed by representatives of the Economic Commission for Latin America (ECLAC) like Raul Prebisch, Celso Furtado or Fernando Enrique Cardoso (future president of Brazil), as well as the 'world-systems' analysis developed by Wallerstein and Arrighi. The economists Andre Gunder Frank and Samir Amin also belong to this school. Naturally, there are differences in the analyses proposed by these authors. However, they share an identical attention to the place of the 'Third World' in the emergence and operation of global capitalism. Politically, the tradition was linked to national liberation and anti-colonial struggles. The 'non-aligned movement' that emerged with the Bandung Conference in 1955 was a major political reference-point for them. Some of its representatives, among them Amin and Wallerstein, were close to Maoism.

In 1977, Brenner published a violent attack on this school in *New Left Review*. For his purposes he used the term – defamatory among representatives of Marxism – 'neo-Smithian', alluding to the author of *The Wealth of Nations*.[130] According to Brenner, the Third Worldists had abandoned placing class relations at the heart of their explanation of the emergence and operation of capitalism. Their principal aim was to refute the 'optimistic' conception of capitalism present in liberalism, particularly Adam Smith. The Third Worldists maintain that the development of world trade on the basis of the division of labour will lead to the development of under-developed regions. The division of labour is supposed to increase productivity, which is thought to increase the wealth produced. For Gunder Frank and Wallerstein, whom Brenner takes as his main targets, capitalism brings about a 'development of under-development' – that is, the development of the centre of the world involves the

---

129   See T. H. Aston and C. H. E. Philpin, eds, *The Brenner Debate: Agrarian Class Structure and Economic Development in Preindustrial Europe*, Cambridge: Cambridge University Press, 1986.

130   See Robert Brenner, 'The Origins of Capitalist Development: A Critique of Neo-Smithian Marxism', *New Left Review*, I/104, July–August 1977.

international
Centre-periphery vs class struggle

under-development of its periphery. As in the theory of 'uneven and combined development', 'under-development' is not a 'lag' in the development of under-developed countries vis-à-vis 'advanced' countries. It is contemporaneous with their advance, in that it is the direct product of it. The development of some thus has as its precondition the under-development of others.

According to Brenner, in their critique of the liberals' optimistic model, the 'neo-Smithians' placed the same explanatory factor at the centre of their analysis – namely, world trade. Whereas for liberals the latter produces wealth and development for all countries, in the view of the 'neo-Smithians' it generates under-development and poverty for those countries 'lagging behind'. But the underlying mechanism is the same, since the origin of development or under-development lies in the expansion of international trade and specialization within it. One consequence of this is that for the Third Worldist economists, the centre-periphery logic is as important, if not more so, than class conflicts in the strict sense. In their analysis of capitalism, the former tends to replace the latter. This idea has crucial political consequences. For example, it leads to advocating 'autarchic' solutions, which consist in 'delinking' the economies of the periphery from the world market and pursuing 'auto-centred' economic development.[131] The policy of industrialization via 'import substitution', which was in vogue in the countries of the South in the 1960s, is a moderate version of this hypothesis. More radical versions are to be found in countries which, like North Korea, have taken the construction of 'socialism in one country' to its ultimate conclusion. According to Brenner, all this is very remote from the classical Leninist strategy, which consisted in working for alliances between the 'weak links' in the periphery and the working classes of the countries of the centre.[132]

For Brenner, capitalism is not principally a matter of international trade and the expansion of the world market: it is a matter of class struggle. According to the 'neo-Smithians', capital accumulation has as its precondition the transfer of profit created in the periphery to the centre of the system. This transfer can occur economically, because the periphery produces goods sold in the centre more cheaply or buys goods produced in the centre at a higher price; or it can occur through force. According to Wallerstein, powerful states have emerged in the western countries in order to guarantee this transfer of profits militarily, if necessary. In Brenner's view, however, the 'neo-Smithians' are wrong to locate the source of capitalist profit in the periphery. It was originally created and is subsequently reproduced in the centre, with the periphery playing a subsidiary role in the matter. Thus, the discovery and exploitation of the Third

---

131   See Samir Amin, *Delinking: Towards a Polycentric World*, trans. Michael Wolfers, London: Zed, 1990.
132   Brenner, 'The Origins of Capitalist Development', p. 92.

World are superfluous in the emergence of capitalism (which does not mean that they did not subsequently contribute to it).

The origin of capitalism lies in the technological innovations introduced into English and, more generally, west European agriculture during the fifteenth and sixteenth centuries. These innovations facilitated an increase in what Marxists call 'relative' surplus-value – that is, the surplus-value generated by increased productivity.[133] The introduction of these innovations, and the productivity growth that flowed from them, was itself due to the state of the class struggle in England at the time. From the fourteenth century, repeated peasant revolts launched an assault on serfdom, which was abolished in the sixteenth century by Queen Elizabeth. This prevented the ruling classes from exploiting the peasantry intensively by increasing 'absolute' surplus-value (for example, by lengthening the work day). For the peasantry was now – in principle, at any rate – a free agent. Other ways had to be found to expand production, which would gradually give rise to the emergence of a new mode of production: capitalism. The main characteristic of the latter, argues Brenner, is its capacity to create profit via increased productivity. There is no need for the periphery to supply it with capital. For Brenner, capitalist development is 'endogenous' or 'self-generated'. This is what has prompted some critics to characterize his theory of capitalism as 'Eurocentric'.[134]

Brenner is the author of a widely discussed analysis of the current crisis of capitalism. In his view, this crisis is inscribed in the *longue durée*. It emerged around 1973 on the occasion of the first oil shock, but the elements that triggered it were in place from the mid-1960s. Like many critical economists, Brenner adopts the theory of 'long waves' of capitalist development elaborated by Kondratiev. This theory maintains that capitalism comprises extended economic sequences lasting several decades, divided into phases of 'expansion' and 'recession'. As regards the contemporary epoch, following a period of growth in the post-war years – the *trente glorieuses* – we entered a phase of deep recession starting in the 1970s. This phase has been characterized by historically low growth rates. Recurrent conjunctural crises must be conceived against the background of this enduring crisis. Starting from this, the problem is to identify the factors that provoked the crisis and the reasons why it has lasted so long.

The crisis we have been experiencing for thirty years is, according to Brenner, a typical 'Marxist' crisis. It is explained by a mechanism formerly highlighted by Marx (and, before him, by the classical British political economists) – namely, the tendency for the profit rate to fall. This Marxist hypothesis

---

133   Ibid., p. 78. See also Ellen Meiksins Wood, *The Origin of Capitalism*, London and New York: Verso, 2002.
134   J. M. Blaut, 'Robert Brenner in the Tunnel of Time', *Antipode*, vol. 26, 1994.

has given rise to numerous debates. Among economists who identify with Marxism today, some contest its validity.[135] However, many economists – Brenner among them – concur in claiming that since the 1970s, capitalism has been undergoing a serious crisis of profitability. This means that the profits which derive from capital investment have fallen sharply, in particular in the manufacturing sector, where the crisis has its origin. To note only a few significant statistics: From 1965 to 1973 – when, according to Brenner, the decline began – the profit rate in the US manufacturing sector fell by 40 per cent. For the G-7 countries as a whole, the drop in the same period amounted to 25 per cent.[136] Between 1950 and 1970, the net growth in profits in the manufacturing sector in the US was more than 24 per cent. Between 1970 and 1993, it was a mere 14 per cent. Moreover, in the period 1990–2000 – allegedly a time of economic boom on account of the advent of 'start-ups' and the so-called dot-coms – the average growth rate in GDP per capita on a world scale was 1.6 per cent. From 1889 to 1989, it was 2.2 per cent.[137] For its part, the expansionary phase of the long wave, extending from the late 1940s to the early 1970s, was marked by unprecedented growth rates.

What is the cause of the descending curve of the profit rate? This is the subject of a vast debate among critical economists. The problem is not exclusively economic, for once the mechanisms that generated the crisis have been identified, the issue arises of the policies to pursue in order to counter it. According to Brenner, the principal explanatory factor lies in international economic competition and uneven development.[138] At the end of the Second World War, the United States was the unchallenged global economic power. The destruction wrought by the war in Europe rendered the continent's countries – with the partial exception of Great Britain – incapable of competing with the United States. US economic hegemony was accompanied by political hegemony, likewise attributable to the war. During the 1960s, Germany and Japan principally, but also France and Italy, were gradually transformed into rivals of the US on the world market. These countries achieved a degree of relatively advanced technological development, by dint of knowledge transfer from the US but also endogenous innovation. They combined this technological development with low wage levels relative to productivity gains, by comparison with wages in the US in the same years.[139] According to Brenner, the still largely rural

135   See Michel Husson, 'Sur la baisse tendancielle du taux de profit', *Note Hussonet*, 20 November 2008 (available at hussonet.free.fr).

136   Robert Brenner, 'The World Economy at the Turn of the Millennium: Toward Boom or Crisis?', *Review of International Political Economy*, no. 8, spring 2001, p. 14.

137   Robert Brenner, 'Towards the Precipice', *London Review of Books*, 6 February 2003.

138   Robert Brenner, *The Economics of Global Turbulence*, London and New York: Verso, 2006, chapter 2.

139   Brenner, 'The World Economy at the Turn of the Millennium', p. 13.

populations of these countries formed a 'reserve army', which temporarily made it possible to discipline wage demands. All this placed Germany and Japan in a perfect position to capture market share from US firms. However, the arrival of new 'entrants' also created a problem of over-capacity of production in the manufacturing sector, which signalled the start of the prolonged decline in the profit rate. Productive capacity now exceeded global demand, which led to a situation of latent over-production and devalorized the capital invested. More-over, the new entrants' technological innovation rendered the fixed capital (machines) previously in use obsolete with increasing rapidity, dragging the profit rate down.

How is it that, once surplus capacity and surplus production have been registered in a sector, investors do not switch their capital to different activities and, in so doing, exploit new profit 'seams'? Here Brenner goes back to one of Marx's arguments concerning the anarchic character of capitalist production – that is, the inability of producers to coordinate their activity. What is ruinous from the standpoint of the overall logic of the system is not necessarily so from the standpoint of each individual capitalist. In the industrial sector, investment in fixed capital is very considerable. By definition, it is difficult to switch, precisely because it is 'fixed', unlike labour, which can be trained to perform new tasks. In these conditions, the rational strategy for each producer is to seek to pull out and withdraw at the expense of the others. The problem is that at an aggregate level such behaviour draws the system into a spiral of general decline in the profit rate. According to Brenner – and Marx before him – this exempli-fies the irrationality of capitalism and the need to counterpose to it a rationally planned mode of production.

Obviously, the dominant classes have not remained passive in the face of this fall in the profit rate. What is commonly called neo-liberalism – a coherent set of public policies first implemented in the mid-1970s (but conceived earlier), whose objective is the restoration of the profit rate by all necessary means – is the answer to this problem on their part. There is a debate among critical econ-omists over whether neo-liberalism has succeeded in checking or even reversing the decline in the profit rate. For Duménil and Lévy, for example, neo-liberal-ism created the conditions for a 'resurgence' of capitalism from the 1980s onwards.[140] It is the fruit of such policies as privatizing public services – which creates new private investment opportunities and hence capital valorization – liberalizing world trade and, more generally, dismantling the welfare state which makes a reduction in the 'cost' of solidarity possible by lowering taxes for the wealthiest fractions of the population.

---

140   See Gérard Duménil and Dominique Lévy, *Capital Resurgent: Roots of the Neoliberal Revolution*, Cambridge (MA): Harvard University Press, 2004.

The resurgence of capitalism also possibly results from its 'financialization' – that is, the emergence of a capitalism whose dominant component is financial. As a result of the fall in real profit rates, capital has increasingly tended to invest in the financial sector and speculation. The deregulation and opening up of the latter, and the facilitation of credit conditions (notably, but not exclusively, in the United States), have generated speculative flows that have allowed investment funds, their clients and their managers to enrich themselves considerably. They have also provoked financial 'bubbles', the last of which to date were the 'telecoms' bubble, which burst in the early 2000s, and the property bubble (so-called sub-primes), which triggered the crisis we are currently experiencing. These financial bubbles derive from what Brenner calls 'stock-market Keynesianism'.[141] The public authorities artificially maintained a high return on financial investments to compensate for the drop in profits in the real economy and encouraged a turn to finance. This yielded high returns, until the day it entered into crisis and thus compounded the recessive trend in the economy as a whole.

According to Brenner, a capitalism wherein finance is dominant is a contradiction in terms.[142] Financial profits must always ultimately be based on profits in the real economy. This does not preclude temporary improvements wholly or partly based on finance, like that experienced by the US in the Clinton era in the 1990s. In the last instance, however, only a major economic crisis can lead to a restoration of the profit rate and thus restart accumulation on new bases. A crisis is a mechanism for destroying capital. In so far as the fall in the profit rate originates in surplus capacity, this mechanism is indispensable for making investment profitable once again. It is interesting to note that Brenner is critical of the notion of spatial fix developed by Harvey. Harvey argues (in a 'Luxemburgist' vein) that crises of capitalism prompt capital to invest in new spaces, to fix its crises by implanting itself in spaces that are still, or are once again (courtesy of war, for example), devoid of capitalist relations. According to Brenner, the 'globalization' of capital – its gradual extension to the entire planet – is indeed the result of the crises it undergoes. At the same time, its implantation in new regions invariably fails to restart accumulation. The productive capacity that has emerged in Asia – especially China – since the 1980s has tended to duplicate the productive capacity already present elsewhere. It is therefore redundant compared with it, not complementary. As a result, far from restoring the rate of profit (as Harvey thinks), it accentuates its decline.

Brenner is firmly opposed to analyses that explain the decline in the profit rate by challenges to capitalism during the 1960s and 70s. This is evident from

---

141   Brenner, 'Towards the Precipice'.
142   Robert Brenner, 'The Economy in a World of Trouble', *Against the Current*, January 2009.

the fact that he dates the onset of the crisis to the mid-1960s, a period when 'anti-systemic' movements (working-class, Third Worldist, counter-cultural) were not yet at their most powerful. In particular, Brenner criticizes the Regulation School's theory of crises.[143] The Regulation School maintains that the crisis of the second half of the 1970s resulted from the pressure put on profit rates by workers. As a result of a growth phase that significantly reduced unemployment, and also because of the influence of working-class political and trade-union organizations, wages and, consequently, labour costs increased, reducing the share of profits accordingly. The 'wage relation' imposed by labour on capital into the 1970s was favourable to labour, until the point when the drop in profitability it induced plunged all economies into crisis. More precisely, in Fordism the organization of work facilitated productivity gains which, combined with the wage relation, allowed for a regular increase in profits and wages. When these gains were exhausted, wages continued to increase because of the wage relation, but profits began to dry up.

Brenner does not deny that during the *trente glorieuses*, or 'golden era', the share of value added was relatively favourable to wage-earners. He also agrees that the dismantling of the workers' movement starting in the late 1970s – the neo-liberal era – made it possible to check the decline in the profit rate. The wage relation therefore does indeed have an impact on the trajectory of profitability. But in no instance is it the principal explanatory factor, which is to be sought (according to Brenner) in uncoordinated international competition between producers. Among the arguments advanced by Brenner to refute the Regulationists is the idea that the crisis has affected all developed countries – both those where the balance of forces was favourable to wage-earners and those where it was not. The former alone should have been affected if the Regulationists' hypothesis was correct. For Brenner this leads to only one conclusion: the origin of the crisis is to be found in the *overall* dynamic of capitalism.

Giovanni Arrighi: A Final 'Systemic Cycle of Accumulation'?

One of the authors characterized above as 'Third Worldist' was the Italian Giovanni Arrighi. However, he spent most of his career in the United States, in particular at the universities of Binghamton in New York and Johns Hopkins in Baltimore. In 1960s Italy, in his formative years, the main Marxist current outside the Communist Party was *operaismo*. Although he interacted with representatives of *operaismo*, Arrighi did not belong to it and his subsequent

---

143   See Robert Boyer, ed., *Théorie de la régulation. L'état des savoirs*, Paris: La Découverte, 2002.

theoretical trajectory differed from Negri's.[144] At the start of the 1970s he set up the 'Gramsci Group', an intellectual and activist collective identifying with the thought of the author of the *Prison Notebooks*.[145] To proclaim descent from Gramsci was unusual on the Italian extra-parliamentary Left of these years because his legacy was invoked and administered by the Communist Party, which meant that those working for a renewal of Marxism generally regarded themselves as anti-Gramscian (opposed to a Gramsci travestied by the PCI). Gramsci has even influenced Arrighi's more recent work, particularly his last book, *Adam Smith in Beijing*, which describes the decline of American 'hegemony' and the rise of China. However, his use of Gramsci's theses is distinct from the way they are usually used in contemporary critical thought – for example, in cultural studies, which tends to regard Gramsci as a thinker of 'culture' and 'superstructures'. Arrighi is firmly situated on the side of the analysis of the base – that is, global economic and social processes. A decisive element in his intellectual formation was his time in Africa, where he taught in the early 1960s. This prompted his interest in problems of development and the impact of imperialism on that continent. One of his important works, published in 1978, was entitled *The Geometry of Imperialism*.[146]

Arrighi is a 'world-systems' theorist, one of the best known after Wallerstein, who is primarily responsible for developing this theory.[147] It draws on Marx and Marxism and has developed in interaction with other variants of 'Third Worldism' – in particular, 'dependency' theory. Another major source of inspiration for world-systems theory is Braudel's economic and social history. World-systems theorists have adopted Braudel's perspective of the '*longue durée*', as well as his concept of 'world-economy', from which the concept of 'world-system' is a generalization. A world-system is defined as a vast geographical entity, a part of the planet composed of one or several continents, which contains several cultural sub-systems, but only one division of labour.[148] In other words, it involves a set of countries – what Wallerstein calls 'cultural subsystems' – which are economically integrated. A world-system can be politically unified and thus assume the form of an empire, as in the case of ancient Rome

---

144   However, it should be noted that the title of Arrighi's last book, *Adam Smith in Beijing*, alludes to a text by Mario Tronti, one of the main representatives of *operaismo*, entitled 'Marx a Detroit'. See Tronti, *Operai e capitale*, Turin: Einaudi, 1966.

145   See the exchange between Arrighi and Harvey published shortly before the former's death: Giovanni Arrighi, 'The Winding Paths of Capital: Interview by David Harvey', *New Left Review*, II/56, March–April 2009.

146   Giovanni Arrighi, *The Geometry of Imperialism: The Limits of Hobson's Paradigm*, London and New York: Verso, 1987.

147   For an introduction see, for example, Immanuel Wallerstein, *World-Systems Analysis: An Introduction*, Durham (NC): Duke University Press, 2004.

148   See Immanuel Wallerstein, *Historical Capitalism*, London and New York: Verso, 1995.

or the Ottoman Empire. It can also be without a political centre or be polycentric, like Europe during the modern era. But in all instances the coherence of the totality is imparted not by politics, but by the single division of labour that obtains in the countries concerned. From the typically Marxist primacy allocated to the economy derives two attributes of world-systems. On the one hand, they are characterized by a centre-periphery logic (to which is added a 'semi-periphery'). The exploitation of the periphery by the centre is the mainspring of the dynamic of capitalist accumulation within them. On the other hand, the theory of world-systems is distinguished by its 'methodological international-ism' – that is, by the fact that it positions the analytical lens directly at the international level, without assigning undue importance to nations.

For Arrighi, capitalism is the outcome of an encounter between two logics, one 'territorial' and the other 'molecular'.[149] According to him, it is a mistake to conceive this system as purely economic. Capitalism contains an irreducible political dimension, which means that the mechanisms for extracting value are always supported by state structures. The world-systems theorists adopt Braudel's distinction between market and capitalism. In their view, the former existed prior to the emergence of the latter; the market economy and capitalism must therefore be regarded as two different instances. Wallerstein even argues that capitalism is opposed to the market – that profit formation requires the existence of monopolies, which are incompatible with competition. Arrighi calls the way that power is projected into space, and exercises control over the populations and natural resources to be found in it, 'territorial' logic. The political space thereby formed is characterized by the fact that it is discontinuous; it is composed of boundaries and sovereignties that are more or less clearly defined. For its part, the 'molecular' logic refers to everything that pertains to the economy – namely, production, trade, financial flows, or the migration of workers. It is called 'molecular' because it progresses gradually, without discontinuities, and tends to undermine boundaries and sovereignties 'from below'.

The relations between these two logics of capitalism are always problematic, rendering the system unstable. Depending on the period, one can prevail over the other. In certain cases the territorial logic is dominant, as in the United States's policy of 'containment' in relation to the Soviet Union during the Cold War. Obviously, this also aimed at keeping open the maximum possible space for US capital to thrive, which means that geopolitics was not the only factor at

---

149   Giovanni Arrighi, *Adam Smith in Beijing: Lineages of the Twenty-First Century*, London and New York: Verso, 2009, pp. 211–12. This distinction was established in collaboration with Harvey and appears for the first time in Giovanni Arrighi, *The Long Twentieth Century: Money, Power and the Origins of Our Time*, London and New York: Verso, 1994, and then in David Harvey, *The New Imperialism*, Oxford: Oxford University Press, 2003. It is inspired by Hannah Arendt, *The Origins of Totalitarianism*, Cleveland and New York: Meridian, 1962.

work. Conversely, in the 'classical' imperialism of the second half of the nine-teenth century, the economic logic prevailed, with states often lagging behind trading companies. But imperialism was naturally also a matter of geopolitics. The tension between these two logics derives from the fact that the molecular logic tends to escape state control, its progression in space being unlimited. States try to follow this progression, by extending their political and military sphere of action as they go along. The problem is that, in so doing, they run the risk of 'imperial over-extension', to adopt an expression of Paul Kennedy's which Arrighi cites approvingly.[150] This concept refers to cases of excessive extension of the distance separating the centre of the world-system from its remotest periph-ery. When this distance grows, the cost of territorial control increases accordingly, to the point of reaching inordinate levels. Over-extension swells military budgets and imperial bureaucracy and diverts profit from the most dynamic sectors of the economy. As a result, it represents one of the causes of the decline of world-systems.

According to Arrighi, since its origins, capitalism has gone through four 'systemic cycles of accumulation'.[151] Each cycle is composed of two phases, which he characterizes as 'material' and 'financial'. The former is a phase of develop-ment in the real economy. During this period, a set of private economic actors, in collaboration with state structures, succeed in initiating a virtuous produc-tive and commercial dynamic, on the basis of a coherent division of labour, which yields rising profits. In time, however, this dynamic inevitably tends towards over-accumulation. Each fraction of capital invested generates less profit, while the competition between economic actors, once channelled by the division of labour, intensifies. It is then that the systemic cycle of accumulation enters into its 'financial' phase. This phase corresponds to what we above called 'financialization' – that is, capital's tendency as a result of the fall in profit rates to take refuge in the financial sphere and speculation. According to Arrighi, financialization is invariably the sign of the decline of a systemic cycle of accu- mulation – the 'autumn of hegemony', in his fine formula – and its replacement by a new cycle. Present-day financialization is no exception to this rule.

Each systemic cycle comprises a hegemonic centre. The centres corre-sponding to the four cycles identified by Arrighi are Genoa (from the fifteenth century to the early seventeenth century), the Low Countries (from the late sixteenth century to the late eighteenth century), Great Britain (from the mid-eighteenth century to mid-twentieth century), and the United States (from the late nineteenth century to the present). Each of these political entities – of

---

150   See Paul Kennedy's book *The Rise and Fall of Great Powers: Economic Change and Military Conflict from 1500 to 2000*, New York: Vintage, 1989.
151   Arrighi, *Adam Smith in Beijing*, p. 230.

which Arrighi observes that none is a 'nation' in the classical sense of the term – presided over a phase of capitalist development by combining territorial and molecular logics in an original way. Thus, Genoese hegemony was essentially molecular; it abstained from territorial conquests. In the sixteenth century the dominant imperial power was Spain, while Genoa was politically unstable and militarily weak. Its hegemony over the early years of capitalism mainly derived from the international mercantile and financial networks it controlled. Great Britain was the first hegemon to have fully applied both logics simultaneously, as indicated by the extent of its colonial empire.[152] An element highlighted by Arrighi is that each hegemonic centre is larger than the last one. To the extent that the diameter of world-systems expands during history, their centre of gravity must also increase in order to sustain or balance the whole. The decisive factor in the dilation of successive hegemons is demographic. The larger the diameter of the world-system, the greater the population required to ensure its dynamism and productivity. The political centre is also the centre of accumulation, which presupposes an ever larger available workforce.

According to Arrighi, we are currently witnessing the decline of the systemic cycle of accumulation dominated by the United States. The defeat suffered by the latter during the Vietnam War was the 'signal crisis' of this decline, the war in Iraq is its 'terminal crisis'. Wars – combined with growing deficits, to which they contribute significantly – play an important role in the transition from one instance of hegemony to the next. For Arrighi, the power of the United States persists to this day, but it represents a typical case of 'domination without hegemony'.[153] The Italian thinker's analysis is close here to that of Robert Cox. 'Domination' is predicated on instances of economic and military superiority that are not accompanied by the consent of the dominated. The latter endure the domination for want of an alternative, but they do not actively collaborate with it, and invariably seek to undermine it. For domination to be converted into hegemony, it is indispensable that it should rest on a mixture of interests that is clearly understood by the dominated – the dominant classes among the dominated populations must have an interest in the domination – and cultural identification. Until the 1970s, the United States combined these elements, which made it an authentic hegemon. But since the Vietnam War, and still more the war in Iraq and the failure of the 'Project for a New American Century', it clearly lacks them.

At the point of the transition from the 'material' phase to the 'financial' phase of the systemic cycle of accumulation, we paradoxically witness the emergence of a 'belle époque'. For the US cycle, this was the Reagan and

---

152   Ibid., p. 241.
153   Ibid., chapter 7.

Clinton decades, which were characterized by a (temporary) return of growth. In the case of the British cycle, the Edwardian epoch of the late nineteenth and early twentieth centuries presented similar characteristics; and analogous periods existed for the Genoese and Dutch cycles. Initially, financialization fictively restores the rate of profit. This stabilizes the situation politically and economically, and re-launches the hegemonic ambitions of the dominant power. The problem is that financialization in no way resolves the problem of over-accumulation and even tends to increase inter-capitalist competition over meagre profit seams. That is why *belles époques* invariably end in wars and revolutionary processes.

For Brenner, the challenges to capitalism in the 1960s and 70s, and, in particular, the workers' movement in the countries of the centre, did not have a decisive impact on the profit rate. Arrighi concurs with him in identifying international competition, and the surplus capacity it generates, as one of the causes of the crisis. However, he disagrees with Brenner as regards the pressure exerted by the wage-earning class on the curve of profitability. According to Arrighi, the period from 1968 to 1973 witnessed a global explosion of wages. During the 1950s and 60s they had increased, but more slowly or in line with labour productivity, which made it possible for firms to maintain their margins. After 1968, however, wages increased much more rapidly and reduced profits accordingly.[154] Added to this is the fact that the crisis which emerged in the early 1970s was inflationary. For Arrighi, this inflation was notably due to the wage increases secured by workers. They compelled governments to increase the mass of money in circulation (and to abandon the gold standard en route), and thus generated inflation.[155] In this sense, it was a symptom of wage-earners' combativeness. This combination of elements allows Arrighi to argue that the pressure exercised by the labour movement did indeed have an impact on the fall in the profit rate. In this he is in agreement with the Regulationists and cognitivists, but opposed to Brenner.

What will succeed the declining US empire? An initial possibility is that the world will experience a long period of 'systemic chaos'. Because of the absence of an unchallenged hegemon capable of stabilizing a new cycle of accumulation, the planet will possibly experience an epoch of wars and intense economic competition. Wallerstein has formulated the hypothesis that the decline of the US cycle is accompanied by a definitive degeneration of capitalism – that, in other words, this fourth systemic cycle of accumulation will be the last.[156] For

154 Arrighi, *The Long Twentieth Century*, p. 305, and *Adam Smith in Beijing*, p. 126.
155 The 'monetarist' counter-revolution, one of whose slogans was 'zero inflation', sought to reverse this balance of forces by restoring profits through reducing inflation.
156 See Immanuel Wallerstein, *Utopistics, or, Historical Choices of the Twenty-First Century*, New York: New Press, 1998, and 'Le capitalisme touche à sa fin', *Le Monde*, 11 October 2008.

Wallerstein, we are entering into a period analogous to the one which, around the sixteenth century, saw the transition from feudalism to capitalism. The idea underlying this hypothesis is that capital has attained such a degree of concentration and monopoly today that profit formation has become increasingly difficult. Obviously, adds Wallerstein, nothing guarantees that the system which will replace capitalism will be more just and less brutal than it. In fact, everything leads us to suppose the opposite.

Arrighi does not go so far as to forecast the disappearance of capitalism. In his view, aside from the possibility of a period of systemic chaos, the emergence of a new world-system under Asian – in particular, Chinese – hegemony cannot be excluded. This is the ultimate significance of the theoretical testament that is *Adam Smith in Beijing*. China's economic development suggests the possibility of a Chinese twenty-first century, with a 'Beijing Consensus' succeeding the 'Washington Consensus'. The whole question is whether China has the ambition to embark on a 'power politics' aimed at eliminating the declining rival in order to supplant it, as the US did to Britain in the past. Arrighi does not exclude the possibility that China will be a hegemonic centre of a new kind, characterized by a 'peaceful ascent'. But it is reasonable to regard this as an audacious hypothesis. As the theorist of international relations John Mearsheimer recalls, never in the course of history has a power deliberately abstained from converting its economic might into military might.[157]

Elmar Altvater: Fossil Capitalism

Elmar Altvater belongs to the small but growing group of economists who believe that the fate of critical economics hinges on its relationship with ecological problems. Altvater is a German economist and was a professor at the Free University of Berlin until the early 2000s. He is an important figure in the anti-globalization movement and a frequent participant in global and regional Social Forums. In particular, he plays an active role in ATTAC-Germany's scientific committee, a national section of the association which emerged belatedly but now counts among the most dynamic. Altvater has co-edited a collective work published by this committee on emissions trading.[158] He is the author of several books on capitalism, notably *The Future of the Market* (1993), *Grenzen der Globalizierung* (*The Limits of Globalization*, co-authored in 1996 with Birgit Mahnkopf), and *Das Ende des Kapitalismus* (2005). In the 1970s he also founded the journal PROKLA, acronym for

---

157   See John Mearsheimer, 'Clash of the Titans', *Foreign Policy*, no. 146, 2005.
158   Elmar Altvater and Achim Brunnengräber, *Ablasshandel gegen Klimawandel?* [*Emissions Trading against Climate Change?*], Hamburg: VSA Verlag, 2008.

Probleme des Klassenkampfs ('Problems of Class Struggle'), whose subtitle is 'Journal of Critical Social Science', and which still appears regularly.[159]

The ecological crisis requires economists to renew their ideas to adapt them to current issues. Altvater's itinerary is interesting in this respect. Hailing from the Marxist 'critique of political economy', he militates actively for relating ecological themes to that paradigm. One of his articles, published in 2003, is significantly entitled 'Is There an Ecological Marxism?' – a question he answers in the affirmative.[160] This research programme is shared by other authors, among them James O'Connor, John Bellamy Foster, Paul Burkett, Jean-Marie Harribey and Ted Benton.

As regards the relationship between critical economists and ecology, two remarks are in order. First of all, as has been said, confronting new problems is a factor in theoretical innovation. The novelty of ecological issues leads critical thinkers to look to references outside the existing critical corpus for the resources with which to think them. Thus, one of the authors to whom some theorists of radical ecology refer is Ilya Prigogine. Nobel Prize winner for chemistry in 1977, he is one of the most innovative scientists of the second half of the twentieth century.[161] He is known for his work in the field of thermodynamics, a discipline widely used (as we shall see) by some 'eco-economists'. From his work in thermodynamics Prigogine has derived a general epistemology that examines the conditions for the equilibrium of a system and its 'self-organization'. Altvater cites him frequently, in particular in support of the hypothesis that capitalism, by dint of the growing expenditure of energy it entails, is tending to become increasingly unstable.

Secondly, when a new problem such as ecology emerges, two attitudes can be envisaged. The first consists in treating it as one variable among others within existing economic models. It seeks to include this variable in economic theories developed in epochs, from the eighteenth century to the first half of the twentieth century, when ecology was not yet a problem. The second attitude involves a critique of the categories of economics – classical and Marxist – from the standpoint of ecology. It amounts to asserting the partially or completely obsolete character of these theories, and the need to develop doctrines commensurate with current ecological challenges. In the second case, what is advocated is, as Kuhn would put it, a paradigm shift. Contemporary critical economists interested in ecology are located on a spectrum extending from one to the other of these positions. All feel the need to

---

159   See the website www.prokla.de.

160   Elmar Altvater, 'Is There an Ecological Marxism?', lecture at the virtual university CLASCO (*Consejo Latinoamericano de Ciencias Sociales*), 2003. Available at www.polwiss. fu-berlin.de.

161   See Ilya Prigogine and Isabelle Stengers, *La Nouvelle alliance*, Paris: Gallimard, 1986.

profoundly transform the conceptual apparatus of critical economics. But obviously this is a complex task; and paradigm shifts cannot be forced. No doubt we shall have to wait for one or two generations of critical thinkers before the mutation is effected completely. This does not prevent today's economists from actively developing theories that incorporate ecology.

Altvater is one of the inventors of the notion of *fossil capitalism*. According to him, capitalism would never have experienced the expansion it has without the intensive exploitation of the fossil energies that are coal, oil and natural gas. In particular, the use of oil on a systemic scale starting in the second half of the nineteenth century made possible what Altvater calls the 'industrial-fossil revolution':

> Without the continuous supply and massive use of fossil energy modern capitalism would be locked into the boundaries of biotic energy (wind, water, bio-mass, muscle-power, etc.). Although something like capitalist social forms occasionally could be found in ancient societies (in Latin America and Asia as well as in Europe), they could not grow and flourish without fossil energy.[162]

Fossil energies, especially oil, have several effects on the development of capitalism. Firstly, oil causes a major alteration in economic and social space-time. It is in the nature of capital to be mobile. As Marx puts it in a sentence we have already cited, 'the world market is contained in the very notion of capital' – which means that capital valorization takes the form of the exploitation of developmental differentials between regions of the world. This mobility would not be effective if based exclusively on biotic energy. The latter would confine capital within narrow spatio-temporal limits, conducive to the blossoming of local 'micro-capitalisms', but not to the world system that has gone on expanding since the second half of the nineteenth century. Altvater employs a concept coined by Harvey to refer to this phenomenon – namely, 'space-time compression'. It refers to the constant acceleration of the speed of capital's circulation, a condition for the stabilization or enhancement of the profit rate. This acceleration results in a 'shrinking' of the world, as a result of the regular introduction of technological innovations in transport and communications. 'Space-time compression' has as its condition of possibility fossil energies – hence the idea that capitalism can only be fossil. Solar energy is too weak and diffuse to bring about this type of compression. The transition to a future solar energy regime would therefore involve a radical change in the spatio-temporal organization of our societies – that is, in the last instance, in capitalism itself.

---

162   Elmar Altvater, 'The Social and Natural Environment of Fossil Capitalism', in Leo Panitch and Colin Leys, eds, *Socialist Register*, vol. 43, London: Merlin, 2007, pp. 6–7.

The influence of oil on capitalism is of another kind as well. In the capital-ist regime, productivity can only be increased by constantly revolutionizing the means of production. This is what, in the section devoted to Brenner, we called 'relative surplus-value', which depends on technological innovations in the production process. For its part, 'absolute surplus-value' results from an intensification of the existing technological regime of production (by length-ening the working day, for example). To say that productivity increases only by dint of constant socio-technical development amounts to claiming that a growing expenditure of energy is the *sine qua non* of profit creation. Alterna-tively put, in order to create profit, productivity must increase, and for it to increase energy use must grow. As Altvater puts it, in the last instance economic growth is simply the result of the transformation of ever more significant quantities of energy and material into commodities.'[163] Two conclu-sions can be drawn from this. Firstly, the *necessary* link between capitalist value and energy use shows that attempts to induce a 'green capitalism' – a capitalism respectful of nature – or 'sustainable development' are doomed in advance (which obviously does not mean that ecological reforms should not be introduced). Secondly, this characteristic of capitalism renders it unstable and self-destructive. The reason for this, of course, is that the available fossil energy diminishes over time.

One of Altvater's sources of inspiration is Nicholas Georgescu-Roegen (1906–94). One of the most influential theorists of ecology today, he was a pioneer of 'degrowth', a current in radical ecology. Georgescu-Roegen was an economist and statistician by training. In the early 1970s he published an influ-ential work entitled *The Entropy Law and the Economic Process*.[164] In it he criticized neo-classical economic theory for its inability to grasp the limits to growth set by nature. This incapacity ultimately derives from the fact that the dominant economic paradigm is based on Newtonian mechanics. According to Georgescu-Roegen, thermodynamics furnishes the most adequate model for economics, because it places the problem of energy depletion at the heart of its models. In particular, Georgescu-Roegen imports into economic analysis the 'second principle of thermodynamics', according to which the energy available or useable in the universe is declining irreversibly. In other words, a quantity of energy employed for a task is definitively lost; it cannot be employed for another task. This is the celebrated function of 'entropy', which gives its title to Georgescu-Roegen's work and allows him to claim that by definition growth is not infinitely possible, because the requisite energy is declining inexorably

163   Elmar Altvater, 'The Growth Obsession', Research Center on Development and International Relations, Working Paper no. 101, 2001, p. 6. Available at http://vbn.aau.dk.

164   Nicholas Georgescu-Roegen, *The Entropy Law and the Economic Process*, Cambridge (MA): Harvard University Press, 1971.

– hence the prioritization by the economist and his followers of the theme of 'degrowth'.

The concept of 'entropy' is adopted by Altvater in a Marxist framework where the law of value, which makes labour the main source of surplus-value, remains valid. His theoretical position is, in reality, ambiguous and on this basis interesting. Thus he can write: 'History consists of the increase of entropy and the associated irreversibility of all processes, whereas capital operates on a logic of reversibility and circularity.'[165] Here we are far removed from the idea stated in the *Communist Manifesto* that 'The history of all hitherto existing society is the history of class struggles.' According to Altvater, history is certainly a matter of class struggle, but it is also a matter of energy loss. This economic-ecological theory is hybrid; it represents a step towards the elaboration of a new theory integrating the old concerns of Marxism and new concerns consequent upon the ecological crisis.

The degree of entropy depends on the prevailing energy regime in the system under consideration. The necessarily 'fossil' character of capitalism entails that its energy use is considerable and that the same is true of its entropy. The global networks of transport and communication which make possible the 'space-time compression' required for capital valorization induce unrestrained oil consumption, one of whose consequences is the climate crisis resulting from excessive emissions of CO_2. We know, moreover, that oil supplies are in the process of running out. According to many experts, the 'Hubbert peak', which refers to the point beyond which oil supplies begin to decline, has already been passed. For others it will come soon. But in all the available scenarios oil will disappear. Moreover, beyond a certain point the cost of extracting oil exceeds its value, as a result of the depth of the deposits or its greater viscosity. To combat the 'industrial-fossil revolution' under whose regime we still live, Altvater calls for the emergence of a 'solar society' based on a 'solar revolution'.[166] It consists in investing massively in renewable forms of energy: sun, water, wind power, geothermal power, bio-mass and so on. Such a revolution is all the more urgent because the rapid development of countries like China and India is increasing entropy. In fact, it is leading to the generalization of western lifestyles, which are highly extravagant in energy consumption.

Altvater makes a distinction between 'wet oil' and 'paper oil'. In addition to being a natural resource with objective physical properties exploited by capital, oil also has a financial value. Alternatively put, it is a commodity which, like all commodities, possesses an 'exchange-value' and a 'use-value'.

165   Altvater, 'The Social and Natural Environment of Fossil Capitalism', p. 7.
166   Altvater, 'The Growth Obsession', p. 15.

This has several consequences. Firstly, it is an object of speculation, which causes prices to fluctuate in a manner unrelated (or indeterminately related) to actual reserves and production. Altvater observes in this connection that the 'financialization' we have referred to throughout this chapter, which is a key characteristic of contemporary capitalism, also affects the oil market. The 'petro-dollars' generated by the exploitation of oil in the Middle East have fuelled the financial sphere since the oil shocks of the 1970s. Another impact of finance on oil is that the 'returns on investment' demanded of firms by their shareholders for the last thirty years can only be achieved by high growth rates. Given the nature of current technology, such growth rates can only be achieved by using an ever greater quantity of (non-renewable) energy. This demonstrates that financial values, seemingly the most abstract and disembodied, have direct consequences for the environment. The idea that contemporary capitalism is a 'cyber-capitalism' operating in a virtual world is demolished by ecological economists. Capitalism is a material mode of production, even when, like today, the financial sphere seems to assume increasing importance.

According to Altvater, we are witnessing the emergence of an 'oil and greenhouse imperialism'. The economist invests the Marxist theme of imperialism with a new significance, by showing that in the current global context it assumes a new meaning on account of the climate crisis. In situations of scarcity, imperialism tends to become increasingly brutal. Natural resources like oil or water being scarcer, the conflicts over them become more radical. This brings about armed conflicts for control of oil-producing regions, of which the war in Iraq is an example. But this also presupposes the emergence of inequalities of a new type within each society – namely, environmental inequalities.[167] Thus, the effects of climate change are borne differently depending on one's social class. Altvater points out that the hurricanes of 2005 – among them Hurricane Katrina, which struck New Orleans – caused $200 billion of material damage.[168] A significant proportion of this damage was inflicted on the popular classes. It is a mistake to regard social history and natural history as two separate histories. They are intimately linked, albeit in complex ways.[169] While the climate crisis seemingly affects humanity indiscriminately – at all events, that is the opinion promoted by the dominant currents in ecology – it is in fact a quintessential class phenomenon.

---

167   These inequalities are the target of the movement for 'environmental justice', which has developed in Anglophone countries in particular. See Carolyn Merchant, *Radical Ecology: The Search for a Liveable World*, London and New York: Routledge, 2005, pp. 170–76.

168   Altvater, 'The Social and Natural Environment of Fossil Capitalism', p. 11.

169   As demonstrated by Mike Davis, *Late Victorian Holocausts*, London and New York: Verso, 2001.

Luc Boltanski: Spirit of Capitalism, Are You There?

An aspect of capitalism we have so far said little about is its ideological dimension. When Marx said of this system that it is a 'social relation', this obviously included an ideological dimension, to which the co-author of *The German Ideology* devoted some of his most profound analyses, and which cannot be conceived separately from analysis of its other dimensions. A contemporary critical thinker who has tackled the problem of ideology in innovative terms is Luc Boltanski, who together with Bruno Latour is probably the most famous living French sociologist internationally. One of Boltanski's most interesting works, co-authored with Eve Chiapello is the imposing *The New Spirit of Capitalism*.[170] The project for this book, and the research programme on neo-capitalism it inaugurated, arose during the great strikes of November–December 1995, which paralyzed France for almost a month. This event represented a mass protest – one of the first in the world – against the neo-liberal variant of capitalism and illustrated the emergence of original forms of resistance to it. The theory of capitalism and its critique is continued by Boltanski in a recent work entitled *De la critique. Précis de sociologie de l'émancipation*.[171] It aims to reintroduce the notion of a 'spirit' of capitalism adopted from the Weber of *The Protestant Ethic and the Spirit of Capitalism* (published in 1904–05), as well as Albert Hirschman, who uses it in particular in *The Passions and the Interests*.[172]

During the 1970s, Boltanski was a close colleague of Bourdieu, with whom he wrote several important texts – in particular, a seminal article entitled 'La production de l'idéologie dominante', published in the journal founded by Bourdieu, *Actes de la recherche en sciences sociales*, and recently reprinted with a new preface by Boltanski.[173] This text anticipated Boltanski's subsequent work on capitalist ideology. The sociological tradition founded by Bourdieu has produced important work in the last decade, particularly after Bourdieu's death in 2002. Thus, one of his best-known inheritors, Loïc Wacquant, professor at the University of California, Berkeley, has produced a theory of 'neo-liberal penal policy' and shown that prison systems throughout the world serve to manage the poverty generated by neo-liberalism and to domesticate the workforce in the labour market. Wacquant has also done important

170   Luc Boltanski and Eve Chiapello, *The New Spirit of Capitalism*, trans. Gregory Elliott, London and New York: Verso, 2005.

171   Luc Boltanski, *On Critique: A Sociology of Emancipation*, trans. Gregory Elliott, Cambridge: Polity, 2011.

172   A.O. Hirschmann, *The Passions and the Interests: Political Arguments for Capitalism before Its Triumph*, Princeton: Princeton University Press, 1977.

173   Boltanski's most recent discussion of his career can be found in 'Critique sociale et émancipation. Entretien avec Laurent Jeanpierre', in *Penser à gauche. Figures de la pensée critique aujourd'hui*, Paris: Amsterdam, 2011.

comparative work aimed at identifying the differences and similarities between the US ghetto and the French *banlieues*.[174] In a different area, in 1999 the sociologist of literature Pascale Casanova published *La République mondiale des lettres*, a book that attracted widespread attention. In it she describes the emergence and functioning of the world literary field, concerning herself with the diffusion of modernism, the relationship between literature and nationalism, and instances of literary consecration like the Nobel Prize.

Boltanski distanced himself from Bourdieu towards the end of the 1980s. This break was made in *De la justification. Les économies de la grandeur*, co-authored with Laurent Thévenot. Its authors break with Bourdieu's critical sociology and seek to develop a sociology *of* critique – that is, a sociology of the ordinary critical operations of social actors.[175] The 1980s and 90s saw North American pragmatism (William James, John Dewey, C. S. Pierce, G. H. Mead) grow in influence in France, as an after-effect of the decline of structuralism and Marxism there. *De la justification* bears the stamp of that influence.[176] A decade earlier, Boltanski devoted a work to the sociology of *cadres* (*cadres* is more or less synonymous in the French context with managers) entitled *Les Cadres. La formation d'un groupe social*. It was influenced by E. P. Thompson's 'constructivist' conception of social classes (to which we shall return), and may even be regarded as the first work in France to evince that influence. For Boltanski, *cadres* are not a class 'in-itself', one of the sociologist's objectives being to overcome the opposition between class 'in-itself' and class 'for-itself'. The emergence of *cadres* in France in the 1930s involved a labour of 'construction' and 'grouping' by various institutions, such as the state (via, for example, the official statistics of INSEE, which counted the category of *cadre*), the trade unions of *cadres*, a specialist press addressed to *cadres*, the integration of *cadres* into wage negotiations with unions representing different categories, and so on. The problem of *cadres* would continue to be a concern of Boltanski's, since the theses developed in *The New Spirit of Capitalism* are based on an analysis of training manuals for *cadres* in neo-liberal firms. For him these manuals contain the quintessence of the new spirit of capitalism, just as ascetic Protestantism contains the quintessence of the original capitalism analyzed by Weber.

One of the contributions made by *The New Spirit of Capitalism* is that it put the word 'capitalism' back into circulation in France. The term had almost

174   Loïc Wacquant, *Urban Outcasts: A Comparative Sociology of Advanced Marginality*, Cambridge: Polity, 2008.

175   Luc Boltanski and Laurent Thévenot, *On Justification: Economies of Worth*, trans. Catherine Porter, Princeton: Princeton University Press, 2006.

176   On the reception of pragmatism in France, see François Dosse, *L'Empire du sens. L'humanisation des sciences humaines*, Paris: La Découverte, 1997.

completely vanished from the public sphere during the neo-liberal decades of the 1980s and 90s, the naturalization of the system ('there is no alternative') having entailed the disappearance of the word referring to it. Boltanski and Chiapello define capitalism in minimal fashion as the 'unlimited accumulation of capital by formally peaceful means'.[177] It is a profoundly absurd system. The 'unlimited' character of accumulation is without foundation or justification: why should it be necessary for capital to be infinitely accumulated, given that human needs are by definition limited? Aristotle called the unlimited accumulation of goods as an end in itself 'chrematistics'. He condemned it and contrasted it with 'economics', or accumulation for a purpose.[178] The essence of capitalism, affirm Boltanski and Chiapello, is chrematistic.

Its absurd character means that capitalism must find something outside itself with which to stimulate individuals' engagement in accumulation. Alternatively put, there is no capitalism without a spirit of capitalism, which supplies people with reasons for conforming to the behaviour required by the system. What Boltanski and Chiapello call 'spirit' of capitalism is the ideology that grounds and justifies engagement in capitalist activity. Obviously, whether one is a wage-earner, employer, or middle manager is not irrelevant to the way in which this spirit operates on the self.

The spirit of capitalism evolves historically. The mobilization of individuals in contemporary globalized capitalism manifestly does not involve the same cognitive and moral content as a century ago. Two principal spirits of capitalism can be identified in the course of history. The first presided over the second half of the nineteenth century. It was embodied by the bourgeois entrepreneur, the conquering captain of industry who took the risk of investing and generated innovation. The mode of organization of firms was paternalist (the entrepreneur was a father figure), the wage-earner's submission to it brought him a certain security in return, while the transmission of capital occurred on a familial basis – hence the importance assigned to class endogamy and the fear of capital being squandered by the erratic behaviour of offspring.

A second spirit is said to have emerged between the 1930s and the 1960s. Its premises were already perceived and analyzed in 'Americanism and Fordism' (1934) by Gramsci, an author to whom Boltanski and Chiapello do not refer, curiously enough, whereas the affinities between his concept of 'hegemony' and their concept of 'spirit' are manifest. (Moreover, Gramsci knew the Italian translation of Weber's *The Protestant Ethic and the Spirit of*

---

177   Boltanski and Chiapello, *The New Spirit of Capitalism*, p. 4.
178   For this distinction see also Jean Baechler, *Le Capitalisme*, 2 vols, Paris: Gallimard, 1995.

Capitalism.) The size of capitalist firms increased markedly compared with the preceding period. A strict Taylorist division of labour was established, and the figures of the rational director and the planning engineer replaced that of the conquering entrepreneur. It was at this stage that the separation between the ownership of capital and the management of firms grew, leading to the establishment of what in the 1960s John Kenneth Galbraith called the 'technostructure'. Boltanski's previous work on the emergence of *cadres* in French capitalism in the first half of the twentieth century is bound up with this new structure of accumulation.

The third spirit is the current spirit: the 'new' spirit of capitalism. It derives from criticism of the previous spirit during the 1960s and 70s, especially around 1968. At this time two types of critique converged to challenge the system: the social critique and the artistic critique.[179] The former, particularly salient in the labour movement, criticizes the material poverty caused by capitalism, as well as the egotism or immorality of those who benefit from it. The novels of Emile Zola immediately come to mind as an example of this form of critique. It demands a more egalitarian distribution of wealth, or a distribution of value added more advantageous to labour. In its radical versions it calls for the overthrow of capitalism. Social critique is a critique of 'exploitation' as an essentially socio-economic phenomenon.

For its part, the artistic critique indicts capitalism for inauthenticity. It challenges the loss of meaning and the standardization of behaviour generated by it. This form of critique, more 'qualitative' than the preceding one (in truth, the quantitative and qualitative have always co-existed in the labour movement), has its origins in bohemian, artistic and student lifestyles. In his work on Flaubert, Bourdieu had already shown how the artistic field was formed in the nineteenth century by inverting the values prevalent in the economic field; or how a 'disinterested' attitude towards the material aspects of existence was the converse of the bourgeois utilitarianism of the age.[180] Rather than exploitation, what is challenged here is therefore alienation.

These two forms of critique have existed since the origins of capitalism, but they have frequently developed separately, with one taking precedence over the other, or one (or both) temporarily disappearing. The potency of the challenge to capitalism around May 1968 consisted in the fact that the two critiques converged. To confine ourselves to the French 1968, it is clear that this event derived its power from the fact that it was both the largest workers' strike in the

---

179   Boltanski and Chiapello's source of inspiration for the distinction is Carlos Grana, *Bohemian versus Bourgeois: French Society and the French Man of Letters in the Nineteenth Century*, New York: Basic, 1964.

180   Pierre Bourdieu, *The Rules of Art: Genesis and Structure of the Literary Field*, trans. Susan Emanuel, Cambridge: Polity, 1996.

history of France and an unprecedented student mobilization, as well as being inseparable from anti-colonialism and feminism.[181]

The critique to which capitalism was subjected compelled its spirit to mutate. It is always (or largely, at any rate) on account of the criticisms made of it that capitalism develops. In some respects this brings Boltanski's conception of the system close to that of Italian *operaismo*. In the latter, it will be recalled, the working class is on the offensive and capital – a 'parasitic' instance – compelled to develop under the blows inflicted on it. According to Boltanski and Chiapello, this is what explains the 'isomorphism' between the structures of capitalism in any epoch and the forms of critique directed at them. The organizations of the labour movement in the early twentieth century resembled capitalist firms in many respects: they were massive, marked by a hierarchical division of labour, and pervaded by a 'positivist' ideology. When the social and artistic critiques challenged mid-century bureaucratized capitalism, they conjointly produced a critique of the parties and trade unions of the 'old' labour movement – the critique represented by the New Left of which we have spoken.

The neo-liberal capitalism – Boltanski and Chiapello call it 'connexionist' – that emerged during the 1970s is a reticular capitalism, not a bureaucratized one. Its globalization is made possible by the new transport and communications technology. It breaks with the strict Taylorist division of labour, replacing the conception/execution (intellectual/manual labour) pair by integrated, autonomous teams and the logic of 'quality control'. Flexibility, within the firm as well as in the labour market, is the key word of this capitalism. Knowledge plays a crucial role in this neo-capitalism, with capital and the state increasingly being 'knowledgeable'. Because of mass unemployment, this capitalism cannot provide wage-earners with the kind of security afforded them during the *trente glorieuses*. Transforming this defect into an advantage, however, it promotes career mobility and consequently only hires wage-earners for a fixed term in the context of 'projects'. Yet career instability makes motivating wage-earners more difficult, since they no longer have reasons to invest emotionally in the firm.

Boltanski and Chiapello's critical argument is that with this new spirit capitalism has recuperated the 'libertarian' demands of 1968. More precisely, it has de-legitimated the social critique by presenting wage rises at a time of globalized competition as unrealistic and adopted for its own purposes the values underlying the artistic critique: fluidity, autonomy, creativity, hostility to bureaucracy and so on. These formerly bohemian values are now those that inspire any self-respecting manager. The bureaucratic hierarchies of yesteryear are regarded as inefficient. The individual's flourishing in the firm is one of the latter's objectives,

---

181   For a reflection on 1968 see Kristin Ross, *May '68 and Its Afterlives*, Chicago: University of Chicago Press, 2002.

effective economic action even having this flourishing as a precondition. The 'start-ups' or 'dot-coms' of the 1990s, or a transnational like Google, illustrate capitalism's recuperation of the libertarian values of 1968.

In an interview published in 2009, ten years after the publication of *The New Spirit of Capitalism*, Boltanski critically reviewed the book's theses. According to him, in the 2000s we have witnessed an aggressive return of Taylorism and work discipline.[182] Not that the 'new spirit of capitalism' was a pure illusion. It did indeed exist, but only for a short time, and its influence was geographically confined to the most 'advanced' capitalism. On a planetary scale, in China or Brazil for example, the classical figure of the Taylorized wage-earner has always predominated. The long-standing crisis in which capitalism has been immersed since the 1970s, and more so since the financial crisis of 2008, has got the better of the 'libertarian' spirit that presided for a decade.

---

182 'La révolte n'est pas un plaisir solitaire. Entretien avec Luc Boltanski et Olivier Besancenot', *Contretemps*, new series, no. 1, 2009.

CHAPTER FIVE

Subjects

This chapter is about the 'subject of emancipation' – that is, the actors who might be plausible vectors of social transformation. As we have said, this question remains a burning one and the candidates for the role are more numerous than ever. The terms in which it is formulated are markedly different from what they once were. But the same problematic runs through contemporary critical theories and those of the 1960s and 70s.

It is important to note that at the time when the organized working class was cast as the principal operator of historical change, the actors involved were plural. Our intention is not to lend credence to some sharp historical break between the period prior to the 1960s, supposedly characterized by an unqualified centrality of the working class, and subsequent years, when society suddenly became 'complex' and demands proliferated and their source diversified. The social world has always been complex. The relative centrality of the working class was, on the one hand, the result of its demographic preponderance and, on the other, the product of a political hegemony constructed over time – since the nineteenth century – by the organizations representing it. What gradually came undone from the second half of the 1950s (or was destroyed, since the neoliberal offensive contributed to this development) was the combination of these two elements. The industrial working class was fragmented, while formerly auxiliary subaltern sectors made their voice heard independently. The outcome was the situation of indeterminacy we are still in today, which is prompting more sophisticated theoretical accounts.

EQUALITY AS EVENT

Jacques Rancière, Alain Badiou and Slavoj Žižek are among the best-known contemporary critical thinkers. Rancière's *La Haine de la démocratie*, Badiou's *De quoi Sarkozy est-il le nom?* and *L'Hypothèse communiste*, and most of Žižek's works – for example, *Welcome to the Desert of the Real!*, whose title is inspired by the film *Matrix* (itself inspired by Baudrillard's theses)[1] – figure prominently in the list of best-selling works in the social sciences in recent years. These are

---

1 See Razmig Keucheyan, 'Les communauté des fans de *Matrix* sur Internet: une étude de sociologie de la connaissance', *L'Année sociologique*, no. 56, 2006.

the most accessible texts in difficult oeuvres. They pertain to their authors' specialism – philosophy – or (to adopt a phrase from Badiou) 'philosophy under the condition of the political'.[2] The size of the readership enjoyed by these three thinkers indicates that present-day critical theories are interacting with some sections of society – in particular, no doubt, those that are most active politically.

At the point of its transformation into poststructuralism, structuralism made a 'turn to the event' – that is, it was led to take the contingent character of social phenomena increasingly into account. It can be argued that this turn was begun by Foucault in his inaugural lecture at the Collège de France in 1970.[3] Thereafter it was notably continued in the oeuvres of Derrida and Deleuze, both of them critics of the 'totalizing' tendencies of structuralism and Marxism.[4]

Rancière and Badiou are products of this history. They are among the youngest representatives of the generation of French philosophers of the 1960s and 70s. Time will tell if it is appropriate to regard them as such, or instead as the first representatives of a new generation of thinkers, distinct from that of Foucault, Althusser, Barthes, Deleuze and Derrida. However that may be, Rancière's theory of the 'part of those with no part' and Badiou's of the 'event' cannot be understood without the thunderclap represented by 1968 and its theoretical effects. The same can be said of Žižek, albeit more indirectly. Younger than Rancière and Badiou, and Slovenian by origin, he pertains to the contemporary French intellectual context by virtue of having studied in France and been influenced by certain of its representatives – in particular, Lacan. But Žižek also belongs to the world of eastern Europe, having been a dissident in his country during the 'socialist' era.

Jacques Rancière: The 'Part of Those with No Part'

Rancière's oeuvre has mainly been concerned with three areas: political theory, the philosophy of education and aesthetics. Like any major oeuvre, however, his disrupts existing categories and leaves no area untouched. A striking feature of Rancière's philosophical work is the innovative connection it makes between problematics that have hitherto remained separate. The notion of the 'distribution of the sensible' developed by him in the domain of aesthetics is thus bound up with what he calls 'police' in the political sphere, allowing him to identify

---

2   See Alain Badiou, *Metapolitics*, trans. Jason Barker, London and New York: Verso, 2005, chapter 1.

3   Alex Callinicos, *The Resources of Critique*, Cambridge: Polity, 2006, p. 84.

4   See Martin Jay, *Marxism and Totality: The Adventures of a Concept from Lukács to Habermas*, Berkeley: University of California Press, 1984, Epilogue ('The Challenge of Post-structuralism').

subterranean links between aesthetics and politics. Likewise, the pedagogical principles he sets out in *Le Maître ignorant* ultimately refer to his axiomatic of the 'equality of intelligence', whose potential political implications can readily be imagined.[5]

Like Balibar, Rancière was originally a follower of Althusser. He was one of the authors of *Lire le Capital*, to which he contributed a chapter entitled 'Le concept de critique et la critique de l'économie politique des *Manuscrits de 1844 au Capital*'. In 1974, Rancière published *La Leçon d'Althusser*, in which he broke with his teacher.[6] The following year he founded the philosophico-political collective and journal *Les Révoltes logiques*. The name was inspired by Rimbaud, whose poem 'Démocratie' (in *Illuminations*) has soldiers in the service of the 'most monstrous exploitation', military and industrial, say: 'We shall massacre the logical revolts.' In these years Rancière, like Badiou, was close to Maoism. However, he was a member of the *Gauche prolétarienne*, whereas the latter belonged to the *Union des communistes de France marxiste-léniniste* (UCFML). Since then Rancière has become the author of a prolific oeuvre, some of which combines (in a different way from Foucault) philosophy and archival material, like *La Nuit des prolétaires*.[7] Other texts are more directly theoretical, like *Aux bords du politique*, *La Mésentente. Politique et philosophie*, or *La Haine de la démocratie*.

Rancière's rupture with Althusser occurred over the issue of the relationship between knowledge and politics. This problem is ubiquitous in Rancière's oeuvre. Althusser's structuralist and 'theoreticist' Marxism distinguishes between 'science' and 'ideology'. The masses are victims of ideology, whose content can vary historically, but which is a constant of history. Only the party and the intellectual equipped with Marxist theory are in a position to strip its veil and access the real movement of history. This assumes that without their input, the masses would remain ignorant of reality, of their own condition. Althusser radicalizes an idea present – in a more political form – in Lenin, according to which consciousness of its historical destiny must be instilled in the working class from without.

In differentiating between science and ideology, the author of *Pour Marx* renewed in twentieth-century conditions an ancient opposition between *episteme* and *doxa* that goes back to Plato. *Doxa* refers to the fallacious commonplace opinion held by the majority, while *episteme* refers to rational knowledge. In

---

5   Jacques Rancière, *The Ignorant Schoolmaster: Five Lessons in Intellectual Emancipation*, trans. Kristin Ross, Stanford: Stanford University Press, 1991.

6   Jacques Rancière, *Althusser's Lesson*, trans. Emiliano Batista, London and New York: Continuum, 2011.

7   Jacques Rancière, *Proletarian Nights: The Workers' Dream in Nineteenth-Century France*, trans. John Drury, London and New York: Verso, 2012.

Plato only the philosopher is capable of making the transition from the one to the other – one reason why the author of the *Republic* was favourable to the philosopher's accession to political power (or to the practice of philosophy by those who held power). In Althusser, the role of the philosopher is played by the party and the Marxist intellectual. But in both cases the problem and the proposed solution are the same. In modern thought, the opposition between *doxa* and *episteme* is present not only in Althusser, but also in the sociology of Bourdieu, on whom Rancière has written a text entitled 'Le sociologue roi', alluding to Plato's 'philosopher king'.[8] For Bourdieu (and Durkheim before him), the sociologist makes an 'epistemological break' with 'preconceptions' – that is, with common sense (connoted negatively) and, by ignoring current opinions, accedes to the objectivity of the social world. In criticizing the avatars of the *doxa/episteme* couple through the ages and across disciplines, Rancière reveals himself to be an anti-Platonist. This separates him from Badiou, who situates his philosophy in a line of descent from Plato.

The distinction between *doxa* and *episteme* has as its corollary mastery – that is, the status and figure of the master. Be he philosopher, sociologist, or Marxist (whether individual or collective – the party), the master is the one who knows how to separate proven knowledge from fallacious belief. Therewith he is in a position to say to those who do not know that they do not know and what they do not know. Thus, having grasped the historical dynamic in its essence, the Marxist theorist is capable of revealing to the masses the truth of their own condition. The master is the one who inserts himself in the gap between *doxa* and *episteme* and derives power from it. Against Althusser and against any mastery, Rancière advances the axiomatic of the 'equality of intelligence'. 'Axiomatic' is to be taken literally: the equality of intelligence, according to Rancière, is neither an empirical state of affairs nor an (attainable or ideal) objective that societies assign themselves. It is a principle – a presupposition – that represents a precondition of any emancipatory action or thought. As Joseph Jacotot, the nineteenth-century theorist of intellectual emancipation whose pedagogical conceptions are the subject of *Le Maître ignorant*, believed, an (ignorant) schoolmaster can teach what he does not know on condition that he creates in pupils an awareness of their intellectual autonomy. It is never a question of replacing the ignorance of the pupil by the knowledge of the master, but of proceeding from knowledge to knowledge. The axiomatic of the 'equality of intelligence' has its starting-point in the abolition of the difference between *doxa* and *episteme* and thereby renders the position of mastery untenable.

---

8   Jacques Rancière, *The Philosopher and His Poor*, ed. Andrew Parker and trans. John Drury, Corinne Oster and Andrew Parker, Durham (NC): Duke University Press, 2003.

What is true of the equality of intelligence also applies to equality *tout court*. Rancière develops a distinction between *police* and *politics*. The former refers to the existing social order – that is, the set of means (often unconscious or implicit) employed to stabilize and preserve the unequal distribution of status and wealth (of 'parts', as Rancière says) in a social body. These means can be physical or psychological; what is ordinarily called 'police' (policemen) is only one component of them. 'Police' is always ultimately based on a 'distribution of the sensible'. In a given society it defines the visible and the invisible, what can be said and what cannot be said, and determines 'that this speech is understood as discourse and another as noise' – as illegitimate speech.[9] The 'distribution of the sensible' consists in a 'world-view' underlying and legitimating the social order. This concept indicates that in Rancière's view a form of aesthetics – in a broad sense irreducible to the artistic regime obtaining in the relevant era – underlies any social order.

'Politics', on the other hand, refers to phases of contestation of 'police'. Such challenges arise when those 'with no part' – those who are not counted in the social order – burst onto the stage of history. This irruption is named by Rancière the 'part of those with no part' – in other words, those who had no part in the initial count. The 'part of those with no part' is in itself empty, since those without a part precisely have no part. It is filled with a political content according to historical circumstances. The appearance of the 'part of those with no part' is a potentiality inscribed – in 'ghostly' form – in the functioning of any 'police'. Rancière says of this potentiality that it is politics itself. The principle cited by those 'with no part' to assert their presence is equality, which they invoke against the 'wrong' of which they are victims. From this we can deduce that for Rancière politics and equality are one and the same thing.

But there is more. While those without a part demonstrate and disrupt the social order, they are not content to demand the part owed them. The part of those with no part is not one part among others, which could reasonably be incorporated into the already existing count of parts. Those without a part demand all parts and are identified with the community as a whole. This is a crucial characteristic of the democratic event according to Rancière:

> It is in the name of the wrong done them by the other parties that the people identify with the whole of the community. Whoever has no part – the poor of ancient times, the third estate, the modern proletariat – cannot in fact have any part other than all or nothing . . . The people are not one class among others. They are the

9   Jacques Rancière, *Disagreement: Politics and Philosophy*, trans. Julie Rose, Minneapolis: University of Minnesota Press, 1998, p. 29. See also Jacques Rancière, *The Politics of Aesthetics: The Distribution of the Sensible*, trans. Gabriel Rockhill, London and New York: Continuum, 2004, p. 12.

class of the wrong that harms the community and establishes it as a 'community' of the just and the unjust.[10]

On account of the wrong done them, when they appear, those without a part start to speak for the whole community. It must be believed that this wrong gives them the right – that is, that it expresses something essential in connection with the latter. At the time of the French Revolution, the Third Estate did not confine itself to demanding its share of wealth and sovereignty. It rid itself of advocates of the social order and invented modern sovereignty by placing 'the people' at its centre. Another example is that the line from the *Internationale* does not say 'We are nothing, let us be *something*', but precisely 'We are nothing, let us be *all*'. In suddenly becoming audible and visible, those without a part undo the current distribution of the sensible and commit the community to a new distribution. For that, the very foundations of the community have to be called into question.

A key element is that the people are *anyone*. Were Rancière less libertarian and more statist, he might adopt Lenin's watchword that 'any cook should be able to govern the country'. The people are not defined by any empirical or sociological characteristics. (For Rancière, sociology is situated on the side of police – that is, the allegedly scientific count of social groups and the parts due them.) It does not refer to any specific section of the population. Certainly, it is composed of those without a part, who are rarely recruited from the ranks of the dominant classes. But there is such an irreducible distance between the position of individuals in the social structure and their practice of politics that political behaviour can never be deduced from this position. In this sense, says Rancière, the people always differs from itself. Without this difference, the administration of things would replace the government of men, as the Saint-Simonian formula adopted by Engels puts it. The role allocated contingency in politics by Rancière indicates the scale of his break with the most scientistic forms of Marxism, of which Althusserian structuralism is one of the last major examples.

The distinction between police and politics is often vague. What Marxists call the 'proletariat' refers, for example, to an actually existing component of society and a (revolutionary) politics. As a result, 'proletariat' is an indissolubly empirical and political concept. The same goes for most politically operative concepts, whose nature is dual. We suggested in the previous chapter that the success of Hardt and Negri's 'multitude' derived from the fact that it captures concrete processes at work in contemporary societies (particularly the fragmentation of the dominated classes) and contains a political project.

Rancière proposes an aetiology of the degeneration to which politics is liable. It is sometimes transformed into 'archi-politics'. This term refers to the

---

10   Rancière, *Disagreement*, p. 9.

temptation to render a community identical to itself by abolishing the contra-dictions it secretes. Totalitarianism, or extreme forms of contemporary 'communitarianism', pertain to this trend. 'Para-politics' is another danger lying in wait for democracy. It refers to the 'de-politicization' of problems, as when neo-liberalism – it was in the neo-liberal context of the 1980s and 90s that Rancière produced his main works – claims to abolish the conflictual dimen-sion of politics and resolve problems in what is allegedly the only possible rational way. A third potential deviation is 'meta-politics'. Unlike 'para-politics', it recognizes the existence of irreducible conflicts in the community. However, it claims that they are external to politics 'in the last instance'. When Marxism argues that the economy is both the source and the solution of apparently polit-ical problems, it engages in meta-politics.

The intrusion of politics in police sets in motion a process that Rancière calls 'disidentification':

> Any subjectification is a disidentification, removal from the naturalness of a place, the opening up of a subject space where anyone can be counted since it is the space where those of no account are counted, where a connection is made between having a part and having no part.[11]

The notion of 'disidentification' attests to the importance assigned identities in contemporary political theory in general and critical thought in particular. In Rancière, it refers to the critique of 'naturalness': the idea that any individual possesses certain social properties by virtue of her place in society and that she must stick to it. Politics is the opposite of identity; it is what puts existing identi-ties in crisis and, by triggering a process of subjectification – the formation of a 'subject' – opens up a space of possibilities, both individual and collective. There is no subject without a distanciation from identities. On this point Rancière concurs with a thesis formulated by the queer theorist Judith Butler. Disidenti-fication refers to concrete political practices – a 'repertoire of action', as sociologists would say. A typical case of 'disidentification' analyzed by Kristin Ross – Rancière's English translator – is the 'social journeys' undertaken around 1968 by revolutionary students to the world of labour and the 'implantation' of a number of them in factories.[12] They were part of the students' desire, made possible by the climate of general disidentification around May 1968, to break with their identity as 'students' and re-identify with different social categories for political ends.[13]

---

11   Ibid., p. 36.
12   See Kristin Ross, *May '68 and Its Afterlives*, Chicago: University of Chicago Press, 2002.
13   On implantation and disidentification, see Robert Linhart, *The Assembly Line*, trans. Margaret Crosland, London: John Calder, 1981.

According to Rancière, equality and its effects are universal. One of the points in common between the three thinkers dealt with in this section is their desire to reactivate a form of universalism in politics. Universalism enjoys rather a bad press today in critical thinking, but also more generally. It is assimilated by what are probably the dominant tendencies within the Left to the 'imperialist' will of the West to impose its point of view on the rest of the world under cover of universality. What is dominant within critical theories is a form of 'multiculturalism' and 'minority thinking' that stresses the relativity of historical phenomena. For his part, Rancière remains firmly attached to the universal, but a universality that is always (in his words) 'local' and 'singular'. Comparing movements in solidarity with Algerian independence in the 1950s and 60s with the relative absence of support for the populations massacred and displaced in Bosnia in the 1990s, he notes that in the first case concrete political links had been created between Algerian and French militants. Each set of militants had recognized in the 'cause of the other' part of their own cause;[14] and international solidarity had thus come to be embodied in concrete political forms.[15]

Thus, Rancière asserts,

[a] political subject is not a group that 'becomes aware' of itself, finds its voice, imposes its weight on society. It is an operator that connects and disconnects different areas, regions, identities, functions, and capacities existing in the configuration of a given experience.[16]

A political subject is always an event. It is neither a social class, nor a sex, nor an 'ethnic' community, even if it can be based on collectives of this type. Nor is it a form of the 'social bond'. A subject consists in the emergence – spontaneous and, in many respects, inexplicable (other than by very general factors like 'wrong') – of equality, and in its disappearance once a new 'distribution of the sensible' has been established. In Rancière's view, a durable politics is a contradiction in terms. From this a simple conclusion follows: politics and democracy are rare.

Alain Badiou: Event, Fidelity, Subject

In some respects, Badiou's thinking is similar to Rancière's. The itinerary of the two philosophers is comparable, running from an initial proximity to Althusserian structuralism – preceded in Badiou's case by a Sartrean moment, whose influence can still be felt today – to a distancing from its most determinist

---

14   One of the striking essays in *On the Shores of Politics*, trans. Liz Heron, London and New York: Verso, 1995, is entitled 'The Cause of the Other'.

15   Rancière, *The Disagreement*, p. 138.

16   Ibid., p. 40.

aspects and a growing insistence on the share of contingency in political proc-esses.[17] Naturally, the event represented by May 1968 weighed heavily in this transition. Badiou's distinction between 'being' and 'event' coincides in certain respects with the contrast between 'police' and 'politics' formulated by Rancière. For all that, Badiou and Rancière are in disagreement on several levels. For example, the former identifies with Platonism – a Platonism that is certainly sometimes disconcerting, but which at the very least characteristically engages in a critique of common sense and the reign of 'opinion'. Rancière does not defend common sense, which in his view forms an integral part of 'police'. However, he does not mobilize against it so highly charged a concept as 'truth', which Badiou has no hesitation in doing. The latter makes a distinction between 'truth' and 'knowledge' that is not without echoes of the Althusserian opposi-tion between 'science' and 'ideology'.

Badiou is a philosophical system-builder. Among contemporary critical thinkers he is unquestionably the one who has adopted this classical task of philosophy most unapologetically. The doctrine elaborated by Badiou is a theory of the 'event'. A theory of great complexity – there can be no question of doing it full justice here – it is laid out in two imposing works, *L'Être et l'événement* (1988) and *Logiques des mondes* (2006), to which should be added *Théorie du sujet*. It also runs through various more thematic works, generally less voluminous and more accessible, like *Saint Paul. La fondation de l'universalisme* (1997), *Abrégé de métapolitique* (1998), *L'Éthique. Essai sur la conscience du mal* (1993), and *Le Siècle* (2005).

Badiou's theory of the event rests on four main categories: being, event, subject and fidelity. In the beginning was being. At its most basic level, it is composed of pure unorganized 'multiples'. These are not 'elementary particles' of the kind studied by modern physics or invoked by classical materialism. They are situated 'beneath' matter, in the sense that what are involved are not real enti-ties but formal properties of being. For Badiou, the fundamental ontology is none other than mathematics, which means that at the most elementary level, being has a formal mode of existence.

'Multiples' acquire an initial degree of ontological consistency when they are structured, or 'counted for one', as Badiou puts it. They are then transformed into 'situations', which are structured 'presentations' of multiples. The consist-ency of reality is consequently dependent on counting operations. Such operations are performed against the background of an original 'vacuum', since the multiples counted are not real entities. They only become such when counted. There exist countless examples of 'situations' – French society is one,

---

17   Badiou's relationship to Althusser is more complex than is conveyed by these few words. See Badiou, *Metapolitics*.

modern art another, the solar system a third. The set of current situations refers to a 'state of the situation'. Badiou plays here on the double meaning of the word 'state', which refers both to a 'structure' and a 'state' in the political sense. It will be recalled that Rancière likewise uses the word 'police' in deliberately ambiguous fashion to refer to a 'distribution of the sensible' and the forces of law and order that ensure its maintenance. From a certain standpoint, Badiou's doctrine may be regarded as a radical form of nominalism. Reality exists only to the extent that it is counted or named. The state of the situation is amenable to being an object of positive knowledge. The latter is situated alongside being; it participates in the counting of its parts.

It can happen that being is suddenly interrupted by an event. To adopt a formula of Nietzsche's used by Badiou in connection with the twentieth century, but whose scope is more general, the event 'breaks the history of the world in two'. Cases of events are diverse, from an amorous encounter, to the discovery of the structure of DNA, to Malevitch's *White on White*, to the Russian Revolution. More precisely, there are four domains in which 'truth procedures' are liable to arise: politics, the sciences, the arts and love. In each of them, the event is absolutely heterogeneous with respect to being; it is unforeseeable and suspends the counting of the multiples that constituted it. The event is on the side of non-being, of what is not counted in the state of the situation. As Badiou says, 'it is of the essence of the event not to be preceded by any sign, and to catch us unawares with its grace, regardless of our vigilance.'[18] The French Revolution is a typical example of an event. We know the details of the processes – economic, political, cultural – at work in the years or decades preceding it. We can mobilize them to explain the conditions in which it occurred. At the same time, this event remains irreducible to the knowledge we possess in connection with it, even retrospectively. For knowledge is on the side of counting the former situation, whereas the event is by definition 'supernumerary'; its essence is to be uncounted. In this sense an event is always more than the sum of the processes it comprises.

Badiou has sometimes been criticized for the 'miraculous' character of his theory of the event.[19] Žižek has even argued that religious revelation is his 'unavowed paradigm' – that is, the model that has secretly governed his work. Badiou's recurrent references to Saint Paul and the road to Damascus lend weight to this hypothesis. Badiou's event is a creator of causality, but it does not itself proceed from any assignable causality. A major inconvenience of this

---

18   Alain Badiou, *Saint Paul: The Foundation of Universalism*, trans. Ray Brassier, Stanford: Stanford University Press, 2003, p. 111.

19   See Daniel Bensaïd, 'Alain Badiou and the Miracle of the Event', in *Think Again, Alain Badiou and the Future of Philosophy*, Peter Hallward, ed., London and New York: Continuum, 2004.

thesis is that it renders any strategic reflection impossible. However uncertain, strategy presupposes opting for a course of action on the basis of processes that are in train. To the extent that the event is supernumerary, any choice of this kind is in principle ungrounded. Badiou's theory of the event is a further example of a characteristic of contemporary critical thinking we have already referred to – namely, the weakness or absence of strategic thinking. However, it is important to indicate that while Badiou's event arises *ex nihilo*, the 'nothing' in question is not situated in some 'beyond'. It is internal to the situation that precedes the event, which is always inconsistent or unstable because it rests on an original vacuum. Thus, although it was not foreseeable, the event of the French Revolution revealed the 'truth' of the *ancien régime* in the sense that the profound inequalities characteristic of the latter contained its seeds.

The 'subject' proceeds from the event. It is one possible consequence of it, which does not mean that it follows mechanically from it. Peter Hallward, author of a standard work on Badiou's thought, defines Badiou's subject as 'an individual transfigured by the truth she proclaims'.[20] The individual exposed to an event is transformed into a subject – that is, she undergoes a process of 'subjectivation' under the condition of the event. For Badiou, subjectivation has (at least) two characteristics. The first is that it is collective. More precisely, Badiou argues that the subjectivation deriving from a political event is always collective. In other domains where 'truth procedures' occur, such as the arts or sciences, it might not be.[21] Moreover, subjectivation does not presuppose any pre-established human essence. It is subsequent to the event and involves a decision on the individual's part to remain faithful to the event. This is what Badiou calls the definition of man as 'programme' – that is, as always open and to come.[22] Here Badiou re-joins the positions of his two masters, Sartre and Althusser. The former's assertion that 'existence precedes essence' consists in believing that human beings construct their own essence when they are already in the world. For Badiou, this construction is carried out in the shadow of a founding event. The conception of man as programme also refers to Althusser's 'theoretical anti-humanism', which represents a radical critique of humanist essentialism (what Badiou dubs 'animal humanism'). Thus, argues Badiou, 'Man is realized not as a fulfilment or as an outcome, but as absent to himself, torn away from what he is, and it is this tearing away which is the basis of every adventurous greatness.'[23]

20   Peter Hallward, *Badiou: A Subject to Truth*, Minneapolis: University of Minnesota Press, 2003, p. 122.

21   Badiou, *Metapolitics*, p. 142.

22   Alain Badiou, *The Century*, trans. Alberto Toscano, Cambridge: Polity, 2007, chapter 13.

23   Ibid., p. 92.

A crucial aspect of Badiou's doctrine is that the identification of an event can only be made subjectively, from inside it. This implies that the existence of an event qua event, and not a mere series of causally intelligible facts, is always uncertain. It needs to be completed by a necessarily subjective act of naming. This act of naming is what Badiou calls an 'interpretative intervention', which he defines as 'any procedure by which a multiple is recognized as an event'.[24] This is where the fourth basic category of Badiou's system – fidelity – comes in:

> An event is never shared, even if the truth we gather from it is universal, because its recognition *as event* is simply at one with the political decision. A politics is a hazardous, militant, and always partially undivided fidelity to evental singularity under a self-authorizing prescription . . . [T]he point from which a politics can be thought – which permits, even after the event, the seizure of its truth – is that of its actors, and not its spectators.[25]

The notion of 'fidelity' is ubiquitous in Badiou. It situates him in a tradition of theological thought, sometimes characterized as 'fideism', which regards the act of faith as constitutive in the relationship to transcendence. Tertullian's '*Credo quia absurdum*' is its most radical expression, asserting that belief in God is more authentic the more reason opposes it. Among the thinkers who belong to this tradition are Pascal, Kierkegaard and Paul Claudel, three authors frequently cited by Badiou. Once fidelity is regarded as central, so too is its opposite – namely, apostasy or renunciation. During a conference on *Logiques des mondes*, Badiou stated that the denial of May 1968 by a number of its protagonists was the real trigger of his reflection on the event.[26]

For Badiou, a genuine subject exists only in fidelity to an event. This implies that many individuals will never be authentic subjects, either because they will not have had the opportunity to be exposed to an event, or because, having been exposed to one, they have not demonstrated fidelity towards it. This is the most aristocratic or Nietzschean dimension of Badiou's thought, which reserves the status of subject for a small number of individuals. There is no shortage of commentators on his work, from the Right and Left alike, who criticize him for this aristocratism.[27] However, it should be noted that for Badiou every person, whatever their origin, is capable of being seized by an event and undergoing a

---

24   Alain Badiou, *Being and Event*, trans. Oliver Feltham, London and New York: Continuum, 2006, p. 202.

25   Badiou, *Metapolitics*, p. 23.

26   'Autour de *Logiques des mondes*', organized by David Rabouin and Frédéric Worms, 24 November 2006, École normale supérieure, Paris.

27   Both Alex Callinicos and Philippe Raynaud, from the Left and from the Right, criticize Badiou for his aristocratism. See Callinicos, *Resources of Critique*, Cambridge: Polity, 2006, p. 101, and Philippe Raynaud, *L'Extrême gauche plurielle*, Paris: Perrin, 2009, p. 153.

process of subjectivation. That said, Badiou's event, like the subjects that emerge from it, is characterized by its rarity. They are always exceptional in kind.

Badiou is a thinker of the universal, but a paradoxical universal. Saint Paul, whom he regards as the founder of universalism, pronounces in the Epistle to the Galatians the famous formula: 'There is neither Jew nor Greek, there is neither bond nor free, there is neither male nor female' (Galatians, 3.28). The Christ-event suspends differences and brings about a 'purely generic multiplicity' that equalizes conditions. This does not prevent Paul from being pragmatic and evincing a tolerant disregard of the differences between the Christian communities whose unity he is working to preserve.[28] However, the key thing is that the Christ-event abolishes identities and gives rise to a universalism addressed to everyone. On the other hand, access to Badiousian universality necessarily occurs via a subjective route. According to the philosopher, truth is always militant. Not that a truth which is valid in itself is subsequently adopted and propagated by convinced apostles. For Badiou, truth only exists in as much as it is militant. The philosopher rejects the relativism prevalent in many contemporary 'postmodern' currents. According to the latter, concepts like 'truth' or the 'universal' are at best fallacious, at worst complicit with western imperialism. For Badiou, they are nothing of the sort. For all that, the universalism developed by the author of *Logiques des mondes* allocates a key role to subjectivity. Far from being a fetter on the emergence of the universal, the latter is a condition of its possibility.

According to Badiou, the 'party form' has been superseded. In the twentieth century, revolutionary politics took the form of parties, which aimed to confront the state on its own ground, seize control of it, and initiate its withering away. This strategic schema ultimately refers to the centrality during the twentieth century of what Badiou calls the 'paradigm of war'.[29] '[T]he twentieth century fulfils the promise of the nineteenth. What the nineteenth century conceived, the twentieth century realizes', claims the philosopher.[30] The problem is that the realization in the here and now of what had previously been a dream led to a brutalization of reality. Unprecedented atrocities were committed, before the revolutionary parties 'routinized' themselves and became 'party-states'. Today, the crucial question is whether a revolutionary politics without a party is possible.[31] Badiou is not a libertarian; he does not plead for the unconstrained blossoming of revolutionary spontaneity. A politics without a party does not betoken a politics without organization. It means a politics without any relationship to the state. Badiou thus refuses to take

---

28   Badiou, *Saint Paul*, p. 98.
29   Badiou, *The Century*, p. 34.
30   Ibid., p. 19.
31   Badiou, *Metapolitics*, pp. 126–7.

part in elections and has abandoned the Leninist paradigm prevalent on the revolutionary Left, whose key feature is the seizure of state power by armed insurrection.

Among the new agents of social transformation, Badiou believes that the *travailleurs sans-papiers* will play a crucial role in the future – not only *sans-papiers* in the developed countries, but also, for example, Chinese peasants who migrate to the cities illegally. The *sans-papiers* focus in themselves all the contradictions of contemporary capitalism and, in that sense, are 'irreconcilable' for Badiou. The wealthy countries have no choice but to employ them clandestinely in order to reduce labour costs and discipline the labour force. At the same time, they are constantly strengthening border controls and organizing charter flights to send them back home, with (it is true) little impact on the scale and direction of migratory flows. To support the struggles of *sans-papiers* consequently amounts to deepening this contradiction, which is inherent in capitalism, thereby increasing its destabilization.

Slavoj Žižek: When Lenin Meets Lacan

Žižek is the unavoidable star of contemporary critical thinking. From Buenos Aires, to New York, New Delhi, Paris and Ljubljana (the city whence he comes), crowds flock to attend his lectures.[32] This attraction is in part attributable to the intellectual 'style' of the Slovenian philosopher. It blends abstruse references to the thought of Schelling and Lacan with examples drawn from popular culture – Hollywood cinema, detective novels or science fiction, jokes of every kind – the whole embellished with semi-provocative quotations from Stalin, Lenin or Mao. This intellectual strategy aims to blur the boundaries between 'high' culture and 'popular' culture. Žižek is the subject or protagonist of several documentaries, including a remarkable *Pervert's Guide to Cinema* (2006) in which he presents his analyses while parodying classic scenes from the history of film.[33] A nightclub in Buenos Aires is also named after him.

Žižek is a highly international philosopher. He completed part of his studies in France, at the University of Paris 8, under the supervision of Jacques-Alain Miller (the son-in-law and intellectual legatee of Lacan), with whom he also underwent psychoanalysis. He writes and publishes in English. Of the thinkers referred to in this book, he is the only one who comes from eastern Europe. For understandable reasons, critical thinking is not at its strongest in that part of the world, even if elements of reconstruction are clearly visible. An in-depth analysis of Žižek's oeuvre would involve understanding in greater detail its relationship

---

32   See Rebecca Mead, 'The Marx Brother', *The New Yorker*, 5 May 2003.
33   See also Astra Taylor's documentary *Žižek!* (2005).

to his country of origin. For to say of an intellectual that he is international does not entail that he is not at the same time the product of a national or regional context. His mode of internationalization is in fact closely correlated with the region he comes from – in particular with its place, economically, politically and culturally, in the contemporary world-system.

A key aspect of Žižek's thinking is his defence of the Cartesian *cogito*. *The Ticklish Subject*, one of his major works (subtitled *The Absent Centre of Political Ontology*), begins with the following declaration: 'A spectre is haunting Western academia . . . the spectre of the Cartesian subject.'[34] The philosopher assimilates the question of the 'subject' to the spectre of communism with which Marx and Engels' *Communist Manifesto* opens. This is to indicate how important an issue it is. As is well known, Descartes formulated a famous philosophical position by declaring '*cogito, ergo sum*' (I think, therefore I am). The idea of a sovereign subject, transparent to itself and rational, is one of the foundations of modernity. It is not only at the heart of the Enlightenment project, but also underlies numerous nineteenth-century emancipatory movements, including liberalism, Marxism and anarchism.[35] Critiques of this conception of the subject have never been wanting, whether issuing from the philosophical tradition (Nietzsche, for example), or from currents like feminism, which early on denounced the 'gendered' character of the *cogito*.[36]

However, the challenge to the Enlightenment, and the theory of the subject accompanying it, took a new turn after the Second World War. The atrocities it witnessed were related to modernity itself. The representatives of the Frankfurt School – Adorno and Horkheimer at their head – thus regarded the gas chambers as the ultimate expression of modern 'instrumental' rationality. Having once served emancipation, reason had backfired and rendered itself complicit with the worst crimes against humanity. Structuralism and poststructuralism, although not (or scarcely) thematizing 'modern barbarism', also developed a critique of humanism. Althusser's 'theoretical anti-humanism', or the 'death of man' prophesied by Foucault, are expressions of it. The poststructuralist viewpoint that dominates 'western academia' (to employ Žižek's term) regards the subject as a 'decentred' entity. In this perspective, an irreducible multiplicity of subjective positions exists, which no 'centre' unifies. The *cogito* has literally disintegrated. Freud's 'discovery' of the unconscious, and the importance assigned to language in philosophy in the second half of the twentieth century,

---

34   Slavoj Žižek, *The Ticklish Subject: The Absent Centre of Political Ontology*, London and New York: Verso, 1999, p. 1.

35   On this see Charles Taylor, *Sources of the Self: The Making of Modern Identity*, Cambridge (MA): Harvard University Press, 1992.

36   See Joan Scott, *Only Paradoxes to Offer: French Feminists and the Rights of Men*, Cambridge (MA): Harvard University Press, 1997.

have consolidated this trend. To borrow a formula from Derrida, the subject is now perceived as a 'function of language'.[37]

Žižek is opposed to the disintegration of the subject. Obviously, this does not lead him to advocate a return pure and simple to modern humanism, in Cartesian or some other form. Žižek subjects the *cogito* to a Lacanian treatment. He interprets everything in the light of the categories of the author of the *Écrits*. For Žižek, the subject is not a 'substance'. It is not a real entity, but a 'void' composed of pure 'negativity'. The subject appears at the interface of the 'Real' and the 'Symbolic'. These two concepts, which Žižek borrows from Lacan, are crucial in his approach. The Real is unknowable by us; it refers to the world prior to any categorization or classification – a pre-linguistic world. The Symbolic is the instance of the ordering of the Real. When people commonly refer to 'reality', it is to the Symbolic that they are referring, because the Real itself is not accessible to us. The Symbolic represents the 'murder of the thing', as Lacan puts it, in the sense that it abolishes the thing qua thing by rendering it intelligible to us (it therewith ceases to be a thing pertaining to the Real). However, the Real never allows itself to be completely symbolized; something in it resists. What psychoanalysis calls 'trauma' refers to cases of the intrusion or violent resurgence of the Real in the order of the Symbolic. Such intrusion is always possible and liable to disrupt the Symbolic. From this standpoint, the Symbolic is therefore necessarily open. It persists in time, but on condition of a resurgence of a conflictual Real.

According to Žižek, the subject is formed in the distance separating the Real from the Symbolic.[38] This distance assumes that the Symbolic differs from the Real, permitting subjectivity to originate. Were the Real and the Symbolic identical, or if the Symbolic was enclosed in itself, no subjective position would be conceivable. According to Žižek, the subject is a 'vanishing mediator'.[39] This concept is adopted from Jameson. In the latter it refers to any phenomenon that allows another phenomenon to emerge and disappears once it has performed that task. Jameson sets the concept to work in his interpretation of Weber's thesis on the Protestant ethic and the spirit of capitalism. For Weber (as read by Jameson) Protestantism represents the condition of emergence of capitalism. However, once the latter emerges, it speeds up the disappearance of Protestantism, because capitalism encourages the process of secularization.[40] Protestantism is therefore a 'vanishing mediator' of capitalism.

---

37   Jacques Derrida, *Speech and Phenomena*, trans. David B. Allison, Evanston: Northwestern University Press, 1973.

38   Tom Myers, *Slavoj Žižek*, London and New York: Routledge, 2003, p. 28.

39   Slavoj Žižek, *For They Know Not What They Do: Enjoyment as a Political Factor*, London and New York: Verso, 2007.

40   See Fredric Jameson, 'The Vanishing Mediator, or Max Weber as Storyteller', in *The Ideologies of Theory: Essays 1971–1986*, Minneapolis: University of Minnesota Press, 1988.

For Žižek, the subject possesses an analogous structure. In as much as it is unknowable, the Real is experienced as 'loss' by the subject. Faced with this nothingness, so as not to sink into madness, the subject constructs the Symbolic.[41] To that end it externalizes itself in a language, the 'word' being the instance by which symbolization is set in motion: 'in pronouncing a word, the subject constructs his being outside himself; he "coagulates" the core of his being in an external sign. In the (verbal) sign, I – as it were – find myself outside myself, I posit my unity outside myself, in a signifier which represents me.'[42] In externalizing itself, the subject creates the object (the Symbolic), but therewith ceases to find itself face to face with it, precisely because it is externalized. The separation between subject and object is therefore abolished, and these two instances are now indissolubly mixed. This implies, among other things, that the place of the subject remains empty. As a result, it can be successively or simultaneously occupied or demanded by the most diverse actors.[43] Like Rancière, Žižek believes that the subject is not a concrete, actually existing collective. It is the condition for concrete individualities or collectives being able to form themselves. But for that to occur, its place must remain formally empty.

A corollary of Žižek's theory of the subject is his conception of ideology. Classically, ideology refers to the gap between reality and the way that individuals represent it to themselves – specifically, in an erroneous or 'ideological' way. This distortion can be ascribed to the class position of individuals or to another cause, but it always occurs without those concerned being aware of it. Philosophical and political critique lodges itself in the gap between these two instances. Its function is to draw the attention of the victims of an ideology to the fact that their representations of reality are mistaken. According to the German philosopher Peter Sloterdijk, who serves as Žižek's starting-point here, this classical model has ceased to work in post-modern societies.[44] The reason is that today individuals know perfectly well that the discourse served up to them by the media and the political class is fallacious. They are no longer dupes, implying that for Sloterdijk, our era is one of general cynicism, which has succeeded the age of ideologies. Such cynicism raises the problem of the effectiveness of critique in the present. If everyone knows that the dominant representation of reality is not the 'true' reality, does critique still have a *raison d'être*?

---

41 Myers, *Slavoj Žižek*, p. 36.

42 Slavoj Žižek, *The Indivisible Remainder: An Essay on Schelling and Related Matters*, London and New York: Verso, 2006, p. 43.

43 Myers, *Slavoj Žižek*, p. 40. The idea that the centre of democratic societies possesses the peculiarity of being empty is adopted by Žižek from Claude Lefort, who formulates it in *L'Invention démocratique*, Paris: Fayard, 1981.

44 Peter Sloterdijk, *Critique of Cynical Reason*, trans. Michael Eldred, London and New York: Verso, 1988.

According to Žižek, Sloterdijk's theory of ideology, like his diagnosis of the age in which we live, is erroneous.[45] The latter is far from being 'post-ideological'. It is true that cynicism is widespread. However, to believe that such cynicism, however general, suffices to pitch us into a post-ideological age is to mistake what ideology is. For ideology is not, in the first instance, a matter of representations. It is a matter of acts. The argument of Pascal's wager makes it possible to clarify this point. It consists in a utility calculation, in the sense of neo-classical economics. It maintains that it is always more advantageous for the individual to believe in God, for if God exists, the benefit to be anticipated from belief is enormous (paradise), just as the cost of unbelief (hell) is enormous. By contrast, it is of little moment whether or not one has believed in God if he does not exist. Every reasonable being must consequently believe in God. The problem, obviously, is that belief cannot be forced. One cannot believe at will; it is necessary to possess genuine faith. Pascal's response to this problem is well known: 'Kneel and pray, and then you will believe.'[46]

The argument of the wager is often interpreted as demonstrating the influence of an individual's behaviour on her mental states. The prayer internalizes its own content, which is gradually transformed into authentic belief thanks to repetition. However, a different interpretation of the wager is possible. According to Žižek, what Pascal's reasoning shows is not that our behaviour is capable of producing representations in our minds. It shows that we often possess representations before knowing that we possess them. Contrary to what she thinks, when the individual gets down on her knees to pray, she already believes in God. When she imagines that she is beginning to believe, in reality she is merely acknowledging a belief already present in her. For what counts is not the mental state, but the act. That is why our age remains saturated with ideologies. Although cynicism reigns, individuals continue to behave as if ideologies were valid. Althusser's theory of 'Ideological State Apparatuses' (ISAs) can be interpreted in the light of this argument.[47] Althusser distinguishes the ISAs – school, church, media, family – from the 'Repressive State Apparatus' (police, army, prisons). The function of the ISAs is to ensure adhesion to the existing order via ideology, by 'naturalizing' this order in the eyes of those subject to it. For Žižek, the ISAs generate adhesion to the system even before the individual perceives it. This involves a belief 'before' belief. The symptom that reveals the existence of this 'pre-belief' is the activity of the individual, who evinces her adhesion to the existing order, however rooted in her a cynical distance from it may be.

45   Slavoj Žižek, 'The Spectre of Ideology', in Žižek, ed., *Mapping Ideology*, London and New York: Verso, 1994; reprinted in Elizabeth Wright and Edmond Wright, eds, *The Žižek Reader*, Oxford: Blackwell, 1999.

46   Blaise Pascal, *Pensées*, Paris: Le Livre de Poche, 2000, §233.

47   Ibid., p. 66.

Žižek identifies with Marxism, which is comparatively rare for an intellectual formed in the former eastern bloc, who was also a dissident in his country during the Soviet era. As a result, he defends determination 'in the last instance' by the economy, which, in a variety of forms, is to be found at the heart of this paradigm from the outset. More precisely, he argues that the form of domination which obtains in the economic sphere – exploitation – possesses primacy over other forms of oppression. Together with his desire to rehabilitate the Cartesian subject, this is a second thesis which sees the philosopher oppose the reigning *doxa* in 'western academia'. The thesis of the determination of the superstructure by the infrastructure dominated critical thinking while the hegemony of Marxism within it lasted – that is, for a long time. From the 1970s onwards, however, the idea that domination is plural progressively became established, to the point of becoming a new *doxa*. Several factors contributed to this development. This period witnessed the proliferation of 'secondary fronts', which undermined the centrality hitherto assigned the confrontation between capital and labour. In addition, various profound socio-technological changes, such as the emergence of mass media, placed culture at the heart of (post)modern life. Bourdieu's sociology is typical of this trend. Bourdieu maintains that the social world is composed of different social 'fields', each of which enjoys 'relative autonomy' from the others. This assumes that particular capitals circulate in each of them, none of which is more important than the others.

According to Žižek, critical thought has gone too far in multiplying forms of domination, to the point where it has become incapable of appreciating the specificity of capitalism as a system. Domination is unquestionably plural. However, what makes capitalism special is that all forms of domination are underpinned by a phenomenon that confers on them the same 'coloration' – namely, the accumulation of capital.[48] Contemporary critical thinkers certainly acknowledge the existence of economic exploitation. But they believe that it involves one form of oppression among others, like male domination or racism. For Žižek, this thesis is erroneous. Exploitation is not one type of oppression among others, but the overall logic underlying them all. That is why the philosopher is highly critical of the prevailing 'multiculturalism', as evinced by his work with the eloquent title of *Plaidoyer en faveur de l'intolérance* ('A Plea for Intolerance').[49]

Žižek adopts the Marxist argument of 'reification' developed, in particular, by Lukács in *History and Class Consciousness* (1923). This is what Lukács argues:

---

48   Slavoj Žižek, 'Holding the Place', in Judith Butler, Ernesto Laclau and Slavoj Žižek, *Contingency, Hegemony and Universality: Contemporary Dialogues on the Left*, London and New York: 2000, p. 320.
49   Slavoj Žižek, *Plaidoyer en faveur de l'intolérance*, Montpellier: Climats, 2007.

where the market economy has been fully developed . . . a man's activity becomes estranged from himself, it turns into a commodity which, subject to the non-human objectivity of the natural laws of society, must go its own way independently of man just like any consumer article.[50]

In capitalism, human activity assumes the status of 'any consumer article' – that is, the status of a commodity. Commodity fetishism contaminates all spheres of human activity and actions. According to Žižek, the conclusion to be drawn from this is simple: 'In short, I am pleading for a "return to the primacy of the economy" not to the detriment of the issues raised by postmodern forms of politicization, but precisely in order to create the conditions for more effective realization of feminist, ecological, and so on, demands.'[51] There is no question of minimizing the importance of feminist, ecological and other struggles. The thesis of determination 'in the last instance' is sometimes represented by its opponents as a wish to diminish these other forms of struggle. According to the philosopher, this is false. Simply put, to the extent that these forms of oppression assume a particular connotation in a capitalist regime, they cannot be separated from the general struggle against reification. It forms the background against which the other struggles are going to unfold; and that is why it must be regarded as central.

Žižek develops a ferocious critique of the theories of 'anti-power' that have proliferated during the 1990s and in the early 2000s. Such theories maintain that the seizure of state power is not merely futile, because power is today disseminated throughout the whole social body and not concentrated in the state, but conducive to catastrophe. They indirectly adopt the 'anti-totalitarian' argument that is a given in the 'new philosophers', arguing that Stalinism, far from being a 'degeneration', was present from the start of the Russian Revolution and perhaps even the French Revolution.

According to Žižek, theorists of anti-power are theorizing defeat in advance.[52] They have internalized and naturalized it to such an extent that they have become incapable of imagining anything but 'temporary zones of autonomy', located on the system's 'margins'.[53] Žižek argues the converse of the critique of 'statocentrism', whose origins, as we have seen, go back (at least) to Foucault. Beyond the New Left and its 'decentred' conception of power, he calls for a re-examination of classical Marxism's conception of power and the state,

---

50   Georg Lukács, *History and Class Consciousness: Studies in Marxist Dialectics*, trans. Rodney Livingstone, London: Merlin, 1971, p. 87.

51   Žižek, *The Ticklish Subject*, p. 356.

52   Ibid., p. 233.

53   On 'temporary zones of autonomy', see Hakim Bey, *T.A.Z.: Temporary Autonomous Zone*, New York: Autonomedia, 1991.

principally that of Lenin. Today, Marx has been widely rehabilitated, after having been denigrated in the 1980s and much of the 90s. For Žižek, it is the figure of Lenin that the radical Left must now reinstate.[54] 'What a true Leninist and a political conservative have in common', claims the philosopher, 'is the fact that they reject what one could call liberal leftist "irresponsibility" (advocating grand projects of solidarity, freedom, and so on, yet ducking out when one has to pay the price for them in the guise of concrete and often "cruel" political measures)'.[55] During the Russian Revolution, Lenin had the courage to assume effective leadership of the state. Far from confining himself to a romantic celebration of the 'October-event', he sought to transpose its effects into an enduring social and political order. That is what explains his proximity to Saint Paul, who likewise worked to make the 'Christ-event' last, by organizing the church. In a provocative formula, Žižek calls this transposition of the event into a durable order 'good terror'. In his view, an authentic event is characterized by the fact that it always comes at a cost.

POST-FEMININITIES

From its inception, feminism has been a field inclined to theoretical innovation. One reason for this perhaps is (as Joan Scott has suggested) that the condition of women in the modern age rests on a basic paradox which is politically difficult to handle, but intellectually stimulating. On the one hand, feminists have argued since at least Olympe de Gouges, the author of the *Déclaration des droits de la femme et de la citoyenne* in 1791, that differences of sex/gender are irrelevant – that at any rate they cannot legitimate women's lack of political rights. On the other hand, in so far as they present themselves in the public sphere as women, calling for women to mobilize to win their rights, feminists in fact introduce that difference into it. This paradoxical toing-and-froing – *Only Paradoxes to Offer* is the title of Scott's book, drawn from a phrase of Olympe de Gouges' – between abolition of difference and its acceptance is one of the main elements (though not the only one) running through the history of feminism. It is also the source of great theoretical sophistication aimed at resolving the paradox, which is far from exhausted today.

Naturally, there can be no question here of doing justice to contemporary feminist output in its entirety.[56] Many currents of feminism will not be dealt

---

54   See Slavoj Žižek, *Žižek on Lenin: Revolution at the Gates – The 1917 Writings*, London and New York: Verso, 2004.

55   Žižek, *The Ticklish Subject*, p. 236.

56   For synthetic introductions to contemporary feminism, readers are referred, for example, to Chris Beasley, *What Is Feminism? An Introduction to Feminist Theory*, London: Sage, 1999, and Elsa Dorlin, *Sexe, genre et sexualités*, Paris: Presses Universitaires de France, 2008.

with, among them black feminism, whose particularity consists in examining the dual oppression of which black women are victims and their relations with those – white women and black men – who are subject to only one of those forms of oppression.[57] Nor will Marxist feminism be mentioned, although it remains influential today, if no doubt less so than in the 1960s and 70s.[58] The peculiarity of Marxist feminism is its combination of analysis of sex/gender with class analysis. From today's feminist corpus we have chosen to present three thinkers who are especially interesting as regards the problematic of the 'subject of emancipation': Donna Haraway, Judith Butler and Gayatri Spivak. These three authors possess the following characteristic in common: they cross 'classical' feminist themes, like the problem of the specificity of women's oppression, with lines of enquiry derived from different intellectual currents. Thus, Spivak is situated at the crossroads of feminism and postcolonialism; Haraway stages an encounter between feminism and the philosophy of science and technology; and Butler reconfigures feminism with concepts from Foucault, Derrida and Lacan. Such forms of theoretical cross-fertilizations indicate to what extent the founding paradox identified by Scott still obtains today.

Donna Haraway: Cyborgs of the World?

Haraway is famous in the Anglo-American world, and her reputation extends to the four corners of the earth. In an unmistakable sign of celebrity, she appears as a character in the second installment of the 'cult' Japanese animated cartoon *Ghost in the Shell*. There are numerous references to her ideas in popular culture, while discussion forums devoted to them on the Internet (and elsewhere) are multiplying. Haraway belongs to the very exclusive club of contemporary thinkers whose theories are subject to a dual appropriation – one academic, the other popular.

Haraway is a biologist by training, which is not without its influence on her theories. She identifies with 'eco-feminism', one of the most interesting intellectual currents to have emerged over recent decades. As its name indicates, eco-feminism aims to conjoin the concerns of feminists and ecologists. It was originally a French creation. Françoise d'Eaubonne, who was also co-founder of the *Front homosexuel d'action révolutionnaire* (FHAR), used the term for the first time in 1974 in her book *Le Féminisme ou la mort*.[59] In it she launched an

---

57 On 'black feminism' see Joy James asnd T. Denesan Sharpley-Whiting, eds., *The Black Feminist Reader*, Cambridge, MA: Wiley-Blackwell, 2000.

58 See Stevi Jackson, 'Marxism and Feminism', in Jacques Bidet and Stathis Kouvelakis, eds, *Critical Companion to Contemporary Marxism*, Leiden and Boston: Brill, 2008.

59 See Carolyn Merchant, *Radical Ecology: The Search for a Liveable World*, London and New York: Routledge, 2005, chapter 8.

appeal to women to carry out an 'ecological revolution' to save the planet. Since then, this current has taken various forms. Some thinkers have established an analogy between the domination of women and that of nature by men, asserting that they are particular instances of the same masculine will to power. On this basis, an author like Karen Warren has developed an ethics – analogous to the ethics of 'care' – intended to be free of sexist bias towards women and nature alike. Other eco-feminist currents have based themselves on the metaphor of 'Mother Earth' – Gaia in Greek mythology or Pachamama in the Quechua language. They often contain a 'spiritual' dimension calling for the restoration of a lost organic unity with the earth beyond the destruction wreaked by modernity. Still other tendencies, partisans of a socialist or Marxist eco-feminism, regard capitalism as the source of women's oppression and the principal cause of the ecological crisis. In this perspective, women's liberation and the establishment of a sustainable mode of production are intimately linked.

The variant of eco-feminism developed by Haraway derives from reflection on technology. It does not unilaterally reject industrial civilization and modernity. But nor does it involve a 'positivist' acceptance of all technological advances. It is opposed to what it calls the 'mythology of origins', which criticizes the present and future in the name of an allegedly pristine past – that is, one exempt from the intrusion of technology into nature. It is equally opposed to the corollary of this mythology – namely, teleology – which regards technology and the social developments it gives rise to as vehicles of progress in themselves. What we need, says Haraway, is a politics of techno-science – in other words, a *techno-politics*. According to her, the 'bio-politics' identified by Foucault as a new era of power that emerged in the nineteenth century, and which is exercised over bodies and populations (contrary to 'disciplinary' power, whose object was territories), is no longer extant. Today, power is techno-scientific and no longer relative to 'naked' life. This means that it is exercised via technology over the technical entities that human beings have become.

According to Haraway, the central emancipatory figure of our time, at once real and utopian, is the *cyborg*. Her most famous text is entitled 'Cyborg Manifesto' and carries the subtitle 'Science, Technology, and Socialist-Feminism in the Late Twentieth Century'.[60] Another famous article by her is entitled 'The Promises of Monsters'. Its subject is the 'hybrid' beings, among them cyborgs and monsters, which populate today's world. A cyborg – contraction of cybernetic organism – is a cross between a human being and a machine that possesses both natural and artificial components. The term has been used in robotics

---

60   See Donna Haraway, 'A Cyborg Manifesto: Science, Technology, and Socialist-Feminism in the Late Twentieth Century', in Haraway, *Simians, Cyborgs and Women: The Reinvention of Nature*, London and New York: Routledge, 1991.

since the 1960s, but its diffusion is also due to its prior use in science fiction. According to Haraway, in some respects we are all cyborgs. Certainly, we are living beings, but we are also composed of 'protheses' that perform various functions in our organisms, some of them vital. Our environment is likewise made up of technical objects that have become unavoidable: computers, vehicles, telecommunications and so forth. With the concept of 'cyborg', Haraway proposes to reconfigure our representation of reality. The latter is no longer composed of human beings on the one hand, and machines on the other, which occasionally enter into relations with one another. An imbrication of the natural and the artificial is now the rule, and their separation is an increasingly rare exception with the passage of time. That is why the elaboration of a new 'ontology', in keeping with technological progress, is indispensable. In particular, it will indicate to us the requisite political tasks in the current context.

Haraway locates her theory of cyborgs in the general history of emancipatory movements. With this theory she aims (in her own words) to 'contribute to socialist-feminist culture'. The initial version of the 'Cyborg Manifesto' was published in 1985 in *Socialist Review*, a journal of US critical Marxism. Obviously, we have not chosen to be cyborgs, which are 'the illegitimate offspring of militarism and patriarchal capitalism'.[61] Technology has always possessed a dark side, its development being bound up with weapons and industrial innovation. Moreover, its 'patriarchal' dimension is clear, since it proceeds from the will to subjugate nature. At the same time, although the ascendancy of cyborgs is ambiguous, nothing rules out exploring their political potential once their existence has been acknowledged. Like a number of contemporary critical thinkers, Haraway subscribes to the strategic paradigm of *détournement*. Its origins go back to the artistic avant-gardes of the twentieth century, especially situationism. It consists in diverting an object or discourse from its original function in order to subvert its content and endow it with a politically or artistically new connotation. Thus, although cyborgs initially went hand in glove with capital, it cannot be excluded that they will make it possible to transcend certain aporiae in which advocates of a radical ecology and socialism are currently trapped.

The emergence of the figure of the cyborg derives from several long-term historical tendencies. First of all, the boundary between the human and the animal has gone on blurring since at least Darwin's *Origin of Species*. The idea that certain characteristics are exclusively peculiar to *homo sapiens* loses its credibility as the life sciences develop. While the cyborg is an amalgam of natural and artificial components, the natural components are therefore both human and animal. Haraway has always paid particular attention to the social

---

61 Ibid., p. 151.

meanings attached to animality, to so-called wild animals as well as pets.[62] Her problematization of the separation between human beings and animals links her to movements promoting animal rights, particularly 'anti-specie-sism'. This tendency in radical ecology maintains that membership in a species is not a relevant criterion for assigning rights. Alternatively put, moral rules – 'thou shalt not kill', for example – which apply to representatives of the human species must also be applied to the representatives of other species. The founding work of contemporary anti-speciesism is Peter Singer's *Animal Liberation*.[63] Even if she differs from him in certain respects, particularly as regards the intellectual tradition to which she belongs (Singer is a utilitarian), Haraway reaches similar conclusions. There is no impassable barrier between species; and this requires us to re-think our relationship with animals and, ultimately, what we call 'nature'.

The division between man and machine has become as blurred as that separating man from animal. The increasing imbrication of the organic and the machinic blurs the categories traditionally employed to understand reality. The disappearance of this dual boundary – man/animal and man/machine – is (according to Haraway) the principal philosophical and political coordinate of the age. *Artefactualism* is what Haraway calls the ontology she elaborates in order to draw all the consequences from this state of affairs. This term refers to the idea that all the entities making up reality are, to various degrees, artefacts – that is, objects that are inseparably organic, technological, symbolic and polit-ical. An artefact is an entity constructed by human hands out of natural materials. Very often, artefacts have a social function, which means that a certain purpose is allocated to them. According to Haraway, artefacts provide a model for thinking about all objects. Her artefactualism is a radical anti-essen-tialism. It maintains that no entity in the world possesses an 'essence' causing it to exist independently of the other entities with which it interacts. An object is always a hybrid, a blend of several things, which amounts to saying that 'essences' do not exist. This anti-essentialism is common to many forms of contemporary critical thought.

Haraway's artefactualism has two important theoretical consequences. Firstly, it is an anti-humanism. If no object in the world possesses an 'essence', human beings do not have one either.[64] Humanism is a doctrine which main-tains that buried beneath the mass of reified and alienated history there is a human essence, and that the role of theoretical and political critique is to further

---

62   See Donna Haraway, *Primate Vision: Gender, Race and Nature in the World of Modern Science*, London and New York: Routledge, 1990.

63   Peter Singer, *Animal Liberation*, London: Pimlico, 1995.

64   Donna Haraway, 'The Promises of Monsters', in Lawrence Grossberg and Cary Nelson, eds, *Cultural Studies*, London and New York: Routledge, 1992, p. 297.

its realization. Haraway is firmly opposed to this idea. To be a cyborg is the opposite of being an essence, even a future one. For the cyborg is by definition composite. As we know, anti-humanism has a history in twentieth-century critical thought. It would be interesting to compare the form of anti-humanism developed by Haraway with that elaborated in the 1960s and 70s by thinkers like Foucault (in *Les Mots et les choses*) and Althusser ('theoretical anti-humanism'). Moreover, we have seen that Badiou's theory of the event likewise identifies with anti-humanism. To our knowledge, to this day there exists no general intellectual history of left-wing anti-humanism.

The second major consequence of Haraway's artefactualism is that for her, 'women' do not exist. The author's anti-humanism is also an anti-feminism – more precisely, a *post-feminism*. Obviously, Haraway is firmly attached to the advancement of women's rights. However, she is critical of feminist currents which argue that the fact of being 'women' in itself confers a shared political destiny on women. Thus, 'There is nothing about being "female" that naturally binds women. There is not even such a state as "being" female, itself a highly complex category constructed in contested sexual scientific discourses and other social practices.'[65] The emergence of a collective female subject is always the result of a construction. To argue, as do some feminist currents, that biology – or even culture – is sufficient to provide a substratum for mobilizing women is mistaken and even politically dangerous. For it lends support to the idea that 'natural' differences between the sexes exist, which has always formed the foundation of sexist discourse 'naturalizing' the division of roles between men and women.

What are the concrete political consequences of the artefactualism advocated by Haraway? Any social mobilization comprises human and non-human actors.[66] The sociology of social movements has erred in attending solely to the humans participating in collective action. For any mobilization includes an infinite variety of entities; and its result depends on their ability to combine their demands effectively. Take the movements defending rain forests, such as we find notably in Latin America.[67] The usual approach consists in thinking that such mobilizations presuppose an ecosystem to be defended – for example, the Amazon – an actor seeking to exploit it – for example, a pharmaceutical

---

65   Haraway, 'A Cyborg Manifesto', p. 155.

66   The distinction between humans and non-humans is developed jointly by Haraway and Bruno Latour, a thinker with whom she has a special theoretical relationship, and who has introduced one of her collections of articles to a French audience. Latour argues that we are currently witnessing a proliferation of 'hybrid' beings, 'blends of nature and culture', rendering the 'great divide' between these two instances, which is at the foundation of modernity, obsolete. See Bruno Latour, *We Have Never Been Modern*, trans. Catherine Porter, Cambridge (MA): Harvard University Press, 1993.

67   Haraway, 'Promises of Monsters', p. 309.

transnational – and a coalition of organizations mobilized against that firm in the name of defending 'nature'.

In fact, the situation is infinitely more complex. Firstly, the Amazon is not an empty space. It has certainly been emptied of some of its indigenous inhabitants, who have been massacred and decimated by microbes since the sixteenth century. But a number of them still live there. So the idea of 'defending' a pristine environment does not make sense. The collective actor that is the Amazon has always been the product of a construction combining humans, non-humans (animals, vegetables), and technical objects (indigenous material civilizations). To oppose the predatory activity of transnational firms thus presupposes giving all the entities involved a say. It remains to be known how all these entities can be brought to 'speak', especially those which are not in a position to do it for themselves (the non-humans). Any collective action thus raises the problem of 'representation', which Haraway argues is always unique and cannot be solved once and for all.

Another instructive example is the fight against AIDS. Haraway describes the association ACT UP as

> a collective built from many articulations among unlike kinds of actors – for example, activists, biomedical machines, government bureaucracies, gay and lesbian worlds, communities of color, scientific conferences, experimental organisms, mayors, international information and action networks.[68]

The list continues for several more lines. The AIDS epidemic has led sufferers and militant groups like ACT UP to intrude in the field of medical expertise and demand to be listened to by doctors. This has disrupted the traditional division of tasks between doctors, who have a monopoly on knowledge and make sick bodies 'speak', and passive patients at the mercy of their medico-institutional power. The epidemic has led to the formation of new 'alliances' – for example, between 'biomedical machines' and the sick, who have learnt to use them and make their own diagnoses. One concept used by Haraway is 'articulation'. 'We articulate, therefore we are' is a watchword she frequently employs. This concept is associated with the Gramscian tradition. For Gramsci, in order to construct a 'historical bloc', the subaltern classes must succeed in articulating their demands under the leadership of a hegemonic class. The position of Haraway, whose use of this concept is certainly fairly free, is interesting in that it includes non-human entities in the terms of the articulation.

As in Rancière, identity and 'disidentification' feature in Haraway. One feature of cyborgs is that they do not correspond to any pre-existing

---

68   Ibid., p. 323.

classification of identities. 'Cyborg' is not in itself an identity, for there are countless ways of being a cyborg. A cyborg is composed to various degrees of organic, machinic and symbolic elements, entailing that every cyborg is unique. Haraway's theory of cyborgs pertains to the critique of the Cartesian 'subject', which, as we saw when presenting Žižek's theses, is fashionable at present. In this sense a cyborg is not an individual. It is multiple – that is, each of its components refers it to a particular filiation. The cyborg is a tangle of filiations at a given moment and in a given place, which in no way presages its composition in different times and places.

Judith Butler: The End of Sexual Identities

Butler is the principal representative of queer theory, one of the most stimulating forms of contemporary feminism or post-feminism. Although developing an approach different from Haraway, less centred on human/animal/machine relations, she approximates to it in as much as she subjects certain presuppositions of feminism to critique – hence the term 'post-feminism'. Butler's best-known – and most controversial[69] – work is *Gender Trouble*, subtitled *Feminism and the Subversion of Identity*. Butler is not the only queer theorist. Among others, we might mention Eve Sedgwick, author in 1990 of *Epistemology of the Closet*, which alludes to the phenomenon of homosexuals 'coming out', Teresa de Lauretis, or David Halperin, author of *Saint Foucault* and specialist on the author of *Histoire de la sexualité*. The queer approach is not only a theory, but a social movement. An organization that identifies with it is Queer Nation, which belongs to the ACT UP movement, and which was created the same year as the release of *Gender Trouble* and *Epistemology of the Closet*. Queer Nation is an activist network committed to the defence of 'LGBTI' (lesbians, gays, bisexuals, transsexuals and intersexes). Like a number of groups in this movement, it advocates 'direct action', which takes the form, in particular, of 'kiss-ins' in public places or the 'outing' of homosexual personalities.

Queer theory adopts the term queer for its own purposes, giving it a positive connotation in a typical strategy of inverting stigmas. More generally, it aims to destabilize sexual identities, whether minority or not. Queer theory is part of the movement of 'de-naturalization' of identities that emerged in the second half of the twentieth century, but whose roots go back to the threshold of the modern age. It represents a particularly radical version of it. In its view, feminism has effectively problematized traditional sexual identities by contesting the idea that patriarchy – male domination – is somehow inscribed in

---

69   For a critique of Butler's positions, see Martha Nussbaum, 'The Professor of Parody', *The New Republic*, 22 February 1999.

nature. However, this problematization has not gone far enough and, what is more, in denaturalizing some identities, feminists have naturalized others. The same is true of the homosexual movement and all minority identity movements. According to queer theorists, it is the very notion of identity that must be rejected. The idea of a 'non-identity' politics has considerable implications from the standpoint of the problematic of the 'subject of emancipation'. It has its origins in Foucault and, in particular, the hypothesis that every 'subject' is constituted by a form of 'power'. Another of its roots is the idea of a 'process without a subject' formulated by Althusser. From the perspective of queer theory, it is important to renounce the position of the subject in order not to afford power any purchase.

Butler subverts a founding distinction of feminism, in particular 'second-wave' feminism (that of the 1960s and 70s) – namely, the distinction between 'gender' and 'sex'. This distinction was notably theorized by Ann Oakley in 1972 in her book *Sex, Gender and Society*.[70] But feminism contained the seeds of it from the outset. Sex refers to the biological differences between men and women, while gender designates the cultural differences that separate them. This distinction is a variant of the more general opposition between nature or the innate (sex) and culture or the acquired (gender), which is ubiquitous in modern intellectual history. One of feminism's inaugural gestures consisted in uncoupling gender from sex and claiming that the social status of women possessed no biological basis. The rationale for this move was that it made it possible to struggle for the abolition of cultural inequalities between genders, regarded as easier to alter than biological inequalities. Assertion of the cultural character of what was previously regarded as natural is at the root of all forms of critique.

Butler concurs with the idea that gender is a cultural construct. But she adds that sex is equally so. In this sense, she goes a step further than 'classical' feminism in asserting the socially constructed character of genders: 'If the immutable character of sex is contested, perhaps this construct called "sex" is as culturally constructed as gender'.[71] Butler contests the existence of an 'immutable' sector of reality that escapes social (power) relations – namely, what Oakley calls 'sex'. In Butler's view, the latter is a cultural construct like gender, if only because the distinction between sex and gender is socio-historically located and consequently there is no reason for the terms composing it not to be equally so. As the title of Butler's book *Bodies That Matter* puts it, bodies are always-already caught up in the symbolic ('matter' signifies both 'material' and 'mean' or 'are

70   Ann Oakley, *Sex, Gender and Society*, London: Gower, 1985.
71   Judith Butler, *Gender Trouble: Feminism and the Subversion of Identity*, London and New York: Routledge, 1990, p. 9.

important'). What Butler ultimately challenges is the separation between nature and culture.

That the distinction between sex and gender is fallacious implies that the categories of 'man' and 'woman' possess no kind of foundation. Classical feminists distinguished gender from sex, claiming that the former was unrelated to the latter. However, in continuing to recognize the existence of an immutable nature, even when unrelated to gender, they ran the risk of it being regarded as the ultimate foundation of male domination. In maintaining the culturally constructed character of sex itself, Butler radicalizes the terms of the debate. 'Man' and 'woman' become floating categories, without real anchorage. Moreover, this applies to all sexual identities, however minoritarian. For Butler, there is no more a masculine or feminine identity than there is a homosexual, bisexual, trans-gender or intersexed one. Any 'differentialism' waving the flag of one of these identities in 'essentialist' fashion is in error. A radical critique of identities is the form taken by Butler's anti-essentialism.

Once the problem is located exclusively at the cultural level, and any consideration of nature is excluded, everything becomes conceivable. For Butler, culture is a quasi-infinitely malleable material (which does not mean that individuals can transform it at will). In this framework it will be possible to argue, for example, that the distinction between 'men' and 'women' develops over the course of history, or that 'man' and 'woman' are not the only two conceivable genders. Alternatively put, these categories do not capture the complexity of the sexual situation of each individual, or of each individual at a given moment of their life. The dichotomy between 'man' and 'woman' can also be regarded as referring to the two ends of a continuum, with each person consequently being more or less man and/or woman. For Butler, 'man' and 'woman' are oppressive, vexatious categories, which trap individuals in sexual identities and practices that limit their potential. She calls for the subversion of established sexual identities and experimentation with new identities.

According to Butler, women did not exist as a unified subject before the emergence of feminism:

> the juridical formation of language and politics that represents women as 'the subject' of feminism is itself a discursive formation and the effect of a given version of representational politics. And the feminist subject turns out to be discursively constituted by the very political system that is supposed to facilitate its emancipation.[72]

---

72   Ibid., p. 3.

Feminism constructs the subject 'women' even as it struggles for its emancipation. It therewith tends to unify a hitherto heterogeneous collective.
Feminism is not the consequence of a pre-existing subject that aspires to
emancipate itself and organizes to this end. It constructs this subject as it
develops and must therefore be regarded as its cause. In this passage, Butler
engages in a critique of what she calls 'representational politics'. It consists in
bringing together the represented – in this instance, women – and a representative – here the feminist movement. 'Representational politics', which is
found in most modern political movements, is problematic. It tends not only
to grant excessive power to a small number of individuals (the representatives), who are supposed to know the interests of the represented and work
towards their realization, but also to homogenize the unique situation of each
of the latter. That is why Butler argues for experimenting with new political
forms, released from the practice of representation.

Butler's challenge to the 'representational politics' leads her to criticize
demands for gay and lesbian marriage.[73] Obviously, in her case this does not
involve opposing the demand on the conservative grounds of the definitionally
heterosexual character of marriage. However, the philosopher claims that the
desire for access to marriage could reinforce an institution which forms one of
the pillars of patriarchy and the oppression of which homosexuals are the
victims. Further, it increases the state's stranglehold on the regulation of sexual
behaviour and definition of a legitimate relationship between two or several
individuals. As such, gay and lesbian marriage risks paradoxically consolidat-
ing a normative sexual-political regime inimical to sexual minorities.
Furthermore, in demanding the same rights as heterosexual couples, homosexual couples cut themselves off from other categories of the population that
are often even more oppressed than they: single mothers and fathers, people
who have multiple amorous relations, trans-genders, intersexes and so forth.
In wishing to be 'included' in marriage, homosexuals in fact distance themselves from these categories. Ultimately, claims Butler, there is no
'representational politics' – that is, desire to accede to normality – which does
not create exclusion. That is why in this particular instance the politically most
correct demand for homosexuals is not access to marriage, but the demand
that marriage should confer no special civil or fiscal rights. In other words, she
advocates abolition of state control of unions.

A quintessential case of subversion of identities is the drag-queen, to whom
Butler devotes some luminous pages.[74] The drag-queen is a flamboyant character,

---

73   Judith Butler, 'Competing Universalities', in Butler, Laclau and Žižek, *Contingency,
Hegemony, Universality*, pp. 175–6.
74   See Butler, *Gender Trouble*, chapter 3.

dressed in outlandish fashion, who performs song-and-dance routines in caba-rets. It can involve a man dressed as a woman, but the converse is also possible (in this case it will be a drag-king). It can also involve a woman disguised as a woman or a man disguised as a man. It is perhaps in these cases that the drag-queen's performance assumes its full significance. Drag-queens play with the boundaries and ambiguities of sexual identities. They deliberately stage the stereotypes of femininity and masculinity by exaggerating them. In this sense, their show is based on playing with clichés, which are reproduced by them ironically – that is, highlighting the fact that they are clichés. Drag-queens fool no one as to their real identity. Like Brechtian 'distanciation', their show is based on a form of complicity with the audience. Their performances expose the 'conventional' and, conse-quently, contingent character of sexual identities. That is why the drag-queen is a highly political figure, who demolishes any idea of the naturalness of identities. According to Butler, the drag-queen's performance is in some respects represent-ative of what we all do in daily life when we conform to the reigning sexual identities. However, we need to learn to introduce into it the same distance and the same irony vis-à-vis those identities as are exhibited by the drag-queen.

For Butler, genders are *performatives* – that is, they constitute their own content. There are not first of all sexes or genders in reality and then a language that refers to them. On the contrary, the object 'sex' or 'gender' is created by the very action of uttering sentences about it. The major modern theorist of perfor-mative utterances was the British philosopher John Austin, on whom Butler draws (freely). In his book *How to Do Things with Words*, Austin examined the semantic structure of sentences like 'I declare you man and wife' or 'I promise to arrive on time', which do not describe a factual state of affairs, but create a present or future reality. The norms of sex/gender possess the same structure. They consist in cultural or discursive rules that produce their object. Unlike many performative utterances, however, the norms of gender must constantly be repeated. It is not enough for the doctor to declare at birth 'It's a boy!' for the boy in question, and those around him, to internalize the norms conforming to that gender. 'Gendered' socialization is conducted throughout life. The perfor-mative character of genders is what ensures the possibility of their subversion. Just like the drag-queen, individuals can introduce distance or difference between themselves and the sexual role they are supposed to play.

Gayatri Spivak: The Silence of the Subaltern

In many ways, Gayatri Chakravorty Spivak is a hybrid theorist. Professor of comparative literature and postcolonial studies at the universities of Columbia and Calcutta (where she was born in 1942), she spent her youth in India, where she completed the first part of her higher education in English literature. Her initial formation may in this respect be regarded as the product of the British colonial heritage.[75] Having emigrated to the United States in the late 1950s, she wrote a thesis on the Irish poet W. B. Yeats under the supervision of Paul de Man at Cornell University. The latter subsequently became one of the members of the 'Yale School' of deconstruction, which derives its name from Derrida's influence on it. This influence was transmitted to Spivak herself. In 1976, she translated one of the French philosopher's important books – *De la grammatologie* – accompanying it with a substantial 'Translator's Preface', which was an important milestone in the reception of Derrida's oeuvre in the United States, and which contributed to its author's reputation.[76] Her constant commuting between India and the Anglo-American world make Spivak a postcolonial intellectual *par excellence*.

Biographical hybridity is accompanied in Spivak by theoretical hybridity. Moreover, it is likely that the latter was the effect of the former – in other words, that personal travel provided the opportunity for theoretical travels.[77] Spivak belongs to the feminist tradition, of which she has however criticized Eurocentric versions, guilty in her view of having ignored the relations between women's condition in western countries and imperialism. She also belongs to the poststructuralist school, particularly its 'deconstructionist' variant. According to the latter, Derrida's concepts are useful for thinking the status of the oppressed in the capitalist periphery. In addition, she has a remarkable knowledge of Marxism and – something rare among poststructuralists – frequently employs categories from it (commodity, exploitation, imperialism) in her analyses. It should be said that Marxism as a movement and doctrine has been particularly dynamic in India. But it is most often as a postcolonial theorist that Spivak is presented. With the late Edward Said, Homi Bhabha, Paul Gilroy and various others, she is one of the leading figures in this school.

Spivak has kept up a critical dialogue with a specifically Indian sector of postcolonial studies – namely, Subaltern Studies. The latter is a radical current in contemporary Indian historiography, which emerged in the 1980s and whose objective is to develop a history 'from below'.[78] It seeks to differentiate

---

75 See Stephen Morton, *Gayatri Chakravorty Spivak*, London and New York: Routledge, 2002, p. 203.

76 See François Cusset, *French Theory: How Foucault, Derrida, Deleuze, & Co. Transformed the Intellectual Life of the United States*, trans. Jeff Fort with Josephine Berganza and Marlon Jones, Minneapolis: University of Minnesota Press, 2008, pp. 109–10.

77 On the problematic of 'traveling theories', see James Clifford, 'Notes on Theory and Travel', in James Clifford *et al.*, *Traveling Theories, Traveling Theorists, Inscriptions*, vol. 5, 1989. See also Edward Said, 'Traveling Theory', in *The World, the Text, the Critic*, Cambridge (MA): Harvard University Press, 1983.

78 On the emergence of Subaltern Studies, see Jean-Loup Amselle, *L'Occident décroché. Enquête sur les postcolonialismes*, Paris: Stock, 2008, in particular Appendix 1. See also Vinayak Chaturvedi, ed., *Mapping Subaltern Studies and the Postcolonial*, London and New York: Verso, 2000.

itself from both British colonial historiography and that developed by the Indian elites in power since the country's independence. Subaltern Studies draw on two theoretical sources. On the one hand, it has been influenced by Gramsci, from whom the term 'subaltern' is taken. Gramsci used it in particular to refer to the peasantry of southern Italy in his considerations on the 'southern question'. On the other hand, the 'subalternists' identify with such British Marxist historians as Hobsbawm, Thompson and Hill, who specialized in taking the social categories absent from official history as their subject. Among the best-known members of Subaltern Studies are Ranajit Guha (a tutelary figure rather than a full member), Dipesh Chakrabarty, Partha Chatterjee and Gyan Prakash. Spivak has contributed to one of the volumes in the 'Subaltern Studies' collection published by Oxford University Press, where these authors come together. With Said and Guha, she has also co-edited and introduced a volume entitled *Selected Subaltern Studies*. One of Spivak's best-known essays, published in 1988 and entitled 'Can the Subaltern Speak?', consists (among other things) in a critique of the epistemology underpinning this tradition.

Subaltern Studies is a heterogeneous intellectual current, with an interesting tendency to hybridize with other currents. Thus, in one of the school's most recent developments, Chakrabarty has begun to reflect on the relationship between postcolonialism and the ecological crisis confronting humanity. In a text entitled 'The Climate of Humanity', the author of *Provincializing Europe* (2009) suggests that climate change makes it possible for the first time to envisage that humanity as such, not one of its components – workers, the colonized, women, or whatever – might become the 'subject' of history. The environmental crisis possesses this particularity, he says, that it concerns human beings without distinction, regardless of their membership in a class, race or gender (even if the way the crisis is experienced depends on such parameters). In fact, argues Chakrabarty, 'Unlike in the crisis of capitalism, there are no lifeboats here for the rich and the privileged.'[79] Coming from postcolonial studies, which have made a speciality of rejecting all forms of universalism, this idea is (to say the least) astonishing. Postcolonial studies in general, and Subaltern Studies in particular, have specialized in criticizing the fallacious universalisms put into circulation by western imperialism that aim to mask its brutal machinations. Were the hybridization between (some sectors of) postcolonialism and political ecology to take, it would not exclude the critique of universalism assuming original contours in the future.

---

79   Dipesh Chakrabarty, 'The Climate of History: Four Theses', *Critical Inquiry*, no. 35, Winter 2009, p. 220.

Let us turn to Spivak. One of her concepts, which has prompted a number of debates in postcolonial studies, as well as among feminists, is *strategic essential-ism*.[80] The critique of essentialism is ubiquitous in contemporary critical thought. It maintains that all identities, whether of gender, class or ethnicity, are socially constructed and consequently contingent. In other words, they do not refer to anything objective or substantive. The concept of strategic essentialism derives from this critique. It agrees that there are no essences in the social world. However, it draws attention to the fact that in everyday life and social struggles individuals frequently refer to such essences, to the extent that they seem diffi-cult to remove.[81] For example, the category of 'woman' put in circulation by classical feminism has generated exclusion in that it has sometimes led the feminist movement to dissociate itself from other oppressed sectors. Such is the criticism of it formulated by Butler. However, the category has also enabled women to mobilize as women – that is, to have a sense of themselves as belong-ing to a dominated group and to work for its emancipation. The concept of strategic essentialism maintains that the provisional fixing of an essence known to be artificial can in some instances be strategically useful. Alternatively put, anti-essentialism can only be theoretical. If it takes effect in practice, it tends to paralyze action, because any action assumes the formation of collectives and collectives tend to 'essentialize' their identities.

The notion of strategic essentialism has been criticized and Spivak has distanced herself from it. Any essentialism, even if only strategic, implies a separation between those included in it and those excluded from it. In a context marked by the theme of the 'clash of civilizations' and the (alleged) return of forms of communitarianism, or at any rate by the promotion of these themes by neo-conservative movements, it is problematic to let it be thought on the Left that some forms of essentialism are legitimate.[82] Even so, it must be acknowl-edged that Spivak has the merit of having raised a real problem. In Butler, Haraway and most contemporary critics of essentialism (whether feminist or not), the issue of the practical conditions for the emergence of collective action is neglected. In particular, what is missing is the issue of how to act collectively without equipping oneself with a minimal collective identity, recognized by all (supporters and opponents) and forming the programmatic and strategic basis of the activist group. For Spivak, obviously, the notion of strategic essentialism does not mean giving carte blanche to any imaginable essentialist impulse. Even if she does not formulate it in such terms, the issue is ultimately not so much whether essences should be dismissed, as opposing good essences to bad ones.

---

80   See, for example, Sara Danius and Stefan Josson, 'An Interview with Gayatri Chakravorty Spivak', *Boundary* 2, no. 20, 1993.

81   Chris Barker, *The Sage Dictionary of Cultural Studies*, London: Sage, 2004, p. 189.

82   Amselle, *L'Occident décroché*, p. 146.

One of Spivak's special interests is the complex and politically explosive relations between the female condition and imperialism. This led her to re-read a series of classics of English literature and expose the 'imperialist unconscious' they contain. Here we can recognize the influence of Edward Said, particularly his work *Orientalism*, published in 1978. According to Spivak, 'It should not be possible to read nineteenth-century British literature without remembering that imperialism, understood as England's social mission, was a crucial part of the cultural representation of England to the English.'[83] This assertion concerns the oeuvres most directly bound up with the colonial problematic (Stevenson, Kipling, Conrad), as well as those seemingly unrelated to it. In particular, Spivak has offered an innovative reading of *Jane Eyre*, Charlotte Brontë's novel published in 1847 (incidentally, the year the *Communist Manifesto* was written). Edward Rochester, future husband of the heroine Jane, was previously married to a woman called Bertha Mason. The latter sinks into madness, is shut up by her husband and ends up perishing in a fire. Bertha Mason is a creole, of Jamaican origin. She is presented by Brontë in terms that locate her on the boundary between animality and humanity, her postures, for example, being compared with those of an animal. Moreover, her death is what allows Jane to marry Rochester. Spivak concludes from this that the emergence of an autonomous feminine subject in the nineteenth century – of which Jane Eyre is regarded as the expression – has as its condition the negation of the autonomy of women from the colonies, their reduction to a pre-human state. This is clear if we think of the fact that women's emancipation from domestic tasks presupposes the support of domestic staff often hailing from the colonies (and dominated social classes). As a result, the history of women's condition and that of imperialism cannot be separated. They must be conceived together – something that feminism has not hitherto sufficiently done.

'Can the Subaltern Speak?' is a classic of postcolonial studies and there are several versions of it. It is a particularly dense text, regarded by some as confused.[84] However that may be, Spivak answers the question posed by her title in the negative. The subaltern cannot speak and the historian cannot find their voice in history. This is what is at issue in Spivak's disagreement with the dominant current of Subaltern Studies. The latter's objective is to unearth the actions and representations of the dominated, those whose trace has been erased by official history. For Spivak, this research programme is a pious wish, for several reasons. Firstly, the author of *A Critique of Postcolonial Reason* criticizes the 'myth of origins' that often implicitly underpins the subalternist

---

83   Gayatri Spivak, 'Three Women's Texts and A Critique of Imperialism', *Critical Inquiry*, no. 12, 1985, p. 243.

84   See Terry Eagleton's critique, 'In the Gaudy Supermarket', *London Review of Books*, 13 May 1999.

epistemology. It is futile to seek to rediscover authentic native cultures under
the sedimented layers of imperialism. Imperialism re-writes everything it
touches, to the extent that nothing found by the colonists on their arrival has
remained intact.[85]

Furthermore, Spivak attacks the concept of the 'specific' intellectual who
only intervenes in politics in the name of competences strictly bound up with a
particular area – for example, for Foucault, madness or prisons – while believing that the oppressed are perfectly capable of speaking for themselves and have
no need of intellectuals to represent them. Spivak argues that Deleuze and
Foucault underestimate the scale and effects of the oppression suffered by
subalterns in the world's peripheral regions. They are simultaneously the object
of several forms of domination – economic, but also (post)colonial, male,
ethnic, spatial and so forth. The position of the poststructuralist philosophers is
at best valid for the dominated classes of the western countries, who have
equipped themselves over the last two centuries with organizations and institutions capable of making their voices heard.[86] Postcolonial subalterns, by
contrast, are so oppressed that they literally have no voice. This presupposes
that postcolonial intellectuals like Spivak herself must to a certain extent
perform a role of representation: 'The subaltern cannot speak . . . Representation has not withered away. The female intellectual as intellectual has a
circumscribed task which she must not disown with a flourish.'[87] The critique
of the representational conception of politics formulated by Haraway is not
adopted by Spivak. A form of 'representational politics' remains on the agenda.

A practice of which Spivak has made interesting analyses is *sati* – the
Hindu religious practice (banned by the British in 1829) of the immolation of
the widow with her dead husband. *Sati* has been the subject of numerous
historical and anthropological analyses. In the debates over it, claims Spivak,
one finds no trace (or virtually none) of the main people involved – the women
themselves – whose point of view is never taken into consideration and who
never appear in the archives. Invoking Derrida and his critique of the 'metaphysics of presence', she argues that the woman is the 'absent centre' of this
debate. She is omnipresent as an object of the debate, but absent even so for
never being regarded as the subject of her own acts. In her analysis, Spivak
claims that the opposition between colonized (connoted positively) and colonizers (connoted negatively), which is frequently found in postcolonial studies,

85 Spivak has had directed at her a criticism frequently made of Said – namely, not
integrating resistance to Orientalism into his history of Orientalism.

86 See Ania Loomba, *Colonialism/Postcolonialism*, London and New York: Routledge,
2005, pp. 194–6.

87 Gayatri Spivak, 'Can the Subaltern Speak?', in Cary Nelson and Lawrence Gossberg,
eds, *Marxism and the Interpretation of Culture*, New York: Macmillan, 1988, p. 308.

is simplistic. The Indian woman is the victim of a dual oppression (at least): she is oppressed as an Indian, certainly, but also as a woman; and the colonists are clearly not the only ones responsible for the latter.

CLASS AGAINST CLASS

In the history of the labour movement and the main doctrine that has accompanied it – Marxism – the division of reality into social classes was long predominant. From the outset, this division was blurred and complicated by the existence of other categories, foremost among which were national and religious categories. Nevertheless, the inseparably cognitive and political operation in which the Left, whether revolutionary or reformist, engaged for more than a century (from the second half of the nineteenth century to the last third of the twentieth) consisted in counterposing social categories to ethnic-national ones.

As readers will appreciate, the whole purpose of Part Two of this book is to demonstrate that a division once hegemonic on the Left is no longer so. The agents of emancipation have multiplied over the decades, while the weight assigned socio-economic determinants, on which the 'classist' conception of reality was based, has decreased. Nevertheless, it is not to be deduced from this that analyses in terms of social classes have disappeared. Contemporary critical thought contains sophisticated theories of social classes, which are probably the more so in that they are now without immediate political stakes, or at least escape the control of working-class organizations. Yet even when critical thinking does contain a class dimension, it is invariably only one factor among others. Thus it will be said that a form of class domination exists, just as forms of male domination or ethnic-racial domination exist, these different forms of domination being placed on the same level. This obviously contravenes the most elementary Marxism. From the standpoint of the latter, socio-economic domination – the confrontation between capital and labour, the commodity form, reification and so on – is not one type of domination among others. In truth, it is not even a type of 'domination'. It is what underpins all forms of domination and confers on them their specificity in the capitalist regime. It is a *logic*, which allows us to regard capitalism as a system. Male domination, for example, pre-exists capitalism, but is (according to Marxists) largely reconfigured by the latter.

Various strategic consequences can be drawn from this. The labour movement in its majority drew the conclusion of the 'centrality' of the relationship between capital and labour, asserting the 'secondary' character of other forms of domination. But there is no necessary implication here, and it is possible to combine the idea that the logic of capital is socio-economic with asserting the need to assign each 'front' the same importance.

E. P. Thompson: The Constructivist Theory of Social Classes

No doubt the most widespread theory of social classes at present is the *constructivist* one. Constructivism is a trend in contemporary social science according to which reality – social and/or material – is 'constructed' or 'socially constructed'. Constructivists invariably combine two ideas. Firstly, they emphasize the influence of social representations on the constitution of the phenomena under consideration. To argue (as does Benedict Anderson) that representations of the nation – the 'imagined community' – have a determining influence on the formation of modern nation-states is typically constructivist. Secondly, constructivists claim that social reality is composed of processes, not essences. Constructivism is an anti-essentialism. When Haraway criticizes the idea that immutable essences of 'nature', 'man' or 'woman' exist, she is associating with this current. More or less radical variants of constructivism exist. Some maintain that only social reality is 'constructed', while others argue that the same is true of material reality.[88]

E. P. Thompson belongs to the first category of constructivists – those who confine 'construction' to social phenomena. The object of construction in his work is social classes. Thompson is one of the major British historians of the twentieth century. He belongs to an earlier generation of thinkers than the one discussed in this book (he was born in 1924). If we have included him, it is because his theory of social classes is one of the most influential in the Anglophone world and beyond (as we have seen with Luc Boltanski), and because it exemplifies one of the current Marxists approaches to class analysis. Among contemporary historians influenced by Thompson, we can identify Peter Linebaugh, James Holstun, Neville Kirk and Marcus Rediker.

Thompson belongs to the group of British Marxist historians that included Hobsbawm, Hill, John Saville, George Rudé, Maurice Dobb and Rodney Hilton.[89] They were all members of, or close to, the British Communist Party. In their respective fields they developed a history 'from below' – that is, a social history of capitalism adopting the standpoint of the subaltern classes. For example, Hill was interested in the history of piracy and its relations with the nascent working class in England in the eighteenth century.[90] For his part, Hobsbawm devoted a book to 'social bandits', of whom the best known is Robin Hood, motivated by a concern for social justice and the redistribution of wealth.

88   See Razmig Keucheyan, *Le Constructivisme. Des origines à nos jours*, Paris: Hermann, 2007.

89   See, for example, Harvey J. Kaye, *The British Marxist Historians*, London: Palgrave Macmillan, 1995.

90   Christopher Hill, 'Radical Pirates?', *Collected Essays*, vol. 3, Brighton: Harvester, 1986.

Like many intellectuals of his generation (but not Hobsbawm), Thompson left the Communist Party in 1956 on the occasion of the Budapest insurrection and Khrushchev's secret speech on Stalin's crimes. He then became an important figure on the anti-Stalinist Left, identifying with a 'humanist' socialism. In particular, he sought to nurture the thinking and practice of this Left by studying the British 'radical' tradition. He wrote a book on William Morris and another on William Blake, in which he showed that the latter had been influenced by political and religious ideas formulated during the English Civil War (in particular, those of the radical religious movement the Muggletonians).[91] Thompson is known for his participation in several polemics that structured the British Left in the 1960s and 70s (the New Left). For example, he opposed the Nairn–Anderson theses on the 'malformed' character of the English bourgeoisie, arguing that it rested on an abusive generalization from the French case. Above all, in an essay of 1978 entitled 'The Poverty of Theory' he attacked structuralism and Althusserianism, criticizing them for ignoring the empirical facts in favour of an exorbitant conception of 'theory'. For Thompson, this polemic provided the opportunity to defend a blend of Marxism and typically British empiricism. In the 1980s, Thompson campaigned for nuclear disarmament.

Thompson was the author in 1963 of a great work of social history entitled *The Making of the English Working Class*.[92] In a historiographical gesture typical of history 'from below', Thompson proposed in this work to uncover forgotten aspects of the history of the English working class in the period 1780–1832, so as to rescue them (in his words) from the 'condescension of posterity'. One of the tasks he assigned himself was to produce a history from the standpoint of the 'tradition of the vanquished', to borrow a phrase from Benjamin. Factually dense, the book was also the opportunity for Thompson to develop an original theory of social classes, which was the converse of the conceptions dominant in Marxism at the time. Thompson was clearly identified with Marxism. However, his theory of classes represents a turning-point in the history of the paradigm, in that it was to inspire the 'post-Marxist' currents which emerged in the second half of the 1970s.

The main target of Thompson's theory of social classes was 'economism' – that is, the idea that social classes are a socio-economic phenomenon existing independently of the consciousness of their members. Referring to the title of his book, the historian thus asserts that 'This book has a clumsy title, but it is one which meets its purpose. *Making*, because it is a study in an active process, which owes as much to agency as to conditioning. The working class . . . was

---

91   E. P. Thompson, *Witness against the Beast: William Blake and the Moral Law*, Cambridge: Cambridge University Press, 1993.

92   E. P. Thompson, *The Making of the English Working Class*, London: Penguin, 1968.

present at its own making.'[93] The working class did not become aware of its own existence after it had come into being. Its birth and consciousness of that birth are one and the same thing, which there are no grounds for separating into an 'objective' (socio-economic) aspect and a 'subjective' aspect (class consciousness). Thompson did not deny that the relations of production have an influence on the formation of social classes. But if they are a necessary condition of it, they are never a sufficient condition. Alternatively put, were there nothing but 'objective' relations of production, there would be no social classes in the sense intended by Thompson.

The decisive element in the emergence of social classes is the formation of an *experience*, a central term in the historian's approach (which associates him with the British empiricist tradition inaugurated by Locke and Hume). An 'experience' is a set of values, representations and affects formed over time by a social class. To each class there corresponds an experience, which is more or less homogeneous depending on the epoch. Experience is in part determined by the position of individuals in the social structure. But the latter is insufficient to account for it, and that is why social classes are not, in the first instance, a matter of 'structure', contrary to what structuralists and various currents of Marxism think. They are a matter of 'lived experience', but a 'lived experience' that is historical and collective.

From Thompson's focus on 'experience' there flows a series of important historical consequences. The first is that in this perspective, social classes are not things, but relations. Social classes do not emerge separately from one another, only subsequently entering into relations of collaboration or conflict. These relations are constitutive of their very being, which means that like the 'ego' in German idealism, social classes 'posit themselves in opposition'. Thus, when the English working class constructed itself in the nineteenth century, it did so by opposing itself, and therefore in referring, to other social classes – for example, the landed aristocracy or the commercial bourgeoisie – by responding to the latter's 'possessive individualism' with its own values, such as solidarity or universality. This does not mean that the evolution of social classes is always synchronic. Discordances exist between their trajectories, but this does not prevent social classes from *co-constructing* themselves – that is, constantly referring to one another, including (and perhaps especially) when they struggle.

A second consequence of Thompsonian 'experience' is that it is always mistaken to speak of social classes in general. In so far as they are dependent on the context of their formation, they are always unique. The fact that they depend in part on the relations of production, and that these relations of production have points in common depending on the epoch and country (capitalism has

---

93   Ibid., p. 8.

enduring features), means that classes share certain characteristics. But 'experience' is by definition relative; classes therefore have to be invoked with maximum spatio-temporal precision. In short, the Italian working class of the 1920s and the Bolivian working class of the 1950s have little in common.

The thesis of the uniqueness of social classes defended by Thompson contradicts a central idea of Marxism – namely, 'universal proletarianization'. This has it that the proletarian condition will gradually extend to more and more people and that it will tend, moreover, to become homogeneous with time. By contrast, Thompson's position implies that the different national proletarian conditions will go on becoming more complex and increasingly heterogeneous. History is an infinite sum of unique 'experiences', whose accumulation singularizes each working class. The thesis of the uniqueness of social classes ensures in addition that there are no laws of history. The 'evolutionistic' Marxism of the Second International, but also the idea defended by Lukács that history is traversed by a phenomenon of universal 'reification', are foreign to Thompson. However, this does not prevent him from acknowledging the existence of similar 'logics' at work in different contexts.

For Thompson, social classes are a dynamic phenomenon. This makes them difficult to apprehend for historians, who always come after the historical reality they study. Affirmation of the dynamic character of classes is the occasion for Thompson to challenge a distinction frequently made by historians and sociologists – namely, that between the working *class* and the working-class *movement*. This distinction rests on the idea that on the one side there is the 'objective' working class, and on the other a labour movement which is set in motion when the working class becomes conscious of itself. The origins of this distinction go back to the contrast between class 'in-itself' and class 'for-itself' in Lenin and Bukharin; and its most recent version is to be found in Bourdieu's distinction between 'probable class' and 'mobilized class'.[94]

For Thompson the distinction is fallacious. The working class does not exist independently of its consciousness of itself. In many respects it *is* this consciousness. Like other classes, whether dominant or dominated, the working class only exists as a movement. The idea of a static social class is, in this sense, a contradiction in terms:

> class happens when some men, as a result of common experiences (inherited or shared), feel and articulate the identity of their interests as between themselves, and as against other men whose interests are different from (and usually opposed to) theirs. The class experience is largely determined by the productive relations into

---

94   See Pierre Bourdieu, 'Social Space and the Genesis of Classes', in Bourdieu, *Language and Social Power*, trans. Gino Raymond and Mathew Adamson, Cambridge: Polity, 1991.

which men are born – or enter involuntarily. Class-consciousness is the way in which these experiences are handled in cultural terms: embodied in traditions, value-systems, ideas, and institutional forms . . . We can see a *logic* in the responses of similar occupational groups undergoing similar experiences, but we cannot predicate any *law*. Consciousness of class arises in the same way in different times and places, but never in just the same way.[95]

The idea of the experiences undergone by a class, which are transformed into a 'culture' and embodied in particular social institutions (parties, trade unions, clubs, cultural and sporting societies), illustrates the way that Thompson defines classes. This theory forms part of a general tendency of (western) Marxism from the mid-twentieth century to concern itself increasingly with superstructural phenomena. For Thompson, a class is perhaps primarily defined by its culture. Its material substratum is not dismissed, but the relative weight of the latter as an explanatory factor is clearly less than in other Marxist analyses of social classes.

David Harvey: The Community of Class and the Class of Community

In the previous chapter, we referred to the way that Harvey conceives the 'new imperialism' and, in particular, the manner in which he brings out capitalism's tendency towards spatial expansion. To his theory of imperialism Harvey adds a subtle theory of social classes. Of all the thinkers mentioned in this book, the author of *The Limits to Capital* is one of the most impressive and one of the closest to the 'totalizing' ambition of the classical Marxists. His works pertain to political economy and sociology, geography (his academic affiliation), and cultural theory, to which he has attended in particular in *The Condition of Postmodernity*.[96] It may be that posterity will one day deem Harvey one of the major representatives of critical thought of the late twentieth and early twenty-first centuries.

An idea present in a number of theories of social classes is that they destroy communities. Social classes are frequently regarded as the collective mode of existence characteristic of modern societies, whereas communities correspond to traditional societies. This idea features in one form or another in a number of classics of economics and sociology – for example, in Ferdinand Tönnies' distinction between 'community' (*Gemeinschaft*) and 'society' (*Gesellschaft*). It is also present in Marx and the Marxists. According to them, capitalism gives

---

95   Thompson, *The Making of the English Working Class*, pp. 8–9.
96   David Harvey, *The Condition of Postmodernity: An Enquiry into the Origins of Cultural Change*, Oxford: Blackwell, 1991.

rise to a rural exodus, one of whose consequences is proletarianization: the transformation of peasants into proletarians. The uprooting of traditional communities by capital abolishes the family mode of production and leads to the formation in the major urban centres of a new kind of collective – namely, social classes. These are distinguished from pre-modern communities in that they are formed in the workplace (factories), now physically separated from the home; that they are based on exploitation – the extraction of surplus-value – and not on a form of 'direct' domination as in pre-modern societies; and that they strip individuals of their former social status. To say of proletarians that they have nothing to lose but their chains signifies that the fact of being prole-tarians has dispossessed them of everything else, including the social bonds that existed in rural communities.

According to Harvey, the relationship between social classes and commu-nities should be re-thought. One of the defects in analyses of social classes to date is their tendency to conceive the latter in an unduly abstract and 'de-terri-torialized' manner. Capitalist modernity is certainly destructive of communities. As we see in contemporary China, for example, it destroys traditional social structures and dumps 'massified' populations into urban centres. But modern cities are also productive of communities, which means that community and class dimensions are always interwoven in them.

To think the interdependence of these two collective modes of being, Harvey uses the phrase 'the community of class and the class of community'.[97] It signifies that membership of a social class consists in more than being subject to the same form of oppression, even if it consists first and foremost in that. Being a member of a class creates a community – that is, a collective culture or identity that leads individuals to share the same relationship to the world. The 'community of class' can, moreover, go beyond the strictly conceived bounda-ries of the class and rub off on other classes. Thus, what is called 'workerism' refers to the way that representatives of other classes – for example, students in the 1970s – adopted (what they believed to be) the culture of the working class. Conversely, there exists a 'class of community', which means that communities are not formed randomly. They contain a class dimension, in particular when they are found in towns and cities. Communities are not formed haphazardly, and if the development of a class culture or identity includes a degree of contin-gency, it is supplied with ballast by 'objective' socio-economic factors. These two aspects of collective existence must therefore be considered together.

In his capacity as a geographer attuned to spatial phenomena, Harvey defines community on a territorial basis, although this does not exclude other dimensions. It involves a spatial entity that refers to a group made up of

97   David Harvey, *Paris, Capital of Modernity*, London and New York: Routledge, 2003, p. 238.

individuals present on the same territory. The community is always formed by bonds of family, friendship and occupation (when the workplace corresponds to the habitat), or neighbourhood, since this bond is among those that lead individuals to group together geographically. Spatiality creates community. The space of community is not only real, but also 'imaginary' – that is, it is the subject of social representations that impact on it through the behaviour they induce. In several of his works Harvey thus highlights the imaginary of the modern city by examining some particular chapter in the history of literature, the plastic arts or cinema, all of them domains in which this imaginary can be apprehended in a special way.

The social representations attaching to the city contain a political dimension. This is what is demonstrated by Harvey's analysis of the Commune in *Paris, Capital of Modernity*.[98] In this book Harvey reconstructs the urban history of Paris in the nineteenth century, particularly between the 1848 Revolution and the 1871 Commune. The striking fact about this period is obviously the profound transformation of the city brought about by Haussmann under the Second Empire. According to Henri Lefebvre, the Commune was an attempt by the people of Paris to re-appropriate urban space against this transformation and the social class – the bourgeoisie – behind it.[99] With Haussmann, the latter took control of urban space economically, politically and militarily. The Prefect of the Seine destroyed the city's 'organic' socio-spatial constitution by building thoroughfares that facilitated troop movements, by developing its transport system (notably by constructing train stations), and by creating new *arrondissements* in 1860. In dispossessing it of its urban experience, he prompted the Parisian population to demand the 'right to the city', to employ a term of Lefebvre's adopted by Harvey.[100] Haussmannization increased spatial segregation – that is, the composition of the quartiers increasingly proceeded on a class basis. Haussmann certainly did not create spatial segregation, which had been a tendency inherent in capitalism for several centuries. However, it was accentuated during the Second Empire, in particular under the impact of geographical specialization in the production of goods and services, and the changes experienced by the property market.[101] This segregation tended to make social classes and (spatial) communities converge. If some quartiers – particularly the Latin Quarter – remained socially mixed, the tendency was towards a separation

---

98   For another approach to the Commune in contemporary critical thought, over which we cannot linger for want of space, see Kristin Ross, *The Emergence of Social Space: Rimbaud and the Paris Commune*, Minneapolis: University of Minnesota Press, 1989.

99   See Henri Lefebvre, *La Proclamation de la Commune*, Paris: Gallimard, 1965.

100   Henri Lefebvre, *Le Droit à la ville*, Paris: Economica, 1968, and David Harvey, 'The Right to the City', *New Left Review*, II/53, September–October 2008.

101   Harvey, *Paris, Capital of Modernity*, p. 241.

between classes. In a word, the latter were *spatialized*. Although Haussmann destroyed traditional communities by ripping the guts out of the quartiers, he therefore also induced the emergence of new communities.

The bourgeoisie's domination of urban space compelled workers to organize and adapt to the new configuration of the city. The originality of this conception of social classes is that it shows that capitalist space is always both an obstacle to be overcome for working-class mobilizations and a resource on which they can draw. The changes undergone by Paris during the Second Empire make the Commune an event different from the 1848 Revolution. In as much as these changes themselves responded (in part) to the latter, we note a reciprocal influence between revolutionary movements and the production of space. This influence is expressed, for example, in a new type of working-class organization created in these years. Under the impetus of Eugène Varlin, the *Fédération des chambres syndicales ouvrières* were founded in the late 1860s, bringing together forty trade unions – recently legalized – citywide. This federation, ancestor of the *Confédération générale du travail*, drew on a powerful old tradition of local mutualism, but was also born out of its instigators' awareness of the need to organize at a more general level. Moreover, Varlin was an active member of the First International – that of Marx and Bakunin – in whose first two congresses, in London and Geneva, he participated. According to Harvey, this *Fédération* and other organizations of the same kind were the fertile ground from which the Commune emerged. Their structuration made it possible to construct the city itself as the theatre of union and political operations. They did not thereby lose their local attachments, which ensured the anchorage of their demands in everyday working-class life.

Other elements attest to the new dialectic between classes and communities during the Commune. Thus, 'municipal liberties' were a key demand of the rebels. Some historians have deduced from this that the Commune was an event with a 'decentralizing' mission. That is, the antagonism did not principally pit workers against the dominant classes, but supporters of increased local power against an oppressive state. According to Harvey, albeit well-attested, the demand for 'municipal liberties' was a class demand in the context of the Commune. If 'decentralization' alone had been at stake, we could not explain why the bourgeoisie and the monarchists – who were partly favourable to it – fled the city so rapidly. If they had to leave, it is because such freedoms were inseparable in the minds of the Communards from an aspiration to equality. In this sense, the emphasis on 'municipal liberties' attests to the fact that the conception of democracy current during the Commune was a territorial one. The political and military importance of working-class districts like Belleville, La Villette and Montmartre during the insurrection is another expression of the increased spatialization of classes from the second half of the nineteenth century. This spatialization had strategically detrimental aspects. During the fighting, recalls Harvey, many workers preferred to defend their districts rather than the walls of the city, which facilitated the task of the *Versaillais*.

Harvey suggests that the 'globalization' of the city under Haussmann contributed to working-class internationalism. The 1848 Revolution had sometimes witnessed the expression of xenophobic sentiments towards foreign workers, coupled (it is true) with demonstrations of solidarity with oppressed peoples, notably the Poles.[102] In subsequent decades the need to raise the issue of emancipation more generally became clear. This necessity was not unconnected with the infrastructural – particularly architectural – changed undergone by societies at the time. As Harvey puts it,

> The space over which community was defined altered as the scale of urbanization changed and spatial barriers were reduced. But it also shifted in response to new class configurations and struggles in which the participants learned that control over space and spatial networks was a source of social power.[103]

The greater the scale and systematization of urbanization, as in the case of Haussmann's Paris, the more the control over space becomes an issue in the struggle between classes. Such control contains both a tactical dimension, indicated during insurrectional periods, and a trade-union dimension, aiming to counteract the effects of the spatial division of labour.

While it is based on historical events, Harvey's theory of social classes can also be used to interpret current events. In late 2001, Argentina experienced one of the most powerful insurrections of recent decades on a world scale. Following an unprecedented crisis, which led to the collapse of its political and economic structures, the country found itself in a quasi-revolutionary situation. That such a conjuncture did not issue in a revolution in due form tells us much about the conditions of possibility of social transformation in advanced capitalist societies. Be that as it may, during this insurrection new social actors emerged. The best known of them were the *piqueteros* – movements of the unemployed and casual workers. Products of the massive lay-off plans of the neo-liberal decade of the 1990s, they are among the most innovative social movements in recent decades. Derived from the Argentinian trade-union tradition, but unable to depend on the factory as the site of militancy because they were composed of unemployed people, the *piqueteros* put in circulation the slogan: '*El barrio es la nueva fabrica*' ('the district is the new

---

102   Ibid., p. 238.
103   Ibid., p. 239.

factory'). Since the factory was inaccessible, popular districts were to be made the launch pad for resistance to neo-liberalism.

What Harvey's theory of social classes demonstrates is that the district has in a sense always been the 'new factory'. In other words, it is a mistake to regard the workplace as the only site for the mobilization of the working class. The community – in the territorial sense – is just as important from this point of view. The implications of grasping popular spaces as spaces of resistance are important. Focusing analysis on the factory means regarding proletarians predominantly as producers. This tendency is evident in many currents of Marxism. By contrast, adding a 'community' dimension to the analysis amounts to making workers plural actors, engaged in production certainly, but irreducible to it. In this regard, Harvey recalls the importance of cafés as sites of political sociability in the years preceding the Commune.[104] Cafés were not only a meeting place between different sectors of the labouring classes, and between the labouring classes and 'bohemia' (journalists, artists, students), but they allowed the workers to experience the most varied modes of existence. As with their days, 'proletarian nights' (to borrow Rancière's phrase) must be included in the analysis.

Erik Olin Wright: Marxism Analyzed

A different way of conceiving social classes is proposed by Erik Olin Wright, a sociologist at the University of Wisconsin, a former Althusserian linked since the 1980s to a school of Marxism far removed from Althusserianism – namely, analytical Marxism. The latter is an attempt to fuse Marxism and methodological individualism. The analytical Marxists seek to endow Marxism with 'micro-foundations' of the kind that underpin neo-classical theory: instrumental rationality of actors, reduction of the social to the individual, cost/benefit analysis, and so on. They seek to free Marxism from what they regard as its most debatable aspect – namely, the 'holistic' conception of social classes and the determinist philosophy of history. This does not mean that they abandon class analysis. On the contrary, their ambition is to re-found the latter on what they consider to be more solid foundations. The best-known analytical Marxists are John Roemer, G. A. Cohen, Jon Elster, Robert Brenner, Adam Przeworski and Philippe van Parijs. Analytical Marxism has practically vanished since the second half of the 1990s. Some of its protagonists, like Cohen and Wright, remain attached to a radically egalitarian perspective, more or less tinged with Marxism. Others, like Elster, have completely aban-

---

104   Ibid., p. 241.

doned it.[105] Of all these authors, Wright is perhaps the one who has remained closest to the initial project of analytical Marxism, even if his ideas too have undergone development.

Ernst Bloch once proposed a penetrating distinction between the 'cold currents' and 'warm currents' in Marxism.[106] The former conceive Marxism as a positive, 'demystifying' science, whose objective is dispassionately to reveal the 'objective' functioning of the social world. Kautsky and Althusser, among others, belong to this group. By contrast, the warm currents confide in utopia and hope and admit the share of subjectivity and even 'belief' involved in Marxism. Benjamin, Marcuse and Goldmann belong to this tradition. Bloch himself is a representative of the warm currents and believed that, while their existence was legitimate, the cold currents should place themselves in the service of the warm. Obviously, we can identify in any Marxist a combination of these two components. For example, Engels, traditionally regarded as having accentuated the 'cold' aspects of Marx's oeuvre, took an interest in pre-modern communism in *Peasant Wars in Germany*.

For his part, Wright situates himself in the cold currents of Marxism. This does not prevent him from formulating a 'utopian' discourse on occasion, but the general tone of his oeuvre is clearly rationalist, not romantic. The epithet 'positivist' would suit him had it not become pejorative, even though it refers to a venerable tradition, outside and inside Marxism alike. An idea running through all of Wright's work is that the sciences – the social variety, at any rate – are capable of decisively aiding human emancipation by exposing the mechanisms that obstruct it. He refers to his research programme as 'emancipatory social science', which encapsulates the relationship he establishes between science and politics.[107] In this respect Wright is a rarity. In the contemporary human sciences the dominant viewpoint is to distrust the modern 'metanarrative' of liberation through knowledge. For a number of authors, knowledge – combined with technology – is the cause of some of the major tragedies of the twentieth century. Wright is perhaps one of the contemporary thinkers who has remained most faithful to this Enlightenment ideal, which was also that of the classical Marxists.

Wright specializes in social class. From the 1980s to the present, he has constantly resisted the tendency of social science to abandon class analysis. This is evident from the titles of his books: *The Debate on Classes, Reconstructing*

105   See Christopher Bertram, 'Analytical Marxism', in Jacques Bidet and Stathis Kouvelakis, eds, *Critical Companion to Contemporary Marxism*, Leiden and Boston: Brill, 2008.

106   Ernst Bloch, *The Principle of Hope*, 3 vols, trans. Neville Plaice, Stephen Plaice and Paul Knight, Oxford: Blackwell, 1986.

107   Erik Olin Wright, 'Compass Points', *New Left Review*, II/41, September–October 2006.

Marxism, Class Counts.[108] In previous decades, social classes were obviously omnipresent. Wright has published numerous empirical works on the development of the class structure in different countries.[109] An interaction between social theory and empirical sociology is one of the distinguishing marks of his oeuvre. It has also led him to make interventions in the domain of normative political philosophy and to discuss, for example, Rawls' theory of justice. For Wright, the problem of social classes is divided into at least four sub-problems: the issues of class structure, the (historical) genesis of classes, class struggle and, finally, class consciousness.

A problem that has attracted the attention of all contemporary theorists of social class is the thorny one of the middle classes. This issue has proved as difficult for critical thinkers as the unanticipated persistence in the twentieth century of nationalism or religion. A key hypothesis among Marxists is social polarization. According to them, society would increasingly be restricted to two social classes – bourgeoisie and proletariat – whose confrontation would result in a transition to socialism. All the classes located between or around them (middle classes, peasantry, lumpenproletariat) were destined to disappear. This prediction has manifestly not come true. The structure of capitalist societies has become denser and more complex, not simplified and polarized. In particular, the middle classes have expanded, particularly since the *trente glorieuses*. The 'petty bourgeoisie' – small shopkeepers or civil servants, for example – have existed since the origins of capitalism. But new social categories have been added to the class structure, among them 'cadres', 'managers' and 'experts' of every sort.

Theorists of social class have adopted various attitudes in the face of this problem.[110] Some have argued that the 'growth of the middle class' is an illusion; that the apparent enlargement of the centre of the social structure in fact conceals a rise in inequalities. This position has attracted renewed interest since the emergence of neo-liberalism, with, for example, the hypothesis of the 'hourglass society'.[111] But it was hardly tenable at the height of the *trente glorieuses*. Other authors, following the example of Nicos Poulantzas, Alvin Gouldner or Serge Mallet, have argued that capitalism has indeed brought about the emergence of social classes of an unprecedented type. The notion of the 'new working class' in fashion in the 1970s, or that of the 'managerial class' (to refer to a

---

108   See, in particular, *Class Counts: Comparative Studies in Class Analysis*, Cambridge: Cambridge University Press, 1996.

109   See, for example, Erik Olin Wright *et al.*, 'The American Class Structure', *The American Sociological Review*, no. 47, 1982.

110   Erik Olin Wright, 'A General Framework for the Analysis of Class Structure', in Wright *et al.*, *The Debate on Classes*, London and New York: Verso, 1989, pp. 3–4.

111   See, for example, Alain Lipietz, *La Société en sablier. Le partage du travail contre la déchirure sociale*, Paris: La Découverte, 1998.

different region of the class structure), are among the attempts to grasp the novelty of this phenomenon.[112] In some cases the new class is a segment of an old social class in the process of becoming autonomous. In others it involves an entirely new class.

Wright has proposed an original solution to this problem, in the form of the concept of 'contradictory class locations'. According to him, the middle classes do not in themselves constitute a class. The individuals who make them up are located in several social classes at once, whose interests are often contradictory. *Cadres* (and managers) exemplify this situation. On the one hand, they are employees – that is, they are not owners of the capital or means of production in the firm for which they work. Obviously, it is now common for these particular types of employee to have an interest in their firm's profits (via stock options, for example), which makes their situation that much more complex. But from the strict standpoint of property relations, they are above all wage-earners. On the other hand, their interests are opposed to those of other employees, because they have power over them within the firm or possess scarce skills which entitle them to sizeable remuneration. These social categories are therefore split.[113] The higher up one goes in the hierarchy of the middle classes – approaching, for example, the CEOs of transnational firms – the more the interests of middle-class employees can be equated with those of capitalists. The lower one descends in that hierarchy, the more their interests resemble those of workers.

The concept of contradictory class locations has numerous consequences, theoretical and political. First of all, it must be noted that the classes which occupy contradictory class locations change in the course of history. While in capitalism it is *cadres*, for example, who are split, in the feudal system it was the bourgeoisie. Its members were split between the aristocracy, on the one hand, which some bourgeois succeeded in entering through the purchase of titles, and the popular classes, on the other. In a 'bureaucratic socialist regime' like the USSR, it is the intelligentsia that is liable to occupy this position. It shares certain advantages with members of the *nomenklatura* (the bureaucracy of the single party), but it is a class distinct from the latter. The social structure is always complex and generates contradictory positions whatever the system.

The contradictory character of class structure raises the problem of class alliances for political movements and revolutions. In a situation of social change, several options present themselves to the classes occupying a contradictory location in the social structure. They can defend the established order

---

112   See, for example, Serge Mallet, *The New Working Class*, trans. Andrée and Bob Shepherd, Nottingham: Spokesman, 1975.
113   Olin Wright, 'A General Framework for the Analysis of Class Structure', pp. 24–6.

by allying with the dominant classes. The veering of the middle classes to the side of the latter is most frequently encountered in modern political history. But they can also believe that their interest lies in social transformation and ally with the popular classes. All large-scale revolutionary phenomena are, according to Wright, underpinned by this mechanism. However that may be, for him the class struggle always involves heterogeneous actors. Consequently, to count on the simplification or polarization of the class structure is mistaken. In this sense, the issue of alliances in not only tactical, but involves a certain conception of what social classes are.

For Wright, the mechanism that underpins the class structure in capitalist societies is exploitation. This concept, once ubiquitous, has almost disappeared from contemporary social science. One would search in vain in the principal sociology journals today for references to it, whatever the country under discussion. If an author happens to allude to it, it is in a vague sense. The current trend, including among thinkers very much on the Left, consists in replacing the concept of exploitation by that of domination, which is supposed to be more inclusive and clear. Thus, the notion of exploitation practically never features in Bourdieu. It is always a question of domination, even when his analyses bear on the economic field. The generalization of the concept of domination at the expense of exploitation coexists with the abandonment of the centrality of the conflict between capital and labour, and with the idea – promoted by Bourdieu and most of today's critical thinkers – that domination is always plural.

According to Wright, capitalism feeds off exploitation, which entails maintaining this concept at the heart of the analysis.[114] Exploitation is a social relation distinct from domination, which cannot be subsumed under the latter. In order to analyze the specificity of exploitation with respect to other forms of oppression, Wright compares the situation of the Amerindians when the European settlers arrived with that of workers in nineteenth-century US society.[115] The Amerindians were the victims of a genocide. This attests to the fact that the settlers had absolutely no need of them economically. A saying of the time thus had it that 'the only good Indian is a dead Indian'. According to Wright, this case refers to a form of 'non-exploitative' oppression: it can extend to the physical elimination of the oppressed population. Exploitation is a very different phenomenon. The exploiter needs the exploited, since the former's own material welfare cannot do without the latter's labour. For this reason, although class massacres can occur, capitalists are to a certain extent compelled to restrain

---

114   For another interesting analysis of exploitation derived from analytical Marxism, see Jon Elster, 'Exploring Exploitation', *Journal of Peace Research*, no. 15, 1978.
115   Olin Wright, *Class Counts*, p. 11.

their violence towards workers. That is why the sentence 'the only good worker is a dead worker' makes no sense.

According to Wright, exploitation is based on three principles.[116] The first is the 'inverse interdependent welfare principle'. It asserts that the welfare of the exploiter causally depends on the misery of the exploited. This implies that the interests of the exploiter and of the exploited are necessarily contradictory; the struggle in which they engage is not a contingent phenomenon. In short, the wealthy are wealthy *because* the poor are poor. Secondly, exploitation rests on the 'exclusion principle'. This principle maintains that the exploited are excluded from the ownership or control of certain resources and significant means of production. It ultimately refers to the (by definition) non-egalitarian distribution of private property under capitalism. Thirdly, exploitation proceeds from the 'appropriation principle'. The individuals who control the means of production appropriate the activity of those who are separated from them. The appropriation principle is what distinguishes the relationship of exploitation from non-exploitative forms of oppression.

Marxism has no monopoly on class analysis. A number of sociologists inspired by the work, for example, of Weber – like Anthony Giddens or John Goldthorpe (both British sociologists) – practice it. However, they do so on the basis of theoretical assumptions different from those of Marxists in general and Wright in particular. For Weberians, social classes are above all a matter of differential opportunities in the market. By dint of their different social statuses, individuals are more or less well-placed to access the available resources. For Marxists, the mechanism underlying social classes does not first of all occur in the market. It operates in the productive sphere, which can certainly then have repercussions in the sphere of commodity circulation.[117] Through the centrality he assigns the productive sphere, Wright takes the opposite position to the dominant trend in contemporary social science. Not that male domination or racial oppression is politically secondary – far from it. But what ultimately defines the capitalist system we live in, and underpins the ensemble of social relations, is exploitation.

Álvaro García Linera: Class, Multitude and Indigenism

Álvaro García Linera's theoretical positions combine several approaches in an original blend. His knowledge and practice of Marxism, like the singular history of the Bolivian labour movement, make him sensitive to the class dimension of social relations. At the same time, he has experienced the influence

---

116   Ibid., p. 10.
117   Ibid., p. 32.

of *operaismo*, especially Negri's theses, leading him to employ the notion of 'multitude' to understand changes in the contemporary world. In addition, the Bolivian indigenist movement, which emerged in a new form in the 1970s, has strongly influenced his ideas. All this makes for a hybrid form of thought, which is certainly characterized by a certain eclecticism, but one that is the quid pro quo of the primacy of action over intellectual activity, strictly conceived, in an unfolding oeuvre.

The Bolivian labour movement was one of the strongest in Latin America. The 1952 Revolution, which yielded the 'national-progressive' regime, was one of the most profound experienced by the continent in the twentieth century, and one in which the proletariat – especially mineworkers – played the most active role. According to García Linera, Bolivia was long characterized by the centrality of the *trade union form*. From the 1940s, the state officially recognized wage-earners' organizations and established a tripartite system of negotiation with employers. For some fifty years, until the implementation of neo-liberal policies from the 1980s, unions were the main vectors for constructing the identity of the Bolivian working class, more so than parties or other types of organization. The Bolivian Workers' Central (COB), founded in 1952 and long dominated by the miners' union, forms the 'backbone' of that class.

The centrality of the union-form in Bolivia from the 1940s until the 1980s assumed several guises. Firstly, in the history of Bolivia we observe an assimilation of political rights to social rights.[118] This means that the accession of the workers to the public sphere takes the form of their unionization. Alternatively put, the political is a function of the social. To be a Bolivian citizen is in this sense – when one belongs to the subaltern classes – to be a union member. The state made it obligatory for each wage-earner to belong to a trade union from 1936. A number of aspects of the everyday life of Bolivians were subsequently managed through this agency. García Linera shows that, via the unions, the construction of the Bolivian working class was supported by the state. Not that it was a creation from scratch by the latter, since the major working-class concentrations in the country's mining zones were a *sui generis* socio-economic fact. But the form taken by the working class largely depended on 'routinized' relations with the state.

García Linera stresses the temporal dimension of class identities. The union-form possesses the particularity that it establishes a *class time*.[119] Where Harvey emphasizes the spatial dimension of social classes – space as a resource

---

118   Álvaro García Linera, *Pour une politique de l'égalité. Communauté et autonomie dans la Bolivie contemporaine*, Paris: Les Prairies ordinaires, 2008, p. 48. See also Álvaro García Linera, 'Indianisme et marxisme. La non-rencontre de deux raisons révolutionnaires', *Contre temps*, new series, no. 4, December 2009.

119   Ibid., p. 44.

and as a product of class relations – García Linera stresses the temporality inherent in membership in a class, in the context of the union-form at any rate. Class time inextricably mixes personal time and collective time. It affords an opportunity for every worker to become part of a collective history – that of the Bolivian working class – composed of social progress, the struggle for national independence, revolutions and resistance to dictatorship. According to García Linera, workers are perceived in Bolivia as 'those who run the country', which places them at the heart of the 'imagined community'.[120] Class time also mobilizes workers for a better future. The permanent contract, which was long the norm in the proletariat, is the juridico-political mechanism whereby everyone saw their situation, and that of their descendants, continually improve. This particular temporality is an integral part of working-class culture. It regulates not only work proper, but also moments of festival, mourning and struggle.

That the working class was hegemonic in Bolivia does not mean that it was the only subaltern category in the country. It means precisely the opposite. That is, this hegemony implies the presence of other social categories on which the working class's model was imposed. In a country more than half of which is made up of Amerindians (Quechua and Aymara), the indigenous population has always represented a demographically imposing category. During the period when the union-form predominated, however, the social question masked the ethnic question. Concretely, it involved the same people, because numerous workers are natives. But in Bolivia, as elsewhere, everything is a question of categories and the development of categories, so that the same individuals can be successively perceived as workers and then natives. Between the 1940s and 80s, the social question (the category of 'worker') was preponderant compared with the ethnic question (the category of 'native'), even if, of course, the latter was not completely obscured. Thus, claims García Linera, while making it possible to establish and institutionalize the narrative of the working class, COB conferred a public existence on other subaltern classes. COB was a framework for the self-construction of social classes, but around the symbols, codes and organizational parameters of the labour movement. The trade-union filiation effaced or displaced other forms of self-organization by the subaltern.[121]

The union-form has been succeeded by the *multitude-form*. In Hardt and Negri, the multitude has primacy over the state. In order to exist, the latter must harness the multitude's potential, its faculties of coordination and cooperation, and the general intellect secreted by its members. In this sense the multitude always possesses the initiative and the state lags behind it. Although drawing on Negri, García Linera inverts this relationship. In his view the

---

120   Ibid., p. 43.
121   Ibid., p. 59.

multitude-form emerges when the state and neo-liberal policies destroy the previous political and economic regime, including the union-form. For him the multitude is therefore a defensive concept, even if, in good Foucauldian logic, any new form of power elicits original forms of resistance. His role as a leader and his knowledge as a field-working sociologist have led him to develop a more concrete concept of multitude than Hardt and Negri's. In the latter, as well as in other theorists of the multitude like Virno, it has a metaphysical air. Another difference separating García Linera from Negri is that for the latter, the multitude is 'postmodern'. It emerges when capitalism has destroyed everything else – namely, the organized working class, nation-states and pre-modern communities. For García Linera, in crushing the working class, neo-liberalism compels its members to fall back on pre-modern social forms. As a result, the multitude must be regarded as a mixture of pre-modernity and postmodernity.

García Linera offers several definitions of the multitude. For example, he speaks of 'an association of associations of diverse classes and social identities, without a single hegemony within it'. He also claims that 'the multitude is essentially an aggregate of *collective individuals* – that is, an association of associations in which each person present does not speak for themselves, but for a local collective entity before which they must account for their actions, decisions and words'.[122] Neo-liberalism is characterized by a dual dynamic of the privatization of public goods and the fragmentation and flexibilization of the labour market. This dual dynamic has several consequences. The abolition of the permanent contract as a norm diversifies the personal trajectories of wage-earners and renders their identities increasingly singular and contingent. It also leads to the reactivation of rural communities, from which the modern labour market had removed labourers. This reactivation enables capitalism to reduce wages and increase profits, since a growing share of the cost of reproducing the labour force is now borne by the community. From this standpoint, neo-liberalism and pre-modernity are excellent bedfellows.

Furthermore, the multitude is distinguished from the working class and the union-form in that it is not underpinned by a form of hegemony. When such hegemony does not exist, what prevails is an 'association of associations' – that is, a mobile set of organizations unified for a given struggle, but whose survival over time is never guaranteed. The idea of an 'association of associations', or a 'movement of movements', is typical of the 1990s and was notably present in the anti-globilization movement.[123] As García Linera puts it, 'Unlike the labour movement in the past, the multitude-form does not possess a

---

122   Ibid., pp. 15, 70.
123   See Tom Mertes, ed., *A Movement of Movements*, London and New York: Verso, 2004.

durable mechanism of convocation and consultation that would make it possible to transform the presence of its components into settled habit.'[124] In this sense the multitude is a more evanescent social form than the working class.

The lack of a 'backbone' in the multitude implies that *class space* takes over from class time. When there exists no mechanism capable of ensuring the movement's stability over time, its mode of unification becomes territorial. This phenomenon is the consequence of the retreat to the communities that we have mentioned. We observe that in many Latin American mobilizations in recent years, structures like 'district' or 'neighbourhood committees' have played a crucial role. Like Harvey and the Argentinian *piqueteros*, García Linera might claim: '*El barrio es la nueva fabrica*'. The difference from Harvey is that García Linera puts the spatio-temporal dimension of social movements into historical perspective. Some of these movements are placed under the sign of time (the labour movement), because their mode of existence is ruled by mechanisms that ensure their temporal stability. Others are placed under the sign of space (current social movements), for in the absence of mechanisms of that kind they are constructed territorially.

The multitude is defined not only by its 'invertebrate' character, but also by the content of the struggles it wages. García Linera notes that these struggles frequently focus on demands relating to 'vital reproduction'. The multitude seeks to contain, or even reverse, the process of generalized commodification characteristic of the neo-liberal period, which extends to what were hitherto public goods. An exemplary instance, at the heart of García Linera's analysis, is the Coordinating Committee for the Defence of Water and Life that conducted the 'water war' in Cochabamba in 2000. Opposed to increased water prices in their towns, its inhabitants rebelled and secured the expulsion of the transnational involved, as well as the 'de-privatization' of the management of water in favour of a municipal firm. This 'users'' movement, bringing together diverse sectors of the population (peasants, natives, civil servants, middle classes, intellectuals), was one of the first cases of a victorious struggle for the collective re-appropriation of a privatized good.[125] It saw the emergence of a 'repertoire of action' widely embraced in the 2000s, which notably included blocking roads and encircling towns. Cochabamba is a city with a strong trade-union tradition, and many ex-miners who have switched to the production of coca leaves – the *cocaleros* – distinguished themselves in the campaign. The accession to power in 2005 of Evo Morales's MAS (Movement

124   García Linera, *Pour une politique de l'égalité*, p. 83.
125   See also Franck Poupeau, 'La guerre de l'eau', *Agone*, nos 26–27, 2002. On contemporary Bolivia see Hervé do Alto and Pablo Stefanoni, *Nous serons des millions. Evo Morales et la gauche au pouvoir en Bolivie*, Paris: Liber/Raisons d'agir, 2008.

towards Socialism) was largely the fruit of these 'wars', which multiplied in subsequent years, in particular with the 'gas war' in 2003, which culminated in the fall of President Sanchez de Lozada.

A third socio-political form highlighted by García Linera is the *community-form*, whose relations with the union-form and the multitude-form he studies. These three forms refer to real processes, but they also possess an 'ideal-typical' character – that is, they are stylized concepts that make it possible to grasp a complex reality. Thus, each concrete social situation must be regarded as a mutable blend of union-form, multitude-form and community-form.

The reactivation of traditional rural communities is bound up with the neo-liberal destruction of the labour market from the 1980s onwards. Another factor that contributed to the resurgence of the community-form was the appearance of a new indigenist 'imaginary' from the 1970s. It emerged under the impetus of Aymara Indians living on the periphery of the big cities who had had access to higher education.[126] As in Anderson's theory of nationalism, to which García Linera explicitly refers, a newly formed elite equipped itself with an idiosyncratic ideology and called for collective mobilization, in this case on an 'ethnic' basis. This new indigenism is not confined to Bolivia. It involves all Latin American countries with indigenous populations. In Bolivia the movement takes the form of 'Katarism', from the name of the rebel native of the eighteenth century, Tupac Katari, whom the MAS regards as one of its ideological 'matrices'.[127]

The traditional form of the indigenous community in the Andean world is the *ayllu*. This refers to a type of community that mixes individual and family property with collective property. It is thought to have its origins in the Inca and even pre-Inca social structure. García Linera underlines the tactical effects of the community-form. The blocking of towns made it possible to 'suffocate' the powers that be until demands were met. The problem is that a long siege of a town is not easy to implement and presupposes strong collective discipline. Such action would not have been possible without the community-form:

> The fact that so many people were able to stay on the roads for so long is explained by the system of rotation immediately put in place. Every 24 hours the mobilized population of a community was replaced by that of a different community, so that the first could rest and devote a few days to agricultural tasks, before returning to the mobilization when its turn came round again.[128]

---

126   García Linera, *Pour une politique de l'égalité*, p. 17.
127   Ibid., p. 28.
128   Ibid., p. 103.

Thus, almost half a million people took part in the siege of La Paz in 2000. The social structure of the actors involved in a struggle therefore has a decisive influence on the tactical repertoire employed on the ground. The union-form makes certain types of strategy possible, the community-form others.

CONFLICTUAL IDENTITIES

The concept of identity is ubiquitous in the contemporary human sciences: it occupies the central place once held by notions such as 'social class' or 'structure'. The 1960s witnessed the gradual emergence of 'identity politics', which sought to struggle against the stigmatization of certain social categories. This politics takes different forms depending on the part of the world concerned. But it is current to varying degrees in all developed countries.

The origins of the concept of identity go back to the classical British empiricists, particularly Locke, who applied it to the problem of the persistence of the person over time.[129] This inextricably descriptive and normative concept (it is bound up with the emergence of the modern concept of personal responsibility) was imported into social science proper around the mid-twentieth century. It initially referred in 'essentialist' mode to supposedly homogeneous social groups. However, it became more flexible with time and it is the 'constructivist' approach to identities that now prevails. The latter rests on a combination of two theses: on the one hand, identities are not states or 'substances', but processes; on the other, identities depend ontologically on the way they are perceived by others.

Nancy Fraser, Axel Honneth, Seyla Benhabib: The Theory of Recognition

These two aspects are present in the theory of 'recognition'. Among the thinkers who develop this theory, Charles Taylor, Axel Honneth, Nancy Fraser and Seyla Benhabib stand out. A number of these authors (not all) regard themselves as inheritors of the Frankfurt School. They are frequently presented as the 'third generation' of that school, following the generation of the founders – Adorno and Horkheimer – and the second generation headed by Habermas and Karl-Otto Apel. The idea of continuing to develop a 'Critical Theory' of capitalism, adapting it to the present, is clearly expressed in their work, as is that of combining normative political philosophy with empirical sociology to analyze society conceived as a 'totality'.[130]

---

129   See Razmig Keucheyan, *Le Constructivisme. Des origines à nos jours*, chapter 3.
130   On the concept of 'totality' in Marxism in general, and the Frankfurt School in particular, see Jay, *Marxism and Totality*.

In the transition from the second generation to the third, Critical Theory has undergone a dual transformation. First of all, it has become more open to women, with several leading figures of the current generation – notably Fraser and Benhabib – being female. Such a development is noticeable in critical thinking in general, even if a majority of authors referred to in this book remain men. Secondly, Critical Theory has left its native land – Germany – and been exported to other parts of the globe, especially North America. It goes without saying that the exile of representatives of the first generation in the United States during the Second World War had some influence in this. Thus, if Honneth, current director of the Institute for Social Research, is German, Fraser is American and Benhabib Turkish (though she teaches at Yale University), while Taylor is Canadian.

What is the theory of recognition? The text that has popularized this theory is an article by Taylor entitled 'The Politics of Recognition'.[131] Born in Montreal to an Anglophone father and a Francophone mother, Taylor is one of the contemporary thinkers of 'multiculturalism'. On this basis he has participated as an 'expert' in commissions on the status of the Quebecois identity in Canada. His conception of recognition has consequently enjoyed a political sounding board. However, the problematic of recognition dates back much further. Hegel – and his master–slave dialectic – is habitually referred to as a source. In particular, Alexandre Kojève's interpretation of it in his *Introduction à la lecture de Hegel* (1947) had a considerable impact in the Francophone and Anglophone worlds alike. Going back still further, a possible source of the theory of recognition is Rousseau. In the *Discours sur l'origine et les fondements de l'inégalité parmi les hommes*, he claimed: 'As soon as men began to value one another, and the idea of consideration had got a footing in the mind, everyone put in his claim to it, and it became impossible to refuse it to any with impunity.'[132] The idea that the (modern) self is based on 'mutual esteem' is at the heart of this theory. Among more contemporary precursors, we find authors such as Sorel, Sartre, Fanon, Mead and Donald Winnicott.

The starting-point for the theory of recognition is simple. Here is how Taylor formulates it: 'a person or group of people can suffer real damage, real distortion, if the people or society around them mirror back to them a confining or demeaning or contemptible picture of themselves. Nonrecognition or misrecognition can inflict harm, can be a form of oppression'.[133] According to Taylor, identities depend for their formation on their being recognized by

131   See Charles Taylor *et al.*, *Multiculturalism and the 'Politics of Recognition'*, Princeton: Princeton University Press, 1994.

132   Jean-Jacques Rousseau, *The Social Contract and the Discourses*, trans. G. D. H. Cole, London: Everyman, 1993, p. 90.

133   Taylor, *Multiculturalism*, p. 25.

others. Their ontology is inter-subjective; they have no existence 'in themselves'. This implies that if they are not recognized, or misrecognized, their formation occurs in adverse conditions. This applies at both the individual and the collective levels (the two are in fact inseparable). Stigmatized social groups are victims of an 'external' oppression that prevents them from acceding to certain statuses, but also an 'internal' one, which leads those concerned to have a 'demeaning' image of themselves. For Taylor, recognition is typical of modern societies. It is underpinned by a basic principle of the latter: the equal dignity of individuals. Recognition is simply recognition of that equal dignity and of the countless ways of life to which it gives rise. By contrast, feudal society was based not on dignity, but honour, which was unequally distributed among individuals.

Once that has been said, numerous questions arise. In particular, what remains indeterminate is the relationship between recognition and demands of an economic kind. The coordinates of this debate were fixed in a dialogue between two representatives of the theory of recognition, Fraser and Honneth. In a book called *Redistribution or Recognition?* they examine the relationship between redistribution, which refers to material inequalities, and recognition, which designates inequalities of status or identity. According to Fraser, struggles against the latter have proliferated since the 1970s. Conversely, movements of an economic character, which had marked the modern period since the Industrial Revolution, seem quantitatively less numerous and politically less legitimate. There are many reasons for this development. The greater complexity of societies has created a need for recognition among a growing number of social groups. In addition, successive waves of globalization have led to an increase in hybridization, but also to a growing perception of cultural differences. However that may be, Fraser does not hesitate to characterize this development as an epochal turning-point in the history of social movements.[134]

Fraser regards this turn as detrimental. It is certainly right to contest any 'economism' claiming that material struggles matter more than identity struggles. Such economism was long dominant in the labour movement, even if qualitative demands were always present there as well. However, 'culturalism', which is symmetrical with economism and which the theories of Taylor and Honneth are not free of in Fraser's view, must also be fought. For the proliferation of identity movements has by no means led to a disappearance of economic inequalities. On the contrary, the latter have continued to grow in the last third of the twentieth century. This leads Fraser to defend a 'dualist' position. Every injustice is composed to varying degrees of material and status elements. Moreover, capitalism is the first system in history to separate these two forms of

---

134   Nancy Fraser and Axel Honneth, *Redistribution or Recognition? A Political-Philosophical Exchange*, London and New York: Verso, 2003, p. 89.

hierarchy to such an extent. Either economic oppression also induces cultural oppression (as in the case of the devaluation of working-class culture), or identity oppression induces economic oppression (as in the case of the structural poverty of blacks in the United States), or these two variables operate in concert, but independently of one another, on the relevant social category.

Gender oppression is typical of the last case. Gender is a hybrid category. It combines economic aspects – since, for example, women's domestic labour is not remunerated, while being a condition of possibility for the male wage-earning class – and symbolic aspects – for our patriarchal societies devalue or negatively connote what is feminine. Obviously, it would be absurd to demand the abolition of the female condition in the same way one demands the abolition of poverty. The demand for the abolition pure and simple of an injustice makes sense only when it pertains exclusively to the economy. Once the dimension of identity or status is at stake, material requirements and status recognition necessarily go together. In this connection, Fraser indicates that the need for recognition also exists in the case of the working class, whose form of oppression is mainly, but not exclusively, economic. In fact, a 'class racism' – wounds to identity resulting from membership in the working class – exists.[135]

Unlike Taylor and Honneth, Fraser regards recognition as a political category, not a moral or psychological one. More precisely, in her view recognition is above all a matter of social justice. If that were not so, how would it be possible to distinguish legitimate forms of recognition (of women, blacks or homosexuals) from illegitimate ones? Can a racist assert his right to be 'recognized' as such if he believes that the lack of recognition harms his identity? Certainly not: racist identity has no justification, because it is illegitimate. At the root of Fraser's conception of recognition we consequently find a political value system. This leads her to state what she believes to be the basic principle of modern democratic politics – namely, 'parity of participation'.[136] This principle asserts that social institutions (whether state institutions or otherwise) must ensure that each person is in a position to interact with others as an 'equal'. It involves the satisfaction of two conditions.[137] Firstly, an objective condition, which ensures each equal person the material resources required to make their voice heard. Any individual or social group in a situation of extreme poverty is obviously not in a position to do so. Secondly, an intersubjective condition, which recognizes the equal value of all ways of life. Fraser presents the principle of 'parity of participation' as a radicalization of

---

135   See, for example, Pierre Bourdieu, 'Le racisme d'intelligence', *Questions de sociologie*, Paris: Minuit, 1980.

136   Fraser and Honneth, *Redistribution or Recognition?*, pp. 36–7.

137   Ibid., p. 37.

the liberal principle of equality. It is interesting to note that Fraser locates her work in the liberal tradition (in the Anglo-American, i.e. historical, sense), claiming that her objective is to radicalize it while incorporating the positive elements it contains. Such an attitude towards liberalism is rare in contemporary critical thought.

Honneth is opposed to Fraser's dualism. The standpoint he develops is 'monistic' in the sense that any injustice is ultimately a matter of recognition for him. Recognition is therefore the central category and redistribution a derivative one. Honneth does not deny the existence of economic inequalities. In a work entitled *Reification* he inscribes his analyses in the tradition of the critique of 'reification' that goes back to Lukács's *History and Class Consciousness*, and which was continued by the original Frankfurt School. In the conclusion to his book, Honneth argues that current societies are taking the path of general commodification (i.e. reification) glimpsed by Lukács early in the twentieth century.[138] When Fraser criticizes Honneth for his 'culturalism', the critique is therefore partly unjustified. The centrepiece of the German philosopher's theoretical apparatus is the argument that human beings are moral animals. On the one hand, this means that they strive for 'self-realization'. Like Taylor, Honneth believes that the latter takes the form of recognition by others. Honneth does not disconnect his theory from a reflection on the 'good life' – that is, a conception of human nature. By contrast, Fraser's (radical) liberalism leads her to refuse to get into a 'substantive' conception of justice, and to favour a form of 'proceduralism' that defines the rules of sociability rather than its content. On the other hand, according to Honneth, any injustice is subjectively lived by the individual as a moral wrong. This also applies to economic injustices. If the labour movement often prioritized demands of a material kind, they did not take a corporatist-sectionalist form; they always referred to values like justice or equality.

Honneth defends the idea that the theory of recognition forms part of a dominated intellectual tradition in modern history, which should be rehabilitated in the face of the dominant tradition. The dominant tradition has its origins in Machiavelli and Hobbes and includes liberalism in all its diversity. It regards the social world as composed of individuals and, what is more, individuals engaged in rational calculation. Honneth's stress on the moral or normative structure of human behaviour adopts the converse position. For him, the capacity of individuals to conceive themselves as such, and engage in rational calculation, presupposes that they have already been recognized as individuals by others.

---

138   Axel Honneth, *Reification: A New Look at an Old Idea*, Oxford: Oxford University Press, 2008, p. 21ff.

The interest of Benhabib's social theory compared with those of Fraser and Honneth is that it investigates the effects of globalization on contemporary inter-subjective processes. Benhabib also identifies with the legacy of the Frankfurt School. Finding her source of inspiration in Habermas's dialogism (the 'theory of communicative action'), she complements it with problematics derived from the oeuvre of Arendt, on whom she has written a book.[139] In addition, like Butler, Haraway, Spivak and Fraser, she participates in contemporary feminist debates.

Benhabib has developed a theory of 'cosmopolitanism'.[140] In some respects it may be regarded as an extension of the theory of recognition to the level of international relations. What are the foundations of cosmopolitanism, for example of the moral rules that govern hospitality to strangers? According to Benhabib, we must not confound cosmopolitan norms with international norms. Since the Treaty of Westphalia (1648), and the emergence of the modern geopolitical order, relations between states have been regulated by international law. The source of the latter ultimately lies in the sovereignty of states, either because it emanates from bilateral treaties or because it is enacted by multilateral organizations whose legitimacy derives from member-states. However, the situation has changed in recent decades. Governmental and non-governmental international organizations have proliferated, migratory movements have increased, and the volume of international regulation has reached significant proportions, to the point of prevailing over national jurisdictions in many cases. Consequently, the issue of the nature of the norms on which this juridical and political globalization is based has become more acute. In particular, the problem has arisen of the relationship between cosmopolitan norms and the citizenship rights enjoyed by persons by virtue of their membership in a nation-state.

The classical liberal answer to the question of the foundations of cosmopolitanism consists in leaving it to human rights. In this perspective, human beings are endowed with natural rights prior to citizenship, which cosmopolitanism merely reveals or actualizes. Benhabib rejects this option, which she regards as 'essentialist' – as assuming a human nature from which human rights proceed. Universalism, claims the author of *The Rights of Others*, can only be dialogical – that is, it can only proceed from the gradual mutual recognition of moral positions that were initially opposed.[141] The solution proposed by

139   Seyla Benhabib, *The Reluctant Modernism of Hannah Arendt*, New York: Rowman & Littlefield, 2003.

140   See, for example, Seyla Benhabib, *Another Cosmopolitanism*, Oxford: Oxford University Press, 2006. See also the works by Ulrich Beck on this issue – for example, Ulrich Beck and Ciaran Cronin, *Cosmopolitan Vision*, Cambridge: Polity, 2006.

141   Benhabib, *Another Cosmopolitanism*, p. 20.

Benhabib rests on the postulate of the emergence of a 'global civil society'. In time it will be able to confer a legitimacy on cosmopolitan norms analogous to that conferred by national civil societies on national rights. Benhabib advances the concept of 'democratic iteration'. Inspired by Derrida's philosophy of language, this concept assumes that any application of a norm involves the introduction of a difference, however minimal, from previous applications of the same norm. The meaning of a norm is never fixed once and for all. New actors can always seize hold of the semantic indeterminacy that surrounds it and give it a new meaning. By recognizing itself and assigning new meanings to existing international regulations, global civil society will thus gradually construct the legitimacy of a new cosmopolitan order.

Achille Mbembe: From Postcolony to Afropolitanism

Africa has a special place in contemporary critical thought. Postcolonial theories are proliferating there that seek to think the current situation of the continent, and to reveal the constructions of identity – the intersection of gender, race and class – that have been at work since decolonization. A striking representative of these theories is Mahmood Mamdani, who is of remote Indian origin, but grew up in Kampala in Uganda (where he continues to teach for part of the year, spending the rest of his time at Columbia University). Mamdani has notably developed a critique of western public opinion, including certain of its 'progressive' sectors, on the conflict in Darfur, arguing that this attitude is inseparable from the war on terrorism initiated by the Bush administration and the radicalization of conflicts it incited.[142]

Another important African theorist is Achille Mbembe. Born at the time of independence fifty years ago, a Cameroonian who did his studies in Paris and then New York before settling in South Africa, Mbembe identifies with a line of African thinkers in the broad, not strictly geographical sense. It includes Leopold Sedar Senghor, Fanon, W. E. B. Du Bois, Aimé Césaire and Edouard Glissant. He is a participant in many debates. In conversation with Spivak, Mbembe positions himself in the field of international postcolonial studies.[143] When he dissects the political economy of contemporary Africa, he interacts with economists or political scientists specializing in the continent. Mbembe has also played the role of general secretary of the Council for the Development of Social Science Research in Africa (CODESRIA). When he denounces the 'neglect of race' in the French republican-universalist tradition, he takes a

142   Mahmood Mamdani, *Saviors and Survivors: Darfur, Politics and the War on Terror*, New York: Doubleday, 2009.

143   Gayatri Spivak, 'Religion, Politics, Theology: A Conversation with Achille Mbembe', *Boundary 2*, vol. 34, no. 2, 2007.

position on controversies that have marked the French Left for twenty years. All this is combined with a theoretical eclecticism typical of contemporary critical thought, which leads him to draw on both poststructuralism and the phenomenology of Merleau-Ponty or Jan Patocka, and on Foucault's biopolitics, transformed by contact with Africa into 'necropolitics' – that is, into a power not over life but over ways of putting to death.[144]

In the modern age, Africa is the 'big Other' (here Mbembe draws on Lacan) of Europe. The continent is 'the mediation that enables the West to accede to its own subconscious and give a public account of its subjectivity'.[145] The constitution of the European individual as a 'subject' had as its condition of possibility the African individual remaining in the state of non-subject, confined somewhere between animality and humanity. Colonization and subjectivation are therefore two processes that must be conceptualized in conjunction, the second being largely dependent on the former. This same argument can be formulated in terms of the philosophy of history. In *Reason in History* (a set of notes and courses from the 1820s), Hegel presents Africa as a continent that is a prisoner of nature, frozen in time, which has not entered into universal history. This makes it possible, *a contrario*, to define European societies as having extricated themselves from the constraints of nature – that is, as historical. Despite the criticisms made of this philosophy of history for half a century, many of the categories still employed by the social sciences, with which they seek to understand Africa, remain impregnated by it. This latent racism is also evident in western politicians. In his 2007 'Dakar Speech', then French president Nicolas Sarkozy thus claimed that 'African people have not entered sufficiently into history . . . Africa's problem is that it lives the present too much in nostalgia for the lost paradise of infancy . . . In this imaginary, where everything always recommences, there is no place for the human adventure or the idea of progress'. Mbembe was one of the Francophone intellectuals who responded strenuously to these statements, indicating their origins in the colonial *episteme*.[146]

The fact that Africa is the 'big Other' of the West does not mean that the relationship between colonized and colonizer can be conceived in a simplistic fashion as opposition. One of Mbembe's contributions is to develop a subtle theory of power, in which Fanon's influence clearly makes itself felt, and which he applies in particular to authoritarian African regimes issued from decolonization. For Mbembe, the structure of power in the postcolony can be analyzed with the concept of 'carnivalization' favoured by Mikhail Bakhtin. In his work

---

144   See Achille Mbembe, 'Nécropolitique', *Raisons politiques*, vol. 21, no. 1, 2006.
145   Achille Mbembe, *On the Postcolony*, Berkeley: University of California Press, 2001, p. 3.
146   See Achille Mbembe *et al.*, *L'Afrique de Nicolas Sarkozy*, Paris: Karthala, 2008.

on Rabelais,[147] Bakhtin argued that during carnivals in the Middle Ages, an inversion occurred in the hierarchies underpinning the social order in normal times. High and low, good and evil, sacred and profane, madman and king are reversed, leading, for example, to the election of a 'pope of fools'. What Bakhtin calls 'carnivalization', which he argues Rabelais's work is an expression of, is therefore a moment – limited in time – of symbolic subversion of the structures and signs of power that is typical of Medieval popular culture.

In postcolonial African regimes, the relationship of individuals to power is similar in kind. It is 'carnivalesque' – that is, of the order neither of sheer resigned acceptance, nor of determined resistance. Thus, says Mbembe, 'citizens developed ways of separating words or phrases from their conventional meanings and using them in quite another sense . . . [T]hey thus built a whole vocabulary, equivocal and ambiguous, parallel to the official discourse.' Or again: 'the public affirmation of the "postcolonized subject" is not necessarily found in acts of "opposition" or "resistance" to the *commandement*. What defines [it] is the ability to engage in baroque practices [which are] fundamentally ambiguous.'[148] The clear distinction between domination and resistance does not operate in the postcolony. The two are inextricably mixed and the boundaries between them shifting.

The whole question is what kinds of identity are induced by this ambiguity towards power. The 'baroque' character of the relationship to power enables the individual to cultivate several identities, to change masks depending on the occasion, to play with words and affects. The resignation of the postcolonial potentate and a change in the nature of power would, from this point of view, involve an impoverishment in identities, since the latter are precisely bound up with the former. According to Mbembe, this is what accounts for Africans' profound ambivalence towards the existing regimes.

Neo-liberalism initiated a new period in the history of the postcolony.[149] In the decades following decolonization, although their income was often linked to fluctuations in the price of raw materials on international markets, the African states possessed a minimum of resources allowing them to ensure their territorial integrity, a monopoly on legitimate violence and, in some cases, a redistribution of wealth. These states entered into crisis in the 1980s, a crisis aggravated by the 'structural adjustment programmes' imposed by the IMF and the World Bank. The intervention of these international bodies set in motion mass privatizations, whereby states were dispossessed of the resources they used to control. This dispossession fuelled a drastic increase in the level of

147 Mikhail Bakhtin, *Rabelais and His World*, trans. Hélène Iswosky, London: Wiley, 1984.
148 Mbembe, *On the Postcolony*, pp. 105, 129.
149 Achille Mbembe, *Sortir de la grande nuit. Essai sur l'Afrique décolonisée*, Paris: La Découverte, 2010, chapter 5.

collective violence: civil wars, separatisms, struggle for state power, and so forth. The state no longer possesses a monopoly on violence. It is increasingly incapable of levying taxes and therefore running its administration. The emergence of 'ethno-regionalisms' and the proliferation of 'internal boundaries' in Africa over the last thirty years cannot be explained outside this context. These ethno-regionalisms lead to a sharpening of the distinction between 'natives' and 'non-natives', which one notices in numerous countries (for example, Ivory Coast), and the rise of deadly indigenisms.

It is interesting to note that depending on the continent, indigenism represents a progressive or, conversely, a reactionary force. As we have seen in our discussion of García Linera, in contemporary Latin America – Bolivia or Ecuador, for example – indigenism is today clearly a progressive force (even if it is not without its problems). In Africa, by contrast, its emergence appears regressive.

As we have said, one of the battle-fields on which Mbembe intervenes is the debate on France's colonial past. For two or three decades France has realized that it was also a colonial power – something that has set off numerous debates on the memory of colonization. French public opinion is gradually becoming conscious of the fact that colonialism and racism represent the 'dark side' of the republican universalism of which the country has presented itself as the bearer since the 1789 Revolution. As Mbembe puts it, France had hitherto decolonized without decolonizing itself.

Mbembe's most stimulating intervention in these debates occurred during the 'banlieue riots' in late 2005. During these riots, which lasted three months and in many respects resembled those that occurred in Britain during the summer of 2011, youth living in the banlieues of the main French cities, many of them issued from sub-Saharan or North African immigration, set fire to cars and urban facilities, and confronted the police in very serious clashes. These riots elicited indignation from all of France's conservative intellectuals (some of them from the ranks of the 'new philosophers' to whom we have referred), who rushed to blame Islam and uncontrolled immigration for the behaviour of youth.

In a remarkable text entitled 'La République et sa bête', Mbembe showed that the riots were simply the continuation of French colonial history.[150] The presence of large immigrant populations in the poor banlieues of major towns is a direct result of colonization. It is on account of the lack of development in their native countries that these populations came to look for work in France after the Second World War. This lack of development is largely due to the colonialism – and neo-colonialism – of which these countries are the victims.

---

150   See Achille Mbembe, 'La République et sa bête', originally posted on the website www. icicmac.com on 7 November 2005.

Moreover, the racial stigmatization of these people, among whom, for example, unemployment runs at 50 per cent among eighteen- to twenty-five-year-olds, is largely explained by the job discrimination they suffer. Such discrimination is itself the consequence of a racism whose origins go back to the representation of the 'African' or the 'Arab' forged in the colonial era. Finally, the policing methods used in the *banlieues*, whether during riots or in normal times, are inherited from the colonial period. During the riots, the government of Dominique de Villepin, who had resisted the Americans at a famous session of the UN Security Council in the run-up to the war in Iraq, reactivated a 'state of emergency' dating from the time of the Algerian War and rarely declared since.

According to Mbembe, the future of Africa lies in *afropolitanism* – a concept coined from a contraction of 'Africa' and 'cosmopolitanism'. It was invented during his time in South Africa, a country he regards as being in the vanguard of the process of cross-fertilization that will give rise to this afropolitanism. Hitherto three main doctrines have served to think and organize the emancipation of Africa. First of all, anti-colonial nationalism, which results from establishing the 'imagined community' (to employ Anderson's term) in the continent. In various forms this doctrine was at the helm during decolonization struggles. A second theory is Marxism, socialist movements having had a real audience in some parts of the continent. The third is pan-Africanism – a form of internationalism limited to Africa – which aimed to create international solidarity on a continental scale beyond the national borders marked out by the colonial powers.

Today, these three doctrines seem outmoded. The nation-state is everywhere in crisis – especially, as we have seen, in Africa. The idea that an 'emergence from the long night' (to paraphrase the title of Mbembe's last book) might occur by relying exclusively on this political structure is dubious. Moreover, nationalism and pan-Africanism (this is less true of Marxism) share a 'cult of origins', according to which, once decolonization has been completed, a kind of intact Africanness will (re-)emerge, enabling the continent to recommence its history on new bases. If postcolonial theories have taught us one thing, it is to mistrust discourses which exalt 'origins' – that is, to reject the idea that it is possible to rediscover a 'virgin' postcolonial identity beneath the colonial experience. Nothing of the sort exists, and origins are always hybrid. That is why, even if he has been influenced by them, Mbembe is critical of the advocates of 'negritude' like Senghor or Césaire. He is also critical of positions like that of the Kenyan writer Ngugi wa Thiong'o. In a book significantly entitled *Decolonising the Mind*,[151] the latter announced that he was giving up writing in English – the

---

[151] Ngugi wa Thiong'o, *Decolonising the Mind: The Politics of Language in African Literature*, Portsmouth: Heinemann, 1986.

language of the colonizer – and called on African writers henceforth to write exclusively in the continent's native languages. For Mbembe, such a project is not only impossible, it is not even desirable.[152] To argue, for example, that French in Africa is merely the language of the colonizer, and that its usage can be purely and simply abolished, is to commit a major political and epistemological error. French has undergone a process of vernacularization – 'creolization', as the Afro-Caribbean writer Edouard Glissant would say – on contact with the continent. It has become immanent in the everyday life of millions of Africans, who recognize it as their language.

Mbembe notes that what is habitually called 'Africa' is today disseminated to all ends of the earth. The continent has produced countless diasporas, from slaves who were victims of the slave trade to doctors or computer specialists caught up in today's brain drain. Conversely, numerous non-black populations – Afrikaners, Jews, Malays, Indians and so forth – have been settled on the continent for generations and are therefore fully-fledged Africans. Afropolitanism is the transnational culture that acknowledges the diversity inherent in 'being African in the world', and aspires to connect it with cosmopolitanisms emanating from different regions of the planet.

Ernesto Laclau: Constructing Antagonisms

Argentinian by origin, professor of political theory at Essex University in England, Ernesto Laclau has developed an approach to the political based on the notion of 'antagonism', regarded as constituting both the foundation and the boundary of the social. While, in principle, antagonism and recognition are opposed, one can advance the hypothesis that the clash between identities, however irreconcilable, always assumes a form of mutual recognition. In this sense, the antagonism conceptualized by Laclau excludes processes like genocide, in which the existence of the other is (literally) negated. It assumes that the opponent is *constructed* as such.

The political theory developed by Laclau is set out in two major books: *Hegemony and Socialist Strategy*, subtitled *Towards a Radical Democratic Politics* and co-authored with his companion, the Belgian philosopher Chantal Mouffe, and published in 1985; and *On Populist Reason*, published in 2005. Among his other works we may cite *Politics and Ideology in Marxist Theory* (1977) and *New Reflections on the Revolution of Our Time* (1990). Laclau is an exemplary case of a globalized critical thinker. A revolutionary activist in his youth in Argentina, he was for a time close to Jorge Abelardo Ramos, the founder of the Argentinian 'National Left'. His Latin American origins clearly

---

152   See Mbembe, *Sortir de la grande nuit*, p. 103.

inform his current conception of the political, especially the problematic of 'populism', which is heavily influenced by his experience of Peronism. But if Laclau sometimes takes a position on his country – recently extending his support to the government of Cristina Kirchner, for example – the intellectual space in which he mainly moves is the Anglo-American world.

The publication in the mid-1980s of *Hegemony and Socialist Strategy* stimulated important debates on the radical Left.[153] At the heart of Laclau and Mouffe's analysis is the Gramscian concept of hegemony.[154] For Laclau and Mouffe, Gramsci is situated at a turning-point in the history of Marxism. The author of the *Prison Notebooks* was conscious of the fact that some of Marxism's key theses had been weakened by the development of capitalism. Hopes of revolution in western Europe had been disappointed. What is more, an 'organized' capitalism emerged in the early twentieth century that Gramsci was one of the first (in 1934) to baptize 'Fordism',[155] and which was different from the 'liberal' capitalism of the *belle époque*. One of the consequences of this new kind of capitalism was the growth, contrary to every (Marxist) expectation, of the category of intermediate *cadres*, bureaucrats and 'intellectuals' of every kind. The introduction of the notion of hegemony into Marxism prior to Gramsci[156] made it possible to revise and adapt this doctrine in accordance with these trends, without calling into question its basic presuppositions. Hegemony makes it possible to grasp the increasing importance of 'cultural' factors in social relations, since it refers to the 'moral' ascendancy of one sector of society over the rest. It also makes it possible to apprehend each political situation in its uniqueness. In the classical Marxists, hegemony (or neighbouring concepts) is essentially a strategic concept.[157] It intervenes for the purposes of thinking cases where the proletariat must make alliances with other classes – the bourgeoisie, the peasantry, the middle classes – while ensuring that their general dynamic is conducive to its interests. It changes nothing in the centrality of social classes in the Marxist view of the world, or the fact that the class which is the vector of historical change is the working class.

In Gramsci, hegemony assumes a different sense, which profoundly changes the Marxist ontology: 'For Gramsci, political subjects are not – strictly speaking

153   Ernesto Laclau and Chantal Mouffe, *Hegemony and Socialist Strategy: Towards a Radical Democratic Politics*, London and New York: Verso, 2001.

154   As indicated in chapter 1, there is a specifically Argentinian Gramscian tradition of which Laclau is a representative.

155   See Antonio Gramsci, *Selections from the Prison Notebooks*, ed. and trans. Quintin Hoare and Geoffrey Nowell Smith, London: Lawrence and Wishart, 1971, Part II, chapter 3.

156   On the concept of hegemony, see Perry Anderson, 'The Antinomies of Antonio Gramsci', *New Left Review*, I/100, November 1976–January 1977.

157   Ernesto Laclau, 'Identity and Hegemony: The Role of Universality in the Constitution of Political Logics', in Butler, Laclau and Žižek, *Contingency, Hegemony and Universality*, p. 52.

– classes, but complex "collective wills"; similarly the ideological elements artic-ulated by a hegemonic class do not have a necessary class belonging.'[158] According to Laclau and Mouffe, Gramsci initiates the gradual emancipation of the concept of hegemony from that of class. This emancipation will reach its conclusion in their own theory. The 'collective wills' mentioned by Gramsci possess two main characteristics. The first is that they are contingent – that is, they are not predetermined by the socio-economic interests of the actors involved. In other words, they are formed in the framework of power relations and on the occasion of concrete social struggles. Moreover, the sectors 'articu-lated' in the context of a hegemonic formation can be of various kinds. They can involve parties and trade unions, but also territorial communities, ethnic groups, or collectives of uncertain identity that construct an identity appropri-ate to the occasion for the struggle.

For Laclau and Mouffe, despite the separation of hegemony from social classes inaugurated by him, Gramsci does not completely abandon some funda-mental aspects of Marxism. In particular, what they call an 'essentialist core' persists in his writings, which ultimately grounds hegemony in a mono-causal logic referring to the class position of the sectors involved. Laclau and Mouffe propose to take the theoretical move initiated by Gramsci to its conclusion and definitively abandon the centrality of classes. The latter can certainly be impor-tant depending on the circumstances. But the primacy allocated them by Marxism in principle is dismissed by Laclau and Mouffe. Several reasons lead them to this conclusion. Firstly, according to them, the social world has been becoming more complex since at least the eighteenth century, rendering it ever more heterogeneous. Far from being consolidated, as forecast by Marxism, the class position of individuals has consequently become more ambiguous. In addition, the industrial working class, once unavoidable in the structuration of social conflicts, has lost its centrality. It has decreased demographically over recent decades. The emergence of 'new social movements', which Laclau and Mouffe invoke in the same way as Fraser, implies that conflictuality is no longer necessarily organized around economic demands bound up with work. At a more fundamental epistemological level, Laclau and Mouffe criticize the 'class essentialism' present in Marxism. Their stress on the contingent character of social groups indicates that they adhere to a form of sociological 'indetermin-ism', according to which the (relative) coherence of actors is always constructed in the course of action and not a priori. Laclau and Mouffe defend a clearly anti-essentialist standpoint.

Abandonment of a class perspective has as its correlate the importance of the notion of antagonism in Laclau and Mouffe: 'Once its identity ceased to be based

---

158   Laclau and Mouffe, *Hegemony and Socialist Strategy*, p. 67.

on a process of infrastructural unity . . . the working class came to depend upon a *split* from the capitalist class which could only be completed in struggle against it . . . "[W]ar" thus becomes the condition for working-class identity'.[159] If no 'essence' underlies the social, the entities that develop in it are necessarily relational – that is, they are constructed with respect to one another or against one another. Interestingly, Laclau and Mouffe maintain that Sorel was the first to develop a conception of the world based on the primacy of conflict. Sorel had a decisive impact on the thinking of Gramsci, who in particular adopted the notion of 'historical bloc' from him. Influenced by Nietzsche and Bergson, Sorel attests to the existence within Marxist and post-Marxist traditions of a 'vitalist' tendency. Laclau and Mouffe are in some respects inheritors of this tendency. Their approach can also be conceived as a radicalization of Thompson's viewpoint. Thompson insists on the fact that class consciousness ('experience') matters as much as, if not more than, the socio-economic condition of workers in determining their class belonging. Like Laclau, he conceives social groups in relational terms – that is, more precisely, in oppositional terms. The difference is that Thompson does not therewith deny that social classes have an objective existence, whereas Laclau abandons this idea. In his view, there is no *a priori* element making it possible to determine where antagonism is going to emerge. It can be constructed anywhere.

On Populist Reason, which appeared simultaneously in English and Spanish in 2005, is one of the most widely discussed critical works at present. It is particularly so in Latin America, where Laclau's theses resonated with the experience of the 'progressive-populist' regimes that emerged in the early 2000s – namely, Hugo Chávez's Venezuela, Evo Morales' Bolivia and Rafael Correa's Ecuador. The emergence of these regimes is to be related to the long-term history of Latin America, which has already had experience of similar regimes in the past. Among them we find Peronism, a specifically Argentinian movement that arose in the late 1940s and which structures the country's political life to this day. The elusive character of this current in many respects – the difficulty of locating it on the traditional coordinates of modern politics – is one of the elements that led Laclau to examine the populist phenomenon. Generally speaking, Laclau's objective is to rehabilitate this phenomenon, habitually regarded as negative. In his view, populism is nothing other than one of the forms assumed by the political in modern democratic societies. More precisely, it is a condition for deepening the central value that governs the latter – namely, equality.

In the beginning was the radical heterogeneity of the social world. For Laclau the latter is characterized by the multiplicity and fragmentation of its components,

---

159   Ibid., p. 39. The centrality of antagonism in Laclau recalls that attributed by Schmitt to the opposition between 'friend' and 'enemy' in his characterization of the political. As such, Laclau is a 'left-wing neo-Schmittian' in the sense defined in Part I.

whose identity is constantly fluctuating. The heterogeneity of the social goes on increasing as societies become more complex. To designate this phenomenon, Laclau uses the phrase 'logic of difference'. Diverse social sectors issued from the economic sphere (trade unions), the community sphere (ethnicities), or others interact with the existing government and institutions, making demands that are specific to them. These demands are sometimes met, in which case the relevant sector goes on engaging in its activities normally. But it can happen that, on grounds of expediency or principle, government and institutions refuse to meet these demands. It is then that the logic of difference is liable to be transformed into a 'logic of equivalence'. The specific character of demands stops being such once they meet with rejection from government. They now possess at least one characteristic in common – that of having been rejected – which creates the conditions for an alliance between them. Populism is ready to make its entrance. Its precondition is the transformation of sectional particularisms into more general demands, which are inscribed in a 'chain of equivalence' creating the link between them.

An 'internal boundary' is then created within the community, which separates the field of power from that of the sectors whose demands have not been met. This boundary, Laclau says, transforms the *plebs* into the *people*. The people are always constituted as such in opposition to an adversary – for example, in the case of Peronism, the 'oligarchy'. To that end, the people often requires its demands to be embodied in the figure of a populist leader. Laclau's use of the notion of 'plebs' – originally, the Roman little people, opposed to the patricians – is similar to that of 'multitude' by Hardt and Negri. Moreover, we note a proliferation in contemporary critical thought of old concepts from Greek or Latin. No doubt it attests to the difficulty in identifying subjects of emancipation in the present conjuncture. The notions of 'plebs' and 'multitude' both refer to indistinct or uncoordinated conditions of the population, composed of irreducible particularisms, and not yet forming a veritable political subject. In Laclau, the transition from the plebs to the people via the transformation of the logic of difference into a logic of equivalence heralds the formation of such a subject. We may note in passing that in Negri, the multitude's mission is to remain a collection of singularities, which never becomes a people, because for him the people is the multitude whose potential has been subjugated by the state.

Populism presupposes the intervention of what Laclau, following certain structuralists and poststructuralists – among them Lévi-Strauss and Derrida – calls 'empty signifiers'. Empty signifiers are symbols, notably but not exclusively linguistic, invested with a different meaning by each sector incorporated into a chain of equivalence. For example, the meanings attached to the idea of 'equality' in French history, in revolutionary periods as well as those of the routine functioning of institutions, are countless. Likewise, in Argentina in the early 1970s, the demand for the 'return of Peron' from his Spanish exile had a different meaning for each sector of Peronism, as indicated by the shoot-out between them at Buenos Aires airport when the general's plane landed in 1973. According to Laclau, it is indispensable that populist signifiers be empty. Were their content fixed, they would be able to embody the imaginary or the interests of only one sector of society. It is precisely its ability to rally different sectors that characterizes populism. It may be that the content of the signifier originally emanated from a fraction of the population. But as the chain of equivalence is extended, it undergoes a process of abstraction that empties it of its substance and allows it to be invested with diverse significations. This leads Laclau to affirm, like Rancière, Badiou and Žižek, that the universal does indeed exist, but that it is an 'empty place'.

A third indispensable element in the emergence of populism is obviously a form of hegemony. This is defined by Laclau as a universal contaminated by particularisms, or as a unity constructed in diversity.[160] In *On Populist Reason*, hegemony is conceived in the form of synecdoche. Synecdoche is a rhetorical figure that consists in taking the part for the whole or conversely (it involves a form of metonymy). In Laclau's theory of populism the notion refers to cases where part of the social totality is substituted for the totality and speaks in its name. When the Bolivian or Mexican natives intrude into their respective national political fields, they do not merely aspire to find a place in the existing political order. They disrupt this order and claim to be the true repository of national legitimacy. They speak in the name of the whole community, not only in that of their interests. For Laclau such is the basic hegemonic operation: 'in the case of populism . . . a frontier of exclusion divides society into two camps. The "people", in that case, is something less than the totality of the members of the community: it is a partial component which nevertheless aspires to be conceived as the only legitimate totality.'[161] Here Laclau approximates Rancière, to whom he explicitly refers. It will be remembered that for Rancière the 'wrong' of which they are the victims permits those 'without a part' to speak in the name of the whole community. Laclau is not saying anything different. Hegemony consists in speaking for the community from one of the 'camps' separated by antagonism. That is what populist logic consists in; and for Laclau it ultimately merges with political logic *tout court*.

Fredric Jameson: Late Capitalism and Schizophrenia

Žižek, it will be remembered, proposes to rehabilitate the 'Cartesian' subject in the face of its 'disintegration' by representatives of poststructuralism, who, according to him, are the reigning masters in the 'western academy'. This leads

---

160   Laclau, 'Identity and Hegemony', p. 50.
161   Laclau, *On Populist Reason*, p. 81.

him to define the subject as 'empty' or pure 'negativity' and to argue that making an (empty) place for it is imperative so that concrete subjects can emerge. One of the thinkers against whom Žižek constructs his philosophico-political position is Jameson. According to Jameson, the subject – like everything else in this world – has a history. 'Always historicize' is an epistemological leitmotif for which he is well known, and applies to the subject as to any other entity.[162] The bourgeois ego, of which the Cartesian subject is a metaphysical prefiguration, emerged and prevailed during the modern age. From the last third of the twentieth century, however, it has been replaced by a new kind of subject, which in actual fact is not a subject as such, because it is fragmented and even constitutively schizophrenic. This subject is the postmodern subject.

Jameson was originally a theorist of literature, and has devoted a number of works to the development of a Marxist aesthetics. Perry Anderson regards him as the culmination of the Western Marxist tradition on account of his capacity, characteristic of that tradition, to bring Marxist categories into interaction with other currents.[163] In this respect it is interesting that the culmination of this tradition should be an American. Jameson's Marxism is eclectic. It incorporates concepts from psychoanalysis, poststructuralism, Greimas's semiotics, Niklas Luhmann's systems theory, Ernest Mandel's political economy, and phenomenology. To what extent this eclecticism succeeds in 'transcending' the elements it comprises in a *sui generis* paradigm is an issue that has been debated by commentators on his oeuvre.[164] Among Jameson's best-known books we might mention *Marxism and Form* (1971), *Brecht and Method* (1998), *A Singular Modernity* (2002), and *The Political Unconscious* (1981), which is without doubt one of the most influential books in contemporary critical thought.[165] Like Žižek, but in a more serious style, Jameson accords popular culture particular attention. From architecture to science fiction, video, and music, no domain eludes his analysis. As another commentator puts it, Jameson seems incapable of forgetting or ignoring anything.[166] Taking account of the totality of sectors is dictated by the historical period in which we live. In effect, it tends to blur the separation between

---

162   This leitmotif is notably sounded in *The Political Unconscious: Narrative as a Socially Symbolic Act*, Routledge: London, 2002. On the problem of 'periodization', see also Fredric Jameson, 'Periodizing the Sixties', in Sohnya Sayres *et al.*, *The Sixties, without Apologies*, Minneapolis: University of Minnesota Press, 1984.

163   Perry Anderson, *The Origins of Postmodernity*, London and New York: Verso, 1998.

164   See Martin Jay, review of *Postmodernism, or The Cultural Logic of Late Capitalism*, in *History and Theory*, vol. 32, 1993.

165   For an introduction to Jameson's trajectory and oeuvre, see Stathis Kouvelakis, 'Fredric Jameson: An Unslaked Thirst for Totalisation', in Bidet and Kouvelakis, eds, *A Critical Companion to Contemporary Marxism*.

166   C. Barry Chabot, 'The Problem of the Postmodern', in Ingeborg Hoesterey, ed., *Zeitgeist in Babel: The Postmodern Controversy*, Bloomington: Indiana University Press, p. 33.

'high' culture and 'popular' culture and obliges the analyst to confront cultural production in all its disordered multiplicity.

Jameson is the author of a famous article published in 1984 and then expanded in 1991 in the form of a (voluminous) work entitled *Postmodernism, or The Cultural Logic of Late Capitalism*. In it he tackles a problem much discussed in recent decades: whether we have entered into 'postmodernity' and whether, consequently, the modern age is at an end. Jameson develops his concept of postmodernism in opposition to two different senses of this notion. The first is that of Lyotard, articulated in *La Condition postmoderne* (1979), whose English translation was prefaced by Jameson.[167] For Lyotard, the main characteristic of postmodernity is the end of 'metanarratives'. During the modern age, individuals subscribed to such values as 'progress' or 'reason', which imparted historical substance and direction to societies. Postmodernity renders these values obsolete. Not every narrative has necessarily disappeared, but those that remain are local narratives of limited scope. The second author opposed by Jameson is Habermas.[168] According to the latter, it is mistaken to characterize our epoch as postmodern. The reason is that modernity is an 'incomplete project' and is such by definition. Habermas's reflection follows in the wake of representatives of the original Frankfurt School, especially the balance sheet they drew from the catastrophes of the twentieth century. The postmodern hypothesis rests in part on the postulate that such catastrophes have irremediably contradicted the ideals of the Enlightenment. For Habermas, however fragile these ideals, it is inconceivable that they be abandoned. The modern project must be reformulated – notably with the concept of 'communicative' reason – but must nevertheless be preserved.

Jameson significantly shifts the terms of this debate. For him, postmodernity is not a 'condition', but a historical period. It has implications for all areas, economics and culture as well as law and politics. Contrary to other construals of the notion, Jameson argues that the completion of modernity leaves no sphere untouched. Like Fraser and Honneth, but on the basis of different theoretical assumptions and objectives, he reactivates the concept of 'totality'.[169] It is one of Lyotard's main targets. 'Metanarratives' always refer to a totality, be it a particular society or humanity as a whole. Their decline entails the renunciation of that category. Conversely, rehabilitating totality assumes maintaining

167   Jean-François Lyotard, *The Postmodern Condition: A Report on Knowledge*, trans. Geoffrey Bennington and Brian Massumi, Minneapolis: University of Minnesota Press, 1984.

168   Jürgen Habermas, 'Modern and Postmodern Architecture', in *The New Conservatism: Cultural Criticism and the Historians' Debate*, ed. and trans. Sherry Weber Nicholsen, Cambridge: Polity, 1989, and 'Modernity versus Postmodernity', *New German Critique*, no. 22, winter 1981.

169   Fredric Jameson, *Postmodernism, or The Cultural Logic of Late Capitalism*, London and New York: Verso, 1991, pp. 332–9.

the possibility of 'metanarratives'. The concept of narrative is central in Jameson. In his view it is not only the condition of any historical reflection, but also what makes it possible to project oneself into the future. For him there is, in particular, one 'metanarrative' that enables us to account for our present situation: Marxism.

According to Jameson, postmodernism corresponds to a phase of capitalist development which he calls 'late capitalism'. This concept has been present in the Marxist tradition since the second half of the twentieth century. It was notably developed by Mandel in his book of that name.[170] According to Mandel, market capitalism (1700–1850) and monopoly capitalism (up to 1960) have been succeeded by a 'third age' of capitalism – precisely 'late' capitalism. It is characterized, *inter alia*, by the rise of multinational firms, a new international division of labour, an explosion of financial markets, the emergence of novel means of communication, and the weakening of the traditional labour movement. Late capitalism does not pitch capitalism into a 'post-industrial' age, as some contemporaries of Mandel believe. However, the changes it introduces in the production process are sufficiently sizeable to justify the hypothesis of a transition to a new phase of accumulation. Incidentally, if Jameson has this age start in the early 1970s, at the time of the first oil shock, for Mandel it begins after the Second World War.[171]

For Jameson, postmodernism represents the 'cultural logic' of late capitalism. The author of *Marxism and Form* rejects the 'standard' Marxist model of the determination of the 'superstructure' by the 'base'. Economic and cultural logics are so interwoven in capitalism that to maintain that one is the 'reflection' of the other is meaningless. From this viewpoint, postmodernism represents not a consequence of late capitalism (which would be its cause), but a 'translation' of the latter into the order of culture. With postmodernism, base and superstructure attain a point of maximum indistinction. Thus, claims Jameson,

> To say that my two terms, the *cultural* and the *economic*, thereby collapse back into one another and say the same thing, in an eclipse of the distinction between base and superstructure that has itself often struck people as significantly characteristic of postmodernism in the first place, is also to suggest that the base, in the third stage of capitalism, generates its superstructures with a new kind of dynamic.[172]

---

170   Ernest Mandel, *Late Capitalism*, trans. Joris de Bres, London: New Left Books, 1975.

171   For a critique of Jameson's periodization of capitalism, see Mike Davis, 'Urban Renaissance and the Spirit of Postmodernism', *New Left Review*, I/151, May–June 1985.

172   Jameson, *Postmodernism*, p. xxi. On this see Adam Roberts, *Fredric Jameson*, London and New York: Routledge, 2000, p. 120.

As a symptom of this fact, Jameson identifies, for example, the growing tendency of the artistic and economic spheres to intermingle. Today, a number of artists openly regard themselves as businessmen, while the language of 'creation' has widely penetrated the economic field. Among the thinkers who have influenced the way in which Jameson conceives the relationship between the 'cultural' and the 'economic' is Goldmann. The author of *Le Dieu caché* sought to identify the 'homologies' between the stages of capitalist development and the literary forms that emerge in them (for example, between 'organized' capitalism and the '*nouveau roman*' in the 1950s and 60s).[173] This style of thinking has been adopted and developed by Jameson.

What are the main characteristics of postmodern culture? A key aspect of this culture is what Jameson calls a 'new depthlessness'. 'Depthlessness' is to be understood here in the literal sense of the lack of any depth or substance, or of what is found on the surface. To illustrate the point, Jameson stages a comparison between Van Gogh's *Old Boots* (1887) and Andy Warhol's *Diamond Dust Shoes* (1980). The first painting represents a peasant's boots. Although they take up the whole canvas, they indirectly refer to a whole peasant world, which viewers are invited to reconstruct imaginatively.[174] Warhol's shoes, by contrast, are superficial in the sense indicated above. No perspective or spatio-temporal markers referring to any world appear in them. Warhol's idea is not, as in modern art, to bare the aesthetic devices that serve to construct the representation of the objects concerned. Everything happens as if objects had been stripped of their very capacity to be represented. In this respect, Jameson evokes the 'death of the world of appearance' and introduces the concept of 'simulacrum' (drawn from Baudrillard) to explain the aesthetic regime in which we now find ourselves.

To postmodern depthlessness there corresponds a new affective structure of individuals. An exciting element in Jameson's work is that, in accordance with the integral historicism he advocates, he elaborates a social history of the emotions in conjunction with the historical periodization mentioned previously. Late capitalism generates not only a culture, but also a new range of emotions, which conditions the type of subject formed today. According to Jameson, we are currently witnessing a 'waning of affect'.[175] This signifies that the major modern affects – anxiety, solitude, alienation – tend to fade. They have been replaced by new nervous conditions, of which the famous 'burnout', or 'postmodern euphoria', are paradigmatic instances. For an emotion as profound as anxiety to be experienced, there must be a subject who experiences it.

173   See Lucien Goldmann, *Towards a Sociology of the Novel*, trans. Alan Sheridan, London: Tavistock, 1977.

174   Jameson, *Postmodernism*, pp. 8–9.

175   Ibid., p. 10.

Furthermore, the subject in question must be endowed with an inner nature. Today, however, the subject is fragmented and schizophrenic, which ultimately means that 'there is no longer a self present to do the feeling'.[176] Does this entail that the history of the emotions is at an end? No. But what now prevails is impersonal 'intensities' that arise fleetingly on the surface of (what were once) individuals.

In the postmodern age, space dominates time. As Hobsbawm has clearly shown, the modern age is a revolutionary one in both the political sphere (since the French Revolution) and the economic sphere (with the Industrial Revolution).[177] One of the consequences of the emergence of postmodernity, according to Jameson, is the waning of this historicity. It results from a loss of collective memory, but also from a growing inability to conceive the future. The waning of historicity has as its counterpart a predominance of space. Postmodern culture, whether television, cinema or architecture, is a visual culture. Sight is the spatial organ *par excellence*, which tends to 'flatten' the set of elements it perceives. In reality, history and time have not really disappeared. They are repressed (in the psychoanalytical sense) by contemporary culture, but continue to operate underground. The task of critical thought – 'utopian' thought, to adopt Jameson's term – is to make a new sense of temporality emerge. This cannot be a return pure and simple to modern temporality; and it is important to register the current structure of capitalism and its cultural logic. But in the absence of a new sense of temporality, no social change is conceivable.

---

176   Ibid., p. 15.
177   See Eric Hobsbawm, *The Age of Revolution: Europe 1789–1848*, London: Weidenfeld and Nicolson, 1962, and *The Age of Capital: 1848–1875*, London: Weidenfeld and Nicolson, 1975.

Conclusion: Worksites

In his profound reflection, dating from 1992, on the then ubiquitous theme of the 'end of history', Perry Anderson sketches out four possible fates for social-ism.[1] The first possibility is that the socialist experience of the period 1848–1989 will seem to future historians an 'anomaly' or 'parenthesis' of the kind repre-sented by the Jesuit state in Paraguay in the seventeenth and eighteenth centuries. For more than a century the Jesuits had organized Guaraní commu-nities in an egalitarian fashion, distributing plots of land equitably and respecting native customs and language. These communities were a source of fascination to a number of thinkers of the time, among them Montesquieu and Voltaire. In the nineteenth century, Cunningham Grahame – a colleague of William Morris – evoked them in his utopian work *A Vanished Arcadia*.[2] Having aroused the hatred of local landowners, these communities were dissolved by a decree of the Spanish crown and the Jesuits were expelled from Paraguay. According to Anderson, it may be that the fate of socialism – in particular, the variant derived from the 1917 October Revolution – will resemble that of the Jesuit state of Paraguay. Three centuries later we know that, for all the respect it elicited, this experiment did not deflect the capitalist and colonialist course of modern history. At most the Guaraní communities are remembered by a few specialists as a moving but ineffectual event, without any legacy. In this eventuality, the fate of socialism would be nothing short of oblivion.

A second possibility is that socialism will undergo a profound reformula-tion in the future. Events will perhaps occur in several decades or centuries that will lead it to merge into a more convincing and effective political project. By way of example, Anderson refers to the relationship between the English and French revolutions. These were retrospectively conceived as part of the same *élan* on the threshold of the modern age. In reality, however, they differed in many respects. Firstly, almost a century and a half separates the Levellers from the Jacobins. The monarchy was restored in England in 1660, and it was not until the end of the subsequent century that a political process of comparable scale occurred in Europe. Secondly, the language of the English revolutionaries

---

1   See Perry Anderson, 'The Ends of History', in Anderson, *A Zone of Engagement*, London and New York: Verso, 1992.

2   This book was one of the sources of inspiration for Roland Joffe's film *The Mission* (1986).

was still essentially religious.[3] By contrast, the French revolutionaries employed a secular political vocabulary. One possibility, argues Anderson, is that in the future events will occur which historians will retrospectively deem to be part of the same long historical cycle as the socialist experiences of the period 1848–1989. But it may be that those who participate in these events will not perceive the link connecting them to socialism. This does not mean that no subterranean or 'objective' relationship will exist between these historical sequences. But it will not figure in the consciousness of protagonists. The resurgence of elements of socialism in a new form presupposes, *inter alia*, a doctrinal transformation of the latter. Certain dogmas, such as the centrality assigned the proletariat or the strategic model of military (Clausewitzian) inspiration that characterized it, will possibly be abandoned. It could be, adds Anderson, that the novel project will be organized around ecological themes, which are likely to assume increasing importance in the future.

A third possible fate of socialism would resemble the link between the French Revolution and subsequent revolutions. Unlike the English Revolution, the French Revolution founded what Anderson calls a 'cumulative' revolutionary tradition. Fifteen years after the Restoration, the streets of Paris were once again lined with barricades. There followed 1848, 1871, the Popular Front, the Resistance and May 1968 – events which, each in its own way, referred to the 'Great Revolution'. The repertoire of action and symbols deployed during the past two centuries largely derives from this original matrix. Doctrinally, modern – especially Marxist – socialism was conceived as continuation and 'supersession' of the Enlightenment and the bourgeoisie. A mutation occurred with Babeuf, without any break in temporal continuity. This is attested at a biographical level as well, the 1848 Revolution having, for example, been conjointly led by old Jacobins (Ledru-Rollin) and new socialists (Louis Blanc). Thus, Anderson says, it may be that in the future the same type of relationship will obtain between socialism and what will succeed it. In a sense, feminism already has this kind of connection with the latter. The labour movement constitutes a source of feminism (obviously, not the only one); August Bebel's *Woman and Socialism* (1883), famous in its day, was one of its founding texts. At the same time, during the twentieth century feminism became increasingly autonomous, 'second-wave' feminism being a largely independent current.

A fourth and final possibility is that the fate of socialism will resemble that of liberalism. Having held sway during the *belle époque*, liberalism entered into a deep crisis with the First World War, from which it recovered only in the second half of the 1970s, when the neo-liberal period began. The violence

---

3   See Christopher Hill, *The World Turned Upside Down: Radical Ideas during the English Revolution*, London: Penguin, 2006.

generated by two world wars, the Bolshevik Revolution, the 1929 depression, the intellectual hegemony of Keynesianism and Marxism, caused it to suffer a prolonged eclipse. From the late 1970s until the middle of the first decade of the 2000s, liberalism enjoyed three decades of unchallenged supremacy, which the current crisis has possibly shaken.[4] It cannot be excluded, claims Anderson, that socialism, like liberalism, will ultimately experience redemption following its eclipse. For that, obviously, it will have to change and, in particular, incorporate certain features of rival doctrines, such as greater respect for individual freedoms. But we would still be dealing with socialism as we have known it, whose main elements would remain intact. This fourth eventuality is close to what Badiou seems to have in mind when he suggests a comparison between the 'communist hypothesis' and scientific activity.[5] A scientific hypothesis is never effective at the first attempt. It is subject to more or less positive 'conjectures and refutations', until the point at which its veracity is established.

The two decades that have passed since Anderson's text appeared make it possible to see the nature of the period we are in more clearly. A first observation is that socialism will not follow the road of the Jesuit state of Paraguay. In other words, future historians will not adjudge it a set of derisory experiences without any posterity as regards the general course of history. The very fact that this eventuality could have been envisaged seems incongruous today (it was far from being so when Anderson was writing). Since the Zapatista insurrection of 1994 and the French strikes of November–December 1995, many struggles have been lost. But they have been fought. New generations have been radicalized, unanticipated oppressed categories have emerged, some states have proclaimed themselves followers of 'twenty-first century socialism', and last but not least the 'Arab Spring' has occurred. And the full social and political effects of the unprecedented economic crisis we have been immersed in since 2007 are still to make themselves felt, including in the western countries. Obviously, there is no question of suggesting that the situation is good. Far from it. However, the long procession of defeats tends to obscure the positive experiences of recent years. Contrary to every expectation, despite the disaster represented by 'real' socialism, socialism does not seem to be doomed in the immediate future to becoming a historical curiosity.

A second observation is that it is unlikely that socialism will be redeemed in the way liberalism was during the last third of the twentieth century. The industrial civilization of which it was the product has certainly not disappeared, contrary to what has been claimed by hasty analyses from various sectors of

---

4   For an analysis of neo-liberal hegemony, see Perry Anderson, 'Renewals', *New Left Review*, II/1, January–February 2000.

5   See Alain Badiou, *The Communist Hypothesis*, trans. David Macey and Steve Corcoran, London and New York: Verso, 2010.

critical thought since the 1960s. But it has been significantly transformed, to the extent that the conditions in which the historical core of the socialist project could emerge have probably disappeared. Consequently, the fate of socialism will perhaps be played out between the second and third of the hypotheses referred to by Anderson. Either the experiences of the 1848–1989 cycle will prove 'cumulative' – that is, they will shortly give rise to massive processes of social transformation. Or more time, and a deeper mutation, will be required for events of this kind to recur. At present, if we must venture a hypothesis, the second eventuality seems more likely. Despite the positive experiences mentioned above, the prospect of their incorporation into a coherent project borne by organized actors seems so remote that it is difficult to see what could impart a 'cumulative' character to them. In this sense, we possibly find ourselves today in a political temporality analogous to the century and a half that separated the English and French revolutions. As Lenin used to say, patience and irony are more than ever revolutionary qualities.

To speed up the passage of time, a start must be made on a programme of work. Among the most important worksites, we shall identify three. The first is the strategic question. Contemporary critical theories sin by their omission of reflection on this. It is attributable to at least two factors. For a start, in order to think and act strategically one must first of all equip oneself with a description, however approximate, of the world in which one is intervening. The world is developing so rapidly today, and its general coordinates are so difficult to fix, that we are still far from possessing a faithful representation of reality that makes it possible to prepare the ground for a coherent strategy of social transformation. Secondly, a strategy is always developed in interaction with social and political movements. As we have seen, however, a structural characteristic of today's critical thinkers is the tenuousness of their relations with the latter. For a genuine 'strategic reason' (in Daniel Bensaïd's words) to be reactivated, it is imperative that this gulf between thinkers and movements be bridged.

A promising strategic track has been identified by Balibar, who suggests that the major 'missed encounter' of the twentieth century was that between its two most important revolutionary 'theorists-practitioners' – namely, Lenin and Gandhi.[6] We cannot exclude the possibility that a new strategic paradigm will emerge in the future from a crossing of their approaches. It would be simplistic to situate Lenin on the side of insurrectionary violence and Gandhi on that of absolute non-violence – if only because India's independence unleashed large-scale violence and, ultimately, the partition of the country, while the revolutionary violence endorsed by Lenin formed part of a 'general economy of

---

6   Étienne Balibar, 'Lenin and Gandhi: A Missed Encounter?', *Radical Philosophy*, no. 172, March–April 2012.

violence' in Russia and Europe that long predated the October Revolution. That is the real meaning of the Lenin's call to 'transform the imperialist war into a revolutionary civil war'. At the same time, the incorporation of Gandhian precepts into a new strategic reason would make it possible to grasp the fact that violence not only always has a human and social cost, but also adversely affects the very identity of those who use it. This idea, claims Balibar, is foreign to Marxism, whose conception of violence was mainly tactical, not ontological. To put a form of 'civil disobedience' on the agenda of critical thinking would, moreover, highlight the increasingly ideological or cultural character of social struggles. Gandhi was a master of the art of the 'war of position', to use Gramsci's term, and many lessons might be learnt from his skill in deploying symbols.

Bensaïd, the most strategically-minded of contemporary critical thinkers, devoted his final efforts before his death in 2010 to picking up the threads of strategic thinking, in conjunction with classical Marxist debates, but also by drawing up a balance sheet of the experience of revolutions and counter-revolutions in Latin America in the second half of the twentieth century (Chile, Brazil, Argentina, Nicaragua and so on) – a continent with which Bensaïd had close links as an activist.[7] According to Bensaïd, two major 'strategic hypotheses' ran through the labour movement from its foundation to the fall of the Berlin Wall: the 'insurrectionary general strike' and the 'protracted people's war'. The first was mainly inspired by the Paris Commune and the Russian Revolution. It unfolded in an urban environment, had as its principal (not exclusive) actor the working class, and sought to seize control of a capital and the power centres located there. The second was inspired by the Chinese and Vietnamese revolutions and had a major influence in the Third Worldist movement. It involved a territorial duality represented by 'liberated zones' and presupposed a more expansive space-time than the preceding hypothesis. All twentieth-century revolutions, says Bensaïd, have blended these two hypotheses to various degrees. The current revolutions in the Arab world illustrate the relevance of this analytical grid, since they combine territorial secession and the emergence of forms of autonomous local government with insurrections in major urban centres.

The key question is whether these hypotheses will continue to structure revolutionary politics in the twenty-first century, especially in countries where parliamentary-democratic traditions more than a century old exist. The Arab revolutions of late 2010–early 2011 were obviously made against dictatorships, not liberal democracies. Bensaïd probably did not accord this problem due importance, even if the 1980s and 90s saw him debate 'critical Eurocommunist' theses (Poulantzas and Christine Buci-Glucksmann) and

---

7   See his autobiography – Daniel Bensaïd, *An Impatient Life: A Memoir*, London and New York: Verso, 2014 (forthcoming).

other varieties of neo-Gramscianism (in particular, Laclau and Mouffe). At all events, the notion of 'strategic crisis' is crucial in Bensaïd, as it was in Lenin. A crisis is the moment *par excellence* when the 'iron circle' of commodity fetishism is broken and the field of possibilities opened up. Bensaïd's conceptualization of crisis naturally issues in the centrality of what he calls the 'party-strategist'. In order to seize the historical opportunities afforded by the crisis, organization is indispensable. As Bensaïd puts it in one of the luminous formulae that were his trademark, the party is not merely 'the result of a cumulative experience, or the modest pedagogue responsible for raising the proletarians up from dark ignorance to the light of reason. It becomes a strategic operator, a sort of gear box and switch of the class struggle.'[8] Obviously, it remains to determine what form a party rallying the oppressed – more precisely, the victims of oppressions of all sorts – and adapted to the challenges of the twenty-first century, should take.

A second worksite involves the ecological question. We have not given this issue the importance it warrants in this book. The reason is that, while it is flourishing at present, political ecology has not yet produced its Marx. In other words, it has not yielded one or several thinkers who perform the two basic operations in which Marx engaged. On the one hand, he produced a (the first) general theory of the total 'social relation' that is capitalism, by integrating into one and the same analytical movement its economic, political, cultural, geographical, epistemological, etc. dimensions. On the other hand, Marx (and Marxists) rendered their thought politically operative – that is, they ensured that their thinking was embodied in real social and political movements. Obviously, Marx himself is the product of a long history, while political ecology is still young.[9] But it is indispensable that a radical ecology, which accomplishes these operations for its own purposes, should appear in the coming years. It goes without saying that, to be effective, it will have to be something other than what is sold under this name in the electoral market, in Europe and elsewhere (the case of the United States is a special one in this respect). An interesting issue will be whether radical ecology develops on bases that are autonomous of Marxism – by promoting, for example, a principle of 'degrowth' foreign to the latter – or whether it will consist in a development of the Marxian materialist axiomatic, as certain authors who re-read Marx in the light of ecological problematics believe.[10]

---

8   Daniel Bensaïd, *La Politique comme art stratégique*, Paris: Syllepse, 2011, p. 41.

9   It only really took off in the second half of the twentieth century, as is demonstrated by Hicham-Stéphane Afeissa, *Qu'est-ce que l'écologie?*, Paris: Vrin, 2009.

10   See John Bellamy Foster, *Marx's Ecology: Materialism and Nature*, New York: Monthly Review Press, 2000, and James O'Connor, *Natural Causes: Essays in Ecological Marxism*, New York: Guilford, 1998.

A third worksite is the rise and increasing autonomy of critical thinking in what used to be called the 'periphery' of the modern world. A hypothesis running through this book is that, since the last third of the twentieth century, forms of critical thought have been disseminated throughout the world. This situation is new, because these theories were until recently a monopoly – certainly not exclusive – of the 'old continent'. However, the globalization of critical thinking possesses the following problematic feature: it is inseparable from its Americanization. The attractiveness of the United States (not merely financial, but also for the promotion and international circulation of oeuvres) is such that, whatever the provenance of thinkers – Latin America, India, China, Africa and so forth – it is difficult for them to resist it. Yet it is likely that the Americanization of critical thinking contains the seeds of its political neutralization.[11] The United States is certainly not the political desert it is sometimes depicted as in Europe. Powerful social movements exist there, among them the movement of illegal immigrants of Hispanic origin that has emerged in the recent years. Rather, the problem lies in the situation of universities and their occupants, which tend on account of their elitist character to be socially and spatially cut off from the rest of society. This socio-spatial segregation of American universities renders the interaction between critical thinkers and political and social movements referred to above even less likely. In this respect, what is required is the emergence of a globalization of critical thinking uncoupled from its Americanization. If a genuinely multi-polar order in the field of critical thinking is still far off, our map suggests that it may emerge in the decades or centuries to come.

---

11   This is the hypothesis defended by Arif Dirlik, 'The Postcolonial Aura: Third World Criticism in the Age of Global Capitalism', *Critical Inquiry*, vol. 20, 1994. See also Mike Davis, *City of Quartz: Excavating the Future in Los Angeles*, London and New York: Verso, 2001.

Index

Marla Holtz